A Study System for Intermediate & Advanced Learners

KANJI IN CONTEXT

中・上級学習者のための漢字と語彙

REFERENCE BOOK

INTER-UNIVERSITY CENTER FOR JAPANESE LANGUAGE STUDIES

KOICHI NISHIGUCHI
TAMAKI KONO

The Japan Times

First edition: October 1994
4th printing: September 1997

English translating & proofreading: Jon McGovern
Editorial assistance: Ledico
Cover art: Hiroko Kobayashi

Published by The Japan Times, Ltd.
5-4, Shibaura 4-chome, Minato-ku, Tokyo 108, Japan

ISBN-7890-0753-7

Printed in Japan

はじめに

　漢字習得のむずかしさは、日本語教育が始まって以来一貫して指摘されてきたことです。1980年代に日本語教育ブームが始まり、さまざまな教科書や教材が世に出されました。そのような中で、初級学習者のための優れた基本漢字学習書も何冊か出版されました。しかしながら、中級ないし上級学習者が基本的な漢字の知識と能力の上にさらに漢字の能力を伸ばしていくための適切な教材は現れませんでした。

　アメリカ・カナダ大学連合日本研究センターでは過去30年にわたって、日本研究を専攻する北米の大学院生に対して上級及び専門的な日本語教育を行ってきましたが、本校でも漢字の指導は長い間教育上の問題となっていました。その問題に対処するために従来よりさまざまな試みがなされてきましたが、1990年夏、本格的な漢字教育システム開発のために特別チームが編成され、以来3年の間に、コンピュータの利用をも視野に入れた新しい漢字教育システムの研究と教材開発、そして試行が集中的に行われました。*Kanji in Context—A Study System for Intermediate and Advanced Learners* はこのようなプロジェクトの成果として生まれたものです。1993年度に本校で使用されたこの教材は、学生から賛辞をもって受け入れられ、めざましい教育成果をあげました。そしてこの度、ジャパンタイムズ社より出版されることとなりました。世界中で日本語を学ぶ人々がますます増えていますが、多くの日本語学習者がこの教材を手にし、日本語習得上の難所である「漢字の壁」を打ち破ることを願ってやみません。

　最後になりましたが、紙面を借りまして、本教材の開発と出版を一貫して支援してくださったブルース・バートン所長、立松喜久子副所長をはじめとするアメリカ・カナダ大学連合日本研究センターの教職員の皆様、ならびに著者らに本教材開発のモティベーションとさまざまな有益なコメントを与えてくれた同センターの学生に感謝の意を表したいと思います。また、本教材の編集作業に知恵と忍耐と細心の注意をもって当たってくださったジャパンタイムズ出版部の関戸千明さんには深く感謝するとともに、仲間として本教材出版の喜びを分かち合いたいと思います。英文校正と翻訳の労を引き受けてくれたジョン・マクガバンさんにも感謝いたします。

1994年9月

アメリカ・カナダ大学連合日本研究センター

西口　光一

河野　玉姫

Preface

Ever since the beginning of Japanese language education for foreigners, the task of learning *kanji* has been one of the major challenges for learners, particularly those whose native language does not make use of the characters. As a result of the rapid growth in the popularity of Japanese language studies that started in the 1980s, an immense volume of various instructional materials has been created over the ensuing years. These materials include several excellent beginning level textbooks for the study of *kanji*, but unfortunately there have been no textbooks that can adequately help intermediate and advanced learners to build upon the foundation of knowledge and proficiency in *kanji* that they have already acquired.

The need for such an upper level textbook has been the concern of the Inter-University Center for Japanese Language Studies (IUC) in Yokohama. For over 30 years, the IUC has been providing advanced Japanese language education to graduate students from universities in North America and professionals who are specializing in Japan-related fields, and throughout this period the instructors have been confronted with the question of how to best educate the students in *kanji*. Various methods were experimented with over the years, leading to the formation in the summer of 1990 of a team of instructors assigned with the task of developing a full-scale system for teaching *kanji*. In the three years that followed, the team conducted intensive research and trials that included investigation of the use of computers in *kanji* education, and the culmination of these efforts was the creation of *Kanji in Context—A Study System for Intermediate and Advanced Learners*. The text was immediately put to use at the IUC for the 1993-94 session, and it received high praise from the students for the effect it had in raising their *kanji* proficiency. It was then decided to have the text be published by The Japan Times, Ltd., with the hope that it would help other Japanese language learners around the world to break through the forbidding "*kanji* barrier."

Before explaining the layout and use of this text, special mention should be given here of the many people whose assistance made this text possible. We extend our warmest appreciation to Dr. Bruce Batten, Director of the Inter-University Center, Ms. Kikuko Tatematsu, Assistant Director, and the entire teaching staff for their support and cooperation in the development of this text, and to the IUC students for the valuable comments and motivation that they provided. We also wish to thank Ms. Chiaki Sekido of The Japan Times, Ltd., for her sage advice, perseverance, and close attention to detail during the editing of this text for publication. Finally, thanks are due to Mr. Jon McGovern for his work in translating and proofreading the text.

September 1994

Inter-University Center for Japanese Language Studies
Koichi Nishiguchi
Tamaki Kono

目 次
(Contents)

この教材の内容と使い方

I. 本教材の概要

Kanji in Context—A Study System for Intermediate and Advanced Learners は、初級のコースを終了した人及び中・上級レベルで学習中の人が、それまでに身につけた漢字や語彙の基礎の上に、さらに多くの漢字と語彙を体系的かつ効率的に学ぶための教材です。本教材は、**参考書**と**ワークブック**の２種類の教材からなっています。

現在出版されている他の漢字教材と比べて、本教材はいくつかの際だった特長を持っています。

□ 中・上級の学習者に対象を絞った初めての教材

現在出版されている漢字教材は，その教材で一から漢字を勉強していくように作られているものが多く、本格的に漢字の学習を始める中級以上の学習者に対象を絞った教材はありませんでした。本教材は、初級の学習を終了した人がさらに漢字の学習を続ける場合や、中・上級の学習者ですでにかなりの数の漢字と語彙を習得しているが、改めて体系的に漢字と語彙を学習したいという場合を基本的に想定して作られています。

□ 漢字を体系的に学ぶことができる

中級以上の段階では、学習者に要求される漢字と語彙が飛躍的に増加します。それを効率よく習得するためには、一つ一つバラバラに覚えるのではなく、漢字や漢字語彙の背後にある体系にも目を向けながら学習する必要があります。

一般に漢字には、形・音・意味の３つの体系があると言われています。形の体系というのは漢字の字形構成の一般規則のこと、音の体系というのは字形構成素に基づく漢字の読みの共通性や類似性、そして、意味の体系というのは同じく字形構成素に基づく漢字の意味の成り立ちの体系のことです。

漢字はこれら３つの要素が有機的に絡み合ったものです。このような漢字の体系に関する知識を適切に習得すれば、新しい漢字や語彙の習得を飛躍的に促進すると同時に、知らない漢字や語彙に出くわした時にその意味や読み方を類推できる力がつきま

す。本教材の**参考書**では、このような漢字の形・音・意味の体系に関する情報が自然に身につくように工夫されています。

□ 漢字の学習だけでなく、漢字語彙の習熟も大きな目標とする

　中・上級の学習者にとっては、新しい漢字の習得もさることながら、漢字語彙を増やし、その正しい用法を身につけることも非常に重要です。しかし、従来の漢字教材はもっぱら個々の漢字が学習の中心で、語彙についてはいくつか示すだけであったり、学習者にはあまり重要でない語が提示されたりしていました。

　これに対し、本教材では、漢字の学習だけでなく、語彙の学習ももう一つの教育目標として明確に定めました。そのために、**参考書**では、日本語学習者に重要と思われる語彙を学習段階を加味しながら選び、提示しました。また、参考書で覚えた語彙は、**ワークブック**で関連語や例文を見ながら、コンテクストの中での使い方が学べるようになっています。

□ 自然に繰り返し学習できる

　これまでの漢字教材では多くの場合、一つの事項は一度だけ提示され、その時に必ず覚えるというアプローチをとってきました。しかし、漢字にしろ漢字語彙にしろ、一度の学習で100％確実に習得できるとは考えられません。

　そのため、本教材では、**参考書**でも**ワークブック**でも、同じ語例や関連語彙が繰り返し提示されます。同じ事項に何度も接することによって、学習者はプレッシャーを感じることなく、確実に漢字と語彙の知識を積み上げていくことができるでしょう。

　では、**参考書**と**ワークブック**について、各々具体的な内容について説明します。なお、詳しい説明を必要としない学習者は、Ⅳ の「本教材の使い方」を読んで学習を始めてください。

II.　参考書の概要

1.　参考書の主な内容

参考書では、主として次のような情報が提示されています。

1) 常用漢字 1,945 字に「誰」と「賂」の 2 字を加えた 1,947 字の漢字（以下、この 1,947 字の漢字を本教材の「学習漢字」と呼びます。）
2) 学習漢字の読み
3) 学習漢字の画数
4) 学習漢字の語例とその読み方および英語訳

2.　学習漢字の選定

1981 年に文部省は、現代日本語を書き表す場合の漢字使用の目安として常用漢字表を発表しました。常用漢字表には、1,945 字の漢字と各々の漢字の標準的な音訓が示されています。現在この常用漢字表は広く社会に受け入れられ、公文書、新聞、雑誌、書籍など現代日本語を書き表す時の基準となっています。

本教材では、この常用漢字表の 1,945 字の漢字すべてと、「誰」と「賂」の 2 字を学習漢字としました。「誰」については、一般的にもしばしば使われ、字形も単純で日本語学習者もたいてい慣れ親しんでいるため、また「賂」については、「賄賂」という語彙の表記は知っていたほうがよいと考えて、学習漢字としました。

3.　学習漢字の水準づけ

本教材では、1,947 字の学習漢字を、日本語の学習段階に対応して 6 つの水準に分けました。その概要は以下の表の通りです。

水　準	学習漢字数	解　　説
第 1 水準	250 字	初級の日本語コースを終了した学習者であれば必ず学習した経験があると考えられる基礎的な漢字。
第 2 水準	100 字 （累計　350 字）	中級の日本語コースで学習している学習者であれば必ず学習した経験があると考えられる漢字。
第 3 水準	850 字 （累計 1,200 字）	中級の日本語コースで一般的に学習されると考えられる漢字。

第4水準	220字 （累計1,420字）	中級の日本語コースでしばしば現れるが一般的とは考えられない漢字、あるいは、上級の日本語コースで一般的に学習されると考えられる漢字。
第5水準	412字 （累計1,832字）	上級の日本語コースでしばしば現れるが一般的とは考えられない漢字。
第6水準	115字 （合計1,947字）	特別な領域や分野の特殊な語彙の中でしか使われない特殊な漢字。この水準の漢字は、自然に関する漢字、歴史・文学に関する漢字、及び極めてまれにしか使われない特殊な漢字の3つのグループに分けられている。

　国立国語研究所が行った調査によると、最も使用頻度の高い500字だけで新聞で使われる漢字の約80%をカバーすることができ、1,000字知っていれば新聞漢字の94%をカバーできるということです。この数字に従えば、本教材の第3水準（1,200字）まで勉強すればおおむね漢字の知識は十分で、第4水準（1,420字）まで勉強すれば、後はもう極めてまれにしか使われない漢字を残すだけということになります。実際のところ、第3水準、あるいは場合によっては第4水準まで学習すれば、漢字及び漢字語彙の知識はほぼ十分で、あとは自分の興味や専門に合わせて実際に新聞や雑誌あるいは本などを読みながら、漢字と漢字語彙の知識を自然に増やしていけばいいでしょう。

4．学習漢字の配列

　3．のように6つの水準に分けた学習漢字は、漢字の重要度や難易度を基本に、字形や意味のつながり、語彙のつながりなど、さまざまな面に配慮して、各水準ごとに方針を立てて配列しました。

　第1水準と**第2水準**では、各学習漢字の語例のうち、一番最初に示した語（**基本語例**：「5．語例の選定と配列」を参照）どうしの意味のつながりを中心に配列しました。

　第3水準と**第4水準**では、以下のような点を総合的に考慮して学習漢字を配列しました。

<＜基本的な方針＞

　・基本語例が学習者にとってなじみがあり、使用頻度も高いと思われる学習漢字から順に提示する。

＜副次的な方針＞

　・重要な熟語を構成する漢字は隣接して提示する。

　・共通の字形要素を持ち、字形がある程度類似している漢字は隣接して提示する。

> ・共通の字形要素を持つわけではないが、字形が類似していて紛らわしい漢字
> は隣接して提示する。
> ・基本語例が一定の語彙グループを形成している場合、そのような漢字はまと
> めて提示する。

　第5水準では、専ら字形要素の共通性に基づいて学習漢字を配列しました。そして、最後の**第6水準**では、各々のグループごとに字形要素の共通性と学習漢字の語例の語彙体系を考慮して学習漢字を配列しました。

　このような結果が巻末の「**学習漢字一覧表**」(p. 280) です。本書の学習漢字はこの表の配列順で提示されています。

5．語例の選定と配列

　語例には、漢字語彙能力の核となり、かつ成人学習者の興味と関心に対応した重要な語彙を精選しました。提示語彙数は約9,000語で、日本語能力試験の1級の漢字語彙の大部分が提示されています。

　各学習漢字の語例のうち、一番最初に示した語例は、その学習漢字を含む最も基本的な語例で、その漢字を学ぶときに必ず覚えてほしい**基本語例**です。それ以降の語例は、漢字の意味や語構成の共通性、読みの共通性と類似性、語例の難易度などを考慮して配列しました。なお、重要と思われる語は、未習の漢字や本書の学習漢字以外の字を含むものでも提示しました（ただし、その場合には [*] や [▲] などの印をつけました——「6．凡例」を参照）。

6. 凡 例

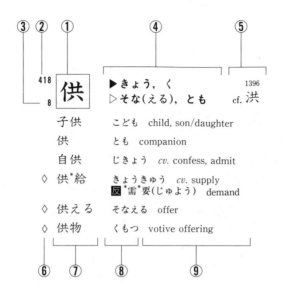

③ ② ①　　　　　④　　　　　⑤

⑥ ⑦　⑧　　⑨

① 見出し字／② 漢字番号／③ 総画数

④ 漢字の読み

1) 常用漢字表にあげられた漢字の読みをすべて提示しました。▶には音読みを、▷には訓読みを示してあります。(　　)内は送りがなの部分です。

2) 細字は、その読みが常用漢字表の「特別なもの又は用法のごく狭いもの」であることを示します。

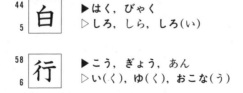

⑤ 形の似ている字に関する情報

場合によっては、形が似ている漢字について注意を促すため、cf. として見出し字部

分の一番右に、類似字とその漢字番号を示してあります。

| 319
4 | 犬 | ▶けん
▷いぬ | 87 124
cf. 大 太 |

⑥ 難易度マーク

学習の便宜のために、語例には難易度を示す印をつけました。

◇……1) 未習漢字を含む語例（ただし、第 1・第 2 水準の漢字(1-350)はすべて既習漢字として扱った）

◇ 大*丈夫　　だいじょうぶ　all right, secure, safe

◇ 和*風　　　わふう　Japanese style　（*は未習漢字を表す。）

2) 既習漢字だけで構成されているが、語彙的に難易度が高いもの

◇ 大いに　　おおいに　very

◇ 落第　　　らくだい　cv. flunk, fail

◇ 公算　　　こうさん　probaility, likelihood

㊜……自然に関する特殊な語彙

㊜*渓谷　　けいこく　valley

㊜麦*芽　　ばくが　malt

㊭……歴史・文学に関する特殊な語彙

㊭大名　　だいみょう　daimyō, feudal lord

㊭文　　　ふみ　letter

㊵……きわめてまれにしか使われない特殊な語彙

㊵*緑青　　ろくしょう　copper/green rust, patina

㊵歩　　　ふ　pawn (in Japanese chess)

これらの印がついている語例は、その漢字を初めて学習している段階では難しいと思われる語彙ですから、覚える必要はありません。まず、無印の語例から学習してください。ワークブックでも、これらの印がついていない語例だけを勉強するようになっています。

なお、◇のついた語のほとんどは、後の段階で再度提示され、その時にもう一度学習できるようになっています。

⑦ 語 例

語例の中に未習漢字や学習漢字以外の漢字が含まれる場合は、それらの漢字に以下の印をつけました。

*……未習漢字（ただし、すぐ次に学習漢字として出てくる場合は無印）

◇ *統一　　とういつ　*cv.* unity

◇ 三つ*角　みつかど　three-way junction

▲……本書の学習漢字以外の漢字

◇ 茶▲碗　　ちゃわん　(rice) bowl, teacup

◇ 大▲阪府　おおさかふ　Osaka Prefecture

⑧ 語例の読み

特殊な読み方をする語例には、以下の印をつけました。

△……その語例が常用漢字表の「付表」の語彙であることを示す。これらは常用漢字表で認められている当て字や熟字訓である。

一人　　　　△ひとり　one person

◇ 二十*歳　△はたち　twenty years old

▲……常用漢字外の読み方であることを示す。

私　　　わたくし，▲わたし　I, me

㊧ 細雪　　▲ささめゆき　light snowfall

⑨ 語例の意味

cv.……熟語動詞(語例に「する」をつけて動詞として使えるもの)であることを示す。

出発　　しゅっぱつ　*cv.* depart, leave

計算　　けいさん　*cv.* calculate, compute

vt. / vi.……英訳からだけでは他動詞／自動詞が判別できない場合に限り、*vt.* または*vi.* を表示した。

続ける　つづける　*vt.* continue

続く　　つづく　*vi.* continue

cf.……漢字の使い方や関連語に関する情報を示した。

子ども　　こども　child, son/daughter　cf. *Kodomo* can be written as 子ども or 子供.

作家　　　さっか　novelist　cf. 筆者(ひっしゃ) writer, 著者(ちょしゃ) author

abbr.……略語であることを示す。

日本銀行　にほんぎんこう　the Bank of Japan　cf. *abbr.* 日銀(にちぎん)

◇ 短*期大学　たんきだいがく　junior college　cf. *abbr.* 短大(たんだい)

反……反対語であることを示す。

◇ 主*観*的な　しゅかんてきな　subjective　反 客*観*的な (きゃっかんてきな) objective

日の出　　　ひので　sunrise　反 日の入り(ひのいり) sunset

⑩ ワークブックとの対応

ワークブックとの対応がすぐわかるように、参考書では、ワークブックの各回ごとに点線で区切り、回数の数字を示してあります。

③

⑪ コラム

漢字と語彙の学習をいっそう促進するため、本書では2種類のコラムを設けました。

●〈漢字の形に気をつけましょう〉のコラム

このコラムでは、同じ構成素をもつ漢字や字形の似ている漢字をいくつかまとめて提示しました。

●語彙に関するコラム

このコラムでは、語彙の学習を促進するために、意味のつながりをもつ語彙をまとめて提示しました。

7. 索　引

漢字学習の便宜のために、参考書には4つの索引が載せてあります。①音訓索引、②字形索引、③総画索引、④語彙索引の4つです。以下、順に使い方を説明します。

（A）漢字の読み方が分かっている場合

① 音訓索引

　漢字の読み方（音読みまたは訓読み）が分かっている時は、音訓索引で漢字を引きます。音訓索引では本書の学習漢字のすべての読み方があいうえお順（五十音順）で提示され、該当する学習漢字と漢字番号がその後ろに示されています。訓読みの場合は送りがなも示されています。

（B）漢字の読み方が分からない場合

　漢字の読み方が分からない場合は、字形索引か総画索引で引きます。

②字形索引

　字形索引では、漢字の形を手がかりとして調べます。

　漢字は、点と線の無秩序な図形ではありません。漢字には、いわば"部品"とも言える字形構成素が多数あり、ほとんどの漢字はそのような部品の組み合わせでできています。組み合わせ方には一定のパターンがあり、構成素の配置によって以下の8つのタイプに分けることができます。

1	◧	レフト（left）	伝	凝	提
2	◨	ライト（right）	別	敬	断
3	⬒	トップ（top）	今	冠	声
4	⬓	ボトム（bottom）	先	基	替
5	◰	トップレフト（top & left）	局	広	戻
6	◱	レフトボトム（left & bottom）	道	起	題
7	◳	トップライト（top & right）	句	載	
8	⊓⊔⊏⊐	エンクロージャー（enclosure）	円	凶	区　国

　字形索引では、このような字形構成素のパターンを使って、以下の手順で漢字を調べます。

1) まず、調べたい漢字をよく見て、字形構成素を見つけます。
2) 巻末の字形構成素チャートでその構成素の番号を調べます。チャートでは、構成素が上記の8つのタイプごとに画数順に並べられていますから、構成素の配置と画数をよく確認して調べてください。
3) 構成素の番号をもとに、字形索引で漢字を調べます。それぞれの字形構成素の項では、画数順で漢字が提示され、その漢字番号が示されています。

調べたい漢字に字形構成素が2つ認められることがよくありますが、そのような場合はどちらの構成素で調べてもかまいません。たとえば「休」の場合、左側の「イ」からでも、右側の「木」からでも引くことができます。あるいは「思」の場合、上の「田」からでも、下の「心」からでも引くことができます。

③ 総画索引
　漢字の中には、「心」「士」「器」「飛」のように、上の8つのパターンに含まれないものもあります。そのような漢字は、すべて総画索引に収録してあります。また、総画索引には、このような字形索引にない189字のほかに、字形索引で引きにくいと思われる漢字30字も入れてあります。　具体的にどんな漢字が含まれているかを知るために、一度総画索引にある漢字を一覧することをお勧めします。

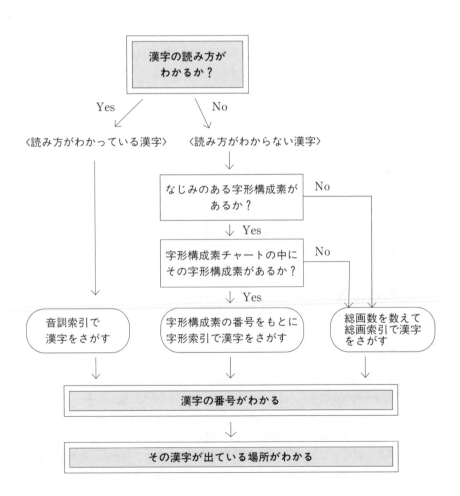

(C) 語彙を探したい場合

④語彙索引

　参考書に収録されているすべての漢字語彙をあいうえお順（五十音順）に並べ、それが掲載されている漢字番号を示しました。この索引を使って掲載箇所を探せば語彙の意味を調べることができますから、参考書を学習辞典のように使うことができます。

III. ワークブックの概要

1. ワークブックの主な内容

　ワークブックでは、毎回、参考書に示された学習漢字を順番に約10字ずつ（第1・2水準では約20字ずつ）取り上げ、語例の使い方に習熟し、漢字語彙を拡充するために役に立つと思われる学習材料をさまざまな形で提示しています。各回は大きく3つのセクションから成り立っています。各セクションの内容は以下の通りです。

　　Ⅰ．学習漢字の語例を含む複合熟語、慣用的な表現、文の構成など
　　Ⅱ．学習漢字の語例の関連及び関連語、表現の対比など
　　Ⅲ．学習漢字の語例を使った実際的な例文

　では、それぞれについて例をあげながら説明します。例の中の下線は参考書で提示された語例であることを示しています。

Ⅰ．このセクションでは、提示されている表現を勉強し、語の基本的な使い方を学習します。

　1）学習漢字の語例を含む複合熟語
　　例）　和平交渉　　団体旅行　　支持率　　技術移転

　2）漢字の語例を含む広い意味での慣用的な表現
　　例）　平和を守る　　公平な態度　　家具付きの家　　約束を守る/破る
　　　　日本人の外国人に対する態度

3) 学習漢字の語例を使った文の構成

  例）　ＸとＹを<u>同等</u>に扱う　　手紙を<u>封筒</u>に入れて送る
　　　　手紙を<u>速達</u>で送る　　大学進学について兄に<u>相談</u>する

Ⅱ．このセクションでは、提示されている表現を勉強し、他の語彙との意味の関連
　　を学習します。

1) 学習漢字の語例の関連及び関連語

  例）　**戦争**と**平和**　　管理職と**平社員**
　　　　事務　　**事務員**　　**事務室**
　　　　会社員　　**銀行員**　　**教員**　　**工員**

2) 表現の対比

  例）　Ｘの意見/提案に<u>反対</u>する　←→　Ｘの意見/提案に<u>賛成</u>する
　　　　<u>損</u>(を)する　←→　<u>得</u>(を)する
　　　　値段　　価格　　**物価**　　**地価**

Ⅲ．このセクションでは、例文をよく読んで、下線で示した語の文中での使い方を
　　学習します。
　　　　例文は、成人学習者が興味を持って学習を進めることができ、かつ、学習漢
　　字の語例の用法を学習するのに最も適当と思われるものを提示しました。下線
　　の語の読み方は右側に示してあります。

2．ワークブックで扱う語例

　ワークブックでは、参考書で提示された語彙のうち、難易度マーク（◊、歴、然、特
→「Ⅱ-6. 凡例」を参照）がついていない語だけを扱っています。マークつきの語例
は、難易度や重要度の点で当該の学習段階に属さないため、扱っていません。
　なお、無印の語例でも、第１・２水準の中の初歩的な語例や、第５・６水準の中の
特殊で使用頻度が低いと思われる語例は、扱っていません。

3．ワークブックと学習水準

　ワークブックの第１巻では、参考書の第１水準から第３水準まで（１-1200）の内容に
対応する学習材料が、また第２巻には第４水準から第６水準まで（1201-1947）の内容
に対応する学習材料が，それぞれ提示されています。

IV. 本教材の使い方

1. 対象レベル

　本教材を使って効果的に学習するためには、基本的に通常の初級コースで学ぶ漢字約200〜300字を習得していることが前提です。もう少し具体的に言うと、本教材の学習漢字のうち、第1水準(1—250)の学習漢字の最初の語例の大部分を読んで理解できるということです。このレベルの学習者であれば、本教材の参考書とワークブックを並行して使用して、効率よく体系的に漢字と語彙を学べるでしょう。

　現在まだ初級段階で勉強している人は、本教材の参考書を使って、教科書で勉強した漢字の知識を整理し、熟語等の語彙を増やすことができます。その場合、ワークブックはある程度漢字と語彙の知識が増えた段階で使い始めればいいでしょう。

2. どこから学習を始めるか

　大まかに言って、本教材の第1水準と第2水準は初級段階、第3水準は中級段階、第4水準は上級段階、そして第5水準と第6水準は超上級段階と言うことができます。学習者は自分の知識・能力や勉強のしかたの好みによってどこから勉強を始めてもかまいませんが、一般的には第1水準の初めから勉強することを薦めます。第1・2水準の漢字の大部分はすでに知っていることと思いますが、漢字語彙の拡充という点できっと役に立つと思います。また、ワークブックでは、第1・2水準は1回に扱う学習漢字数を多くして、効率的に学習が進められるようにしてあります。

3. 本教材を使った漢字と漢字語彙の学習

　本教材を十分に活用していただくために、ここでは本教材の特長を生かした基本的な学習方法について解説します。しかし、人によって好きな勉強方法が異なりますので、本教材に慣れてきたら、学習者は各々自分に合ったやり方で本教材を使ってください。

┌─<学習者はワークブックの各回で、以下のような要領で勉強を進めてください>─

ステップ1　学習漢字の基本的知識の形成

　参考書で学習漢字の最初の語例の意味と読み、及びそれを構成している漢字を確実に覚えてください。この知識が各学習漢字の知識の基本になります。

ステップ2　学習漢字の意味と用法の理解

　参考書で学習漢字の語例を勉強し、学習漢字の意味と用法を理解してください。

ステップ3　学習漢字の語例の学習

　参考書の中の無印の語例の意味と読みを覚えてください。◇、歴、然、特などの印がついている語例は進んだ段階の語例なので、覚えなくてもかまいません。

ステップ4　語例の使い方と関連語の学習

　ワークブックで学習漢字の語例の使い方や関連語を勉強してください。そして下線が引いてある語（参考書の中の無印の語例）(注) の意味と読みと使い方を確実に覚えてください。万が一分からない場合は、もう一度参考書にもどって勉強してください。

　　　(注)第3水準と第4水準では、参考書の中の無印の語例をすべてワークブックに載せましたが、第1水準と第2水準では無印の語例のうち初歩的な語例を除いた事項のみを、第5水準と第6水準では無印の語例のうち特に重要と思われる事項のみをワークブックに載せました。

ステップ5　習得の確認

　日本語の先生あるいは友達に簡単なクイズを作ってもらい、知識の習得を確認してください。クイズの問題は、参考書の中の無印の語例から選んでください。

Introduction

I. Overview of Text

Kanji in Context—A Study System for Intermediate and Advanced Learners has been designed to allow learners who have just completed a beginning course or are currently studying at the intermediate or advanced level to systematically and efficiently expand the foundation of *kanji* and vocabulary that they have acquired. This text is divided into two halves, a reference book and a 2-volume workbook.

Kanji in Context has several distinct features not found in other *kanji* textbooks currently available:

☐ The first textbook specifically designed for intermediate and advanced learners

Until now, *kanji* textbooks have always been designed so that study commences with the very basics, and there have been no textbooks to help intermediate and advanced learners begin an in-depth study of the characters. In response to this deficiency, *Kanji in Context* has been created specifically for learners who have just completed a beginning course or have already learned a fair number of *kanji* at the intermediate or advanced level but would like to amplify their knowledge of *kanji* and *kanji*-based vocabulary in a systematic fashion.

☐ *Kanji* can be learned in a systematic fashion

At the intermediate level and above, the number of *kanji* needed by learners rises sharply. In order to effectively meet this growing need, it is not adequate to learn each new character randomly; rather, it is also necessary to study the systematic connections that lie behind *kanji* and *kanji*-based vocabulary. In general, there are three basic elements to *kanji*: form, sound, and meaning. Form refers to the principles behind the structure of *kanji* (the components and their positions within a character); sound to the shared connections and similarities in the readings of particular *kanji*, as based on their components; and meaning to the underlying system of meaning in *kanji*, as based on their components.

These three elements are organically intertwined within the *kanji*, and a proper knowledge of them will not only bring a dramatic increase in the speed at which new *kanji* and vocabulary are digested, but will also foster the ability to infer the meaning and reading of previously unencountered *kanji* and vocabulary. The reference book of this text has been designed so that the principles of form, sound, and meaning behind the *kanji* will be automatically acquired as the characters are studied.

☐ Focus of study is not on *kanji* only, but also on *kanji*-based vocabulary

In addition to the acquisition of new *kanji*, it is also important for intermediate and advanced learners to learn new *kanji*-based vocabulary and their correct usage. However, traditional *kanji* textbooks have focused excessively on the study of characters one by one, providing only a sprinkling of vocabulary which, more than often, have little practical use for learners.

In contrast, this text goes beyond mere study of *kanji* to include the acquisition of vocabulary as one of its objectives. Thus the reference book contains an abundant collection of essential vocabulary, all of which have been selected with the different stages of learning in mind. Moreover, the usage of the vocabulary in the reference book can be learned in context through the example sentences and related vocabulary in both volumes of the workbook.

☐ *Kanji* can be easily acquired by repeated exposure

In the majority of *kanji* textbooks, each *kanji* or word is presented only once, an approach based on the assumption that it will be fully mastered at the time it appears. However, a single presentation leaves no guarantee that the character or word will be effectively acquired by the learner. For this reason, the same target vocabulary and related words are repeatedly presented in both the reference book and the workbook. The frequent contact with a particular *kanji* or word will reinforce its acquisition, while at the same time relieving learners of the pressure experienced under the single-presentation approach.

Now follows a description of the contents of the reference book and the workbook. Learners who do not need to go over these details should at least read "IV. How to Use *Kanji in Context*" before commencing their study.

II. Overview of Reference Book

1. Main Contents

The reference book presents the following information:

1) 1,947 *kanji*: all 1,945 *Jōyō Kanji* plus 誰 and 賂
2) The readings of these *kanji*
3) The number of strokes in these *kanji*
4) Vocabulary using the *kanji*, and the corresponding *kana* reading and English equivalent

2. Selection of the *Kanji* in This Text

In 1981 the Japanese Ministry of Education published the *Jōyō Kanji Hyō*, a list standardizing the use of *kanji* in modern written Japanese. 1,945 characters were selected, and their *on* and *kun* readings (Chinese-derived and Japanese readings) were delimited. The authority of this list has deeply permeated Japanese society to the point where it now serves as the standard for modern *kanji* usage in official documents, newspapers, magazines, books, and the like.

All 1,945 *Jōyō Kanji* have been included in this text, as well as two additional characters, 誰 and 賂. 誰 has been included since it is often used and since its simple form is easily recognized by most Japanese language learners, whereas 賂 has been included since learners should be familiar with the writing of the compound 賄賂.

3. *Kanji* Levels

The 1,947 *kanji* appearing in the reference book have been divided into six levels corresponding to the following stages of learning:

Level	No. of *Kanji*	Stage
1	250	These are elementary *kanji* that a learner who has completed a beginning course is expected to have already studied.
2	100 (subtotal: 350)	These are *kanji* that an inter-mediate learner is expected to have already studied.
3	850 (subtotal: 1,200)	These are *kanji* that are generally taught in an intermediate course.
4	220 (subtotal: 1,420)	These are *kanji* that may be covered in certain intermediate courses but are not necessarily common to such courses, or *kanji* that are generally taught in advanced courses.
5	412 (subtotal: 1,832)	These are *kanji* that may be covered in certain advanced courses but are not necessarily common to such courses.
6	115 (total: 1,947)	These are special *kanji* which appear only in the vocabulary or terminology of particular fields. The *kanji* in this level are divided into three categories: *kanji* related to nature, *kanji* related to history or literature, and *kanji* which are very rarely used.

According to a study by the National Language Research Institute, the 500 most often used *kanji* represent roughly 80% of the *kanji* found in newspapers, and 94%

of newspaper *kanji* can be covered by 1,000 characters. In accordance with this finding, mastery of the 1,200 *kanji* in Levels 1-3 of this text makes for a broad, adequate knowledge of *kanji*. If Level 4 *kanji* are also mastered, then the only *kanji* remaining are those which are rarely used. In fact, study up through Level 3 (or, depending on the circumstances, up through Level 4), should give you a more or less sufficient knowledge of *kanji* and useful vocabulary. All you need to do for the next step is to naturally increase this knowledge by actually reading newspaper and magazine articles and books related to your interests or field of study.

4. Arrangement of Entries

Not only have the *kanji* in this text been divided into six levels, but they have also been arranged in special order within each level according to a variety of factors, particularly their importance and difficulty, as well as connections in form, meaning, and related vocabulary. In addition, various strategies of arrangement have been applied to the levels as explained below.

Levels 1 & 2: The entries have been arranged mainly around the connections in meaning between each entry's first vocabulary word (the "key word"— see "5. Selection and Arrangement of Vocabulary" below).

Levels 3 & 4: The entries have been arranged comprehensively according the following strategies:

Main strategy: The entries are arranged in order of familiarity and frequency of use of each entry's key word.

Secondary strategies:
- *Kanji* that go together to make up important compounds are placed together.
- *Kanji* that share common components and are similar in form are placed together.
- *Kanji* that do not share common components but are similar enough in form that they might be confused are placed together.
- *Kanji* whose key words make up a distinct group are placed together.

Level 5: The entries are arranged mainly according to similarities in form.

Level 6: The entries are mainly arranged mainly according to similarities in form and vocabulary.

The overall arrangement produced by the above strategies can be seen by perusing the condensed listing of the entries at the end of the text (p. 280).

5. Selection and Arrangement of Vocabulary

The vocabulary in this text represent the core of *kanji*-based vocabulary, and were carefully selected as the most essential words which meet the needs and interests of adult learners. There are approximately 9,000 words, covering the majority of *kanji*-based vocabulary that appear on Level 1 of the Japanese Language Proficiency Test. The first word of the vocabulary listing of an entry is the key word for that particular *kanji*, the most fundamental word that uses the *kanji* and should definitely be memorized when learning the *kanji*. The vocabulary that follow the key word are arranged according to various factors, including similarities in the meaning of the *kanji* as used in the vocabulary, similarities in structure, similarities in reading, and degree of difficulty. Amongst the vocabulary are compounds that contain *kanji* that have not yet been covered in the text to that point or *kanji* that are not covered at all in the text, but were considered important enough to warrant their inclusion in the vocabulary listing. Such vocabulary have been marked with special symbols, such as * or ▲ (see 6. below).

6. Explanation of Entries

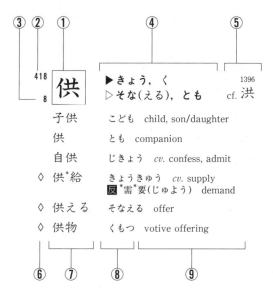

① ***Kanji* entry**

② **Number of order in text**

③ **Stroke number**

④ **Readings**

1) All the readings listed in the *Jōyō Kanji Hyō* are given. ▶ marks the *on* readings, and ▷ marks the *kun* readings. *Okurigana* are placed in parentheses.

2) Readings which according to the *Jōyō kanji Hyō* are limited in usage or to special cases are printed in light font.

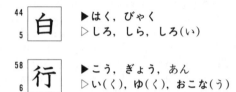

⑤ *Kanji* **similar in appearance**

In some cases, *kanji* that are similar in appearance to a particular *kanji* entry are listed on the right side of the heading along with their number in the text, so as to prevent confusion.

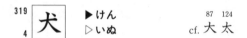

⑥ **Notation of difficulty**

Difficult vocabulary have been marked with special symbols for clear reference.

◇······1) Vocabulary which contain a *kanji* that has not yet been studied in the text. (Note that all the *kanji* in Levels 1 and 2 are treated as previously studied characters.)

◇ 大*丈夫　だいじょうぶ　all right, secure, safe
◇ 和*風　わふう　Japanese style
(* denotes the *kanji* which has not yet been studied.)

2) Vocabulary which are made up of previously studied *kanji* but are considered difficult words.

◇ 大いに　おおいに　very
◇ 落第　らくだい　*cv.* flunk, fail

（然）……Special vocabulary related to nature.

      （然）＊渓谷　　けいこく　valley
      （然）麦＊芽　　ばくが　malt

（歴）……Special vocabulary related to history or literature.

      （歴）大名　　だいみょう　*daimyō*, feudal lord
      （歴）文　　ふみ　letter

（特）……Special vocabulary which are used very rarely.

      （特）＊緑青　　ろくしょう　copper/green rust, patina
      （特）歩　　ふ　pawn (in Japanese chess)

Since the vocabulary marked with these symbols are considered difficult in one's first encounter with them, there is no need to memorize them right away. Instead, start with the vocabulary that are not marked with these symbols (the workbook covers only the unmarked vocabulary). Most of the vocabulary marked with ◊ appear again later in the text so that they can be studied once more.

⑦ **Appearance in text**

Vocabulary which contain a *kanji* that has not yet appeared as an entry or a *kanji* which does not appear as an entry at all are marked with the following symbols:

＊ ……*Kanji* which have not yet appeared as an entry (*kanji* which soon appear thereafter as an entry are left unmarked).

      ◊ ＊統一　　とういつ　*cv.* unity
      ◊ 三つ＊角　　みつかど　three-way junction

▲ ……*Kanji* which do not appear as an entry in the text.

      ◊ 茶▲碗　　ちゃわん　(rice) bowl, teacup
      ◊ 大▲阪府　　おおさかふ　Osaka Prefecture

⑧ **Special readings**

The following symbols have been added to vocabulary which have a special reading:

△ ……Supplementary readings which appear in the appendix to the *Jōyō Kanji*. These represent *ateji* and *jukujikun* which are recognized as *Jōyō Kanji* readings.

      一人　　△ひとり　one person
      ◊ 二十＊歳　　△はたち　twenty years old

私　　　　わたくし, ▲わたし　I, me
歴 細雪　　▲ささめゆき　light snowfall

⑨ Meaning

cv.······This denotes compound verbs (compounds which can be used as verbs by the addition of *suru*).

出発　　しゅっぱつ　*cv.* depart, leave
計算　　けいさん　*cv.* calculate, compute

vt./vi.······These are used to indicate whether a verb is transitive or intransitive in cases where it cannot be determined from the English translation alone.

続ける　　つづける　*vt.* continue
続く　　　つづく　*vi.* continue

cf.······This marks notes on usage or related vocabulary.

子ども　　こども　child, son/daughter　cf. *Kodomo*
　　　　　can be written as 子ども or 子供.
作家　　さっか　novelist　cf. 筆者(ひっしゃ) writer,
　　　　　著者(ちょしゃ) author

abbr.······This denotes abbreviations of compounds.

日本銀行　　にほんぎんこう　the Bank of Japan　cf. *abbr.* 日銀(にちぎん)
◊　短*期大学　たんきだいがく　junior college　cf. *abbr.* 短大(たんだい)

反······This denotes antonyms.

◊　主*観*的な　しゅかんてきな　subjective　反客*観*的な
　　　　　　　(きゃっかんてきな)　objective
日の出　　ひので　sunrise　反日の入り(ひのいり) sunset

⑩ Cross reference with workbook

Each section of the reference book corresponding to a lesson in the workbook is marked off with a dotted line, and the number of the corrosponding lesson is also given.

③

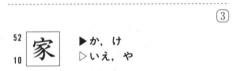

⑪ **Columns**

In order to help you further expand your knowledge of *kanji* and *kanji*-based vocabulary, two different types of informative columns have been included in this text.

■ Easily Confused *Kanji*
Kanji which can be easily confused due to common components or similarity in appearance are presented together in this column.

■ Related Vocabulary
Vocabulary which are connected in meaning are presented together in this column.

7. Index

Four types of indexes have been included to allow for speedy reference: *on-kun*, form, stroke, and vocabulary. These indexes can be used as described below.

(A) When the reading is known:

***On-Kun* Index**
This index can be used to look up a *kanji* when you know either its *on* or *kun* reading. All the readings for *kanji* entries are contained in the index (arranged in *a-i-u-e-o* order), with the corresponding *kanji* and its number of order in the text. *Okurigana* are included for the *kun* readings.

(B) When the reading is not known:

Either the form index or the stroke index can be used to look up a *kanji* when you do not know the reading.

Form Index
In this index, use the structure of the *kanji* to help you find its location. As most learners know, *kanji* are not random collections of dots and lines; instead, most of them are made up of distinct components. There are a large number of such components, and there is a set pattern to how they are combined to form a *kanji*. The location of the main component can take one of the following eight types of positions.

1	レフト (left)	伝	凝	提
2	ライト (right)	別	敬	断
3	トップ (top)	今	冠	声
4	ボトム (bottom)	先	基	替
5	トップレフト (top & left)	局	広	戻
6	レフトボトム (left & bottom)	道	起	題

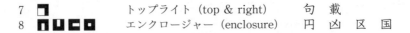8   エンクロージャー (enclosure)   円　凶　区　国

The above types of position are used to look up a *kanji* with the form index as follows:

1) Determine which component is the main component of the *kanji* that you wish to find.
2) Look up the number of the main component by referring to the chart at the end of this text. The main components for each of the eight position types are arranged in order of stroke number, so it will be necessary to carefully check the main component's position and stroke number in order to use this index.
3) Use the component number to find the *kanji* in the index. The *kanji* are arranged under each component heading according to stroke number, and their entry nember is given.

There are many cases where two components of a *kanji* are recognized as its main component, and either one can be used in this index to look up the *kanji*. For example, in the case of 休, both イ on the left and 木 on the right can be used to look up the character. In the same manner, the *kanji* 思 can be referenced with its top component 田 or its bottom component 心.

Stroke Index
There are some *kanji* that do not fit into the eight position types, such as 心, 土, 器, and 飛. All these *kanji* (185 characters) not found in the form index are included in the stroke index. Also found in the stroke index are *kanji* which are considered difficult to find through the form index (30 characters). It would be a good idea to go over the stroke index at least once in order to familiarize yourself with what sort of *kanji* are listed.

(C) Looking up vocabulary:

Vocabulary Index
All the vocabulary contained in the reference book are listed in *a-i-u-e-o* order in the vocabulary index with the corresponding entry number of the *kanji* under which they appear. Thus the reference book can serve as a dictionary through the use of the vocabulary index to look up the location of a particular word to find its meaning.

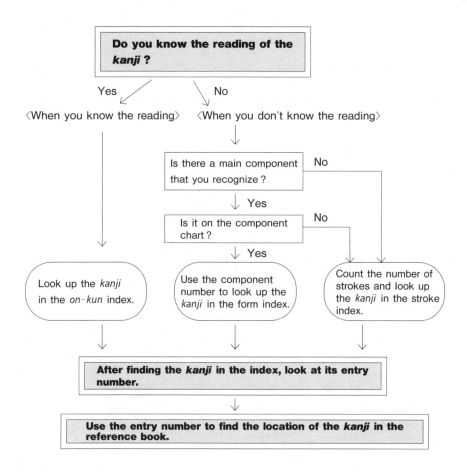

III. Overview of Workbook

1. Main Contents

Each lesson of both volumes of the workbook focuses on approximately 10 *kanji* (approximately 20 for Levels 1 and 2) from the reference book in the order that they appear, and provides a variety of approaches to help you master the usage of the target vocabulary and expand your overall understanding of *kanji*-based vocabulary. Each lesson is divided into three major sections as listed below:

Section I: Double compounds, idiomatic expressions, and sentence patterns
               that use the vocabulary.
Section II: Related vocabulary, other related words, contrasting expressions.
Section III: Example sentences using the vocabulary.

Now follow some examples of the material presented in each of the above sections.
Underlined words are the vocabulary from the reference book.

Section I
In this section, the basic usage of the vocabulary is learned by studying expressions
containing them.

1) Double compounds containing the vocabulary, e.g.;

　　和平交渉　　団体旅行　支持率　　技術移転

2) Broad idiomatic expressions using the vocabulary, e.g.;

　　平和を守る　　公平な態度　　約束を守る/破る
　　日本人の外国人に対する態度

3) Sentence patterns using the vocabulary, e.g.;

　　ＸとＹを同等に扱う　　手紙を封筒に入れて送る
　　手紙を速達で送る　　大学進学について兄に相談する

Section II
In this section, the connections in meaning between the vocabulary and related
words are studied.

1) Related target vocabulary and other related words, e.g.;

　　戦争と平和　　　管理職と平社員
　　事務　　　事務員　　事務室
　　会社員　　銀行員　　教員　　　工員

2) Contrasting expressions, e.g.;　　　・

　　Ｘの意見/提案に反対する　⟷　Ｘの意見/提案に賛成する
　　損(を)する　⟷　得(を)する
　　値段　　価格　　物価　　地価

Section III
In this section, the usage of the vocabulary is learned in the context of example
sentences. The example sentences have been chosen so as to be of interest to adult
learners, and they are the most appropriate examples for learning proper usage of
the vocabulary. The readings of the underlined vocabulary are given on the right
of the sentences.

2. Vocabulary Covered in Workbook

The vocabulary treated in the workbook are only the ones in the reference book that do not bear any of the symbols for difficult words (◇, 然, 歴, 特: see II. 6 "Explanation of Entries"). The marked vocabulary have not been included because they do not belong to a corresponding stage of study. In addition, some unmarked vocabulary have not been included in the workbook: very basic vocabulary found in Levels 1 and 2, and rarely used special vocabulary found in Levels 5 and 6.

3. Division of Workbook

The first volume of the workbook covers Levels 1-3 of the reference book (*kanji* no. 1-1200), and the second volume covers Levels 4-6 (*kanji* no. 1201-1947).

IV. How to Use *Kanji in Context*

1. Target Level

One of the assumptions for the effective use of *Kanji in Context* is that the learner has mastered the 200-300 *kanji* normally taught in a typical beginning course. In terms of this text, you should already be familiar with most of the key words for the *kanji* entries in Level 1 (*kanji* no. 1-250). If you have mastered these *kanji*, then you should be able to make effective use of the reference book and the workbook together to systematically learn the *kanji* and vocabulary presented.

If you are still at the beginning level, you can quickly increase your knowledge of compounds and other vocabulary by using the reference guide to systematically organize the *kanji* that you study in your beginning course textbook. As for the workbook, you should perhaps wait until you have increased your knowledge of *kanji* and vocabulary to a certain extent before you start using it.

2. Where to Start

For the most part, Levels 1 and 2 of the *kanji* entries in the reference book represent the beginning level of study, Level 3 represents the intermediate level, Level 4 represents the advanced level, and Levels 5 and 6 represent the post-advanced level. While it is possible for you to enter this text at any point in accordance with your current level of proficiency and preferred study method, generally it will be best to start at the beginning with Level 1. Although you are most likely already familiar with a large number of the *kanji* in Levels 1 and 2, study of these levels is sure to help expand your knowledge of *kanji*-based vocabulary. In addition, the lessons in the workbook corresponding to Levels 1 and 2 contain more *kanji* than the other lessons so that you can quickly and efficiently proceed with your studies.

3. Studying *Kanji* and *Kanji*-Based Vocabulary with *Kanji in Context*

Below are some pointers that will help you to get the most out of the special design of this text. However, as everyone has his or her own preferred study method, feel free to study this text in the manner that best serves your needs after you have become acquainted with its set-up.

Step 1: Acquire a fundamental knowledge of the *kanji* entries
Fully memorize the meaning and reading of the key words in the reference book and the *kanji* from which they are composed. This study gives you a fundamental knowledge of the *kanji*.

Step 2: Learn the meaning and usage of the *kanji* entries
Go over the vocabulary listed for each entry in the reference book to learn the meaning and usage of the *kanji*.

Step 3: Study the vocabulary
Memorize the meaning and reading for all the unmarked vocabulary in the reference book. Since the vocabulary marked with ◇, 然, 歴, and 特 are vocabulary for a more advanced stage of study, there is no need to learn them right away.

Step 4: Study the usage of the vocabulary and learn related words
Use the workbook to study the usage of the vocabulary from the reference book and other words related to the vocabulary. Be sure to fully memorize the meaning, reading, and usage of all the underlined words (the unmarked vocabulary from the reference book). If you are unable to recall the meaning or reading for a particular word, then go back to the reference book to get this information.

> Note: All the unmarked vocabulary from Levels 3 and 4 in the reference book are covered in the workbook, but only the unmarked vocabulary in Levels 1 and 2 which are not very basic words and the unmarked vocabulary in Levels 5 and 6 which are essential are taken up in the workbook.

Step 5: Check your mastery
Have your Japanese teacher or a friend make simple quizzes for you to check your mastery of the material. Use just the unmarked vocabulary in the reference book for the quizzes.

第１水準

(Level 1)

1-250

①

1 1	一	▶いち，いつ ▷ひと，ひと（つ）

一　　　　　　　いち　one

一分　　　　　　いっぷん　one minute

◇ *統一　　　　とういつ　*cv.* unify

◇ 一*般*的な　　いっぱんてきな　general, usual, ordinary

◇ *唯一の　　　ゆいいつの　sole

一人　　　　　△ひとり　one person

一人一人　　　△ひとりひとり　one (person) by one, one (person) at a time

一つ　　　　　ひとつ　one (thing)

一目で　　　　ひとめで　at a glance

一日　　　　　△ついたち　the first (day of a month)

一日　　　　　いちにち　one day

2 2	二	▶に ▷ふた，ふた（つ）

二　　　　　　　に　two

二分　　　　　　にふん　two minutes

二人　　　　　△ふたり　two persons

二つ　　　　　ふたつ　two (things)

二日　　　　　△ふつか　the second (day of a month), two days

二十日　　　　△はつか　the twentieth (day of a month)

◇ 二十*歳　　　△はたち　twenty years old

3 3	三	▶さん ▷み，み（つ），みっ（つ）

三　　　　　　　さん　three

三分　　　　　　さんぷん　three minutes

三人　　　　　　さんにん　three persons

三つ　　　　　みっつ　three (things)

三日　　　　　みっか　the third (day of a month), three days

◇ 三つ*角　　　みつかど　three-way junction

◇ 三日月　　　みかづき　crescent moon

4 5	四	▶し ▷よ，よ（つ），よっ（つ），よん

四　　　　　　　よん，し　four

四分　　　　　　よんぷん　four minutes

四人　　　　　　よにん　four persons

四つ　　　　　よっつ　four (things)

四日　　　　　よっか　four days

四月四日　　　しがつよっか　April 4

◇ 四つ*角　　　よつかど　crossroads, four-way junction

〈数え方(1)〉

一分（いっぷん）　二分（にふん）　三分（さんぷん）　四分（よんぷん）　五分（ごふん）

六分（ろっぷん）　七分（ななふん）　八分（はちふん/はっぷん）　九分（きゅうふん）

十分（じっぷん/じゅっぷん）

一人（ひとり）　二人（ふたり）　三人（さんにん）　四人（よにん）　五人（ごにん）

六人（ろくにん）　七人（しちにん/ななにん）　八人（はちにん）　九人（きゅうにん/くにん）

十人（じゅうにん）

5
4

| 五 | ▶ご |
| | ▷いつ，いつ(つ) |

五	ご　five
五分	ごふん　five minutes
五人	ごにん　five persons
五つ	いつつ　five (things)
五日	いつか　the fifth (day of a month), five days

6
4

| 六 | ▶ろく |
| | ▷む，む(つ)，むっ(つ)，むい |

六	ろく　six
六分	ろっぷん　six minutes
六人	ろくにん　six persons
六つ	むっつ　six (things)
六日	むいか　the sixth (day of a month), six days
六つ切り	むつぎり　cutting into six pieces

7
2

| 七 | ▶しち |
| | ▷なな，なな(つ)，なの |

七	しち，なな　seven
七分	ななふん　seven minutes
七人	ななにん　seven persons
七つ	ななつ　seven (things)

| 七日 | なのか　the seventh (day of a month), seven days |
| ◊ 七夕 | △たなばた　the Festival of the Weaver, the Star Festival |

8
2

| 八 | ▶はち |
| | ▷や，や(つ)，やっ(つ)，よう |

八	はち　eight
八分	はちふん　eight minutes
八人	はちにん　eight persons
八つ	やっつ　eight (things)
八日	ようか　the eighth (day of a month), eight days
八百屋	△やおや　fruit and vegetable shop
◊ 八つ*当たり	やつあたり　cv. take out one's anger on someone
◊ 八重*桜	やえざくら　double-flowered cherry tree

9
2

| 九 | ▶きゅう，く |
| | ▷ここの，ここの(つ) |

九	きゅう，く　nine
九分	きゅうふん　nine minutes
九人	きゅうにん　nine persons
九つ	ここのつ　nine (things)
九日	ここのか　nine days
九月九日	くがつここのか　September 9

〈数え方(2)〉
かぞ かた

一つ(ひとつ)　二つ(ふたつ)　三つ(みっつ)　四つ(よっつ)　五つ(いつつ)

六つ(むっつ)　七つ(ななつ)　八つ(やっつ)　九つ(ここのつ)　十(とお)

一日(ついたち)　二日(ふつか)　三日(みっか)　四日(よっか)　五日(いつか)

六日(むいか)　七日(なのか)　八日(ようか)　九日(ここのか)　十日(とおか)

二十日(はつか)

10 十 (2)
▶じゅう，じっ
▷とお，と

十	じゅう ten
十分	じっぷん，じゅっぷん ten minutes
十分(に)	じゅうぶん(に) in full, thoroughly
十人	じゅうにん ten persons
◊ 十*字*架	じゅうじか cross
十	とお ten (things)
十日	とおか the tenth (day of a month), ten days
◊ 十重	とえ tenfold
二十日	△はつか the twentieth (day of a month), twenty days
◊ 二十*歳	△はたち twenty years old

11 百 (6)
▶ひゃく

百	ひゃく one hundred
百円	ひゃくえん one hundred yen
～百	～ひゃく ～ hundred
三百六十五日	さんびゃくろくじゅうごにち 365 days
八百屋	△やおや fruit and vegetable shop

12 千 (3)
▶せん
▷ち

千	せん one thousand
千円	せんえん one thousand yen
～千	～せん ～ thousand
◊ 千*島*列*島	ちしまれっとう the Kuril Islands

13 万 (3)
▶まん，ばん

一万	いちまん ten thousand
一万円	いちまんえん ten thousand yen
◊ 万年*筆	まんねんひつ fountain pen
万一	まんいち by any chance, if anything should happen
◊ 万全の	ばんぜんの thorough, all possible (means/etc.)

14 円 (4)
▶えん
▷まる(い)

一万円	いちまんえん ten thousand yen
円	えん yen
円高	えんだか rise in the exchange rate of the yen
円安	えんやす fall in the exchange rate of the yen
◊ 円い	まるい circular cf. 丸い(まるい) round, circular

15 人 (2)
▶じん，にん
▷ひと

アメリカ人	アメリカじん an American
中国人	ちゅうごくじん a Chinese
日本人	にほんじん a Japanese
外国人	がいこくじん foreigner

─〈百から一万〉─────

百(ひゃく)　二百(にひゃく)　三百(さんびゃく)　四百(よんひゃく)　五百(ごひゃく)　六百(ろっぴゃく)　七百(ななひゃく)　八百(はっぴゃく)　九百(きゅうひゃく)

千(せん)　二千(にせん)　三千(さんぜん)　四千(よんせん)　五千(ごせん)　六千(ろくせん)　七千(ななせん)　八千(はっせん)　九千(きゅうせん)　一万(いちまん)

一人	△ひとり　one person
二人	△ふたり　two persons
三人	さんにん　three persons
五、六人	ごろくにん　five or six persons
人	ひと　person
男の人	おとこのひと　man
女の人	おんなのひと　woman
人々	ひとびと　people
大人	△おとな　adult
◇*仲人	△なこうど　go-between, match-maker
◇*素人	△しろうと　amateur
◇*玄人	△くろうと　expert

16 / 4　日　▶にち，じつ　▷ひ，か

日曜日	にちようび　Sunday
その日	そのひ　that day
日ざし	ひざし　sunlight
毎日	まいにち　every day
日本	にほん，にっぽん　Japan
休日	きゅうじつ　day off, holiday
◇*祝日	しゅくじつ　national holiday
一日	△ついたち　the first (day of a month)
二日	△ふつか　the second (day of a month), two days
三日	みっか　the third (day of a month), three days
◇*昨日	さくじつ，△きのう　yesterday
今日	△きょう　today

明日	みょうにち，△あす，▲あした　tomorrow

17 / 4　月　▶げつ，がつ　▷つき

月曜日	げつようび　Monday
月	つき　month, moon
月見	つきみ　moon-viewing
三日月	みかづき　crescent moon
一月	いちがつ　January
一か月	いっかげつ　one month
五月晴れ	△さつきばれ　fine weather in May
歴 五月雨	△さみだれ　early summer rain

18 / 4　火　▶か，　▷ひ，ほ

火曜日	かようび　Tuesday
火	ひ　fire, flame
火事	かじ　fire, conflagration
◇火*星	かせい　Mars
◇火*影	ほかげ　light of a fire/flame

19 / 4　水　▶すい　▷みず

水曜日	すいようび　Wednesday
水	みず　water
水道	すいどう　waterworks, water service, tap water
◇水*星	すいせい　Mercury
◇*清水寺	きよみずでら　Kiyomizu Temple (in Kyoto)

〈「々」の使い方〉

々, as in 人々, is a sign to repeat the preceding *kanji*.

ex. 木々（きぎ）　時々（ときどき）　方々（かたがた，ほうぼう）

20 木 4
▶ぼく，もく
▷き，こ

木曜日	もくようび	Thursday
木	き	tree
木々	きぎ	trees
大木	たいぼく	big tree
◇ 木*星	もくせい	Jupiter
◇ 木*綿	△もめん	cotton
◇ 木立	こだち	grove/thicket of trees

21 金 8
▶きん，こん
▷かね，かな

金曜日	きんようび	Friday
金	きん	gold
金	かね	money
お金持ち	おかねもち	rich person
◇ 金*星	きんせい	Venus
◇ 金物屋	かなものや	hardware store
◇ 金*堂	こんどう	main hall of a temple, golden pavillion
◇ *黄金	おうごん，こがね	gold

22 土 3
▶ど，と
▷つち

土曜日	どようび	Saturday
土	つち	soil, earth
土地	とち	land
◇ 土*星	どせい	Saturn
◇ お土*産	△おみやげ	souvenir

23 曜 18
▶よう

日曜日	にちようび	Sunday
曜日	ようび	day (of the week)

24 年 6
▶ねん
▷とし

来年	らいねん	next year
去年	きょねん	last year
今年	△ことし	this year
年	とし	year, age
二千年	にせんねん	(the year) 2000, two thousand years
三年生	さんねんせい	third-year student
年月	ねんげつ，としつき	months and years, time
年中	ねんじゅう	the whole year, throughout the year
生年月日	せいねんがっぴ	date of birth
年金	ねんきん	pension

25 時 10
▶じ
▷とき

一時	いちじ	one o'clock
時間	じかん	time
〜時間	〜じかん	〜 hour(s)
時々	ときどき	sometimes
時	とき	time
時計	△とけい	clock, watch
◇ 時雨	△しぐれ	rain shower in late autumn or early winter

26 分 4
▶ぶん，ふん，ぶ
▷わ(ける)，わ(かれる)，わ(か る)，わ(かつ)

〜分	〜ふん	〜 minute(s)
十分な	じゅうぶんな	enough, sufficient
水分	すいぶん	moisture, water
分かる	わかる	understand, realize, find out
分ける	わける	share, divide

分かれる　わかれる　branch off from ~ cf. *別れる（わかれる）part from, separate from a person

五分五分　ごぶごぶ　fifty-fifty

◇ 分かつ　わかつ　share

②

27
4
| 今 | ▶こん，きん |
| | ▷いま |

今　いま　now

今週　こんしゅう　this week

今月　こんげつ　this month

今日　こんにち　today, nowadays

今日　△きょう　today

今年　△ことし　this year

今朝　△けさ　this morning

歴 今上*陛下　きんじょうへいか　the reigning emperor

28
4
| 午 | ▶ご |

午前　ごぜん　morning

午後　ごご　afternoon

午後5時　ごごごじ　five o'clock p. m.

29
9
| 前 | ▶ぜん |
| | ▷まえ |

前　まえ　in front of, before

名前　なまえ　name

人前で　ひとまえで　in public

一人前　いちにんまえ　grown-up, independent, full-fledged

午前　ごぜん　morning

30
9
| 後 | ▶ご，こう |
| | ▷うし（ろ），あと，のち，おく（れる） |

午後　ごご　afternoon

その後　そのご，そのあと　after that

前後　ぜんご　front and behind, before and after, about

明後日　みょうごにち，▲あさって　the day after tomorrow

後ろ　うしろ　behind, back

後で　あとで　later

～（した）後　～（した）あと　after ~

後ほど　のちほど　later

後れる　おくれる　be behind (in one's work/schedule/etc.) cf. 遅れる（おくれる）be late (for)

後続の　こうぞくの　following (vehicle/etc.)

31
3
| 上 | ▶じょう，しょう |
| | ▷うえ，うわ，かみ，あ（げる），あ（がる），のぼ（る），のぼ（せる），のぼ（す） |

上　うえ　top; on, above

上着　うわぎ　coat, jacket

上手な　△じょうずな　skilled, good (tennis player/drawing/etc.)

地上　ちじょう　on the ground

川上　かわかみ　upper reaches of a river, upstream

◇ *値上げ　ねあげ　price increase; cv. raise prices

上げる　あげる　raise

上がる　あがる　rise, go up

上り電車　のぼりでんしゃ　inbound train

上る　のぼる　rise, go up (stairs) cf. *登る（のぼる）go up, climb

◇ 上回る　うわまわる　be more than, surpass

◇ 上せる　のぼせる　have a rush of blood to the head, be crazy about (a man/woman)

◇ 上す　のぼす　put on, put something on (top of)

歴 上人　しょうにん　saint

32 3	下	▶か, げ ▷した, しも, もと, さ(げる), さ(がる), くだ(る), くだ(す), くだ(さる), お(ろす), お(りる)

地下鉄	ちかてつ　subway
下	した　bottom; under, beneath
下書き	したがき　rough copy, draft; cv. draft
◇*靴下	くつした　sock
◇ 下見	したみ　preliminary visit
川下	かわしも　lower reaches of a river, downstream
～の下で	～のもとで　under the supervision of ～
下水	げすい　sewage, drainage
下車	げしゃ　cv. get off (a train)
上下	じょうげ　up and down, top and bottom; cv. go up and down
◇*値下げ	ねさげ　price reduction; cv. lower prices
下げる	さげる　bring down, lower
下ろす	おろす　put down　cf. 降ろす (おろす) unload, drop off (a passenger)
下りる	おりる　go down　cf. 降りる (おりる) get off (a train/etc.)
下り電車	くだりでんしゃ　outbound train
下る	くだる　go down, fall
下さる	くださる　give (honorific)
見下す	みくだす　despise, look down on (in contempt)
下手な	△へたな　unskillful, poor (tennis player/drawing/etc.)

33 4	中	▶ちゅう ▷なか

中	なか　the inside; in the middle
中学校	ちゅうがっこう　junior high school
中国	ちゅうごく　China
中東	ちゅうとう　the Middle East
中年の	ちゅうねんの　middle-aged
日中	にっちゅう　in the daytime
◇ 日中*関*係	にっちゅうかんけい　Sino-Japanese relations
一日中	いちにちじゅう　all day long
世界中	せかいじゅう　throughout the world
◇ 心中	しんじゅう　double suicide; cv. commit suicide together
◇ 中小*企業	ちゅうしょうきぎょう　small and medium-sized enterprises

34 15	横	▶おう ▷よこ

横	よこ　side, beside
横切る	よこぎる　cross
◇ 横*顔	よこがお　profile
◇ 横*断	おうだん　cv. cross, go across

35 5	右	▶う, ゆう ▷みぎ

右	みぎ　right
右手	みぎて　right hand/arm
右足	みぎあし　right foot/leg
◇ 右*翼	うよく　the right wing, rightist
左右する	さゆうする　control, affect

36 5	左	▶さ ▷ひだり

左	ひだり　left
左手	ひだりて　left hand/arm
左足	ひだりあし　left foot/leg
左右する	さゆうする　control, affect
◇ 左*翼	さよく　the left wing, leftist

37 5	**本**	▶ほん ▷もと

	本	ほん　book
	〜本	〜ほん　counter for long objects
	日本	にほん，にっぽん　Japan
	本心	ほんしん　one's real intention, one's right mind
	本来	ほんらい　originally, from the first
◇	本*当に	ほんとうに　truly, really
◇	本*当の	ほんとうの　true, real
◇	本	もと　the beginning, the origin

38 6	**机**	▶き ▷つくえ

| | 机 | つくえ　desk |
| ◇ | 机上の*空*論 | きじょうのくうろん　armchair theory |

39 8	**東**	▶とう ▷ひがし

	東	ひがし　east
	東ヨーロッパ	ひがしヨーロッパ　Eastern Europe
	東アジア	ひがしアジア　East Asia
	中東	ちゅうとう　the Middle East
	東京	とうきょう　Tokyo
◇	東*洋	とうよう　the East
◇	*関東	かんとう　the Kanto region

40 6	**西**	▶せい，さい ▷にし

	西	にし　west
	西ヨーロッパ	にしヨーロッパ　Western Europe
	西アジア	にしアジア　West Asia
	東西南北	とうざいなんぼく　north, south, east, and west

| ◇ | 西*洋 | せいよう　the West |
| ◇ | *関西 | かんさい　the Kansai region |

41 9	**南**	▶なん，な ▷みなみ

	南	みなみ　south
	南アメリカ	みなみアメリカ　South America
	東南アジア	とうなんアジア　Southeast Asia
	南下	なんか　cv. go south
歴	南*無*妙*法*蓮*華*経	なむみょうほうれんげきょう　chant of the Tendai and Nichiren sects of Buddhism, taken from the Lotus Sutra

42 5	**北**	▶ほく ▷きた

	北	きた　north
	北アメリカ	きたアメリカ　North America
	北風	きたかぜ　north wind
	東北	とうほく　the Tohoku region, (the) northeast
	北海道	ほっかいどう　Hokkaido
	南北問題	なんぼくもんだい　the North-South problem
◇	北方*領土	ほっぽうりょうど　the Northern Territories

43 4	**方**	▶ほう ▷かた

	方	ほう　direction, way
◇	方*向	ほうこう　direction
	方々	ほうぼう　here and there, various places
	食べ方	たべかた　way of eating, table manners
	あの方	あのかた　the person over there (honorific)
	行方	△ゆくえ　whereabouts

44	白	▶はく，びゃく
5		▷しろ，しら，しろ(い)

白い	しろい	white
白	しろ	white
真っ白(い/な/の)	まっしろ(い/な/の)	pure white, as white as snow
白人	はくじん	white person, Caucasian
明白な	めいはくな	clear, obvious
◇ 白夜	びゃくや	nights under the midnight sun
◇ 白む	しらむ	grow light

45	黒	▶こく
11		▷くろ，くろ(い)

黒い	くろい	black
黒	くろ	black
白黒テレビ	しろくろテレビ	black-and-white television
◇ 黒*字	くろじ	surplus, black (as in "be in the black")
	反赤*字(あかじ)	deficit, red (as in "be in the red")
真っ黒な	まっくろな	pitch-black
黒人	こくじん	black person

46	赤	▶せき，しゃく
7		▷あか，あか(い)，あか(らむ)，あか(らめる)

赤い	あかい	red
赤	あか	red
赤らめる	あからめる	blush
真っ赤な	△まっかな	bright/deep red
赤道	せきどう	the equator
◇ 赤外*線	せきがいせん	infrared light
◇ 赤十*字	せきじゅうじ	the Red Cross
◇ 赤*銅色	しゃくどういろ	bronze(-colored)

47	青	▶せい，しょう
8		▷あお，あお(い)

青い	あおい	blue
青	あお	blue
青白い	あおじろい	pale
真っ青な	△まっさおな	deep blue, pale
◇ 青春時*代	せいしゅんじだい	youth, springtime of life
◇ 青少年	せいしょうねん	juveniles, young people
特 *緑青	ろくしょう	copper/green rust, patina

48	先	▶せん
6		▷さき

先生	せんせい	teacher, master
先週	せんしゅう	last week
先々週	せんせんしゅう	the week before last
先月	せんげつ	last month
先々月	せんせんげつ	the month before last
先日	せんじつ	the other day
先に	さきに	previously, beforehand
先ほど	さきほど	a little while ago

49	生	▶せい，しょう
5		▷い(きる)，い(かす)，い(ける)，う(まれる)，う(む)，お(う)，は(える)，は(やす)，き，なま

先生	せんせい	teacher, master
学生	がくせい	student
◇ 生*徒	せいと	pupil, student
◇ 生*活	せいかつ	living, life
◇ 生長	せいちょう	growth (of a plant)
一生	いっしょう	one's (whole) life

◇ *誕生日	たんじょうび	birthday
生まれる	うまれる	be born
生む	うむ	yield, produce cf. *産む（うむ）bear
生きる	いきる	live
生き生きした	いきいきした	lively, fresh
生かす	いかす	make the most of, make the best use of
生け花	いけばな	the art of flower arrangement
生ビール	なまビール	draft beer
◇ 生*野*菜	なまやさい	fresh vegetables
生える	はえる	grow, come out
◇ *芝生	△しばふ	lawn, plot of grass
◇ 生地	きじ	cloth
◇ 生*糸	きいと	raw silk
◇ 生い立ち	おいたち	one's background, one's personal history, one's origin

50 **8** 学 ▶がく ▷まな(ぶ)

学校	がっこう	school
学生	がくせい	student
大学	だいがく	university, college
学長	がくちょう	president (of a university), provost
～学部	～がくぶ	department of ～, school of ～
入学	にゅうがく	cv. enter a school
学ぶ	まなぶ	learn

51 **10** 校 ▶こう

学校	がっこう	school
小学校	しょうがっこう	elementary school
中学校	ちゅうがっこう	junior high school

| 高校 | こうこう | high school |
| 校長 | こうちょう | principal, schoolmaster |

③

52 **10** 家 ▶か, け ▷いえ, や

家	いえ, ▲うち	house, home
家族	かぞく	family
◇ 家*庭	かてい	family, home
家事	かじ	housework, housekeeping
家内	かない	my wife
国家	こっか	state, nation
作家	さっか	novelist, author
ロックフェラー家	ロックフェラーけ	the Rockefeller family
大家さん	おおやさん	landlord, owner of a rented house/apartment

53 **11** 部 ▶ぶ

部屋	△へや	room
部長	ぶちょう	department head
人事部	じんじぶ	personnel department
部下	ぶか	subordinate, one's men
◇ 本部	ほんぶ	headquarters, head office
外部の	がいぶの	outside, external
内部の	ないぶの	inside, internal
全部	ぜんぶ	all
一部	いちぶ	a portion, a part of
部分	ぶぶん	one portion, one part
大部分	だいぶぶん	most of ～, the bulk of ～

54 屋 9 ▶おく ▷や

本屋	ほんや	bookstore
花屋	はなや	flower shop
八百屋	△やおや	fruit and vegetable shop
部屋	△へや	room
小屋	こや	hut, shed
◇ 屋*根	やね	roof
屋上	おくじょう	housetop, roof
屋内プール	おくないプール	indoor (swimming) pool
屋外	おくがい	outdoor, open-air
◇ 家屋	かおく	houses
歴 母屋	△おもや	main building/house

55 店 8 ▶てん ▷みせ

店	みせ	store, shop
店長	てんちょう	store manager
本店	ほんてん	the main office/store
◇*支店	してん	branch office/store
◇*支店長	してんちょう	branch manager
夜店	よみせ	night stall/stand
◇ 店屋	みせや	shops and stores

56 駅 14 ▶えき

駅	えき	station
駅前	えきまえ	in front of the station
東京駅	とうきょうえき	Tokyo Station
駅長	えきちょう	stationmaster

57 銀 14 ▶ぎん

銀行	ぎんこう	bank
日本銀行	にほんぎんこう	the Bank of Japan cf. *abbr.* 日銀(にちぎん)
銀	ぎん	silver
水銀	すいぎん	mercury
銀色	ぎんいろ	silver, silvery

58 行 6 ▶こう，ぎょう，あん ▷い(く)，ゆ(く)，おこな(う)

銀行	ぎんこう	bank
旅行	りょこう	trip; *cv.* make a trip, travel
行動	こうどう	*cv.* act, behave, conduct
行く	いく，ゆく	go
行方	△ゆくえ	whereabouts
行う	おこなう	do, carry out, hold cf. 行われる(おこなわれる) be carried out, be held
◇ 行い	おこない	act, action, behavior
行事	ぎょうじ	event
◇ 行*政	ぎょうせい	administration
行	ぎょう	line (in a text)
～行目	～ぎょうめ	line (one/two/etc.)
歴 行*脚	あんぎゃ	pilgrimage; *cv.* make a pilgrimage

59 会 6 ▶かい，え ▷あ(う)

会社	かいしゃ	company
社会	しゃかい	society
会話	かいわ	conversation
国会	こっかい	the Diet
学会	がっかい	academic conference
大会	たいかい	convention, general meeting, tournament, rally
会う	あう	meet
◇ 会*釈	えしゃく	*cv.* bow slightly
◇ 会*得	えとく	*cv.* understand (the meaning of), learn how to do

60 社 7	▶しゃ ▷やしろ

会社	かいしゃ　company
社会	しゃかい　society
社長	しゃちょう　company president
社*員	しゃいん　company employee
本社	ほんしゃ　headquarters, main office
支社	ししゃ　branch (office)
歴 社	やしろ　Shinto shrine

61 電 13	▶でん

電車	でんしゃ　train
電話	でんわ　telephone
電気	でんき　electricity
発電	はつでん　(electric) power generation; *cv.* generate electricity
電子	でんし　electron
◇ 電*池	でんち　battery

62 車 7	▶しゃ ▷くるま

電車	でんしゃ　train
自転車	じてんしゃ　bicycle
車	くるま　car
歴 山車	△だし　float, festival car

63 自 6	▶じ，し ▷みずか(ら)

自動車	じどうしゃ　car
自転車	じてんしゃ　bicycle
自分	じぶん　self, oneself, I
自分で	じぶんで　by oneself, personally
◇ 自*由	じゆう　freedom, liberty
◇ 自*然	しぜん　nature
◇ 自ら	みずから　(for) oneself, in person

64 動 11	▶どう ▷うご(く)，うご(かす)

自動車	じどうしゃ　car
自動	じどう　automatic
動く	うごく　move
動物	どうぶつ　animal cf. *植物(しょくぶつ) plants
行動	こうどう　*cv.* act, behave, conduct

65 転 11	▶てん ▷ころ(がる)，ころ(げる)，ころ(がす)，ころ(ぶ)

自転車	じてんしゃ　bicycle
運転	うんてん　*cv.* drive, work, operate
転ぶ	ころぶ　tumble, fall down
転がす	ころがす　roll (a stone/tire/ etc.)
転がる	ころがる　roll (over), tumble
転々とする	てんてんとする　go rolling, wander (from one place/job to another)

66 道 12	▶どう，とう ▷みち

道	みち　road
水道	すいどう　waterworks, water service, tap water
国道	こくどう　national road
◇ 道*路	どうろ　road
北*海道	ほっかいどう　Hokkaido

茶道	さどう，ちゃどう　the art of the tea ceremony　cf. *華道(かどう) the art of flower arrangement, *剣道(けんどう) kendō, swordsmanship, *柔道(じゅうどう) judo
◇*神道	しんとう　Shintoism

67　男　7
▶だん，なん
▷おとこ

男の人	おとこのひと　man
男	おとこ　man
山男	やまおとこ　mountaineer, alpinist, woodsman
◇男*性	だんせい　male, man
長男	ちょうなん　the eldest son

68　女　3
▶じょ，にょ，にょう
▷おんな，め

女の人	おんなのひと　woman
女	おんな　woman
◇女*性	じょせい　female, woman
長女	ちょうじょ　the eldest daughter
◇女*房	にょうぼう　my wife
◇*老若男女	ろうじゃくなんにょ，ろうにゃくなんにょ　men and women of all ages
◇女人	にょにん　woman
◇女*神	めがみ　goddess
歴*乙女	△おとめ　maiden, (young) girl, virgin
◇海女	△あま　woman diver (for pearls/oysters/etc.)

69　子　3
▶し，す
▷こ

子ども	こども　child, son/daughter　cf. Kodomo is normally written as こども、or 子供.
男の子	おとこのこ　boy

女の子	おんなのこ　girl
◇*迷子	△まいご　lost child
◇*息子	△むすこ　son
帰国子女	きこくしじょ　children who have returned to Japan after living abroad for some time
◇男子社*員	だんししゃいん　male employee (of a company)
◇女子社*員	じょししゃいん　female employee
◇*扇子	せんす　folding fan

70　主　5
▶しゅ，す
▷ぬし，おも

主人	しゅじん　master, proprietor, my husband
主語	しゅご　subject　cf. *述語(じゅつご) predicate
主題	しゅだい　subject, theme
◇主*観*的な	しゅかんてきな　subjective 反客*観*的な(きゃっかんてきな) objective
主な	おもな　main
持ち主	もちぬし　owner
地主	じぬし　landlord, landowner
◇*坊主	ぼうず　Buddhist priest, shaven head, boy

71　奥　12
▶おう
▷おく

奥さん	おくさん　(your/his) wife
奥	おく　inside, inner part
山奥	やまおく　deep in the mountains
奥行き	おくゆき　depth
◇奥*義	おうぎ　secrets

72 私 7	▶し ▷わたくし
私	わたくし，▲わたし　I, me
私立大学	しりつだいがく　private university/college　cf. 国立大学（こくりつだいがく）national university/college, 公立高校（こうりつこうこう）public high school

73 父 4	▶ふ ▷ちち
父	ちち　father
お父さん	△おとうさん　father (polite)
父母	ふぼ　father and mother

74 母 5	▶ぼ ▷はは
母	はは　mother
お母さん	△おかあさん　mother (polite)
母国語	ぼこくご　mother tongue
◇ *乳母	△うば　wet nurse
歴 母屋	△おもや　main building/house

75 兄 5	▶けい，きょう ▷あに
兄	あに　elder brother
お兄さん	△おにいさん　elder brother (polite)
兄弟	きょうだい　brother(s) and sister(s)
父兄	ふけい　parents

76 弟 7	▶てい，だい，で ▷おとうと
弟	おとうと　younger brother
兄弟	きょうだい　brother(s) and sister(s)
◇ 子弟	してい　children
◇ 弟子	でし　disciple

77 姉 8	▶し ▷あね
姉	あね　elder sister
お姉さん	△おねえさん　elder sister (polite)
姉妹	しまい　sister

78 妹 8	▶まい ▷いもうと
妹	いもうと　younger sister
姉妹	しまい　sisters
◇ 姉妹*都*市	しまいとし　sister city

79 友 4	▶ゆう ▷とも
友だち	ともだち　friend　cf. *Tomodachi* is normally written as 友達.
友人	ゆうじん　friend (more formal than 友だち)
◇ 友好*関*係	ゆうこうかんけい　friendly relations

④

80 何 7	▶か ▷なに，なん
何	なに　what
何時	なんじ　what time　cf. 何人，何回，何日，etc.
何でも	なんでも　whatever
何で	なんで　why (used in casual speech)
何とか	なんとか　one way or another, somehow
◇ *幾何学	きかがく　geometry

81 誰 15	▷だれ

cf. 誰 is not a *Jōyō Kanji*, but it has been included in this text.

| 誰 | だれ　who |

82 名 6	▶めい，みょう ▷な
名前	なまえ　name
人名	じんめい　personal name
地名	ちめい　place name
名人	めいじん　master, expert
◇ *仮名	△かな　kana, Japanese syllabary
◇ 名残	△なごり　traces, remains
歴 大名	だいみょう　daimyō, feudal lord

83 高 10	▶こう ▷たか(い)，たか，たか(まる)，たか(める)
高い	たかい　high, expensive
円高	えんだか　rise in the exchange rate of the yen
売上高	うりあげだか　sales, turnover
高校	こうこう　high school
◇ 高気*圧	こうきあつ　high (atmospheric) pressure
高まる	たかまる　rise, be raised

84 安 6	▶あん ▷やす(い)
安い	やすい　cheap, inexpensive
ドル安	ドルやす　fall in the exchange rate of the dollar
安心	あんしん　cv. feel relieved, stop worrying, feel at ease 反 心*配 (しんぱい) cv. be worried, be anxious
安全	あんぜん　safety
◇ *不安	ふあん　anxiety

85 新 13	▶しん ▷あたら(しい)，あら(た)，にい
新しい	あたらしい　new

新聞	しんぶん　newspaper
新車	しんしゃ　new car cf. 中古車 (ちゅうこしゃ) used car
新入生	しんにゅうせい　new student
◇ 新入社*員	しんにゅうしゃいん　new employee
新たな	あらたな　new
歴 新*妻	にいづま　newly married wife

86 古 5	▶こ ▷ふる(い)，ふる(す)
古い	ふるい　old
古本	ふるほん　used book
使い古す	つかいふるす　wear out (by use)
中古車	ちゅうこしゃ　used car
◇ 古*典文学	こてんぶんがく　classical literature
◇ 古文	こぶん　ancient writings, classics
◇ 古今東西	ここんとうざい　all ages and countries

87 大 3	▶だい，たい ▷おお，おお(きい)，おお(いに)
大きい	おおきい　big, large
◇ 大水	おおみず　flood cf. *洪水 (こうずい) flood
◇ 大いに	おおいに　very
大学	だいがく　university, college
大小	だいしょう　large and small, size
◇ 大*丈夫	だいじょうぶ　all right, secure, safe
◇ 大*豆	だいず　soybean
大国	たいこく　big/powerful nation
大金	たいきん　large amount of money
大した	たいした　great, serious, important, considerable (as in 大した問題ではない)

大して	たいして　not very ～, not so much ～
大人	△おとな　adult
歴 大*和朝*廷	△やまとちょうてい　*Yamato Chōtei*, the ancient Japanese Imperial Court
歴 大*和*絵	△やまとえ　*Yamato-e* painting

88
3 小　▶しょう　▷ちい(さい)，こ，お

小さい	ちいさい　small, little
小学校	しょうがっこう　elementary school
大小	だいしょう　large and small, size
小人	しょうにん　children (used in bus fares/etc.)
小人	しょうじん　insignificant person, small-minded person
小人	こびと　dwarf
◇ 小*指	こゆび　the little finger, the little toe
◇ 小*鳥	ことり　little bird
小切手	こぎって　check
小川	おがわ　(small) stream
◇ 小*豆	△あずき　adzuki bean

89
8 長　▶ちょう　▷なが(い)

長い	ながい　long
社長	しゃちょう　company president
部長	ぶちょう　department head
長時間	ちょうじかん　for a long time
長所	ちょうしょ　strong point, merit 反 短所(たんしょ) weak point, shortcoming
長年	ながねん　for a long time

90
12 短　▶たん　▷みじか(い)

短い	みじかい　short
短気な	たんきな　quick-tempered
短所	たんしょ　weak point, shortcoming
長短	ちょうたん　strong points and weak points
◇ 短*期大学	たんきだいがく　junior college cf. *abbr.* 短大(たんだい)
◇ 短*期の	たんきの　short-term

91
12 朝　▶ちょう　▷あさ

朝	あさ　morning
朝ごはん	あさごはん　breakfast
毎朝	まいあさ　every morning
朝日新聞	あさひしんぶん　*Asahi Shimbun* (a newspaper)
朝食	ちょうしょく　breakfast
今朝	△けさ　this morning

92
9 昼　▶ちゅう　▷ひる

昼	ひる　daytime, noon, midday
昼ごはん	ひるごはん　lunch
昼休み	ひるやすみ　lunch break
昼間	ひるま　daytime
昼食	ちゅうしょく　lunch

93
8 夜　▶や　▷よ，よる

夜	よる　night
夜明け	よあけ　dawn, daybreak
夜中	よなか　in the night
今夜	こんや　tonight
夜食	やしょく　midnight snack

◇ 夜行*列車　やこうれっしゃ　overnight train

◇ *昨夜　さくや, ▲ゆうべ　last evening, last night

94 晩 12 ▶ばん

晩　ばん　evening, night

晩ごはん　ばんごはん　dinner, supper

今晩　こんばん　tonight

毎晩　まいばん　every night

一晩　ひとばん　one night

一晩中　ひとばんじゅう　all night (long)

◇ 晩年　ばんねん　late in life, one's later years

95 夕 3 ▶せき ▷ゆう

夕方　ゆうがた　evening

夕日　ゆうひ　evening/setting sun

◇ 夕べ　ゆうべ　evening

◇ 七夕　△たなばた　the Festival of the Weaver, the Star Festival

◇ 一朝一夕　いっちょういっせき　in a day, in a short time

96 春 9 ▶しゅん ▷はる

春　はる　spring

春休み　はるやすみ　spring vacation

春分の日　しゅんぶんのひ　Vernal Equinox Day

◇ 立春　りっしゅん　the first day of spring (in the lunar calendar)

◇ 青春時*代　せいしゅんじだい　youth, the springtime of life

売春　ばいしゅん　cv. prostitute

◇ 春画　しゅんが　pornographic picture

97 夏 10 ▶か, げ ▷なつ

夏　なつ　summer

夏休み　なつやすみ　summer vacation

◇ 春夏秋冬　しゅんかしゅうとう　the four seasons

◇ 夏*至　げし　the summer solstice

98 秋 9 ▶しゅう ▷あき

秋　あき　autumn, fall

秋風　あきかぜ　autumn breeze

秋分の日　しゅうぶんのひ　Autumnal Equinox Day

99 冬 5 ▶とう ▷ふゆ

冬　ふゆ　winter

冬休み　ふゆやすみ　winter vacation

◇ 冬*空　ふゆぞら　winter sky, wintry weather

◇ 冬*眠　とうみん　cv. hibernate

100 山 3 ▶さん ▷やま

山　やま　mountain

入山　にゅうざん　cv. begin to climb a mountain

下山　げざん　cv. climb down a mountain

火山　かざん　volcano

◇ 山水画　さんすいが　(Chinese-style) landscape paintings

歴 山車　△だし　float, festival car

◇ *築山　△つきやま　small artificial hill (in a landscape garden)

101 川 3	▶せん ▷かわ	
	川	かわ river
	～川	～がわ ～ River
	川上	かわかみ upper reaches of a river, upstream
	川下	かわしも lower reaches of a river, downstream
	小川	おがわ (small) stream
◇	川原	△かわら dry riverbed
◇	*河川	かせん rivers
歴	川*柳	せんりゅう *senryū*, short humorous verse

102 石 5	▶せき, しゃく, こく ▷いし	
	石	いし stone
	小石	こいし small stone
	石田	いしだ (surname)
	石けん	せっけん soap cf. 石けん can be written as 石鹸, but 鹸 is not a *Jōyō Kanji*.
◇	*宝石	ほうせき jewel, precious stone
◇	*磁石	じしゃく magnet, compass
歴	～石	～こく *koku* (unit of volume, approx. 180*l*)

103 田 5	▶でん ▷た	
	山田	やまだ (surname)
	田中	たなか (surname)
	田	た rice field
	水田	すいでん paddy field, (rice) paddy
◇	*油田	ゆでん oil field
◇	田*舎	△いなか the country, countryside, one's hometown

⑤

104 多 6	▶た ▷おお(い)	
	多い	おおい abundant, plenty
	多少	たしょう to a certain extent, somewhat; quantity, amount
◇	多*数の	たすうの many, a lot of

105 少 4	▶しょう ▷すく(ない), すこ(し)	
	少ない	すくない few
	少し	すこし a little, a few
	少年	しょうねん boy
	少女	しょうじょ girl
	少々	しょうしょう a little, a bit
◇	少*数の	しょうすうの a little, a few
◇	*減少	げんしょう *cv.* reduce

106 明 8	▶めい, みょう ▷あ(かり), あか(るい), あか(るむ), あか(らむ), あき(らか), あ(ける), あ(く), あ(くる), あ(かす)	
	明るい	あかるい bright, light, cheerful
◇	明るむ	あかるむ become light
	明らかな	あきらかな clear, obvious
	明白な	めいはくな clear, obvious
	説明	せつめい *cv.* explain
◇	*証明	しょうめい *cv.* prove, certify; proof, evidence
	明日	みょうにち, △あす, ▲あした tomorrow
	夜が明ける	よがあける day breaks
	夜明け	よあけ dawn, daybreak
	明け方	あけがた dawn, daybreak

明くる日	あくるひ	the next day
明かり	あかり	light
◇ 明かす	あかす	stay up all night, reveal (one's identity/intentions)

107 暗 13
▶あん
▷くら(い)

暗い	くらい	dark, gloomy
暗室	あんしつ	(photo) darkroom
明暗	めいあん	light and shade
◇ 暗*示	あんじ	*cv.* hint, suggest

108 低 7
▶てい
▷ひく(い), ひく(まる), ひく(める)

低い	ひくい	low, short
高低	こうてい	rise and fall, pitch, undulations
◇ 低気*圧	ていきあつ	low (atmospheric) pressure
◇ 低める	ひくめる	lower

109 近 7
▶きん
▷ちか(い)

近い	ちかい	near
近道	ちかみち	shortcut
近づく	ちかづく	approach, come near
近々	ちかぢか	shortly, before long
近所	きんじょ	neighborhood
近日中に	きんじつちゅうに	soon, one of these days
◇ 近*代*化	きんだいか	modernization

110 遠 13
▶えん, おん
▷とお(い)

遠い	とおい	far
◇ *永遠の	えいえんの	eternal
◇ 遠足	えんそく	(a day) excursion, (school) trip

◇ 遠心力	えんしんりょく	centrifugal force
◇ 遠近*法	えんきんほう	perspective drawing
特 *久遠の	くおんの	eternal

111 強 11
▶きょう, ごう
▷つよ(い), つよ(まる), つよ(める), し(いる)

強い	つよい	strong
強まる	つよまる	become strong
強み	つよみ	strong point
勉強	べんきょう	*cv.* study
強力な	きょうりょくな	strong, powerful
◇ 強*制	きょうせい	*cv.* compel, force
強引な	ごういんな	forcible, overbearing
◇ 強いる	しいる	compel, force

112 弱 10
▶じゃく
▷よわ(い), よわ(る), よわ(まる), よわ(める)

弱い	よわい	weak
弱まる	よわまる	become weak
◇ 弱*点	じゃくてん	weak point
◇ 弱*肉強食	じゃくにくきょうしょく	(a world where) the weak are victims of the strong

113 広 5
▶こう
▷ひろ(い), ひろ(まる), ひろ(める), ひろ(がる), ひろ(げる)

広い	ひろい	wide, broad, large
広場	ひろば	plaza, (public) square, open space
広まる	ひろまる	*vi.* spread, be diffused, become popular
広がる	ひろがる	*vi.* spread, extend, stretch

広める	ひろめる	*vt.* spread, diffuse, disseminate, make something popular
広げる	ひろげる	*vt.* widen, unfold, unroll, spread, extend, expand
広々とした	ひろびろとした	wide, spacious
広大な	こうだいな	vast

114 / 11 悪 ▶あく，お
▷わる(い)

悪い	わるい	bad, wrong, evil, harmful
悪口を言う	わるくち/わるぐちをいう	speak ill of
悪人	あくにん	wicked/bad person
悪意	あくい	ill will, malice
◇ 悪*化	あっか	*cv.vi.* worsen
◇*憎悪	ぞうお	hatred; *cv.* hate
◇*嫌悪*感	けんおかん	hatred, disgust

115 / 9 重 ▶じゅう，ちょう
▷え，おも(い)，かさ(ねる)，かさ(なる)

重い	おもい	heavy, weighty, serious (illness/injury)
体重	たいじゅう	body weight
重力	じゅうりょく	gravity
重大な	じゅうだいな	serious, important, grave
◇ 重*工業	じゅうこうぎょう	heavy industry
◇ 重*点	じゅうてん	important point, priority, emphasis
◇ 重*役	じゅうやく	company director
◇ 重体	じゅうたい	seriously injured/ill, in a critical/serious condition
◇*貴重な	きちょうな	precious, valuable
◇*慎重な	しんちょうな	prudent, careful, cautious

◇ 重*複	ちょうふく	*cv.* be repeated/duplicated, overlap
◇ 二重*否定	にじゅうひてい	double negative
重ねる	かさねる	pile up, repeat
◇ 八重*桜	やえざくら	double-flowered cherry tree

116 / 12 軽 ▶けい
▷かる(い)，かろ(やか)

軽い	かるい	light, slight (illness/injury)
手軽な	てがるな	easy, simple
気軽に	きがるに	easily, without reserve
◇ 軽やかに	かろやかに	joyously, merrily
軽食	けいしょく	light meal
軽自動車	けいじどうしゃ	compact car
◇ 軽*工業	けいこうぎょう	light industry
◇ 軽*率な	けいそつな	careless, thoughtless, rash, hasty

117 / 6 早 ▶そう，さっ
▷はや(い)，はや(める)，はや(まる)

早い	はやい	early
早める	はやめる	move (the date) forward
◇*素早い	すばやい	quick, agile, nimble
早朝	そうちょう	early in the morning
◇ 早春	そうしゅん	early spring
◇ 早*速	さっそく	immediately, right away
◇ 早急に	さっきゅうに	immediately

118 / 12 遅 ▶ち
▷おく(れる)，おく(らす)，おそ(い)

遅い	おそい	late, slow

遅れる	おくれる	be late, be overdue, behind the times
遅らす	おくらす	delay, put off
◇ 遅*刻	ちこく	cv. be late

<table>
<tr><td>119
暑
12</td><td colspan="2">▶しょ
▷あつ(い)</td></tr>
</table>

暑い	あつい	hot
残暑	ざんしょ	late summer heat
◇ 暑中見*舞い	しょちゅうみまい	midsummer greeting card
◇*避暑地	ひしょち	summer retreat

<table>
<tr><td>120
寒
12</td><td colspan="2">▶かん
▷さむ(い)</td></tr>
</table>

寒い	さむい	cold
寒気	さむけ	chill, (have) the shivers
◇ 寒気	かんき	the cold, coldness
◇ 寒*村	かんそん	lonely/impoverished village
◇ 寒*天	かんてん	agar
◇*厳寒の	げんかんの	severely cold, coldest

<table>
<tr><td>121
深
11</td><td colspan="2">▶しん
▷ふか(い), ふか(める), ふか(まる)</td></tr>
</table>

深い	ふかい	deep, thick
深める	ふかめる	deepen, promote (better understanding/etc.)
深まる	ふかまる	get deeper, deepen
◇ 深夜*放送	しんやほうそう	late-night/all-night broadcasting
◇ 水深	すいしん	water depth

<table>
<tr><td>122
浅
9</td><td colspan="2">▶せん
▷あさ(い)</td></tr>
</table>

浅い	あさい	shallow, slight
◇ 浅*薄な	せんぱくな	shallow

<table>
<tr><td>123
細
11</td><td colspan="2">▶さい
▷ほそ(い), ほそ(る), こま(か), こま(かい)</td></tr>
</table>

細い	ほそい	thin, fine, slim, slender
やせ細る	やせほそる	become thin, become emaciated
細かい	こまかい	fine (line), detailed, trifling, small (change)
細部	さいぶ	details
明細書	めいさいしょ	detailed statement
歴 細雪	▲ささめゆき	light snowfall

<table>
<tr><td>124
太
4</td><td colspan="2">▶たい, た
▷ふと(い), ふと(る)</td></tr>
</table>

太い	ふとい	thick, big
太る	ふとる	grow fat
◇ 太*陽	たいよう	the sun
◇ 太*郎	たろう	(male given name)
◇*丸太	まるた	log
歴 太*刀	^たち	sword

<table>
<tr><td>125
若
8</td><td colspan="2">▶じゃく, にゃく
▷わか(い), も(しくは)</td></tr>
</table>

若い	わかい	young
若々しい	わかわかしい	youthful
若者	わかもの	young person
若手(の)	わかて(の)	young (actor/etc.)
◇ 若人	^わこうど	young person
◇ 若年*労働者	じゃくねんろうどうしゃ	young worker
◇*老若男女	ろうじゃくなんにょ, ろうにゃくなんにょ	men and women of all ages
◇ 若しくは	もしくは	or, otherwise

126 6	忙	▶ぼう ▷いそが(しい)
	忙しい	いそがしい　busy
	多忙な	たぼうな　busy
◊	忙*殺される	ぼうさつされる　be very busy (with work)

- ⑥

127 13	寝	▶しん ▷ね(る), ね(かす)
	寝る	ねる　fall asleep, go to bed, lie down
	昼寝	ひるね　nap
	寝かす	ねかす　put (a child) to bed, lay down
	寝室	しんしつ　bedroom
◊	寝*台車	しんだいしゃ　sleeping car

128 10	起	▶き ▷お(きる), お(こす), お(こる)
	起きる	おきる　get up, happen, occur
	早起きする	はやおきする　get up early
	起こす	おこす　wake up (a person), raise, sit up, bring about
	起こる	おこる　happen, occur
	起立	きりつ　cv. stand up
◊	起*源	きげん　origin, beginning

129 8	始	▶し ▷はじ(まる), はじ(める)
	始まる	はじまる　begin, start, commence
	始まり	はじまり　beginning
	始める	はじめる　begin, start, commence
	始め	はじめ　outset, beginning
	開始	かいし　cv. begin, start, commence

	始発	しはつ　the first train/bus of the day

130 11	終	▶しゅう ▷お(わる), お(える)
	終わる	おわる　end, be completed
	終える	おえる　end, finish, complete
◊	終*了	しゅうりょう　cv. end
	終電	しゅうでん　the last train of the day
◊	終*点	しゅうてん　terminal
	終日	しゅうじつ　all day (long)
	始終	しじゅう　all the time

131 9	食	▶しょく, じき ▷く(う), く(らう), た(べる)
	食べる	たべる　eat
	食べ物	たべもの　food
	食事	しょくじ　meal
	朝食	ちょうしょく　breakfast
	昼食	ちゅうしょく　lunch
	夕食	ゆうしょく　dinner, supper
	食料	しょくりょう　food, provisions
	食う	くう　eat　cf. Kuu can be written as 喰う, but 喰 is not a Jōyō Kanji.
◊	*断食	だんじき　fast, fasting; cv. fast
◊	▲乞食	こじき　beggar

132 12	飲	▶いん ▷の(む)
	飲む	のむ　drink, take (medicine), swallow
	飲(み)物	のみもの　drink, beverage
	飲み水	のみみず　drinking water
	飲料水	いんりょうすい　drinking water
	飲食店	いんしょくてん　restaurant

飲酒運転　いんしゅうんてん　drunken driving

133 来 7
▶らい
▷く(る), きた(る), きた(す)

来る　くる　come
来月　らいげつ　next month
来年　らいねん　next year
来日　らいにち　cv. come to Japan
本来　ほんらい　originally, from the first
来る〜日　きたる〜にち/か　this coming 〜(date)
◇ 来す　きたす　cause, bring about, lead to

134 帰 10
▶き
▷かえ(る), かえ(す)

帰る　かえる　go back, return, leave (from work/etc.)
日帰り旅行　ひがえりりょこう　day trip
帰国　きこく　cv. return to one's country

135 乗 9
▶じょう
▷の(る), の(せる)

乗る　のる　get on, ride, take (a bus/plane/etc.)
◇ 乗り物*酔い　のりものよい　motion sickness, carsickness, seasickness
◇ 乗車*券　じょうしゃけん　train/bus ticket
歴 大乗*仏教　だいじょうぶっきょう　Mahayana Buddhism
歴 小乗*仏教　しょうじょうぶっきょう　Hinayana/Theravada Buddhism

136 降 10
▶こう
▷お(りる), お(ろす), ふ(る)

降りる　おりる　get off (train/bus/etc.)

乗り降り　のりおり　getting on and off
降ろす　おろす　unload, drop off (a passenger)
降車口　こうしゃぐち　exit on a train/bus
降る　ふる　fall, rain
◇ 降雨*量　こううりょう　(amount of) rainfall
◇ 下降　かこう　cv. descend

137 作 7
▶さく, さ
▷つく(る)

作る　つくる　make, produce
手作りの　てづくりの　handmade
作文　さくぶん　composition
作家　さっか　novelist cf. 筆者(ひっしゃ) writer, 著者 (ちょしゃ) author
作者　さくしゃ　writer
名作　めいさく　masterpiece, fine piece (of art)
◇ 作*品　さくひん　(artistic/fictional/etc.) work
◇ 作物　さくもつ　crop, agricultural product
動作　どうさ　action, movement, motion
◇ 作*法　さほう　manners, form, etiquette

138 休 6
▶きゅう
▷やす(む), やす(まる), やす(める)

休む　やすむ　rest, have a day off, be absent (from school/work)
夏休み　なつやすみ　summer vacation
お休み(なさい)　おやすみ(なさい)　Good night.
一休み　ひとやすみ　short break
休める　やすめる　rest, give a rest
休日　きゅうじつ　holiday, day off

連休　　　れんきゅう　consecutive holidays

◇　週休二日*制　しゅうきゅうふつかせい the five-day workweek system

139
7　見　　▶けん
　　　　　▷み(る), み(える), み(せる)

見る　　　みる　look, watch, see

見上げる　みあげる　look up

見下ろす　みおろす　look down (from the roof/etc.)

見下す　　みくだす　despise, look down on (in contempt)

見方　　　みかた　point of view

見本　　　みほん　sample

見える　　みえる　(can) be seen, (can) see, be in sight, appear (honorific)

見せる　　みせる　show

意見　　　いけん　opinion, idea, suggestion

見学　　　けんがく　cv. visit (a factory/etc.) to learn something

140
10　勉　　▶べん

勉強　　　べんきょう　cv. study

勉学　　　べんがく　study

◇*勤勉な　きんべんな　hardworking, industrious

141
7　住　　▶じゅう
　　　　　▷す(む), す(まう)

住む　　　すむ　live

住所　　　じゅうしょ　address

◇　住*民　じゅうみん　inhabitants, residents

◇　住*宅　じゅうたく　house, residence

◇　住まい　すまい　house, dwelling

142
9　持　　▶じ
　　　　　▷も(つ)

持つ　　　もつ　have, take, hold, carry

持ち上げる　もちあげる　lift (up), hold up, flatter, praise

気持ち　　きもち　feeling, sensation, mood

◇*支持　しじ　cv. support

143
8　知　　▶ち
　　　　　▷し(る)

知る　　　しる　know, learn, notice, be acquainted

知人　　　ちじん　acquaintance, friend

知事　　　ちじ　(prefectural) governor

◇　知*識　ちしき　knowledge, information

144
10　酒　　▶しゅ
　　　　　▷さけ, さか

酒　　　　さけ　liquor, sake

酒屋　　　さかや　liquor shop

◇　酒場　さかば　bar, pub

日本酒　　にほんしゅ　Japanese sake

飲酒運転　いんしゅうんてん　drunken driving

◇　お*神酒　△おみき　sake offered to the gods

145
9　茶　　▶ちゃ, さ

お茶　　　おちゃ　tea, Japanese tea

◇*紅茶　こうちゃ　black tea

◇　茶▲碗　ちゃわん　(rice) bowl, teacup

茶色　　　ちゃいろ　brown

茶の間　　ちゃのま　living room

茶室　　　ちゃしつ　tea-ceremony room/house

茶道　　　さどう, ちゃどう　the art of the tea ceremony

146 地 6　▶ち，じ

地下鉄	ちかてつ	subway, under-ground railway
地下水	ちかすい	ground water
土地	とち	land
地名	ちめい	place name
地方	ちほう	region, district, province, countryside
◇*居心地がいい △いごこちがいい		comfortable/cozy (room), feel at home
◇ 地*震	じしん	earthquake
◇ 地*面	じめん	surface of the earth, land, ground
◇ 意気地のない △いくじのない		timid, cowardly

147 鉄 13　▶てつ

地下鉄	ちかてつ	subway, under-ground railway
私鉄	してつ	private railway
鉄道	てつどう	railroad
鉄	てつ	iron

148 者 8　▶しゃ ▷もの

学者	がくしゃ	scholar
医者	いしゃ	doctor
前者	ぜんしゃ	the former
後者	こうしゃ	the latter
◇*第三者	だいさんしゃ	third person, outsider
若者	わかもの	young person
うちの者	うちのもの	member of one's family/group cf. よその者 (よそのもの) outsider to one's family/group

149 所 8　▶しょ ▷ところ

近所	きんじょ	neighborhood
住所	じゅうしょ	address
場所	ばしょ	place
研究所	けんきゅうじょ	(research) laboratory, research institute
所長	しょちょう	head/chief/manager (of an office)
名所	めいしょ	famous place/sight
発電所	はつでんしょ	electric power plant
長所	ちょうしょ	strong point, merit
短所	たんしょ	weak point, shortcoming
◇ 所*得	しょとく	income
◇*台所	だいどころ	kitchen

150 外 5　▶がい，げ ▷そと，ほか，はず(す)，はず(れる)

外国	がいこく	foreign country
外国人	がいこくじん	foreigner
外国語	がいこくご	foreign language
外来語	がいらいご	loan word
外出	がいしゅつ	cv. go out
*海外旅行	かいがいりょこう	traveling abroad, overseas trip
外	そと	outside
外の	ほかの	another cf. *Hokano* can be written as 他の, but the use of this character for *hoka* is not officially recognized in the *Jōyō Kanji*.
外す	はずす	take off, remove, unfasten
外れる	はずれる	come off/undone, miss (the target)
◇ 外*科	げか	surgery

151 国 8	▶こく ▷くに	
外国	がいこく	foreign country
母国語	ぼこくご	mother tongue
大国	たいこく	big/powerful nation
小国	しょうこく	small nation
中国	ちゅうごく	China
◇▲韓国	かんこく	the Republic of Korea, (South) Korea
四国	しこく	Shikoku
国家	こっか	nation
国	くに	country, nation

152 内 4	▶ない，だい ▷うち	
国内旅行	こくないりょこう	travel within a country
館内	かんない	in the building
◇*構内	こうない	in the station building
家内	かない	my wife
内外	ないがい	inside and outside
◇ 内*側	うちがわ	inside
◇*境内	けいだい	precinct (of a temple/shrine)

153 旅 10	▶りょ ▷たび	
旅行	りょこう	trip, travel; *cv.* make a trip, travel
旅館	りょかん	Japanese-style inn
旅	たび	journey, trip, travel
旅先	たびさき	destination, place where one is staying while on a journey
◇ 旅人	たびびと	traveler

154 語 14	▶ご ▷かた（る），かた（らう）	
日本語	にほんご	Japanese (language)
英語	えいご	English (language)
中国語	ちゅうごくご	Chinese (language)
外国語	がいこくご	foreign language
語学	ごがく	(foreign) language study
言語	げんご	language, speech
国語	こくご	(the Japanese) language (as a school subject)
物語	ものがたり	tale, story, narrative
◇ 語る	かたる	talk, chat, tell (a story)
◇ 語り手	かたりて	narrator, storyteller
◇ 物語る	ものがたる	narrate, show (the fact that ～)

155 英 8	▶えい	
英語	えいご	English (language)
英会話	えいかいわ	English conversation
英国	えいこく	the United Kingdom
◇ 大英*帝国	だいえいていこく	the British Empire
◇ 英*才*教*育	えいさいきょういく	special education for the gifted

⑦

156 世 5	▶せい，せ ▷よ	
世界	せかい	world
世話	せわ	care (as in "take care of")
◇ 世*代	せだい	generation
二世	にせい	second generation (immigrant/etc.)
中世	ちゅうせい	the Middle Ages, the medieval period

この世	このよ	this world, the present life
あの世	あのよ	the next world, the afterlife
世の中	よのなか	the world, life

157 界 9 ▶かい

世界	せかい	world
文学界	ぶんがくかい	literary world
◇*政界	せいかい	political world
◇*財界	ざいかい	financial world
◇*限界	げんかい	limit, bounds

158 倍 10 ▶ばい
cf. 部 53

| 倍 | ばい | double, twice, two times |
| ～倍 | ～ばい | ～fold, ～ magnification |

159 半 5 ▶はん ▷なか(ば)

十二時半	じゅうにじはん	twelve-thirty
半年	はんとし	a half year
半分	はんぶん	half
前半	ぜんはん	the first half
後半	こうはん	the second half
大半	たいはん	the greater part of, the larger portion of, the majority of, for the most part
◇ 三十*代半ば	さんじゅうだいなかば	one's middle thirties

160 全 6 ▶ぜん ▷まった(く)

| 全部 | ぜんぶ | all |
| 日本全国 | にほんぜんこく | all over Japan, all parts of Japan cf. 世界*各国(せかいかっこく) many countries |

◇ 全体主*義	ぜんたいしゅぎ	totalitarianism
全く	まったく	quite, entirely, thoroughly, completely
◇ 全うする	まっとうする	accomplish, fulfill

161 間 12 ▶かん，けん ▷あいだ，ま

時間	じかん	time
年間	ねんかん	yearly, a year
夜間	やかん	at night, night (school)
間	あいだ	interval, space, gap, distance
日本間	にほんま	Japanese-style room
◇*洋間	ようま	Western-style room
茶の間	ちゃのま	living room
人間	にんげん	human being, mankind
◇ 世間	せけん	the world, people

162 回 6 ▶かい，え ▷まわ(る)，まわ(す)

～回	～かい	～ time(s)
前回	ぜんかい	last time
今回	こんかい	this time
*次回	じかい	next time
回答	かいとう	cv. reply, answer
回る	まわる	turn (round), go (round)
回り道	まわりみち	detour, roundabout way
特 回*向	えこう	cv. hold a memorial service

28

163 週 11　▶しゅう

先週	せんしゅう	last week
今週	こんしゅう	this week
来週	らいしゅう	next week
〜週間	〜しゅうかん	〜 week(s)
◊ 週*末	しゅうまつ	weekend
◊ 週休二日*制	しゅうきゅうふつかせい	the five-day workweek system

164 毎 6　▶まい

毎日	まいにち	every day
毎週	まいしゅう	every week
毎月	まいつき	every month
毎年	まいとし, まいねん	every year

165 体 7　▶たい, てい　▷からだ

体	からだ	body
体力	たいりょく	physical strength
◊ 体*格	たいかく	physique, build
大体	だいたい	on the whole, by and large, roughly, for the most part; main (points)
一体	いったい	What on earth (did you do/etc.)
一体になる	いったいになる	become one with, be united
世間体	せけんてい	appearance
◊ 体*裁	ていさい	appearance, form, style

166 頭 16　▶とう, ず, と　▷あたま, かしら

頭	あたま	head
頭痛	ずつう	headache
先頭	せんとう	the forefront, the head, the lead, the top
◊ 〜頭	〜とう	(counter for big animals)
◊ 東京*音頭	とうきょうおんど	*Tōkyō Ondo*, Tokyo Dance Song
◊ 頭文*字	かしらもじ	the first letter (of a word), initials

167 口 3　▶こう, く　▷くち

口	くち	mouth
入(り)口	いりぐち	entrance
出口	でぐち	exit
早口で	はやくちで	(speak) fast
◊ 火口	かこう	(volcanic) crater
◊ 口*述*試*験	こうじゅつしけん	oral examination
◊ *異口同*音に	いくどうおんに	with one voice, with one accord

168 目 5　▶もく, ぼく　▷め, ま

目	め	eye
お目にかかる	おめにかかる	see (honorific)
目安	めやす	standard, yardstick, criterion
目上の人	めうえのひと	one's superior, one's senior
目下の人	めしたのひと	one's inferior, one's junior
目前	もくぜん	before one's eye, immediate, impending
◊ 目*的	もくてき	purpose
◊ 目*標	もくひょう	goal, objective
◊ *面目	めんぼく	face, honor, reputation
◊ 目の*当たりに	まのあたりに	before one's eyes

169　耳　6
▶じ
▷みみ

耳	みみ　ear
早耳	はやみみ　sharp-eared
◇ 耳*鼻*科	じびか　otolaryngology

170　手　4
▶しゅ
▷て，た

手	て　hand
切手	きって　(postage) stamp
手前	てまえ　this side
手間	てま　time, labor, effort
手伝う	△てつだう　help, assist
上手な	△じょうずな　skilled, good (tennis player/drawing/etc.)
下手な	△へたな　unskillful, poor (tennis player/drawing/etc.)
◇*選手	せんしゅ　athlete, player
◇ 手*綱	たづな　reins

171　足　7
▶そく
▷あし，た(りる)，た(る)，た(す)

足	あし　foot, leg, paw
～足	～そく　～ pair(s) of (shoes/socks/etc.)
◇*不足	ふそく　shortage, insufficiency; cv.vi. lack, be short of
◇ 水*不足	みずぶそく　water shortage
足りる	たりる　be enough, be sufficient
足す	たす　add, supply
◇ 足*袋	△たび　Japanese-style socks

172　心　4
▶しん
▷こころ

心	こころ　mind, heart, spirit
本心	ほんしん　one's real intention/mind
中心	ちゅうしん　center, middle
◇*関心	かんしん　concern, interest
◇*感心	かんしん　cv. admire, be very impressed
◇*感心な	かんしんな　admirable
◇ 心中	しんじゅう　double suicide; cv. commit suicide together
◇*居心地がいい	△いごこちがいい　comfortable/cozy (room), feel at home

173　力　2
▶りょく，りき
▷ちから

力	ちから　power, force, (physical) strength
力仕事	ちからしごと　physical labor, job that requires muscle power
力強い	ちからづよい　powerful, mighty, strong
学力	がくりょく　academic ability
体力	たいりょく　(physical) strength
全力で	ぜんりょくで　with all one's might, to the best of one's ability
◇*能力	のうりょく　ability, capacity
◇*努力	どりょく　effort; cv. make efforts
◇*権力	けんりょく　power, authority
◇*原子力発電所	げんしりょくはつでんしょ　nuclear power plant
◇*馬力	ばりき　horsepower, energy (to do work)
◇ 力*量	りきりょう　ability

174　立　5
▶りつ，りゅう
▷た(つ)，た(てる)

立つ	たつ　stand up
立ち上がる	たちあがる　stand up, stand up and take action, rise (up)
立ち止まる	たちどまる　stop, halt, pause

目立つ	めだつ　stand out, be conspicuous
立場	たちば　position, standpoint, situation
夕立	ゆうだち　sudden shower in the late afternoon
立食パーティー	りっしょくパーティー buffet-style dinner party
国立大学	こくりつだいがく　national university
中立国	ちゅうりつこく　neutral country
◇*建立される	こんりゅうされる　be built

175　座　10　▶ざ　▷すわ(る)

座る	すわる　sit down
座席	ざせき　seat
口座	こうざ　bank account

176　歩　8　▶ほ，ぶ，ふ　▷ある(く)，あゆ(む)

歩く	あるく　walk
歩道	ほどう　sidewalk
歩行者	ほこうしゃ　pedestrian
～歩	～ほ　～ step(s)
進歩	しんぽ　*cv.* improve, advance; progress, advance, improvement
◇ 歩合	ぶあい　percentage, commission
◇ 歩み	あゆみ　walking, history (of a company/school/etc.)
特 歩	ふ　pawn (in Japanese chess)

177　走　7　▶そう　▷はし(る)

走る	はしる　run
◇ 走者	そうしゃ　runner
◇*競走	きょうそう　*cv.* run in a race

◇*師走	△しわす　December

178　話　13　▶わ　▷はな(す)，はなし

話す	はなす　talk, tell, speak
話し手	はなして　speaker
話し中	はなしちゅう　(the line is) busy
話し合う	はなしあう　talk, discuss
話し合い	はなしあい　talk, discussion
立ち話	たちばなし　stand chatting/talking
電話	でんわ　telephone
会話	かいわ　conversation

179　聞　14　▶ぶん，もん　▷き(く)，き(こえる)

聞く	きく　hear, listen
聞き手	ききて　hearer, listener
聞こえる	きこえる　(can) be heard, (can) hear
新聞	しんぶん　newspaper
◇ 前*代*未聞の	ぜんだいみもんの unheard-of, unprecedented

180　読　14　▶どく，とく，とう　▷よ(む)

読む	よむ　read
読書	どくしょ　*cv.* read books
読者	どくしゃ　reader
◇ 読*経	△どきょう　*cv.* chant a sutra
◇*句読*点	くとうてん　punctuation marks
◇ 読本	とくほん　reader (as in a textbook)

181　書　10　▶しょ　▷か(く)

書く	かく　write
書き手	かきて　writer

書き取り	かきとり	dictation, *kanji* quiz
前書き	まえがき	preface
読書	どくしょ	*cv.* read books
書名	しょめい	title (of a book)
書店	しょてん	bookstore
書道	しょどう	calligraphy
◇ 書物	しょもつ	books

182 **借** 10

▶しゃく
▷か(りる)

借りる	かりる	borrow, rent
借り	かり	debt
借金	しゃっきん	debt, loan; *cv.* borrow money
借家	しゃくや	rented house
◇ 貸借	たいしゃく	*cv.* lend and borrow; debt and credit

183 **貸** 12

▶たい
▷か(す)

貸す	かす	lend, loan
貸家	かしや	house for rent
貸間	かしま	room for rent
貸し	かし	debt (as in "I am in his debt.")
貸(し)出し	かしだし	lending, loan
◇ 貸借	たいしゃく	*cv.* lend and borrow; debt and credit

184 **返** 7

▶へん
▷かえ(す), かえ(る)

返す	かえす	return, give something back
送り返す	おくりかえす	send back, return
返事	へんじ	*cv.* answer, reply
◇ 返*却	へんきゃく	*cv.* return, repay

185 **出** 5

▶しゅつ, すい
▷で(る), だ(す)

出る	でる	go out, attend
出口	でぐち	exit
日の出	ひので	sunrise 反日の入り(ひのいり) sunset
出かける	でかける	go out
出す	だす	put out, take out
見出し	みだし	headline, dictionary entry
出発	しゅっぱつ	*cv.* depart, leave
外出	がいしゅつ	*cv.* go out
出国	しゅっこく	*cv.* depart from a country
出席	しゅっせき	*cv.* attend (a class/meeting/etc.), be present
◇ *提出	ていしゅつ	*cv.* present, submit
◇ 出*納*係	すいとうがかり	cashier, teller

186 **入** 2

▶にゅう
▷い(る), い(れる), はい(る)

入る	はいる	enter
入れる	いれる	put in, let in
気に入る	きにいる	like, be pleased (with)
入(り)口	いりぐち	entrance
日の入り	ひのいり	sunset
入学	にゅうがく	*cv.* enter a school
入社	にゅうしゃ	*cv.* enter/join a company
入院	にゅういん	*cv.* be sent to a hospital, be hospitalized
入国	にゅうこく	*cv.* enter a country, be admitted into a country
入場	にゅうじょう	*cv.* enter, be admitted
◇ *収入	しゅうにゅう	income
◇ 参入	さんにゅう	*cv.* enter (a market)

187 7
売
▶ばい
▷う(る)，う(れる)

売る	うる	sell
売り場	うりば	sales counter, department where something is sold
売り切れる	うりきれる	be sold out
売(り)上(げ)	うりあげ	sales, proceeds
小売(り)店	こうりてん	retail store
◊ 前売(り)*券	まえうりけん	advance ticket
◊ 売(り)手*市場	うりてしじょう	sellers' market
売れる	うれる	sell (well) cf. ～はよく売れる sell well
売れ行き	うれゆき	sales
売店	ばいてん	stand, kiosk, stall
売春	ばいしゅん	cv. prostitute
◊*販売	はんばい	cv. sell

188 12
買
▶ばい
▷か(う)

買う	かう	buy
買(い)物	かいもの	shopping
◊ 買(い)手*市場	かいてしじょう	buyers' market
売買	ばいばい	cv. buy and sell, trade/deal in
◊ 買*収	ばいしゅう	cv. buy up, purchase, bribe

189 5
払
▶ふつ
▷はら(う)

払う	はらう	pay
◊*支払う	しはらう	pay
◊*支払(い)	しはらい	payment
前払(い)	まえばらい	advance payment
◊ 払*底	ふってい	cv. become scarce, run short

◊ 払▲拭	ふっしょく	cv. sweep away, wipe out

190 12
着
▶ちゃく，じゃく
▷き(る)，き(せる)，つ(く)，つ(ける)

着る	きる	put on, wear
着せる	きせる	dress someone
着物	きもの	kimono
下着	したぎ	underwear
水着	みずぎ	swimsuit, bathing suit
着く	つく	reach, arrive
到着	とうちゃく	cv. reach, arrive
～着	～ちゃく	arriving at (time)
～着	～ちゃく	counter for clothes
着々と	ちゃくちゃくと	steadily, step by step
着手	ちゃくしゅ	cv. start to do, start on
◊*愛着	あいちゃく，あいじゃく	love, attachment, affection
◊*執着	しゅうちゃく，しゅうじゃく	cv. be attached, stick (to)

191 11
脱
▶だつ
▷ぬ(ぐ)，ぬ(げる)

脱ぐ	ぬぐ	take off (clothes/shoes/etc.)
脱水	だっすい	cv. spin-dry (the laundry)
◊ 脱水*症*状	だっすいしょうじょう	dehydration
◊ 脱出	だっしゅつ	cv. escape, get out of
◊ 脱*線	だっせん	cv. be derailed, run off the track, digress (from the subject)
◊ 脱*獄	だつごく	cv. escape from prison

192 働 13	▶どう ▷はたら（く）	
働く	はたらく	work
働き	はたらき	work, workings
働き手	はたらきて	worker
◇*労働	ろうどう	work, labor
◇*労働者	ろうどうしゃ	worker, laborer
◇*労働*組合	ろうどうくみあい	labor union
◇*労働人口	ろうどうじんこう	working population, work force
◇*労働力	ろうどうりょく	manpower, work force, labor force
◇*労働力*不足	ろうどうりょくぶそく	labor shortage

193 泳 8	▶えい ▷およ（ぐ）	
泳ぐ	およぐ	swim
水泳	すいえい	swimming
遠泳	えんえい	long-distance swimming
◇*平泳ぎ	ひらおよぎ	breaststroke

194 写 5	▶しゃ ▷うつ（す），うつ（る）	
写す	うつす	copy, take (a picture)
写真	しゃしん	photograph, picture
写真家	しゃしんか	photographer
◇ 写生	しゃせい	cv. sketch

195 待 9	▶たい ▷ま（つ）	
待つ	まつ	wait
待ち合わせ（を）する	まちあわせ（を）する	arrange to meet, meet (at)
待ち合わせる	まちあわせる	arrange to meet, meet (at)
待合室	まちあいしつ	waiting room

◇*期待	きたい	cv. hope for, expect
◇*招待	しょうたい	cv. invite

196 遊 12	▶ゆう，ゆ ▷あそ（ぶ）	
遊ぶ	あそぶ	play
遊園地	ゆうえんち	amusement park, recreation grounds
遊歩道	ゆうほどう	promenade
◇ 物見遊山	ものみゆさん	pleasure trip

197 呼 8	▶こ ▷よ（ぶ）	
呼ぶ	よぶ	call, call out to
呼び出す	よびだす	ask to come, call up (on the phone), summon
◇ 呼*吸	こきゅう	cv. breathe cf. *息をする（いきをする）breathe

⑨

198 洗 9	▶せん ▷あら（う）	
洗う	あらう	wash
お手洗い	おてあらい	lavatory, toilet
洗濯	せんたく	cv. do laundry
洗濯機	せんたくき	washing machine
水洗トイレ	すいせんトイレ	flush toilet
◇ 洗*脳	せんのう	cv. brainwash

199 使 8	▶し ▷つか（う）	
使う	つかう	use
使い方	つかいかた	how to use, method of use
◇ 使用*法	しようほう	how to use, method of use
大使	たいし	ambassador
歴 使者	ししゃ	messenger

200 14	歌	▶か ▷うた，うた(う)

歌	うた	song
歌う	うたう	sing
歌手	かしゅ	singer
国歌	こっか	national anthem
校歌	こうか	school song
短歌	たんか	*tanka*, Japanese poem of thirty-one syllables
◇*和歌	わか	*waka*, Japanese poem of thiry-one syllables

201 11	習	▶しゅう ▷なら(う)

習う	ならう	learn
学習	がくしゅう	*cv.* learn
自習	じしゅう	*cv.vi.* study by oneself
◇*予習	よしゅう	*cv.* prepare one's lessons
◇*復習	ふくしゅう	*cv.* review
◇ 習*得	しゅうとく	*cv.* master
◇ 習*字	しゅうじ	calligraphy, penmanship

202 9	思	▶し ▷おも(う)

思う	おもう	think, guess, believe, feel, consider
思い出す	おもいだす	remember
思い出	おもいで	memories
思いつく	おもいつく	think of, hit on (an idea)
思いがけない	おもいがけない	unexpected
思い(っ)きり	おもい(っ)きり	to one's heart content, as hard as one can
思わず	おもわず	unconsciously, in spite of oneself

| 思考力 | しこうりょく | ability to think |
| 意思決定 | いしけってい | decision making |

203 7	言	▶げん，ごん ▷い(う)，こと

言う	いう	say, talk about, tell
◇ 言い*訳	いいわけ	excuse
伝言	でんごん	message; *cv.* give/send a message
言語	げんご	language
方言	ほうげん	dialect
◇ 言*葉	ことば	language
一言	ひとこと	a word, single word

204 10	通	▶つう，つ ▷とお(る)，とお(す)，かよ(う)

通る	とおる	go along, pass through/along
通り	とおり	street
大通り	おおどおり	big street
～通り	～どおり	～ street/avenue
人通り	ひとどおり	pedestrian traffic
(～した)通り	(～した)とおり	as (promised/one is told/etc.)
一通り	ひととおり	once
～通り	～とおり	～ ways (of doing something)
通う	かよう	go to (school/work), go to and from
通学	つうがく	*cv.* attend/go to school
◇ 通*勤	つうきん	*cv.* commute, go to one's office
通行	つうこう	traffic; *cv.* pass, go past/through
通知	つうち	*cv.* notify, announce
文通	ぶんつう	*cv.* correspond (by letters)

◇	*交通	こうつう　traffic, transportation
	通じる	つうじる　be understood, be connected, run, be open to traffic
◇	通	つう　connoisseur, expert
◇	通夜	つや　wake, vigil

205 渡 12 ▶と ▷わた(る)，わた(す)

	渡る	わたる　go across, go over
	渡す	わたす　lay/build across, hand (over)
◇	渡*米	とべい　cv. go to America
◇	渡*航*費	とこうひ　overseas travel expenses
歴	渡来人	とらいじん　foreigners who came to ancient Japan, bringing certain expertise

206 送 9 ▶そう ▷おく(る)

	送る	おくる　send
	見送る	みおくる　see someone off
	見送り	みおくり　seeing someone off
	送り返す	おくりかえす　send back, return
◇	送り*仮名	おくりがな　conjugational/declensional ending added in *kana* after a *kanji*
	送金	そうきん　cv. remit/send money
	運送会社	うんそうがいしゃ　shipping/freight company
◇	送*別会	そうべつかい　farewell party
◇	*放送局	ほうそうきょく　broadcasting station, radio/TV station

207 泊 8 ▶はく ▷と(まる)，と(める)

	泊まる	とまる　stay, stop
	二泊三日	にはくみっか　(trip of) three days and two nights
◇	宿泊*費	しゅくはくひ　charges for accommodations

⑩

208 覚 12 ▶かく ▷おぼ(える)，さ(ます)，さ(める)

	覚える	おぼえる　remember, memorize
	覚えている	おぼえている　remember, have/keep/bear something in mind
	目が覚める	めがさめる　vi. wake up
	目を覚ます	めをさます　vi. wake up
	目覚まし時計	めざましどけい　alarm (clock)
	知覚	ちかく　cv. perceive
◇	*感覚	かんかく　sense, sensation, feeling

209 忘 7 ▶ぼう ▷わす(れる)

	忘れる	わすれる　forget
	忘れ物	わすれもの　thing left behind
	忘年会	ぼうねんかい　year-end (dinner) party

210 調 15 ▶ちょう ▷しら(べる)，ととの(う)，ととの(える)

	調べる	しらべる　study, investigate, examine
	調子がいい	ちょうしがいい　be in good health, be in good order
	強調	きょうちょう　cv. emphasize cf. 重*視（じゅうし）cv. attach importance to, regard as important

◇ 調える　　　ととのえる　prepare something, make arrangements, supply

211
続 **13**　　▶ぞく
▷つづ(く), つづ(ける)

続ける　　　つづける　*vt.* continue

話し続ける　　はなしつづける　continue talking/speaking

続く　　　つづく　*vi.* continue

降り続く　　　ふりつづく　continue raining cf. *-tsuzuku* is used only in 降り続く. *-tsuzukeru* is used for other verbs.

続き　　　つづき　continuation, continuance, sequel

手続き　　　てつづき　procedures

連続　　　れんぞく　continuation, series; *cv.* continue, be consecutive

続々と　　　ぞくぞくと　one after another, in rapid succession

◇ *相続　　　そうぞく　*cv.* inherit, succeed

◇ *継続　　　けいぞく　*cv.* continue

212
考 **6**　　▶こう
▷かんが(える)

考える　　　かんがえる　think, consider, meditate

考え方　　　かんがえかた　way of thinking, thought, idea

考え　　　かんがえ　idea, thought, plan, opinion, intention

思考　　　しこう　thinking; *cv.vi.* think

参考書　　　さんこうしょ　reference book

考古学　　　こうこがく　archeology

◇ 考*慮　　　こうりょ　*cv.* consider, take into consideration

213
答 **12**　　▶とう
▷こた(える), こたえ

答える　　　こたえる　answer, reply, respond

答(え)　　　こたえ　answer, reply, response

回答　　　かいとう　reply, answer; *cv.* reply, answer, respond

解答　　　かいとう　answer, solution; *cv.* answer, solve

◇ 答*弁　　　とうべん　*cv.* reply, answer, (at an assembly)

214
教 **11**　　▶きょう
▷おし(える), おそ(わる)

教える　　　おしえる　teach, tell

教え方　　　おしえかた　teaching method

教わる　　　おそわる　be taught, be told

教室　　　きょうしつ　classroom

教授　　　きょうじゅ　professor; *cv.* teach

◇ 教*育　　　きょういく　education; *cv.* educate

教会　　　きょうかい　church

キリスト教　　　キリストきょう　Christianity

◇ *宗教　　　しゅうきょう　religion

215
開 **12**　　▶かい
▷ひら(く), ひら(ける), あ(く), あ(ける)

開ける　　　あける　*vt.* open, make room for, vacate, empty

開く　　　あく　*vi.* open, become empty/vacant, be through with, be free (as in not busy, have no plans)

開店　　　かいてん　*cv.* open a store

開始　　　かいし　*cv.* start, begin

開会　　　かいかい　*cv.* open a meeting, go into session

◇ 開会*式　　　かいかいしき　opening ceremony

開通　　　かいつう　*cv.vi.* be open to traffic

開く　　　ひらく　open, unfold, found, establish, hold (a meeting/party), bloom, blossom

◇ *海開き　　　うみびらき　opening a beach to the public for the summer

開発	かいはつ	cv. develop
◇ *展開	てんかい	cv. develop, unfold

216 閉 11
▶へい
▷と(じる)，と(ざす)，し(める)，し(まる)

閉める	しめる	shut, close
閉まる	しまる	be shut/closed, shut, close
閉じる	とじる	close
閉店	へいてん	cv. close a shop
閉会	へいかい	cv. close a meeting, adjourn
◇ 閉会*式	へいかいしき	closing ceremony
開閉	かいへい	cv. open and close
◇ 閉*鎖	へいさ	cv. close (a road/port/ etc.)
◇ 閉ざす	とざす	shut (one's mouth/a gate/etc.)

217 止 4
▶し
▷と(まる)，と(める)

止める	とめる	stop, turn off
止まる	とまる	stop, halt, be parked
通行止め	つうこうどめ	No Thorough-fare
中止	ちゅうし	cv. stop, suspend, discontinue, cancel
◇ *禁止	きんし	cv. forbid, prohibit, place a ban on
歴 *波止場	△はとば	wharf, pier

218 焼 12
▶しょう
▷や(く)，や(ける)

焼く	やく	burn, roast, bake, broil, grill, toast, bake, fire (pottery), scorch, be jealous
焼ける	やける	be burnt, be baked, be toasted, be roasted, be suntanned
日焼け	ひやけ	cv. be suntanned
夕焼け	ゆうやけ	evening glow
全焼	ぜんしょう	cv. be burned down, be reduced to ashes
◇ 焼*失	しょうしつ	cv. be burned down, be consumed by fire

219 消 10
▶しょう
▷け(す)，き(える)

消す	けす	extinguish, switch off (a light), turn off (the gas), erase, wipe out, cross out
取り消す	とりけす	cancel
消しゴム	けしゴム	eraser
消える	きえる	disappear, go out (as in a light/candle), melt (away), die away
◇ 消火*器	しょうかき	fire extinguisher
◇ 消*化	しょうか	cv. digest
◇ 消*費者	しょうひしゃ	consumer

220 直 8
▶ちょく
▷じき，ただ(ちに)，なお(す)，なお(る)

直す	なおす	repair, fix, correct, revise, improve cf. *治す(なおす) cure, heal
見直す	みなおす	reconsider, come to have a better opinion of
直る	なおる	be repaired, be fixed cf. *治る(なおる) get well, be cured
直通電話	ちょくつうでんわ	direct (phone) line
直流	ちょくりゅう	direct current, DC 反*交流(こうりゅう) alter-nating current, AC
直行便	ちょっこうびん	direct flight
直前	ちょくぜん	immediately be-fore
直後	ちょくご	immediately after
◇ *工場直売	こうじょうちょくばい	selling directly from the factory
◇ 直*接	ちょくせつ	directly

◇ *率直な　　　そっちょくな　honest, frank, candid, straightforward

◇ *正直な　　　しょうじきな　honest

◇ 直に　　　　じきに　soon, in a short time, before long; immediately

◇ 直ちに　　　ただちに　immediately, right away

| 221 並 8 | ▶へい ▷なみ, なら(べる), なら(ぶ), なら(びに) |

並べる　　　ならべる　line (things) up, put side by side, display, list

並ぶ　　　　ならぶ　stand in a line, line up, be parallel

並木　　　　なみき　row of trees (along a road/etc.)

◇ 並びに　　　ならびに　and, as well as

◇ 並行して　　へいこうして　(do another thing) at the same time

| 222 変 9 | ▶へん ▷か(える), か(わる) |

変える　　　かえる　vt. change, alter, reform (a system), amend (a regulation)

変わる　　　かわる　vi. change, be altered, vary, be amended, be revised, change into

大変な　　　たいへんな　serious, grave, terrible, dreadful

変な　　　　へんな　odd, strange, queer

◇ 変*化　　　へんか　cv. change, vary, transform; transition

| 223 残 10 | ▶ざん ▷のこ(る), のこ(す) |

残す　　　　のこす　leave (behind), save (for later use)

残る　　　　のこる　remain, stay

残らず　　　のこらず　completely, without exception

残り　　　　のこり　remainder, remnant, surplus

◇ 残りご*飯　のこりごはん　leftover rice/ food

残業　　　　ざんぎょう　overtime work; cv. work overtime

残金　　　　ざんきん　remainder, balance

◇ 残*念な　　ざんねんな　be regrettable, be unfortunate

◇ 名残　　　　△なごり　traces, remains

| 224 集 12 | ▶しゅう ▷あつ(まる), あつ(める), つど(う) |

集める　　　あつめる　bring together, gather, collect, call together

集まる　　　あつまる　gather, get together, meet, crowd, be concentrated

集会　　　　しゅうかい　meeting, gathering, assembly

集金　　　　しゅうきん　cv. collect money/ bills

集合　　　　しゅうごう　cv. gather, meet, assemble

集中　　　　しゅうちゅう　cv. concentrate, centralize, center on, focus on

◇ *収集　　　しゅうしゅう　cv. collect, gather

◇ *特集　　　とくしゅう　special feature; cv. feature

◇ *特集*号　　とくしゅうごう　special issue

◇ 全集　　　　ぜんしゅう　the complete works (of)

◇ 集う　　　　つどう　gather, get together, meet

| 225 倒 10 | ▶とう ▷たお(れる), たお(す) |

倒す　　　　たおす　knock down, push over, fell, beat, defeat, kill, overthrow, topple

倒れる　　　たおれる　fall over, collapse, break down, die, be killed, be overthrown

◇ 倒*産　　　とうさん　cv. go bankrupt; bankruptcy, financial failure

⑪

226 11		▶ゆう	

郵便局	ゆうびんきょく post office
郵送	ゆうそう *cv.* mail

227 9	便	▶べん, びん ▷たよ(り)	

郵便局	ゆうびんきょく post office
◇ 定*期便	ていきびん regular service (a flight/etc.)
◇ 便乗*値上げ	びんじょうねあげ jumping on the bandwagon and increasing prices
◇ 便▲箋	びんせん letter pad
便利な	べんりな useful, handy
便所	べんじょ lavatory
◇ 小便	しょうべん urine
◇ 便り	たより letter, correspondence, news, tidings

228 7	局	▶きょく	

郵便局	ゆうびんきょく post office
◇*放送局	ほうそうきょく TV station, radio station
◇ 北*米局	ほくべいきょく Bureau for North America
局長	きょくちょう bureau chief
結局	けっきょく finally, in the end
◇*政局	せいきょく political situation

229 10		▶びょう, へい ▷や(む), やまい	

病院	びょういん hospital
病気	びょうき illness, sickness, disease
病気の	びょうきの ill, sick
病人	びょうにん sick person cf.*患者 (かんじゃ) patient

重病	じゅうびょう serious illness/disease
◇*不*治の病	ふちのやまい, ふじのやまい incurable/fatal disease
◇ 病む	やむ fall ill, become sick, suffer from
◇*疾病	しっぺい illness, sickness, disease

230 10	院	▶いん	

病院	びょういん hospital
大学院	だいがくいん graduate school
入院	にゅういん *cv.* be sent to a hospital, be hospitalized
退院	たいいん *cv.* leave the hospital, be discharged from the hospital

231 11	窓	▶そう ▷まど	

窓	まど window
窓口	まどぐち (teller's/etc.) window
同窓会	どうそうかい alumni association

232 8	雨	▶う ▷あめ, あま	

雨	あめ rain
大雨	おおあめ heavy rain
雨水	あまみず rainwater
◇ 雨*具	あまぐ rainwear, raincoat, umbrella
◇ 雨*量	うりょう precipitation, rainfall
◇*梅雨	△つゆ the rainy season
◇*梅雨前*線	ばいうぜんせん warm front of early summer rain
◇ 小雨	こさめ light rain, drizzle
◇ 春雨	はるさめ spring rain, drizzle
◇*霧雨	きりさめ misty rain

| 歴 | 五月雨 | △さみだれ　early summer rain |
| ◇ | 時雨 | △しぐれ　(rain) shower (in late autumn and early winter) |

233 京 8
▶きょう，けい

東京	とうきょう　Tokyo
京都	きょうと　Kyoto
上京	じょうきょう　cv. go to Tokyo
帰京	ききょう　cv. return to Tokyo
◇ 京▲阪*神地方	けいはんしんちほう Osaka and its neighboring regions

234 映 9
▶えい
▷うつ（る），うつ（す），は（える）

映画	えいが　movie
上映	じょうえい　cv. show (a movie)
映る	うつる　be reflected
映す	うつす　reflect, project
◇ 映える	はえる　shine, look nice

235 画 8
▶が，かく

映画	えいが　movie
画家	がか　painter, artist
日本画	にほんが　Japanese-style painting
◇*絵画	かいが　picture, drawing, painting
◇*洋画	ようが　Western-style painting, foreign film
◇*邦画	ほうが　Japanese film
計画	けいかく　cv. create a plan/project

236 仕 5
▶し，じ
▷つか（える）

仕事	しごと　work, business, job
仕上げる	しあげる　finish (off/up), complete
仕上がる	しあがる　be finished, be completed, be ready
◇ 仕立てる	したてる　make (clothes), tailor
◇ 仕える	つかえる　serve (a person), work under/for
◇*給仕	きゅうじ　waiter, waitress; cv. wait

237 事 8
▶じ，ず
▷こと

仕事	しごと　work, business, job
出来事	できごと　event, happening, occurrence
見事な	みごとな　beautiful, splendid, masterful
物事	ものごと　things, matters, everything
家事	かじ　housework, housekeeping
火事	かじ　fire
人事	じんじ　personnel affairs
大事な	だいじな　important
◇ 事*件	じけん　incident, affair, matter, case, trouble
◇ 好事家	こうずか　dilettante

238 質 15
▶しつ，しち，ち

質問	しつもん　question; cv. ask questions
質	しつ　quality cf. *量（りょう）quantity
本質	ほんしつ　real nature, substance, essence
◇*品質	ひんしつ　quality of a product cf. *性*能（せいのう）capacity/performance (of a machine)

◊	地質	ちしつ　nature of the soil, geological features
	人質	ひとじち　hostage
◊	質屋	しちや　pawnshop
◊	言質	△げんち　pledge, word (as in "get one's word")

239 / 11　問　▶もん　▷と(う)，と(い)，とん

質問	しつもん　question; cv. ask questions
問題	もんだい　problem, issue, question (in an exam)
学問	がくもん　learning, study, studies
問答	もんどう　cv. ask questions and give answers
問い	とい　question
問い合わせる	といあわせる　make inquiries (at an office), inquire
問い合わせ	といあわせ　inquiry
◊ 問屋	とんや, といや　wholesale store

240 / 10　料　▶りょう

料理	りょうり　cv. cook; cuisine
料金	りょうきん　charge, fee, fare
送料	そうりょう　postage, cost of sending
有料道路	ゆうりょうどうろ　toll road
◊ 食料*品	しょくりょうひん　food, groceries

241 / 11　理　▶り

料理	りょうり　cv. cook; cuisine
理解	りかい　cv. understand, comprehend　cf. 分かる(わかる)　understand, realize, find out
心理	しんり　psychology
心理学	しんりがく　psychology

	地理	ちり　geography
	物理学	ぶつりがく　physics
◊	物理*的に	ぶつりてきに　physically
◊	理*論	りろん　theory
◊	*論理	ろんり　logic

242 / 10　真　▶しん　▷ま

写真	しゃしん　photograph, picture
真理	しんり　truth
◊ 真*空	しんくう　vacuum
真っ白な	まっしろな　pure white, snow-white
真っ黒な	まっくろな　pitch-black
真っ赤な	△まっかな　bright/deep red
真っ青な	△まっさおな　deep blue, pale
真っ暗な	まっくらな　pitch-dark
◊ 真ん*丸い/な	まんまるい/な　(perfectly) round
真ん中	まんなか　the middle, the center, the heart
真っ先に	まっさきに　at the very beginning, first of all

243 / 10　紙　▶し　▷かみ

手紙	てがみ　letter
紙	かみ　paper
新聞紙	しんぶんし　newspaper
コピー用紙	コピーようし　copying paper
白紙	はくし　blank sheet
◊ *和紙	わし　Japanese paper

244 / 6　好　▶こう　▷この(む)，す(く)

好きな	すきな　favorite; be fond of

大好きな　だいすきな (most) favorite; be very fond of

好き好きだ　すきずきだ be a matter of taste

好意　こうい goodwill, good wishes, kindness, favor

好調な　こうちょうな in good condition, satisfactory

◊ 友好*的な　ゆうこうてきな friendly

◊ 好人物　こうじんぶつ good-natured person

好む　このむ like, be fond of cf. 気に入る(きにいる) get/grow fond of

好み　このみ preference

245 **元** ▶げん, がん
4 ▷もと

元気な　げんきな healthy, be in good spirits

◊ 二元*論　にげんろん dualism

足元　あしもと at one's feet, (one's) step

地元の　じもとの local/home (team, etc.)

◊ 家元　いえもと head/master of a school (of flower arrangement/tea ceremony/etc.)

◊ 元来　がんらい originally, primarily, by nature

◊ 元▲旦　がんたん the first day of the year

246 **気** ▶き, け
6

元気な　げんきな healthy, in good spirits

気持ち　きもち feeling, mood, sensation

気に入る　きにいる get/grow fond of

電気　でんき electricity

人気　にんき popularity, popular

人気　ひとけ sign/presense of people

大気　たいき atmosphere

気体　きたい gas

◊ 気*候　きこう weather, climate

◊ *浮気　△うわき cv. have an affair, be unfaithful to one's spouse

◊ 人気のない　ひとけのない deserted, empty

◊ 気*配　けはい indication, sign

◊ 火の気　ひのけ fire, heat

◊ 意気地のない　△いくじのない timid, cowardly

247 **静** ▶せい, じょう
14 ▷しず, しず(か), しず(まる), しず(める)

静かな　しずかな quiet, silent, calm, peaceful

静まる　しずまる calm down

◊ 静けさ　しずけさ stillness, silence, calm, peace

◊ *冷静な　れいせいな cool-headed

静電気　せいでんき static electricity

◊ 静*脈　じょうみゃく vein

248 **利** ▶り
7 ▷き(く)

便利な　べんりな useful, handy

利用　りよう cv. use

勝利　しょうり victory

利口な　りこうな wise, clever

利子　りし interest (on a loan/etc.)

◊ 利*息　りそく interest (on a loan/etc.)

◊ 利*益　りえき profit

右利き　みぎきき right-handed

左利き　ひだりきき left-handed

◊ *砂利　△じゃり gravel, pebbles

249 親 16 ▶しん
▷おや，した（しい），した（しむ）

親切な	しんせつな　kind
◇ *両親	りょうしん　father and mother, parents
父親	ちちおや　father
母親	ははおや　mother
親	おや　parent(s)
親子	おやこ　parent(s) and child(ren)
◇ 親*指	おやゆび　thumb
親しい	したしい　close, intimate

| 親友 | しんゆう　close friend |
| 親日家 | しんにちか　Japanophile, pro-Japanese person |

250 切 4 ▶せつ，さい
▷き（る），き（れる）

切る	きる　cut
切手	きって　(postage) stamp
親切な	しんせつな　kind
大切な	たいせつな　important　cf. 大事な（だいじな）　important
◇ 一切	いっさい　all, the whole, everything; not anything, not at all

44

第 2 水準

(Level 2)

251-350

⑫

251 笑 10	▶しょう ▷わら(う)，え(む)

笑う	わらう laugh, smile
笑い	わらい laughter
苦笑	くしょう *cv.* smile wryly, give a forced laugh
◇ *微笑	びしょう *cv.* smile
◇ 笑*顔	△えがお smiling face
◇ 笑み	えみ smile

252 泣 8	▶きゅう ▷な(く)

泣く	なく cry
◇ 泣き*声	なきごえ cry, tearful voice
◇ *号泣	ごうきゅう *cv.* cry bitterly

253 喜 12	▶き ▷よろこ(ぶ)

| 喜ぶ | よろこぶ be glad, be pleased |
| ◇ 喜*劇 | きげき comedy 反 悲*劇(ひげき) tragedy, tragic event |

254 困 7	▶こん ▷こま(る)

| 困る | こまる have difficulty/trouble, be in/get into trouble, be embarrassed |
| ◇ 困*難な | こんなんな difficult, hard |

255 怒 9	▶ど ▷いか(る)，おこ(る)

| 怒る | おこる，いかる become angry |
| ◇ *激怒 | げきど *cv.* be enraged, fly into a rage |

256 押 8	▶おう ▷お(す)，お(さえる)

| 押す | おす push, press |

押し入れ	おしいれ closet
押さえる	おさえる press/hold down, stop, restrain
◇ 押*収	おうしゅう *cv.* seize, confiscate

257 引 4	▶いん ▷ひ(く)，ひ(ける)

引く	ひく pull, draw (curtain/bowstring/etc.)
長引く	ながびく be prolonged, be protracted
引き返す	ひきかえす turn/come back, return
引き出す	ひきだす pull out, take out, withdraw
引き出し	ひきだし drawer
引っかかる	ひっかかる be caught in/by ～, be cheated
引っかける	ひっかける hang/suspend on ～, trap, cheat
引き分け	ひきわけ draw, tie (as in game)
取(り)引(き)	とりひき trading, deal
◇ *字引	じびき dictionary cf. *辞書 (じしょ)，rather than *字引，is used in modern Japanese.
引力	いんりょく gravity, gravitational force
引用	いんよう *cv.* cite
引退	いんたい *cv.* retire
強引な	ごういんな overbearing, coercive, pushy

258 死 6	▶し ▷し(ぬ)

死ぬ	しぬ die, be killed
死人	しにん dead person, the dead
死者	ししゃ the deceased, the dead
死体	したい dead body, corpse, cadaver
死	し death

◇ 死*亡	しぼう	*cv.* die, be killed

259
7 吹　　▶すい
　　　▷ふ(く)

吹く	ふく	blow, exhale
◇ 吹*雪	△ふぶき	snowstorm, blizzard
◇ *息吹	△いぶき	a breath (of spring), an emanation (of youth)
◇ 吹*奏楽	すいそうがく	wind-instrument music

260
9 急　　▶きゅう
　　　▷いそ(ぐ)

急ぐ	いそぐ	hurry (up), hasten
急に	きゅうに	suddenly
急行	きゅうこう	express (train); *cv.vi.* go in haste
急用	きゅうよう	urgent business
◇ 急*速な	きゅうそくな	rapid

261
9 咲　　▷さ(く)

咲く	さく	bloom, blossom
返り咲く	かえりざく	come back (to power)

262
13 置　　▶ち
　　　▷お(く)

置く	おく	put, place
置物	おきもの	ornament (for an alcovel/entranceway/etc.)
物置	ものおき	storeroom
◇ *位置	いち	position, location; *cv.* be located

263
12 勝　　▶しょう
　　　▷か(つ)、まさ(る)

勝つ	かつ	win
勝者	しょうしゃ	winner
勝利	しょうり	victory
連勝	れんしょう	consecutive victories; *cv.* keep on winning
◇ *優勝	ゆうしょう	*cv.* win (the championship/the pennant/etc.)
◇ 勝る	まさる	be superior

264
15 選　　▶せん
　　　▷えら(ぶ)

選ぶ	えらぶ	choose, select, elect
選出	せんしゅつ	*cv.* elect
選手	せんしゅ	athlete
◇ 選*挙	せんきょ	election; *cv.* elect

265
9 飛　　▶ひ
　　　▷と(ぶ)、と(ばす)

飛ぶ	とぶ	fly, jump, hop
飛び出す	とびだす	run out, jump out
飛行機	ひこうき	airplane
飛行場	ひこうじょう	airfield cf. 空港(くうこう) airport

266
15 踏　　▶とう
　　　▷ふ(む)、ふ(まえる)

踏む	ふむ	step on, tread on
踏切	ふみきり	railroad crossing
◇ *雑踏	ざっとう	crowd
◇ *舞*踏会	ぶとうかい	ball, dance
◇ 踏まえる	ふまえる	be based on

⑬

267
11 進　　▶しん
　　　▷すす(む)、すす(める)

進む	すすむ	advance, move forward, make progress
進学	しんがく	*cv.* enter the next stage of education, go on to the next grade

前進	ぜんしん	*cv.* go ahead, advance
進歩	しんぽ	*cv.* advance
先進国	せんしんこく	advanced country

268 盗 11
▶とう
▷ぬす(む)

盗む	ぬすむ	steal
強盗	ごうとう	burglar, robber
盗作	とうさく	plagiarism

269 受 8
▶じゅ
▷う(ける)，う(かる)

受ける	うける	receive, be given
引き受ける	ひきうける	undertake, accept (a job/assignment/etc.)
受け取る	うけとる	receive, accept, understand
◇ 受け*身	うけみ	passiveness, passivity, passive voice
◇ 受*付	うけつけ	reception/information desk, acceptance, receipt
授受	じゅじゅ	*cv.* give and receive
◇ 受理	じゅり	*cv.* accept, receive
受かる	うかる	pass (an exam)

270 取 8
▶しゅ
▷と(る)

取る	とる	take, get, hold
取り出す	とりだす	take out
取り入れる	とりいれる	accept, adopt, borrow, harvest
受け取る	うけとる	get, receive, accept, interpret, understand
◇ 取*材	しゅざい	*cv.* collect/gather (news material/data/etc.)

271 合 6
▶ごう，がっ，かつ
▷あ(う)，あ(わす)，あ(わせる)

合う	あう	fit, suit, match
間に合う	まにあう	be in time, be enough
お見合い	おみあい	*cv.* meet a prospective marriage partner
合わせる	あわせる	put together, add, tune (to)
会合	かいごう	meeting, gathering; *cv.* meet, gather
集合	しゅうごう	*cv.* meet, gather, assemble
合意	ごうい	agreement; *cv.* agree
◇ 合*格	ごうかく	*cv.* pass (an entrance/certificate exam)
◇ 合*併	がっぺい	*cv.* merger
歴 合*戦	かっせん	battle

272 吸 6
▶きゅう
▷す(う)

吸う	すう	smoke, inhale, suck (blood), absorb
吸い取る	すいとる	absorb, suck up, soak up, squeeze (money out of someone/etc.)
呼吸	こきゅう	respiration, breathing; *cv.* breathe cf. *息をする (いきをする) breathe
◇ 吸*収	きゅうしゅう	*cv.* absorb, assimilate

273 拾 9
▶しゅう，じゅう
▷ひろ(う)

拾う	ひろう	pick up, gather
◇ 拾*得物	しゅうとくぶつ	a find, something found
◇ 拾万円	じゅうまんえん	one hundred thousand yen

274
誘
14
▶ゆう
▷さそ（う）

誘う　　　　さそう　invite

◇ 誘発　　　　ゆうはつ　cv. induce, cause, trigger

◇ 誘*惑　　　ゆうわく　cv. tempt, allure

◇*勧誘　　　かんゆう　cv. invite, persuade, induce

◇ 誘*拐　　　ゆうかい　cv. kidnap

275
疲
10
▶ひ
▷つか（れる），つか（らす）

疲れる　　　つかれる　be tired, grow weary

疲れ　　　　つかれ　tiredness, fatigue, weariness

気疲れ　　　きづかれ　cv. be mentally tired, worry, be bored

◇ 疲*労　　　ひろう　tiredness, fatigue, weariness; cv. be tired

276
比
4
▶ひ
▷くら（べる）

比べる　　　くらべる　compare

見比べる　　みくらべる　compare (visually)

比重　　　　ひじゅう　weight

◇ 比*較　　　ひかく　cv. compare

◇ 比*例　　　ひれい　cv. be proportional, be in proportion to

277
決
7
▶けつ
▷き（める），き（まる）

決める　　　きめる　decide, judge

決定　　　　けってい　cv. decide, settle, determine

◇ 決定*的な　けっていてきな　definite, final, decisive

決心　　　　けっしん　cv. determine, be determined, make up one's mind, resolve

決して　　　けっして　never

278
伝
6
▶でん
▷つた（わる），つた（える），つた（う）

伝える　　　つたえる　tell, report, communicate

手伝う　　　△てつだう　help, assist

◇ 言い伝え　いいつたえ　legend, tradition

伝う　　　　つたう　go along

伝言　　　　でんごん　message; cv. give/send a message

◇ 伝*統　　　でんとう　tradition

◇ 伝説　　　でんせつ　legend

279
流
10
▶りゅう，る
▷なが（れる），なが（す）

流れる　　　ながれる　flow

流す　　　　ながす　pour, let flow, drain, spread (rumors), broadcast

上流　　　　じょうりゅう　upper stream, upper class

◇ 上流*階*級　じょうりゅうかいきゅう　upper class

中流　　　　ちゅうりゅう　middle stream, middle class

下流　　　　かりゅう　lower stream

一流ホテル　いちりゅうホテル　top-ranking hotel, one of the best hotels

流行　　　　りゅうこう　fashion, vogue, craze, fad, popularity; cv. be in fashion, be popular/prevalent/epidemic

◇ 流*布　　　るふ　cv. circulate, spread

⑭

280
落
12
▶らく
▷お（ちる），お（とす）

落ちる　　　おちる　fall, drop

落ち着く　　おちつく　settle down, calm down

落とす　　　おとす　drop, throw down, lose

落とし物　おとしもの　lost article/property

落石　らくせき　falling rock(s)

転落　てんらく　cv. fall, roll/tumble down

◇ 落*雷　らくらい　lightning strike

◇*墜落　ついらく　cv. fall, crash

---

281 晴 12　▶せい
▷は(れる)，は(らす)

晴れる　はれる　clear (up), feel refreshed/better

晴れ　はれ　fine weather

秋晴れ　あきばれ　fine autumn day

◇*快晴　かいせい　fine weather

◇ 晴*天　せいてん　fine weather, clear sky

---

282 投 7　▶とう
▷な(げる)

投げる　なげる　throw, pitch, give up

投手　とうしゅ　pitcher

投書　とうしょ　contribution, letter from a reader (to the editor); cv.vi. contribute (a letter/poem/etc.) to a publication

◇ 投*資　とうし　cv. invest

◇ 投*票　とうひょう　cv. vote, cast a ballot

◇ 投機　とうき　speculation, venture

---

283 逃 9　▶とう
▷に(げる)，に(がす)，のが(す)，のが(れる)

逃げる　にげる　run away, get away, escape

逃げ出す　にげだす　run away, flee

逃走　とうそう　cv. run away, escape

逃がす　にがす　release, set free, let escape

取り逃がす　とりにがす　fail to catch

逃す　のがす　fail to use (an opportunity)

見逃す　みのがす　miss, overlook, pass over, let go unchallenged/unpunished

◇ 逃れる　のがれる　escape, get away

---

284 過 12　▶か
▷す(ぎる)，す(ごす)，あやま(つ)，あやま(ち)

過ぎる　すぎる　pass, go past, elapse

通り過ぎる　とおりすぎる　go past, pass (a place/etc.)

飲み過ぎ　のみすぎ　drinking too much, excessive drinking

食べ過ぎ　たべすぎ　eating too much, excessive eating

通過　つうか　cv. pass (through)

◇ 過半*数　かはんすう　majority, more than half

◇ 過*労死　かろうし　early death caused by overwork

◇ 過*程　かてい　process

◇ 過*失　かしつ　error, fault

過ごす　すごす　spend (a day/a vacation/etc.)

◇ 過ち　あやまち　error, fault

---

285 捨 11　▶しゃ
▷す(てる)

捨てる　すてる　throw away, dispose of

見捨てる　みすてる　walk out on, forsake

捨て犬　すていぬ　abandoned dog

四捨五入　ししゃごにゅう　round off (to the nearest whole number)

◇ 取捨選*択　しゅしゃせんたく　cv. sort out, choose, select

286 発 9　▶はつ，ほつ

出発	しゅっぱつ	cv. depart, leave
発車	はっしゃ	cv. depart (as in trains or buses)
～発	～はつ	departing from ～
～発	～はつ	departing at ～ (time)
発明	はつめい	cv. invent
発見	はっけん	cv. discover
発行	はっこう	cv. issue, publish
◇ 発足	ほっそく	cv. be inaugurated, start
◇ 発起人	ほっきにん	proposer, promoter

287 到 8　▶とう

到着	とうちゃく	cv. arrive
◇ 到*底	とうてい	cannot possibly, (not) at all
◇ 到来	とうらい	cv. come, arrive

288 計 9　▶けい
▷はか(る)，はか(らう)

計画	けいかく	cv. create a plan/project
時計	△とけい	watch, clock
会計	かいけい	accounting
家計	かけい	household budget
合計	ごうけい	cv. add up, total; sum, total
◇ 計る	はかる	measure, plot, design

289 定 8　▶てい，じょう
▷さだ(める)，さだ(まる)，さだ(か)

決定	けってい	cv. decide, determine
意思決定	いしけってい	decision-making

安定	あんてい	cv. be stable/steady
安定した	あんていした	stable
◇ *不安定な	ふあんていな	unstable
定食	ていしょく	set meal
定年	ていねん	retirement age
定休日	ていきゅうび	regular day off
◇ 定める	さだめる	decide (on), determine, appoint, lay down (a rule)
◇ 定かではない	さだかではない	unknown
◇ 定石	じょうせき	standard move (in the games of *go* and *shōgi*), standard method

⑮

290 注 8　▶ちゅう
▷そそ(ぐ)

注意	ちゅうい	cv. warn, caution, take notice of
注目	ちゅうもく	cv. pay attention, watch, keep one's eyes on
注文	ちゅうもん	cv. order
発注	はっちゅう	cv. place an order
◇ 注ぐ	そそぐ	pour

291 意 13　▶い

注意	ちゅうい	cv. warn, caution, take notice of
意見	いけん	opinion
用意	ようい	cv. prepare
好意	こうい	good will, good wishes, kindness, favor
意外な	いがいな	unexpected, unforeseen
意地悪な	いじわるな	mean, spiteful
生意気な	なまいきな	conceited, impertinent, insolent

292 説 14	▶せつ，ぜい ▷と(く)	
説明	せつめい	cv. explain
解説	かいせつ	cv. explain, comment on
小説	しょうせつ	novel
社説	しゃせつ	editorial
説教	せっきょう	cv. preach (a sermon), lecture (a child)
◇ 説*得	せっとく	cv. persuade
◇ *仮説	かせつ	hypothesis
◇ *演説	えんぜつ	(political) speech; cv. deliver a (political) speech
◇ 遊説	ゆうぜい	cv. make an election tour, go canvassing (for votes)
◇ 説く	とく	explain, expound, advocate, persuade

293 解 13	▶かい，げ ▷と(く)，と(かす)，と(ける)	
理解	りかい	cv. understand, comprehend cf. 分かる (わかる) understand, realize, find out
見解	けんかい	comment, opinion
解決	かいけつ	cv. solve, settle
解く	とく	solve
解ける	とける	come untied, melt away
解かす	とかす	melt (snow/ice/etc.)
◇ 解脱	げだつ	emancipation from worldly attachments, salvation from earthly bondage; cv. be emancipated

294 参 8	▶さん ▷まい(る)	
参加	さんか	cv. participate, take part in
参考書	さんこうしょ	reference book
持参	じさん	cv. bring
お参り	おまいり	cv. visit a shrine/temple

295 加 5	▶か ▷くわ(える)，くわ(わる)	
参加	さんか	cv. participate, take part in
◇ 加*工	かこう	cv. process (food/etc.)
加入	かにゅう	cv. join (a club/association/etc.)
◇ 加*盟	かめい	cv. join (a league/federation/etc.)
◇ 加*熱	かねつ	cv. heat
加える	くわえる	add (one number to another), inflict (damage)
加わる	くわわる	join, take part in, increase

296 練 14	▶れん ▷ね(る)	
練習	れんしゅう	cv. practice, drill, rehearse
洗練された	せんれんされた	sophisticated
◇ *訓練	くんれん	training, drill
◇ *熟練*労働者	じゅくれんろうどうしゃ	skilled worker
◇ 練る	ねる	knead, elaborate (a scheme)

297 研 9	▶けん ▷と(ぐ)	
研究	けんきゅう	cv. study, research
研究所	けんきゅうじょ	(research) laboratory, research institute
◇ 研*修	けんしゅう	study and training; cv. be trained
◇ 研*修所	けんしゅうじょ	training center
◇ 研ぐ	とぐ	cv. sharpen (a knife)

298
7　究　▶きゅう
　　　▷きわ（める）

研究	けんきゅう	cv. study, research
究明	きゅうめい	cv. look deep into, investigate, inquire into
◇ 究める	きわめる	master, investigate thoroughly, get at the truth

299
10　連　▶れん
　　　▷つら（なる），つら（ねる），つ（れる）

連絡	れんらく	cv. contact
連続	れんぞく	continuation, series; cv. continue, be consecutive
◇ 国*際連合	こくさいれんごう	the United Nations cf. abbr. 国連（こくれん）
◇ 連*想	れんそう	cv. be reminded of; association (of ideas)
◇ *関連	かんれん	relations, connection; cv. be connected/associated/correlated cf. *関*係（かんけい） relations, relationship
◇ *関連した	かんれんした	related, relevant
◇ ～に*関連して	～にかんれんして	in connection with, in relation to, with reference to
連れていく	つれていく	take someone along
◇ 連なる	つらなる	range, lie/stand/in a row, be strung out

300
12　絡　▶らく
　　　▷から（む），から（まる）

連絡	れんらく	cv. contact
◇ 絡む	からむ	coil around, become entwined
◇ 絡まる	からまる	become entangled
◇ ～絡みの	～がらみの	related to

301
17　濯　▶たく

洗濯	せんたく	cv. do the laundry
洗濯機	せんたくき	washing machine
洗濯物	せんたくもの	laundry

302
12　結　▶けつ
　　　▷むす（ぶ），ゆ（う），ゆ（わえる）

結婚	けっこん	cv. marry, get married
結ぶ	むすぶ	tie, fasten (together), bind, enter (a relationship with)
結合	けつごう	cv. combine, unite
終結	しゅうけつ	cv. end, conclude
◇ 結*論	けつろん	conclusion
◇ 結*納	ゆいのう	betrothal presents
◇ 結う	ゆう	dress/do up (one's hair), tie (up), fasten
◇ 結わえる	ゆわえる	bind, fasten, tie

303
11　婚　▶こん

結婚	けっこん	cv. marry, get married
新婚旅行	しんこんりょこう	honeymoon
◇ 婚*約	こんやく	cv. get engaged
◇ *離婚	りこん	cv. divorce, get divorced

304
12　運　▶うん
　　　▷はこ（ぶ）

運転	うんてん	cv. drive (a car/etc.), operate a (machine)
運転手	うんてんしゅ	driver
運動	うんどう	motion, movement, exercise, athletics, (social) movement, campaign; cv. exercise

運ぶ	はこぶ carry, convey, transport, take (something to a place), make progress
運送会社	うんそうがいしゃ delivery company
運	うん fortune

305
案
10

▶あん

案内	あんない cv. show around, show the way, give a tour of; guidance, invitation
案	あん plan, idea
名案	めいあん good idea
◇*提案	ていあん cv. propose
案外	あんがい unexpectedly

⑯

306
卒
8

▶そつ

卒業	そつぎょう cv. graduate
卒業生	そつぎょうせい graduate
大卒(者)	だいそつ(しゃ) college/university graduate cf. 中卒(者), 高卒(者)
新卒	しんそつ recent graduate

307
業
13

▶ぎょう, ごう
▷わざ

卒業	そつぎょう cv. graduate
授業	じゅぎょう class
事業	じぎょう business
休業	きゅうぎょう cv. close a business (for a holiday/etc.), suspend business/operations
◇*職業	しょくぎょう profession, job
◇*産業	さんぎょう industry
◇*実業家	じつぎょうか businessman, entrepreneur

◇ 自業自*得	じごうじとく the natural consequences of one's evil deed, getting one's just deserts
◇ 早業	はやわざ quick feat/trick

308
用
5

▶よう
▷もち(いる)

利用	りよう cv. use
使用	しよう cv. use
通用	つうよう cv. be available, be good, be valid
用事	ようじ business, errand, engagement
用	よう business, errand, engagement (in casual speech)
用意	ようい cv. prepare
用心	ようじん cv. be careful, be on the alert
用語	ようご (technical) term
◇ 用*途	ようと use
◇*費用	ひよう cost
◇ 用いる	もちいる use, employ, adopt

309
去
5

▶きょ, こ
▷さ(る)

去年	きょねん last year
過去	かこ past cf. *未来(みらい) future, *現*在(げんざい)present
立ち去る	たちさる leave (a place)

310
趣
15

▶しゅ
▷おもむき

趣味	しゅみ interest, hobby
◇ 趣	おもむき grace, elegance, charm

311
味
8

▶み
▷あじ, あじ(わう)

趣味	しゅみ interest, hobby
意味	いみ meaning, significance; cv. mean

◇ *興味　　　きょうみ　interest

地味な　　　じみな　plain, simple, quiet 反 *派手な（はでな）showy, bright

◇ *風*邪気味だ　かぜぎみだ　have a slight cold

◇ 気味が悪い　きみがわるい　weird, uncanny, creepy

◇ 正味　　　しょうみ　net (weight/quantity/etc.), full (as in "eight full hours")

味　　　あじ　taste, flavor

味わう　　　あじわう　taste, experience, go through

調味料　　　ちょうみりょう　seasoning

味覚　　　みかく　the sense of taste

◇ 三味*線　△しゃみせん　*shamisen*, a three-stringed banjo-like instrument

---

312 授 **11**　▶じゅ　▷さず(ける), さず(かる)

授業　　　じゅぎょう　class

教授　　　きょうじゅ　professor

授受　　　じゅじゅ　*cv.* give and receive

◇ 授ける　さずける　grant (a license), confer (a title), award (a prize)

---

313 橋 **16**　▶きょう　▷はし

橋　　　はし　bridge

日本橋　　　にほんばし　Nihonbashi (a place in Tokyo)

日本橋　　　にっぽんばし　Nipponbashi (a place in Osaka)

歩道橋　　　ほどうきょう　pedestrian bridge

鉄橋　　　てっきょう　railway bridge

---

314 花 **7**　▶か　▷はな

花　　　はな　flower

花屋　　　はなや　florist, flower shop, flower stall

生け花　　　いけばな　the art of flower arrangement

お花見　　　おはなみ　cherry blossom viewing

花火　　　はなび　firework

◇ 花*壇　　　かだん　flower bed

---

315 薬 **16**　▶やく　▷くすり

薬　　　くすり　drug, medicine

薬屋　　　くすりや　pharmacy, drugstore

薬局　　　やっきょく　pharmacy

薬学　　　やくがく　pharmacy, pharmaceutics

◇ 薬味　　　やくみ　spice

---

316 色 **6**　▶しょく, しき　▷いろ

色　　　いろ　color

茶色　　　ちゃいろ　brown

〜色の　　　〜いろの　〜 colored

色紙　　　いろがみ　colored paper

色づく　　　いろづく　turn color (as in leaves)

色っぽい　　　いろっぽい　erotic, seductive, sexy

◇ 色気　　　いろけ　sex appeal

◇ 色気がある　いろけがある　be very interested in, have an inclination for, sexy

◇ 好色な　　　こうしょくな　lustful, erotic

色紙　　　しきし　square piece of fancy paper (for writing a poem/etc.)

◇ 色*彩　　　しきさい　hue, tint, coloring, color

◇ *原色　　　げんしょく　primary color

◇ *特色　　　とくしょく　distinguishing characteristics

◇ *景色　　　△けしき　view, landscape

317 服 8 ▶ふく

服	ふく clothes
◇*洋服	ようふく Western-style clothes
◇*和服	わふく Japanese-style clothes, kimono
◇ 服*装	ふくそう (a way of) dressing, clothes
◇*征服	せいふく cv. conquer
◇ 着服	ちゃくふく cv. embezzle

318 客 9 ▶きゃく，かく

客	きゃく guest, customer
客間	きゃくま guest room (in a house)
乗客	じょうきゃく passenger
旅客機	りょかくき passenger airplane
◇ お客*様	おきゃくさま guest, customer (honorific)
◇ 客*観*的な	きゃっかんてきな objective 反 主*観*的な（しゅかんてきな）subjective

319 犬 4 ▶けん ▷いぬ 87 124 cf. 大 太

犬	いぬ dog
小犬／子犬	こいぬ puppy
◇*野犬	やけん stray dog

320 文 4 ▶ぶん，もん ▷ふみ

文	ぶん sentence, passage
作文	さくぶん composition, essay
文学	ぶんがく literature
文体	ぶんたい style
文語	ぶんご literary language/expression

文明	ぶんめい civilization
◇ 文*化	ぶんか culture
◇ 人文*科学	じんぶんかがく humanities
◇ 文*字	もじ letter (of the alphabet/etc.)
◇ 文*盲*率	もんもうりつ illiteracy rate cf.*識*字*率（しきじりつ）literacy rate
歴 文	ふみ letter

321 物 8 ▶ぶつ，もつ ▷もの

飲(み)物	のみもの drink, beverage
食べ物	たべもの food
物	もの thing, object, substance, article
本物	ほんもの genuine article, real thing
◇*偽物	にせもの imitation, sham, fake
名物	めいぶつ local specialty, well-known product
生き物	いきもの living thing, creature, animal, life
動物	どうぶつ animal
◇*植物	しょくぶつ plant
生物	せいぶつ living thing, organism
生物学	せいぶつがく biology
◇ 物理*的に	ぶつりてきに physically
物理学	ぶつりがく physics
物質	ぶっしつ matter, substance
◇ 物*価	ぶっか prices
食物	しょくもつ food

⑰

322 族 11 ▶ぞく

家族	かぞく family
部族	ぶぞく tribe

◇ *民族　　　　　みんぞく　people, ethnic group

◇ 族*議*員　　　ぞくぎいん　Diet member who works on policy-making in a particular field

323
4

公

▶こう
▷おおやけ

公園　　　　　こうえん　park, square

公立高校　　　こうりつこうこう　public high school

◇ 公*共*施*設　こうきょうしせつ　public/community facilities

◇ 公*共事業　　こうきょうじぎょう　government enterprise

◇ 公*共*交通システム　こうきょうこうつうシステム　public transportation system

◇ 公言　　　　　こうげん　cv. declare

◇ 公*平な　　　こうへいな　fair, impartial

◇ 公*正な　　　こうせいな　just, fair, righteous

◇ 公の　　　　　おおやけの　public, official, formal

主人公　　　　しゅじんこう　main character (of a story/etc.)

324
13

園

▶えん
▷その

公園　　　　　こうえん　park, square

動物園　　　　どうぶつえん　zoo

◇ *植物園　　　しょくぶつえん　botanical garden

遊園地　　　　ゆうえんち　amusement park

◇ 日本*庭園　　にほんていえん　Japanese garden

◇ 園*芸　　　　えんげい　gardening

◇ 花園　　　　　はなぞの　flower garden

325
7

医

▶い

医者　　　　　いしゃ　doctor

◇ 医*師　　　　いし　doctor

医学　　　　　いがく　medical science

医学部　　　　いがくぶ　medical department

名医　　　　　めいい　great doctor, skilled physician

女医　　　　　じょい　woman doctor

326
11

宿

▶しゅく
▷やど，やど(る)，やど(す)

宿題　　　　　しゅくだい　homework

下宿　　　　　げしゅく　lodging; cv. lodge, rent a room

◇ 宿*泊　　　　しゅくはく　cv. stay at, lodge

宿　　　　　　やど　inn, lodgings

雨宿り　　　　あまやどり　cv. take cover from the rain (under the eaves of a house)

◇ 宿す　　　　　やどす　be pregnant

327
18

題

▶だい

宿題　　　　　しゅくだい　homework

問題　　　　　もんだい　issue, problem, question (in a exam)

出題　　　　　しゅつだい　cv. make questions (for an exam)

話題　　　　　わだい　topic, subject (of a conversation)

題名　　　　　だいめい　title

328
6

寺

▶じ
▷てら

寺　　　　　　てら　temple

山寺　　　　　やまでら　mountain temple

◇ 寺院　　　　　じいん　temple

329
7

図

▶ず，と
▷はか(る)

図書館　　　　としょかん　library

地図　　　　　ちず　map

図	ず	figure, diagram
◇ 図*表	ずひょう	figures and diagrams
◇ 図*形	ずけい	figure
合図	あいず	signal, sign
意図	いと	intention; *cv.* intend
◇ 図る	はかる	plot, scheme, design

330 館 16 ▶かん

図書館	としょかん	library
旅館	りょかん	Japanese-style inn
学生会館	がくせいかいかん	students' hall
水族館	すいぞくかん	aquarium
館長	かんちょう	director (of a museum/aquarium/etc.), chief librarian
本館	ほんかん	main building
◇*別館	べっかん	annex

331 室 9 ▶しつ ▷むろ

教室	きょうしつ	classroom
研究室	けんきゅうしつ	office (of a professor/researcher)
病室	びょうしつ	sickroom
客室	きゃくしつ	guest room, passenger cabin
待合室	まちあいしつ	waiting room
室内	しつない	indoor, indoors, in a room
◇*洋室	ようしつ	Western-style room
◇*和室	わしつ	Japanese-style room
歴 室町時代	むろまちじだい	Muromachi era, 14-16th century

332 席 10 ▶せき

出席	しゅっせき	*cv.* attend (a class/meeting/etc.), be present
◇*欠席	けっせき	*cv.* be absent (from school/etc.)
席	せき	seat
座席	ざせき	seat
着席	ちゃくせき	*cv.* be seated, sit down
主席	しゅせき	the Chairman (of the Chinese Communist Party)
◇*首席	しゅせき	top/first in the class

333 度 9 ▶ど, と, たく ▷たび

～度	～ど	～ time(s), ～ degree(s)
今度	こんど	shortly, soon, this time, next time
毎度	まいど	each time, always
年度	ねんど	(school/fiscal/etc.) year
高度な	こうどな	high, advanced, high-grade
◇ 高度*経*済*成長	こうどけいざいせいちょう	high economic growth
◇*温度	おんど	temperature
◇*速度	そくど	speed
◇*制度	せいど	system
◇*限度	げんど	limit, limitation
度々	たびたび	many times, over and over
この度	このたび	this time, now
◇*支度	したく	preparation; *cv.* get ready
歴*法度	はっと	regulations

334 機 16 ▶き ▷はた

飛行機	ひこうき	airplane

機内	きない	inside an airplane
機内食	きないしょく	inflight meal
◇ 機*関	きかん	organization, institution, engine
◇ 機*関車	きかんしゃ	locomotive
◇ 機*械	きかい	machine
機会	きかい	opportunity, occasion
◇ 機	はた	loom

335 場 12 ▶じょう ▷ば

場所	ばしょ	place, venue
場合	ばあい	occasion, case
場	ば	field, place, spot, space, room, scene
立場	たちば	standpoint, one's ground, point of view, viewpoint
◇ *市場	いちば	marketplace
◇ *工場	こうば	small factory
◇ *工場	こうじょう	factory
飛行場	ひこうじょう	airfield cf. *空*港(くうこう) airport
出場	しゅつじょう	cv. take part, participate
◇ *市場	しじょう	market

336 県 9 ▶けん

県	けん	prefecture, prefectural government
～県	～けん	～ Prefecture
県立(の)	けんりつ(の)	prefectural
県道	けんどう	prefectural road
◇ 県*庁	けんちょう	prefectural office

337 府 8 ▶ふ

京都府	きょうとふ	Kyoto Prefecture
◇ 大`阪府	おおさかふ	Osaka Prefecture
府立(の)	ふりつ(の)	prefectural (used only for Osaka and Kyoto)
◇ 府*庁	ふちょう	prefectural office (used only for Osaka and Kyoto)
◇ *幕府	ばくふ	the Shogunate government

338 都 11 ▶と, つ ▷みやこ

東京都	とうきょうと	the Tokyo metropolitan area
都立(の)	とりつ(の)	metropolitan
都内	とない	within Tokyo
都道府県	とどうふけん	the Tokyo metropolitan area, Hokkaido, Osaka, Kyoto, and the prefectures
都会	とかい	city
◇ *首都	しゅと	capital
◇ 都*庁	とちょう	Tokyo Metropolitan Government (Office)
◇ 都	みやこ	capital cf. *首都(しゅと), rather than 都, is used in modern Japanese.
都合	つごう	convenience, circumstances; cv. arrange (for), see to (something)

⑱

339 暖 13 ▶だん ▷あたた(か), あたた(かい), あたた(まる), あたた(める)

暖かい	あたたかい	warm
暖める	あたためる	vt. warm, heat
暖まる	あたたまる	get warm, be warmed
暖冬	だんとう	mild winter
◇ 暖*房	だんぼう	heating; cv. heat (a room)
◇ *温暖な	おんだんな	warm, mild, temperate

340 涼 11 ▶りょう
▷すず(しい)，すず(む)

涼しい	すずしい	cool
◇ 夕涼み	ゆうすずみ	enjoying the cool of evening, cooling off in the evening
◇ 涼む	すずむ	cool oneself, cool off
◇ 涼*風	りょうふう	cool/refreshing breeze
◇*清涼飲料(水)	せいりょういんりょう(すい)	refreshing beverage, soft drink

341 悲 12 ▶ひ
▷かな(しい)，かな(しむ)

悲しい	かなしい	sad, sorrowful
悲しむ	かなしむ	feel sad, lament, deplore
悲*劇	ひげき	tragedy, tragic event 反 喜*劇（きげき）comedy
悲運	ひうん	misfortune, bad luck

342 苦 8 ▶く
▷くる(しい)，くる(しむ)，くる(しめる)，にが(い)，にが(る)

苦しい	くるしい	painful, difficult, hard
重苦しい	おもくるしい	oppressive, gloomy
苦しむ	くるしむ	suffer, be in pain
苦しめる	くるしめる	cause pain, cause distress, torment, annoy
苦心	くしん	cv. take pains, work hard
◇ 苦*労	くろう	cv. suffer, trouble, labor
苦い	にがい	bitter
◇ 苦り切る	にがりきる	be disgusted/displeased

343 楽 13 ▶がく，らく
▷たの(しい)，たの(しむ)

楽しい	たのしい	fun, enjoyable
楽しみ	たのしみ	pleasure, joy, fun
楽しむ	たのしむ	enjoy, have fun
音楽	おんがく	music
◇ 楽*器	がっき	musical instrument
楽な	らくな	easy, comfortable
気楽に	きらくに	without worry/hesitation
安楽死	あんらくし	euthanasia, mercy killing
楽園	らくえん	paradise
◇*快楽主*義	かいらくしゅぎ	hedonism, epicureanism
◇*娯楽	ごらく	amusement, recreation
◇*神楽	△かぐら	kagura, Shinto sacred music and dance

344 辛 7 ▶しん
▷から(い)

辛い	からい	(spicy) hot, salty
辛口の	からくちの	dry (wine/beer/ etc.)
◇*塩辛い	しおからい	salty
◇ 辛うじて	かろうじて	barely, narrowly, with difficulty
◇*香辛料	こうしんりょう	spices

345 甘 5 ▶かん
▷あま(い)，あま(える)，あま(やかす)

甘い	あまい	sweet
甘える	あまえる	behave like a spoiled child, demand attention
甘やかす	あまやかす	indulge, pamper, spoil
甘口の	あまくちの	sweet (wine/sake/ etc.)
◇ 甘味料	かんみりょう	sweetener
◇ 甘*美な	かんびな	sweet

346 痛 12	▶つう ▷いた(い), いた(む), いた(める)

痛い	いたい　hurt, be painful
痛み	いたみ　pain, ache
痛む	いたむ　hurt, ache, have a pain
痛ましい	いたましい　pitiful, sad, miserable
痛手	いたで　damage
頭痛	ずつう　headache
苦痛	くつう　pain, agony
◇ 痛*快な	つうかいな　delightful, exciting, thrilling

347 有 6	▶ゆう, う ▷あ(る)

有名な	ゆうめいな　famous
国有地	こくゆうち　national land
私有地	しゆうち　privately-owned land
所有	しょゆう　cv. own
有る	ある　exist
有り金	ありがね　money on hand, all the money one has
◇ 有*無	うむ　existence, presence, yes or no
◇ *希有な	けうな　rare, uncommon

348 退 9	▶たい ▷しりぞ(く), しりぞ(ける)

退屈な	たいくつな　tedious, boring, monotonous
早退	そうたい　cv. leave school/the office early
退院	たいいん　cv. leave the hospital, be discharged from the hospital
退学	たいがく　cv. withdraw from school
退席	たいせき　cv. leave one's seat/the room
引退	いんたい　cv. retire (from active life)
◇ 退*却	たいきゃく　cv. retreat, withdraw
◇ 退く	しりぞく　retreat, step back, withdraw, retire
◇ 立ち退く	たちのく　move out, evacuate, vacate, withdraw

349 屈 8	▶くつ

退屈な	たいくつな　tedious, boring, monotonous
理屈	りくつ　argument, theory, reason, logic
◇ *不屈の	ふくつの　indomitable, unyielding
◇ 屈する	くっする　yield to, give in to
◇ 屈*伸	くっしん　bending and stretching (exercises)
◇ 屈*辱	くつじょく　humiliation, disgrace, insult

350 同 6	▶どう ▷おな(じ)

同じ	おなじ　same, identical
同一の	どういつの　same, identical
同一人物	どういつじんぶつ　the same person
同時に	どうじに　at the same time
同意	どうい　cv. agree, consent
◇ 同*情	どうじょう　cv. sympathize
◇ 同*居	どうきょ　cv. live together 反 *別居(べっきょ) cv. live separately
◇ *共同*声明	きょうどうせいめい　joint communique
◇ *協同*組合	きょうどうくみあい　cooperative
◇ *混同	こんどう　cv. confuse (something for something else)

第 3 水準
(Level 3)

351-1200

⑲

351 平 5　▶へい，びょう
▷たい(ら)，ひら

平和	へいわ　peace
和平	わへい　peace (conference/etc.)
平行な	へいこうな　parallel
◇ 水平*線	すいへいせん　horizon
平日	へいじつ　week days
平気な	へいきな　calm, indifferent
公平な	こうへいな　fair
◇*不公平な	ふこうへいな　unfair
◇*不平	ふへい　complaint
◇ 平*等	びょうどう　equality
平らな	たいらな　flat
平社員	ひらしゃいん　ordinary employee, non-managerial employee
歴 平家物語	へいけものがたり　*Heike Monogatari, The Historic Romance of the Taira Family*

352 和 8　▶わ，お
▷やわ(らぐ)，やわ(らげる)，なご(む)，なご(やか)

平和	へいわ　peace
和	わ　peace, harmony
和文	わぶん　Japanese script, writing in Japanese
◇ 和*風	わふう　Japanese style
◇*不和	ふわ　disharmony, discord
◇ 和らげる	やわらげる　pacify, soften
◇ 和やかな	なごやかな　congenial
歴 和*尚	おしょう　Buddhist priest
歴 大和	△やまと　*Yamato*, ancient Japan

353 等 12　▶とう
▷ひと(しい)

平等	びょうどう　equality
同等の	どうとうの　equal
上等な/の	じょうとうな/の　one of the best, fine, superior
等分	とうぶん　*cv.* divide into equal parts; equal parts
◇ 高等教*育	こうとうきょういく　higher education
◇ 一等	いっとう　first class
◇ 等しい	ひとしい　be equal to

354 第 11　▶だい

第一に	だいいちに　first, first of all
第〜	だい〜　No. 〜 (prefix for ordinals)
第一人者	だいいちにんしゃ　the leading person (in a field/etc.)
第三者	だいさんしゃ　third person/party
◇*次第に	しだいに　gradually
◇ 〜*次第	〜しだい　as soon as 〜, depending on 〜
◇ 落第	らくだい　*cv.* flunk, fail

355 筆 12　▶ひつ
▷ふで

万年筆	まんねんひつ　fountain pen
筆	ふで　writing brush
自筆	じひつ　one's own handwriting
◇*鉛筆	えんぴつ　pencil
◇ 筆*記*試*験	ひっきしけん　written examination

356 算 14　▶さん

| 計算 | けいさん　*cv.* calculate, compute |

足し算	たしざん	addition
引き算	ひきざん	subtraction
暗算	あんざん	mental arithmetic/calculation; *cv.* calculate in one's head
◇ *予算	よさん	budget
◇ 算*数	さんすう	arithmetic
◇ 公算	こうさん	probability, likelihood

357 符 11　▶ ふ　　　　570　cf. 荷

切符	きっぷ	ticket
◇ *音符	おんぷ	musical note
◇ 符*号	ふごう	mark, sign

358 簡 18　▶ かん

簡単な	かんたんな	easy, brief
◇ 簡*潔な	かんけつな	concise
◇ 簡*素な	かんそな	plain, simple
◇ 簡*略な	かんりゃくな	simple, brief
書簡	しょかん	letter

359 単 9　▶ たん

単語	たんご	word
単なる	たんなる	mere
◇ 単に	たんに	only, merely, simply
◇ 単*数	たんすう	singular 反 *複*数（ふくすう）plural
◇ 単*位	たんい	unit, denomination
◇ 単*独で	たんどくで	by oneself

360 戦 13　▶ せん　▷ いくさ，たたか（う）

戦争	せんそう	war; *cv.* fight, go to war

内戦	ないせん	civil war
休戦	きゅうせん	cease-fire, *cv.* hold a cease-fire
戦前	せんぜん	prewar, before the war
戦後	せんご	postwar, after the war
◇ 第二*次（世界）大戦	だいにじ（せかい）たいせん	World War II
戦う	たたかう	fight
歴 戦	いくさ	war, battle

361 争 6　▶ そう　▷ あらそ（う）

戦争	せんそう	war; *cv.* fight, go to war
言い争う	いいあらそう	quarrel, argue
◇ *論争	ろんそう	argument, controversy; *cv.* argue, dispute
◇ 争*点	そうてん	point of contention, issue
◇ 争*議	そうぎ	dispute, strike

⑳

362 反 4　▶ はん，ほん，たん　▷ そ（る），そ（らす）

反対	はんたい	*cv.* object
反日運動	はんにちうんどう	anti-Japanese movement
反発	はんぱつ	*cv.* repulse, repel, oppose
◇ 反*省	はんせい	*cv.* reflect upon, examine one's conscience
◇ 反*面	はんめん	on the other hand
◇ *謀反	むほん	rebellion
◇ 反る	そる	bend
◇ 反らす	そらす	bend
特 反物	たんもの	a roll of cloth

363 対 7 ▶たい, つい

反対	はんたい *cv.* object
対立	たいりつ *cv.vi.* be opposed to/ confronted with
対話	たいわ dialogue; *cv.* have a dialogue
〜に対する	〜にたいする to 〜, toward 〜, against 〜
◇ 一対の	いっついの a pair of

364 村 7 ▶そん ▷むら

村	むら village
村長	そんちょう village mayor
◇ 村*民	そんみん villager
◇ *市*町村	しちょうそん cities, towns, and villages

365 付 5 ▶ふ ▷つ(く), つ(ける)

付く	つく be attached, stick to
日付	ひづけ date (of a letter/document/etc.)
付近の	ふきんの adjacent, nearby, neighboring
◇ *交付	こうふ *cv.* deliver, hand over

366 団 6 ▶だん, とん

団体	だんたい group (of tourists/etc.)
集団	しゅうだん group, mob, mass (suicide/etc.) cf. 集団心理 (しゅうだんしんり) group psychology; グループ has a wider usage than 団体 or 集団.
団結	だんけつ *cv.* be united, stand together
◇ 団地	だんち housing complex
◇ *布団	ふとん futon
◇ 座*布団	ざぶとん floor cushion

367 寸 3 ▶すん

寸	すん *sun* (old Japanese measure of length, 3.03 cm)
◇ 寸*法	すんぽう measurements, size
◇ 一寸	▲ちょっと for a while

368 支 4 ▶し ▷ささ(える)

支店	してん branch (office/store)
支社	ししゃ branch (office)
支部	しぶ branch, local chapter
支出	ししゅつ expenditure, disbursement; *cv.* pay out, expend
支持	しじ *cv.* support (a political party/etc.)
支持者	しじしゃ supporter
◇ 支*給	しきゅう *cv.* supply (money/food/etc.)
支える	ささえる support
◇ 差し支える	△さしつかえる interfere

〈漢字の形に気をつけましょう・1〉

| 368 支 | 369 技 | 972 *枝 | 1443 *岐 |

| 本店と支店 | 技術の進歩 | 木の*枝 えだ | 分*岐点 ぶんきてん |

369	技	▶ぎ
7		▷わざ

	技術	ぎじゅつ technique, technology
◇	技*師	ぎし engineer cf. エンジニア has a wider usage than 技師.
◇	技*能	ぎのう skill
◇	技	わざ art, skill

370	術	▶じゅつ
11		

	技術	ぎじゅつ technique, technology
	手術	しゅじゅつ (surgical) operation; cv. have an operation, operate (on a patient)
	手術室	しゅじゅつしつ operating room
	学術用語	がくじゅつようご technical term

371	街	▶がい, かい
12		▷まち

	街	まち street
	地下街	ちかがい underground shopping mall
◇	五*番街	ごばんがい Fifth Avenue
歴	街道	かいどう high road

372	封	▶ふう, ほう
9		

| | 封筒 | ふうとう envelope |
| | 開封 | かいふう cv. open (a letter) |

| ◇ | 封*鎖 | ふうさ cv. block up, blockade |
| ◇ | 封*建*制度 | ほうけんせいど feudalism |

373	筒	▶とう
12		▷つつ

	封筒	ふうとう envelope
	水筒	すいとう canteen, flask
◇	筒	つつ pipe, tube, cylinder

㉑

374	竹	▶ちく
6		▷たけ

| | 竹 | たけ bamboo |
| ◇ | 竹*林 | たけばやし, ちくりん bamboo grove |

375	替	▶たい
12		▷か(える), か(わる)

	両替	りょうがえ exchanging/changing money; cv. exchange/change money
	替える	かえる replace
	着替え	きがえ a change of clothes
	着替える	きかえる, きがえる change one's clothes
	取り替える	とりかえる change (parts/etc.)
◇	*代替エネルギー	だいたいエネルギー alternative energy source

〈漢字の形に気をつけましょう・2〉

	370	371	1388	1449
	術	街	*衝	*衡

手術	地下街	*衝*突する	*貿*易*不*均*衡
		しょう とつ	ぼう えき ふ きん こう

376 賛 15 ▶さん

賛成	さんせい	cv. agree
◇ 賛*美歌	さんびか	hymn, psalm
◇*賞賛	しょうさん	cv. praise, admire

377 成 6 ▶せい, じょう ▷な(る), な(す)

成功	せいこう	cv. succeed
成長	せいちょう	cv. grow, mature
成立	せいりつ	cv. be established/founded
成人	せいじん	adult; cv. become an adult
◇ 成分	せいぶん	ingredient, component
成り立つ	なりたつ	be composed of
◇ 成し*遂げる	なしとげる	accomplish
特 成*就	じょうじゅ	cv. accomplish, attain

378 功 5 ▶こう, く

成功	せいこう	cv. succeed
◇ 功*労者	こうろうしゃ	a person who performed distinguished services
◇ 功*徳	くどく	charitable act

379 工 3 ▶こう, く

| 工場 | こうじょう | factory |
| 工場 | こうば | small factory |

工事	こうじ	construction; cv. construct
人工の	じんこうの	manmade, artificial
電子工学	でんしこうがく	electronic engineering
◇ 大工	だいく	carpenter
◇ 細工	さいく	craftsmanship; cv. manipulate (a situation)

380 的 8 ▶てき ▷まと

目的	もくてき	purpose, aim
技術的な	ぎじゅつてきな	technological
人工的な	じんこうてきな	artificial
◇*民主的な	みんしゅてきな	democratic
◇ 理*想的な	りそうてきな	ideal
〜的な	〜てきな	〜tic, 〜al, etc.
的	まと	target

381 約 9 ▶やく

約束	やくそく	cv. promise
公約	こうやく	public pledge, (campaign) promise; cv. pledge publicly
先約	せんやく	previous engagement
約〜	やく〜	about, approximately

382 束 7 ▶そく ▷たば

| 約束 | やくそく | cv. promise |

〈漢字の形に気をつけましょう・3〉

380	381	1335	1917	1014
的	約	*釣	*勺	*均

社会的な立場　　約束する　　*釣りをする　　*勺　　平*均
　　　　　　　　　　　　　　　　つ　　　　　しゃく　　へい きん

結束	けっそく	cv. unite, stand together
束	たば	bundle
花束	はなたば	bouquet
◊ 束ねる	たばねる	tie in a bundle

383 **速** 10 ▶そく
▷はや(い), はや(める), すみ(やか)

速い	はやい	fast, quick, swift
速度	そくど	speed, velocity
速力	そくりょく	speed, velocity
時速	じそく	speed per hour cf. *秒速 (びょうそく), 分速 (ふんそく), 時速 (じそく)
加速	かそく	cv. accelerate
◊ 加速度	かそくど	acceleration
◊ 高速道*路	こうそくどうろ	expressway, freeway
早速	さっそく	right away
◊ 速やかに	すみやかに	immediately, promptly

384 **達** 12 ▶たつ

速達	そくたつ	express mail, special delivery
上達	じょうたつ	cv.vi. improve
発達	はったつ	cv. develop
達成	たっせい	cv. achieve
友達	△ともだち	friend
◊ 結*論に達する	けつろんにたっする	reach a conclusion

㉒

385 **違** 13 ▶い
▷ちが(う), ちが(える)

間違い	まちがい	mistake, error, accident, mishap
間違って	まちがって	erroneously

間違える	まちがえる	make a mistake
違う	ちがう	be different, be wrong
違い	ちがい	difference
違反	いはん	cv. violate (a law/treaty/etc.)
◊ 違*法	いほう	illegal
◊ 違*憲	いけん	unconstitutional
◊ *相違*点	そういてん	difference

386 **逆** 9 ▶ぎゃく
▷さか, さか(らう)

逆の	ぎゃくの	reverse
逆説	ぎゃくせつ	paradox
◊ 反逆	はんぎゃく	cv. rebel
逆らう	さからう	oppose, go against
◊ 逆さ(ま)	さかさ(ま)	upside-down, inverted

387 **整** 16 ▶せい
▷ととの(える), ととの(う)

整理	せいり	cv. arrange
調整	ちょうせい	cv. adjust
◊ 整*然と	せいぜんと	in an orderly fashion
◊ 整*数	せいすう	integer, integral number
◊ 整える	ととのえる	arrange

388 **務** 11 ▶む
▷つと(める)

事務	じむ	clerical work
事務室	じむしつ	administration office
◊ 事務*員	じむいん	office clerk
外務省	がいむしょう	the Ministry of Foreign Affairs
国務省	こくむしょう	the State Department (of the U.S. government)
◊ 公務*員	こうむいん	public official/servant

◇ 務める　つとめる　work, serve

389
省 9
▶せい，しょう
▷かえり（みる），はぶ（く）

外務省　がいむしょう　the Ministry of Foreign Affairs

文部省　もんぶしょう　the Ministry of Education

省エネルギー　しょうエネルギー　energy conservation

反省　はんせい　*cv.* reflect upon, examine one's conscience

◇ 省*略　しょうりゃく　*cv.* omit

◇ 省く　はぶく　save (time/effort/etc.)

◇ 省みる　かえりみる　reflect upon

390
談 15
▶だん

相談　そうだん　*cv.* consult, talk over

会談　かいだん　conference, talk; *cv.* talk together, have a conference

談話　だんわ　conversation, talk; *cv.* talk, chat

対談　たいだん　face-to-face talk, conversation; *cv.* have a conversation

391
相 9
▶そう，しょう
▷あい

相談　そうだん　*cv.* consult, talk over

相続　そうぞく　*cv.* inherit, succeed

◇*首相　しゅしょう　prime minister

外相　がいしょう　*abbr.* foreign minister

文相　ぶんしょう　*abbr.* minister of education

相手　あいて　the other party, partner, opponent

相変わらず　あいかわらず　as usual, as ever, as before

392
想 13
▶そう，そ
1287
cf. 憩

理想　りそう　ideal

思想　しそう　idea, thought

連想　れんそう　*cv.* be reminded of; association (of ideas)

発想　はっそう　idea, conception

◇*空想　くうそう　fantasy, daydream

◇ 回想　かいそう　*cv.* look back on, recollect

◇*予想　よそう　*cv.* foresee

◇*愛想　あいそ　amiability

393
首 9
▶しゅ
▷くび

首　くび　neck, head

手首　てくび　wrist

首席　しゅせき　top/first in the class

首相　しゅしょう　prime minister

国家元首　こっかげんしゅ　sovereign of a nation, head of state

部首　ぶしゅ　radical of a Chinese character

394
身 7
▶しん
▷み

出身　しゅっしん　(be) from, place of origin

自身　じしん　(one's) self

心身　しんしん　mind and body

全身　ぜんしん　whole body

◇ 単身*赴*任　たんしんふにん　*cv.* take up a post in a distant place, leaving one's family behind

身分　みぶん　one's social standing

中身　なかみ　contents

⟨23⟩

395 員 ▶いん
10

社員	しゃいん company worker
会社員	かいしゃいん company worker
銀行員	ぎんこういん bank employee
教員	きょういん teacher
工員	こういん factory worker
会員	かいいん member (of a club/society)
全員	ぜんいん all members, entire staff
定員	ていいん (seating) capacity, quota
◇ 人員*削*減	じんいんさくげん personnel cut/reduction, layoff

396 損 ▶そん
13　　　▷そこ(なう)，そこ(ねる)

損	そん loss, deficit; cv. lose
◇ 損*失	そんしつ loss, deficit
◇ 損なう	そこなう hurt, damage

397 別 ▶べつ
7　　　▷わか(れる)

別の	べつの different, separate, another
◇ *区別	くべつ cv. distinguish, differentiate
◇ 別*居	べっきょ cv. live apart
別人	べつじん different person

◇ *差別	さべつ cv. discriminate
◇ 別*荘	べっそう country villa, country cottage, summer house
別れる	わかれる part from, separate from a person

398 特 ▶とく
10

特別な	とくべつな special, particular
特急	とっきゅう special express (train)
特色	とくしょく distinguishing characteristics
特長	とくちょう special characteristic
◇ 特*徴	とくちょう distinctive feature
特売	とくばい bargain sale
特に	とくに specially, particularly
特有の	とくゆうの characteristic of, peculiar to
◇ *独特の	どくとくの peculiar, original, unique

399 点 ▶てん
9

点	てん point
百点	ひゃくてん full marks, perfect score (on a test)
出発点	しゅっぱつてん starting point
◇ *原点	げんてん origin (of coordinates/axes)
◇ 点*字	てんじ braille
点火	てんか cv. ignite

〈漢字の形に気をつけましょう・4〉

328	195	142	398	1878
寺	待	持	特	*侍
お寺	友達を待つ	バッグを持つ	特別なやり方	*侍 さむらい

71

◇ 点*検　　てんけん　cv. check

◇ 点々と　　てんてんと　here and there, spo-radically, in drops

400	無	▶む, ぶ
12		▷な(い)

無理な　　むりな　impossible

無名の　　むめいの　unknown

無地の　　むじの　plain, unfigured

無料の　　むりょうの　free (of charge)

無口な　　むくちな　taciturn, reticent

無心に　　むしんに　innocently

無事に　　ぶじに　safely, with no problems

無い　　ない　not have, not exist

401	然	▶ぜん, ねん
12		

自然　　しぜん　nature

当然　　とうぜん　naturally, as a matter of course

全然　　ぜんぜん　not at all

◇*必然的な　ひつぜんてきな　natural, inevitable

◇*天然ガス　てんねんガス　natural gas

402	当	▶とう
6		▷あ(たる), あ(てる)

本当の　　ほんとうの　true

当分　　とうぶん　for the time being cf. しばらく for a while

当時　　とうじ　at that time

見当　　けんとう　estimate

手当　　てあて　allowance, medical treatment;　cv. treat (a cut/burn/etc.)

当たる　　あたる　hit

日当たりがいい　ひあたりがいい　be sunny, have lots of sunshine

当たり前　　あたりまえ　natural, proper

当てはめる　あてはめる　apply (a rule/etc.)

一人当たり　ひとりあたり　per person, per capita

◇ 心当たり　こころあたり　idea

403	予	▶よ
4		

予定　　よてい　plan, schedule; cv. make a plan, prearrange

予約　　よやく　reservation, appointment;　cv. reserve, make an appointment

予想　　よそう　cv. expect, foresee

◇ 地*震予知　じしんよち　earthquake prediction

◇*天気予*報　てんきよほう　weather forecast

404	野	▶や
11		▷の

分野　　ぶんや　field (of studies/etc.)

野生の　　やせいの　wild

◇ 野*菜　　やさい　vegetable

平野　　へいや　plain, flat land

野原　　のはら　field, plain

㉔

405	原	▶げん
10		▷はら

原因　　げんいん　cause, reason

原理　　げんり　principle

原料　　げんりょう　raw material

原書　　げんしょ　the text, the original

原案　　げんあん　original plan/proposal/bill

原野　　げんや　(uncultivated) field, plain

◇ 原始時*代　げんしじだい　primitive age

野原	のはら	field, plain
◇*河原/川原	△かわら	dry riverbed
◇*海原	△うなばら	ocean, sea

406 ▶いん
6 　　　▷よ(る)

原因	げんいん	cause, reason
死因	しいん	cause of death
◇*要因	よういん	factor
◇ 因*果*関*係	いんがかんけい	causal relationship
◇ 因る	よる	be caused by, be due to

407 正 ▶せい, しょう
5 　　▷ただ(しい), ただ(す), まさ

正しい	ただしい	right, correct, just
正解	せいかい	right answer; *cv.* answer correctly
校正	こうせい	*cv.* proofread
◇*訂正	ていせい	*cv.* correct
◇ 正*義	せいぎ	justice
◇ 正*確な	せいかくな	exact, precise
正直な	しょうじきな	honest
正午	しょうご	noon
お正月	おしょうがつ	the New Year
◇ 正*面	しょうめん	front, facade
◇ 正*夢	まさゆめ	prophetic dream, a dream which later comes true
◇ 正に	まさに	exactly, surely, certainly

◇ 正す	ただす	rectify, correct

408 幾 ▶き
12 　　▷いく

幾つ	いくつ	how many
幾つかの	いくつかの	a couple of, several
◇ 幾分	いくぶん	somewhat, to some extent
◇ 幾何学	きかがく	geometry

409 糸 ▶し
6 　　▷いと

糸	いと	thread
生糸	きいと	raw silk
◇ 綿糸	めんし	cotton thread

410 級 ▶きゅう
9

高級な	こうきゅうな	high-grade
同級生	どうきゅうせい	classmate
初級	しょきゅう	elementary level
中級	ちゅうきゅう	intermediate level
上級	じょうきゅう	advanced level
◇ 学級	がっきゅう	class (level)

411 能 ▶のう
10

能力	のうりょく	ability, capacity
本能	ほんのう	instinct
能	のう	Noh drama

〈漢字の形に気をつけましょう・5〉

254	406	1717
困	因	*囚
困る	原因	*囚人 しゅう じん

◇ 能*面　　のうめん　Noh mask

---

412 可 5　　▶か

可能な　　かのうな　possible

可決　　かけつ　*cv.* approve

◇ 可能*性　　かのうせい　possibility

◇*不可能な　　ふかのうな　impossible

◇*不可*欠な　　ふかけつな　indispensable

◇*不可*分な/の　　ふかぶんな/の　indivisible

---

413 代 5　　▶だい，たい
▷か（わる），か（える），よ，しろ

世代　　せだい　generation

時代　　じだい　era, period

古代　　こだい　ancient times, antiquity

◇*現代　　げんだい　modern, contemporary; modern times, the present age

～年代　　～ねんだい　～ties (as in "the sixties")

代理　　だいり　*cv.* act for, represent; proxy, deputy

代金　　だいきん　price, charge

◇*交代　　こうたい　*cv.* take turns

お代わり　　おかわり　second helping, another cup

代わりに　　かわりに　in place of, in return/exchange for

◇ 千代田*区　　ちよだく　Chiyoda Ward (in Tokyo)

◇ 飲み代　　のみしろ　money for drinking

---

414 化 4　　▶か，け
▷ば（ける），ば（かす）

文化　　ぶんか　culture

化学　　かがく　chemistry

強化　　きょうか　*cv.* strengthen

合理化　　ごうりか　*cv.* rationalize

◇*民主化　　みんしゅか　*cv.* democratize

◇ 自*由化　　じゆうか　*cv.* deregulate

～化　　～か　～ize, ～en, etc.

◇ 化*粧　　けしょう　*cv.* make up, put on make up

◇ 化ける　　ばける　take another form, disguise oneself

---

415 他 5　　▶た

他の　　たの，▲ほかの　another, other cf. 外の is the normal way to write *hokano*.

他人　　たにん　other persons

他国　　たこく　other countries

その他　　そのた　etc., miscellaneous

他方　　たほう　the other party/direction, on the other hand

---

416 仏 4　　▶ぶつ
▷ほとけ

仏教　　ぶっきょう　Buddhism

大仏　　だいぶつ　large statue of Buddha

◇ 日仏*関*係　　▲にちふつかんけい　Japanese-French relations

◇ 仏　　ほとけ　Buddha

〈漢字の形に気をつけましょう・6〉

409　410　243　744
糸　級　紙　*氏

くもの糸　　高級車　　手紙　　*氏名
　　　　　　　　　　　　　　しめい

㉕

417
7
位
▶い
▷くらい

地位　　ちい　(social) position, rank, status

学位　　がくい　academic degree

位置　　いち　position, location; *cv.* be located　cf. 地位(ちい)(social) position, rank, status

◇ 位　　くらい　position, rank

418
8
供
▶きょう, く　　　　1396
▷そな(える), とも　cf. 洪

子供　　こども　child, son/daughter

供　　とも　companion

自供　　じきょう　*cv.* confess, admit

◇ 供*給　きょうきゅう　*cv.* supply 反*需*要(じゅよう) demand

◇ 供える　そなえる　offer

◇ 供物　くもつ　votive offering

419
6
共
▶きょう
▷とも

共通の　きょうつうの　mutual, common

共通点　きょうつうてん　something in common

男女共学　だんじょきょうがく　coeducation

公共の　こうきょうの　public

公共事業　こうきょうじぎょう　government enterprise

共和国　きょうわこく　republic

共に　ともに　both, together

420
5
以
▶い

～以上　～いじょう　more than ～

～以下　～いか　less than ～

～以内　～いない　within ～

以前　いぜん　formerly

421
8
性
▶せい, しょう

女性　じょせい　woman, female

男性　だんせい　man, male

性　せい　sexuality

性別　せいべつ　gender

◇ 中性洗*剤　ちゅうせいせんざい　neutral detergent

本性　ほんしょう　true nature

422
4
不
▶ふ, ぶ

水不足　みずぶそく　water shortage

不足　ふそく　insufficiency, shortage; *cv.vi.* lack, be short of

不安な　ふあんな　uneasy, insecure

不十分な　ふじゅうぶんな　inadequate

不正な　ふせいな　unlawful

不利な　ふりな　disadvantageous

不運　ふうん　misfortune

不通になる　ふつうになる　be cut off, be interrupted

行方不明 △ゆくえふめい　missing

不気味な　ぶきみな　weird

◇ 不可　ふか　failure (in an exam/etc.)

423
5
必
▶ひつ
▷かなら(ず)

必要な　ひつような　necessary

必死に　ひっしに　desperately

必然的な　ひつぜんてきな　natural, inevitable

必ず　かならず　surely, without fail

必ずしも　かならずしも　not always

424	要	9	▶よう ▷い(る)

必要な	ひつような	necessary
重要な	じゅうような	important
主要な	しゅような	major
要点	ようてん	main point
要約	ようやく	cv. summarize
◇ 要*素	ようそ	element, factor
◇ 要*求	ようきゅう	cv. demand, request
◇ 要するに	ようするに	in short
◇ 要る	いる	be required/needed

425	価	8	▶か ▷あたい

物価	ぶっか	prices
地価	ちか	land prices
単価	たんか	unit price
定価	ていか	manufacturer's recommended price
高価な	こうかな	expensive
◇ 価*格	かかく	price
◇ 価	あたい	value

426	値	10	▶ち ▷ね，あたい

値上げ	ねあげ	price increase; cv. raise prices
値下げ	ねさげ	price reduction; cv. lower prices
◇ 値*段	ねだん	price
価値	かち	value, worth
◇ 値	あたい	value, worth

427	普	12	▶ふ

普通の	ふつうの	common, ordinary
◇ 普*段の	ふだんの	usual
◇ 普*段着	ふだんぎ	everyday clothes
◇ 普*遍的な	ふへんてきな	universal
◇ *普及	ふきゅう	cv. diffuse, spread

428	昔	8	▶せき，しゃく ▷むかし

昔	むかし	long ago, before (in contrast to "at present")
昔話	むかしばなし	old tale
大昔	おおむかし	ancient times
◇ 昔日	せきじつ	old days
歴 今昔物語	こんじゃくものがたり	Konjaku Monogatari (a collection of folktales edited in the 11th century)

429	増	14	▶ぞう ▷ま(す)，ふ(える)，ふ(やす)

増える	ふえる	vi. increase
増やす	ふやす	vt. increase
増加	ぞうか	cv.vi. increase
増大	ぞうだい	cv.vi. expand, increase
倍増	ばいぞう	cv. double
◇ 増*税	ぞうぜい	tax increase/hike; cv. increase/raise taxes
◇ 増*産	ぞうさん	expansion of production; cv. expand production
◇ 増す	ます	vi. increase

430	減	12	▶げん ▷へ(る)，へ(らす)

減る	へる	vi. decrease
減らす	へらす	vt. decrease

| 減少 | げんしょう | *cv.vi.* decrease |

半減　はんげん　*cv.* reduce by half, take off half, decrease by half

増減　ぞうげん　*cv.* increase and decrease

加減　かげん　addition and subtraction, state, condition; *cv.* regulate, adjust

◇ 減*税　げんぜい　tax reduction/cut; *cv.* reduce/cut taxes

◇ 減*産　げんさん　reduction of production; *cv.* reduce production

431　感　13　▶かん

感じる　かんじる　feel, sense

感想　かんそう　impressions, one's thoughts

感心　かんしん　*cv.* be impressed

五感　ごかん　the five senses

感受性　かんじゅせい　sensibility, sensitivity

◇ 感*情　かんじょう　feelings, emotion

432　留　10　▶りゅう, る　▷と(める), と(まる)

留学　りゅうがく　*cv.* study abroad

書留　かきとめ　registered mail

◇ 留*守　るす　absence from home

◇ 留*守*番電話　るすばんでんわ　answering machine

◇ 留める　とめる　stop, detain, fix in one position

433　貿　12　▶ぼう

貿易　ぼうえき　trade; *cv.* trade, do business with

◇ 貿易*摩*擦　ぼうえきまさつ　trade friction

434　易　8　▶えき, い　▷やさ(しい)　cf. 賜 場　1898　335

貿易　ぼうえき　trade; *cv.* trade, do business with

易しい　やさしい　easy

◇ *容易な　よういな　easy, simple

◇ *難易度　なんいど　degree of difficulty

◇ *交易　こうえき　trade, commerce, barter; *cv.* trade, exchange, barter

◇ 易者　えきしゃ　fortune-teller

435　量　12　▶りょう　▷はか(る)

量　りょう　quantity, amount　反 質(しつ) quality

大量の　たいりょうの　large amount of

少量の　しょうりょうの　small amount of

分量　ぶんりょう　quantity

雨量　うりょう　amount of rainfall

重量　じゅうりょう　weight (of a vehicle/machine/etc.)

◇ 大量生*産　たいりょうせいさん　mass production; *cv.* mass produce

◇ 量る　はかる　measure (amount/weight)

436　裏　13　▶り　▷うら

裏　うら　reverse side, back

裏返す　うらがえす　turn inside out

裏口　うらぐち　back door, rear entrance

裏切る　うらぎる　betray

表裏のない　ひょうりのない　single-minded

表裏一体の　ひょうりいったいの　one and indivisible

437 **表** ▶ひょう
8 ▷おもて, あらわ(す), あらわ(れる)

表　　　おもて　surface, front

裏表のある人　うらおもてのあるひと double-dealer, hypocrite

表　　　ひょう　table, chart

表紙　　ひょうし　cover (of a book/magazine)

発表　　はっぴょう　cv. announce, make public, present (findings/etc.)

公表　　こうひょう　cv. make public, publicly announce

代表的な　だいひょうてきな　representative, typical

◊ 表*情　ひょうじょう　facial expression

表す　　あらわす　express

表れる　あらわれる　be expressed

表れ　　あらわれ　manisfestation, expression

438 **面** ▶めん
9 ▷おも, おもて, つら

面白い　おもしろい　interesting

面　　　めん　mask, surface, aspect

表面　　ひょうめん　surface, exterior

水面　　すいめん　surface of the water

洗面所　せんめんじょ　lavatory, washroom, toilet

場面　　ばめん　situation, scene

面倒　　めんどう　care, trouble

〜方面　ほうめん　〜 direction, 〜 side

面会人　めんかいにん　visitor to a hospitalized/imprisoned person

面目　　めんぼく　face, honor, dignity

◊ 面*影　おもかげ　looks, trace

◊ 面　　おもて　face, surface

◊ 面　　つら　surface, face (impolite)

㉗

439 **最** ▶さい
12 ▷もっと(も)

最近　　さいきん　lately, recently

最初　　さいしょ　start, beginning

最後　　さいご　end, last

最高の　さいこうの　best

最低の　さいていの　worst

(〜の)最中に　(〜の)さいちゅうに　in the midst of 〜

最も　　もっとも　most

◊ 最*寄りの　△もよりの　nearest, nearby

440 **初** ▶しょ
7 ▷はじ(め), はじ(めて), はつ, うい, そ(める)

初め　　はじめ　beginning

初めに　はじめに　first

初めて　はじめて　for the first time

最初　　さいしょ　start, beginning

初歩　　しょほ　the rudiments, the ABCs

〈「最〜」の表現〉

最新の (さいしんの)　　　最古の (さいこの)

最大の (さいだいの)　　　最小の (さいしょうの)

最*良の (さいりょうの)　　最悪の (さいあくの)

初日の出	はつひので　the first sunrise of the year
◇ 初*恋	はつこい　one's first love
◇ 書き初め	かきぞめ　first (calligraphy) writing of the New Year
◇ 初々しい	ういういしい　innocent, naive

441 刀 2　▶とう　▷かたな　1774　cf. 刃

| 刀 | かたな　sword |
| 日本刀 | にほんとう　Japanese sword |

442 号 5　▶ごう

〜号	〜ごう　〜 issue (of a magazine/journal/etc.)
今週号	こんしゅうごう　this week's issue
先週号	せんしゅうごう　last week's issue
3号室	さんごうしつ　Room No. 3
号外	ごうがい　an extra (edition of a newspaper)
年号	ねんごう　name of a reign era
◇*番号	ばんごう　(identification) number
◇*信号	しんごう　traffic signal

443 労 7　▶ろう

労働時間	ろうどうじかん　working hours
労働	ろうどう　work, labor
労働力	ろうどうりょく　labor, labor force
労働者	ろうどうしゃ　worker, laborer
◇ 労働*組合	ろうどうくみあい　labor union
労力	ろうりょく　trouble, effort
心労	しんろう　worry, concern

444 協 8　▶きょう

協力	きょうりょく　cv. cooperate
協力者	きょうりょくしゃ　collaborator
協同	きょうどう　cooperation, collaboration; cv. cooperate, collaborate
協会	きょうかい　society, association
◇ 日*米協会	にちべいきょうかい　the U.S.-Japan Society
生協	せいきょう　co-op
◇*農協	のうきょう　agricultural cooperative

445 門 8　▶もん　▷かど

門	もん　gate
正門	せいもん　front gate
名門	めいもん　distinguished/illustrious family
入門	にゅうもん　introduction, primer; cv. become a pupil
部門	ぶもん　group, branch, section
◇*専門	せんもん　specialty, area of expertise
◇ 門*松	かどまつ　pine branch decoration for the New Year

446 関 14　▶かん　▷せき

関係	かんけい　relation, relationship; cv. be related/connected
関連	かんれん　relationship, connection; cv. be connected/associated/correlated
関心	かんしん　interest, concern cf. *興味(きょうみ) interest
関東	かんとう　the Kanto region
関西	かんさい　the Kansai region
歴 関所	せきしょ　border gate (in the Edo period)

447　係　9

▶けい
▷かか（る），かかり

関係	かんけい	relation, relationship; *cv.* be related/connected
係（り）	かかり	person in charge
係長	かかりちょう	section chief
◇ 係る	かかる	be related to

448　孫　10

▶そん
▷まご

| 孫 | まご | grandchild |
| 子孫 | しそん | offspring |

449　系　7

▶けい

日系人	にっけいじん	a person of Japanese descent
体系	たいけい	system
◇ 系*統	けいとう	system, lineage
◇ 太*陽系	たいようけい	solar system
◇ 系*列子会社	けいれつこがいしゃ	subsidiary company

450　懸　20

▶けん，け
▷か（ける），か（かる）

懸案	けんあん	pending issue
◇ 一生懸*命（に）	いっしょうけんめい（に）	with all one's efforts
◇ 懸*念	けねん	*cv.* worry
◇ *命懸けの	いのちがけの	desperate

451　態　14

▶たい

態度	たいど	attitude, behavior, one's position/stance
事態	じたい	state of affairs
生態系	せいたいけい	ecosystem
◇ *実態	じったい	actual situation

452　池　6

▶ち
▷いけ

| 池 | いけ | pond |
| 電池 | でんち | battery |

453　湖　12

▶こ
▷みずうみ

湖	みずうみ	lake
ミシガン湖	ミシガンこ	Lake Michigan
湖水	こすい	lake water
湖面	こめん	the surface of a lake

454　海　9

▶かい
▷うみ

海	うみ	sea, ocean
海外	かいがい	overseas
日本海	にほんかい	the Japan Sea
東シナ海	ひがしシナかい	the East China Sea

〈漢字の形に気をつけましょう・7〉

146	415	452
地	他	池
地下鉄	他人	池

◇ 海*洋　　　　かいよう　ocean　cf. 太平*洋（たいへいよう）the Pacific Ocean, 大西*洋（たいせいよう）the Atlantic Ocean

◇ 海原　　　　△うなばら　ocean, sea

◇ 海女　　　　△あま　woman diver (for pearls/oysters/etc.)

455
島 ▶とう
10　　 ▷しま

島　　　　　しま　island

島国　　　　しまぐに　island country

◇ 島*民　　　とうみん　islander

無人島　　　むじんとう　uninhabited island

半島　　　　はんとう　peninsula

◇ *淡*路島　　あわじしま　Awaji Island (the largest island in the Seto Inland Sea)

456
岸 ▶がん
8　　 ▷きし

西海岸　　　にしかいがん　west coast

東海岸　　　ひがしかいがん　east coast

海岸　　　　かいがん　coast, beach

対岸　　　　たいがん　opposite bank

岸　　　　　きし　riverbank, shore

457
岩 ▶がん
8　　 ▷いわ

岩　　　　　いわ　rock

岩石　　　　がんせき　stone, rock

458
谷 ▶こく
7　　 ▷たに

谷　　　　　たに　valley

谷間　　　　たにま　ravine

谷川　　　　たにがわ　mountain stream

◇ 谷*底　　　たにぞこ　the bottom of a ravine

⦿*渓谷　　　けいこく　valley

◇ 四ツ谷　　▲よつや　Yotsuya (a place in Tokyo)

◇ 長谷川　　▲はせがわ　(surname)

459
林 ▶りん
8　　 ▷はやし

林　　　　　はやし　small forest

山林　　　　さんりん　mountain forest

林業　　　　りんぎょう　forestry

460
森 ▶しん
12　　 ▷もり

森　　　　　もり　woods, forest

森林　　　　しんりん　forest

461
空 ▶くう
8　　 ▷そら，あ（く），あ（ける），から

空　　　　　そら　sky

青空　　　　あおぞら　blue sky, open-air (market/concert/etc.)

大空　　　　おおぞら　sky, firmament

空気　　　　くうき　air

空間　　　　くうかん　space

空中　　　　くうちゅう　in the air

空く　　　　あく　become unoccupied

空室　　　　くうしつ　unoccupied room

空車　　　　くうしゃ　empty cab

空の　　　　からの　empty

空っぽの　　からっぽの　empty

空手　　　　からて　karate

462
天 ▶てん
4　　 ▷あめ，あま

天気　　　　てんき　weather

天文学　　　てんもんがく　astronomy

天国　　　　てんごく　heaven, paradise

天性の　　　てんせいの　natural (attribute), innate

◇ 天の川　　あまのがわ　the Milky Way

◇ 天下り　　あまくだり　appointment of a former government official to a high post in a company (through influence from above)

◇ 天の下　　あめのした，あまのした　this world

463 星
9
▶せい，しょう
▷ほし

星　　　　　ほし　star

星空　　　　ほしぞら　starry sky

流れ星　　　ながれぼし　meteor

火星　　　　かせい　Mars

金星　　　　きんせい　Venus

歴 明星　　　みょうじょう　Venus

464 光
6
▶こう
▷ひか(る)，ひかり

光　　　　　ひかり　light

光る　　　　ひかる　shine, glitter

日光　　　　にっこう　sunlight, sunshine; Nikko (a tourist spot north of Tokyo)

◇ 光*線　　こうせん　ray/beam of light

465 風
9
▶ふう，ふ
▷かぜ，かざ

風　　　　　かぜ　wind

そよ風　　　そよかぜ　gentle breeze

風土　　　　ふうど　climate

◇ 風*向き　かざむき　direction of wind

◇ 風▲呂　　ふろ　bath

歴 風土記　　ふどき　old records and descriptions of a region's culture and geographic features

◇ 風*邪　　△かぜ　a cold

466 虫
6
▶ちゅう
▷むし

虫　　　　　むし　bug, insect

◇ *毛虫　　けむし　hairy caterpillar

◇ 虫*歯　　むしば　decayed tooth, cavity

◇ *害虫　　がいちゅう　harmful insect

◇ *殺虫*剤　さっちゅうざい　insecticide

29

467 凡
3
▶ぼん，はん

平凡な　　　へいぼんな　commonplace

凡人　　　　ぼんじん　ordinary person

◇ 凡*例　　はんれい　introductory notes, map legend

468 冗
4
▶じょう

冗談　　　　じょうだん　joke

◇ 冗長な　　じょうちょうな　lengthy, verbose

469 個
10
▶こ

個人　　　　こじん　individual

◇ 個人主*義　こじんしゅぎ　individualism

個性　　　　こせい　individuality, one's personality

個別的な　　こべつてきな　individual, specific

〜個　　　　〜こ　(counter for various objects)

470 固
8
▶こ
▷かた(める)，かた(まる)，かた(い)

固い　　　　かたい　hard

固まる　　　かたまる　harden

固体	こたい	solid
固定	こてい	*cv.* fix, settle
強固な	きょうこな	firm, solid, strong
固有の	こゆうの	peculiar, inherent, characteristic of
◇ 固執	こしつ	*cv.* hold fast to, persist in, insist on

471 豆 7　▶とう，ず　▷まめ

豆	まめ	beans, peas
コーヒー豆	コーヒーまめ	coffee beans
◇*枝豆	えだまめ	green soybeans, cooked green soybeans (often eaten as a snack with beer)
◇*納豆	なっとう	fermented soybeans
◇ 豆*腐	とうふ	tofu, soybean curd
◇ 大豆	だいず	soybean
◇ 小豆	△あずき	adzuki bean

472 登 12　▶とう，と　▷のぼ(る)

登る	のぼる	climb
登山	とざん	mountain climbing; *cv.* climb a mountain
◇ 登*録	とうろく	*cv.* register
◇ 登場	とうじょう	*cv.* appear (as in a character in a play/novel/etc.)
◇ 登用	とうよう	*cv.* promote, appoint

473 祭 11　▶さい　▷まつ(る)，まつり

(お)祭(り)	(お)まつり	festival
秋祭(り)	あきまつり	fall festival
文化祭	ぶんかさい	cultural festival
百年祭	ひゃくねんさい	100th anniversary
◇*祝祭日	しゅくさいじつ	national holiday
◇ 祭る	まつる	deify, enshrine

474 際 14　▶さい　▷きわ

国際的な	こくさいてきな	international
学際的な	がくさいてきな	interdisciplinary
◇*交際	こうさい	*cv.* keep company with, associate with
◇*実際	じっさい	as a matter of fact, in fact
◇ 水際	みずぎわ	water's edge
◇ 際だつ	きわだつ	stand out

475 察 14　▶さつ

警察	けいさつ	police
◇*観察	かんさつ	*cv.* observe
◇ 考察	こうさつ	*cv.* examine, study (as an academic inquiry)
◇*視察	しさつ	*cv.* visit to observe/inspect
◇*検察*庁	けんさつちょう	the Public Prosecutor's Office

476 警 19　▶けい

警察	けいさつ	police
◇ 警*官	けいかん	police officer
◇ 警*告	けいこく	*cv.* warn, caution, advise
◇ 警*報	けいほう	warning (signal), alarm (signal)
◇ 警*備	けいび	*cv.* guard, defend
◇ 警*視*庁	けいしちょう	Tokyo Metropolitan Police

477 驚 22　▶きょう　▷おどろ(く)，おどろか(す)

| 驚く | おどろく | be surprised |
| 驚かす | おどろかす | surprise |

◇ 驚*異的な　きょういてきな　astonishing

◇ 驚*嘆　きょうたん　cv. be astonished

- -

㉚

478
12　**敬**　▶けい
　　　　▷うやま（う）

尊敬　そんけい　cv. respect, look up to

敬意　けいい　respect

敬語　けいご　honorific expressions

◇ 敬*老の日　けいろうのひ　Respect-for-the-Aged Day

◇ 敬*具　けいぐ　Sincerely yours (closing word for letters)

◇ 敬遠　けいえん　cv. keep at a distance

◇ 敬う　うやまう　respect, hold in high esteem

479
12　**尊**　▶そん
　　　　▷たっと（い），とうと（い），
　　　　　たっと（ぶ），とうと（ぶ）

尊敬　そんけい　cv. respect, look up to

尊重　そんちょう　cv. respect, value

自尊心　じそんしん　pride

尊大な　そんだいな　arrogant

◇ 尊ぶ　たっとぶ, とうとぶ　respect, honor

◇ 尊い　たっとい, とうとい　noble, precious

480
15　**導**　▶どう
　　　　▷みちび（く）

半導体　はんどうたい　semiconductor

導入　どうにゅう　cv. introduce (a new system/technology/etc.)

先導　せんどう　cv. initiate, lead

◇*指導　しどう　cv. lead, guide, instruct

◇*指導者　しどうしゃ　leader

◇ 主導*権　しゅどうけん　initiative, leadership

導く　みちびく　lead

481
11　**停**　▶てい
　　　　　　　　　　　　　1652
　　　　　　　　　　　　cf. 亭

バス停　バスてい　bus stop

停留所　ていりゅうじょ　bus stop

停止　ていし　cv. stop, suspend (service/etc.)

停車　ていしゃ　cv. stop (as in buses or trains)

停電　ていでん　power failure/cut; cv. have a power failure

◇*各駅停車　かくえきていしゃ　local train

◇ 調停　ちょうてい　cv. mediate

◇ 停*滞　ていたい　cv. stagnate

482
6　**件**　▶けん

事件　じけん　incident

用件　ようけん　business (as in "get down to business")

件　けん　matter

◇*条件　じょうけん　condition

483
4　**牛**　▶ぎゅう
　　　　▷うし

牛　うし　cow, bull, cattle

子牛　こうし　calf

牛小屋　うしごや　cowshed, barn

水牛　すいぎゅう　water buffalo

野牛　やぎゅう　buffalo

484
10　**馬**　▶ば
　　　　▷うま，ま

馬　うま　horse

小馬/子馬　こうま　pony

馬小屋　うまごや　stable

馬車　ばしゃ　horse-drawn carriage

馬力	ばりき	horse power
馬術	ばじゅつ	horseback riding
出馬	しゅつば	cv. stand as a candidate, run for (the Diet)

485 魚 11　▶ぎょ　▷うお, さかな

魚	さかな	fish
魚屋	さかなや	fish shop
金魚	きんぎょ	goldfish
◇ 魚*市場	うおいちば	fish market

486 鳥 11　▶ちょう　▷とり

鳥	とり	bird
小鳥	ことり	little bird
野鳥	やちょう	wild bird
白鳥	はくちょう	swan
一石二鳥	いっせきにちょう	killing two birds with one stone
◇ 鳥*居	とりい	Shinto shrine archway

487 鳴 14　▶めい　▷な(く), な(る), な(らす)

鳴く	なく	(birds:) sing, (other animals:) meow, neigh, croak, etc.
◇ 鳴き*声	なきごえ	singing of a bird
鳴る	なる	ring
◇*共鳴	きょうめい	cv. resonate, sympathize

488 羊 6　▶よう　▷ひつじ

羊	ひつじ	sheep
小羊/子羊	こひつじ	baby sheep
羊毛	ようもう	wool

489 群 13　▶ぐん　▷む(れる), む(れ), むら

群集	ぐんしゅう	crowd, multitude, throng
群集心理	ぐんしゅうしんり	mob psychology
◇ 群*衆	ぐんしゅう	large group of people
◇*抜群の	ばつぐんの	outstanding, distinguished (performance)
群れ	むれ	herd, flock, group
◇ 群れる	むれる	flock, crowd
◇ 群がる	むらがる	crowd, gather, swarm

490 毛 4　▶もう　▷け

毛	け	hair
毛糸	けいと	woolen yarn
まゆ毛	まゆげ	eyebrow
羊毛	ようもう	wool
不毛な	ふもうな	unproductive, barren, sterile

〈漢字の形に気をつけましょう・8〉

455　486　487
島　鳥　鳴

*向こうの島まで泳いでいく　鳥が鳴く
　む

491 羽　6　▶う
▷は, はね

羽毛	うもう	down, feathers, plumage
◇ 羽田空*港	はねだくうこう	Haneda Airport
羽	はね	wing
◇ 羽*根	はね	feather, plumage
〜羽	〜わ/ば/ぱ	(counter for birds) cf. 1羽(いちわ), 2羽(にわ), 3羽(さんば), 6羽(ろっぱ)
歴 羽音	はおと	fluttering (of birds/moths/etc.)

㉛

492 翌　11　▶よく

翌日	よくじつ	the following day
翌週	よくしゅう	the following week
翌月	よくげつ	the following month
翌年	よくねん, よくとし	the following year
翌朝	よくちょう, よくあさ	the next morning

493 義　13　▶ぎ

社会主義	しゃかいしゅぎ	socialism
個人主義	こじんしゅぎ	individualism
◇*民主主義	みんしゅしゅぎ	democracy
◇ 共*産主義	きょうさんしゅぎ	communism
〜主義	〜しゅぎ	〜cy, 〜ism
義務	ぎむ	obligation, duty cf.*権利(けんり) right
同義語	どうぎご	synonym
◇*類義語	るいぎご	synonym

494 議　20　▶ぎ

会議	かいぎ	meeting, conference
議長	ぎちょう	chairperson
議会	ぎかい	congress, parliament
議員	ぎいん	member of an assembly/the Diet/Congress/etc.
協議	きょうぎ	cv. confer
不思議な	ふしぎな	strange, mysterious

495 講　17　▶こう

講義	こうぎ	lecture; cv. give a lecture
休講	きゅうこう	cv. cancel a lecture
◇ 講*師	こうし	lecturer
◇ 講*演	こうえん	lecture; cv. give a lecture
◇ 講*堂	こうどう	lecture hall/auditorium (of a school)
◇ 講和*条約	こうわじょうやく	peace treaty

〈漢字の形に気をつけましょう・9〉

496	497	498	499	1579	1458
論	倫	輪	輸	*諭	*愉

議論する　　不倫の関係　　三輪車　　輸出と輸入　　子供を*諭す
　　　　　　　　　　　　　　　　　　　　　　　　　　　　さと

*愉*快な*仲間
ゆ かい　なか ま

496 論 15 ▶ろん

理論	りろん	theory
論理	ろんり	logic
議論	ぎろん	cv. discuss, argue
世論	よろん，せろん	public opinion
◇ 世論調*査	よろんちょうさ	public opinion survey/poll
論文	ろんぶん	thesis, essay
結論	けつろん	conclusion
〜論	〜ろん	〜 theory, theory of 〜 e.g., 進化論（しんかろん）theory of evolution, *資本論（しほんろん）the Capital
論じる	ろんじる	discuss

497 倫 10 ▶りん

倫理	りんり	ethics, morals
倫理学	りんりがく	ethics
不倫の	ふりんの	illicit, immoral

498 輪 15 ▶りん ▷わ

三輪車	さんりんしゃ	tricycle cf. 一輪車（いちりんしゃ），二輪車（にりんしゃ），三輪車（さんりんしゃ），四輪車（よんりんしゃ）
車輪	しゃりん	wheel
◇ *競輪	けいりん	bicycle race
◇ *指輪	ゆびわ	(finger) ring

499 輸 16 ▶ゆ

輸入	ゆにゅう	cv. import
輸出	ゆしゅつ	cv. export
輸送	ゆそう	cv. transport
空輸	くうゆ	cv. send by air
◇ 運輸省	うんゆしょう	Ministry of Transportation

500 較 13 ▶かく

| 比較 | ひかく | cv. compare |
| 比較的 | ひかくてき | rather, comparatively |

501 効 8 ▶こう ▷き(く)

効果	こうか	effect, effectiveness
効果的な	こうかてきな	effective
有効な	ゆうこうな	effective, valid
無効の	むこうの	invalid
効力	こうりょく	effectiveness
◇ 時効	じこう	prescription (in a statute of limitations)
効く	きく	be effective, work
効き目	ききめ	effectiveness (of a medicine)

502 果 8 ▶か ▷は(たす)，は(てる)，は(て)

| 結果 | けっか | result |

〈漢字の形に気をつけましょう・10〉

| 51 校 | 504 交 | 501 効 | 503 郊 |

学校　　交通手*段　　効果的な教え方　　郊外に住む
しゅ だん

成果	せいか	result, performance
効果	こうか	effect, effectiveness
◇ 果*汁	かじゅう	fruit juice
果物	△くだもの	fruit
果たす	はたす	accomplish, fulfill
◇ 果たして	はたして	at all (as in "Is it useful at all?")
◇ 果てる	はてる	die
◇ 地の果て	ちのはて	end of the land

㉜

503 郊　9　▶こう

郊外	こうがい	suburbs, outskirts
近郊	きんこう	suburbs, outskirts, environs

504 交　6　▶こう
▷まじ(わる)，まじ(える)，ま(じる)，ま(ざる)，ま(ぜる)，か(う)，か(わす)

交通	こうつう	traffic
外交	がいこう	diplomacy
国交	こっこう	diplomatic relations
◇ 交ざる	まざる	be mixed
◇ 交わす	かわす	exchange
◇ 交わる	まじわる	have an exchange

505 渉　11　▶しょう

交渉	こうしょう	*cv.* negotiate

506 干　3　▶かん
▷ほ(す)，ひ(る)

干渉	かんしょう	*cv.* interfere, meddle
干す	ほす	dry
特 干る	ひる	get dry, parch

507 汗　6　▶かん
▷あせ

汗	あせ	sweat
◇ *冷汗	ひやあせ	cold sweat
◇ 発汗	はっかん	*cv.* perspire

508 軒　10　▶けん
▷のき

〜軒	〜けん	(counter for houses)
◇ 軒並み	のきなみ	at every house, from one item to another
◇ 軒	のき	eaves
◇ 軒先	のきさき	edge of the eaves, front of the house

509 形　7　▶けい，ぎょう
▷かた，かたち

人形	にんぎょう	doll
形	かたち	shape, form, figure
◇ 三*角形	さんかくけい	triangle
正方形	せいほうけい	square
長方形	ちょうほうけい	rectangle
無形の	むけいの	invisible, intangible
◇ 手形	てがた	draft (as in "pay by draft")

510 枠　8　▷わく
1069
cf. 粋

枠	わく	frame, quota
窓枠	まどわく	window frame
輸入枠	ゆにゅうわく	import quota
◇ 枠*組	わくぐみ	framework

511 械　11　▶かい

機械	きかい	machine

機械化	きかいか	mechanization; *cv.* mechanize, introduce machinery

512 **識** 19 ▶しき

知識	ちしき	knowledge
意識	いしき	consciousness, awareness; *cv.* be conscious/aware, feel
識別	しきべつ	*cv.* discriminate (something from another), discern
◇*常識	じょうしき	common sense
◇*認識	にんしき	*cv.* recognize, understand, perceive

513 **職** 18 ▶しょく

職業	しょくぎょう	occupation, profession
職場	しょくば	place of work, workplace
職員	しょくいん	personnel, staff, staff member
職	しょく	job
職人	しょくにん	artisan, workman
◇*現職の	げんしょくの	current (Diet member/governor/mayor/etc.)
無職の	むしょくの	unemployed

514 **就** 12 ▶しゅう, じゅ ▷つ(く), つ(ける)

就職	しゅうしょく	*cv.* find work
就業時間	しゅうぎょうじかん	working hours
◇ 就*任	しゅうにん	*cv.* assume (a post)
◇ 就く	つく	take a seat, take office, get a job
◇ 成就	じょうじゅ	*cv.* accomplish, attain

③③

515 **経** 11 ▶けい, きょう ▷へ(る)

経済	けいざい	economy
経理	けいり	accounting
◇ 経*験	けいけん	*cv.* experience, go through
◇ 経*歴	けいれき	one's personal history
◇*神経	しんけい	nervous system, nerve
◇ 経*由	けいゆ	*cv.* go via/by way of/through
◇ 経度	けいど	longitude 反*緯度(いど) latitude
◇ (お)経	(お)きょう	sutra
◇ 経る	へる	go through

516 **済** 11 ▶さい ▷す(む), す(ます)

経済	けいざい	economy
返済	へんさい	*cv.* repay, return
決済	けっさい	*cv.* settle (bills)
使用済みの	しようずみの	used (battery/plastic bag/etc.)

〈漢字の形に気をつけましょう・11〉

408 幾　334 機　511 械　1334 *戒

幾つ時計を持っていますか　機械　*戒*律
かい りつ

89

済む	すむ	come to an end

517 活 9 ▶かつ

生活	せいかつ	life; *cv.* live, make a living
活動	かつどう	activity; *cv.* be active, take an active part
活気	かっき	vigor, liveliness
活力	かつりょく	vitality, (vital) energy
活性化	かっせいか	*cv.* activate, vitalize
活発な	かっぱつな	lively, active
活用	かつよう	*cv.* make (full) use
◇ 活*字	かつじ	printing/movable type

518 法 8 ▶ほう, はっ, ほっ

方法	ほうほう	method
文法	ぶんぽう	grammar
法案	ほうあん	bill, legislative proposal
法律	ほうりつ	law, act
特 法*被	はっぴ	a worker's livery coat (now often worn in festivals)
特 法主	ほっしゅ	head of a religious sect

519 律 9 ▶りつ, りち

法律	ほうりつ	law, act
◇*規律	きりつ	order, discipline

◇ 自律*神経	じりつしんけい	autonomic nerve
◇ 律*儀な	りちぎな	honest, loyal

520 往 8 ▶おう

往復切符	おうふくきっぷ	round-trip ticket
往来	おうらい	traffic, coming and going; *cv.* come and go
立ち往生	たちおうじょう	*cv.* be brought to a standstill/halt, be stalled
往々にして	おうおうにして	often

521 復 12 ▶ふく

往復切符	おうふくきっぷ	round-trip ticket
往復	おうふく	*cv.* go to a place and return, run between
回復	かいふく	*cv.* recover
復習	ふくしゅう	*cv.* review
反復	はんぷく	*cv.* repeat
◇ 復活	ふっかつ	*cv.* revive, come back to life
◇ 復*興	ふっこう	*cv.* revive, restore

522 複 14 ▶ふく

複雑な	ふくざつな	complicated, complex
複写機	ふくしゃき	copying machine cf. コピー機 is normally used.

〈漢字の形に気をつけましょう・12〉

521	522	1088
復	複	*腹
往復切符	複雑な仕事	*腹痛 ふくつう

重複	ちょうふく	*cv.* overlap, duplicate
◇ 複合*汚*染	ふくごうおせん	combined pollution
◇ 複*数の	ふくすうの	plural 反単*数の (たんすうの) singular
◇ 複*製	ふくせい	copy, reproduction

523 / 14　雑　▶ざつ，ぞう

雑誌	ざっし	magazine, journal
◇ 雑*音	ざつおん	noise
◇ 雑*草	ざっそう	weeds
◇ 雑木林	ぞうきばやし	coppice

524 / 14　誌　▶し

| 雑誌 | ざっし | magazine, journal |
| 日誌 | にっし | daily record |

㉞

525 / 12　勤　▶きん，ごん　▷つと(める)，つと(まる)

勤める	つとめる	work for
通勤	つうきん	*cv.* commute
出勤	しゅっきん	*cv.* go to work
勤務時間	きんむじかん	working hours
転勤	てんきん	*cv.* be transferred to another office of the company
歴 勤行	ごんぎょう	(Buddhist) religious service

526 / 18　難　▶なん　▷かた(い)，むずか(しい)

難しい	むずかしい	difficult
難解な	なんかいな	difficult (to understand)
難易度	なんいど	degree of difficulty
困難	こんなん	hardship, difficulty
難病	なんびょう	intractable disease
難点	なんてん	defect
◇ *非難	ひなん	*cv.* blame, criticize
◇ 難*民	なんみん	refugee
◇ 盗難	とうなん	burglary, robbery
◇ *許し難い	ゆるしがたい	unforgivable

527 / 13　漢　▶かん

漢字	かんじ	*kanji*, Chinese character
漢文	かんぶん	Chinese writing, Chinese classics
◇ 漢和*辞*典	かんわじてん	Japanese dictionary of Chinese characters
門外漢	もんがいかん	outsider (to a field)
◇ *熱*血漢	ねっけつかん	hot-blooded man
歴 漢	かん	Han dynasty

528 / 6　字　▶じ　▷あざ

| 漢字 | かんじ | *kanji*, Chinese character |

〈漢字の形に気をつけましょう・13〉

525	526	527	1436	1582
勤	難	漢	*嘆	*謹
勤務時間	難しい漢字	感*嘆する かん たん	*謹*賀新年 きん が	

数字	すうじ number
ローマ字	ローマじ Roman alphabet
文字	もじ letter (of the alphabet/etc.)
字	じ letter, character
赤十字	せきじゅうじ the Red Cross
名字	みょうじ surname, last name
特 字	あざ section of a town/village

529 数 13
▶すう，す
▷かず，かぞ（える）

数字	すうじ numeral, figures
数学	すうがく mathematics
人数	にんずう number of people
点数	てんすう points (obtained)
分数	ぶんすう fraction (in mathematics)
無数の	むすうの countless, innumerable
単数の	たんすうの singular
複数の	ふくすうの plural
手数料	てすうりょう fee, charge
数	かず number
数える	かぞえる count
◇ 数*奇屋橋	すきやばし Sukiyabashi (a place near Ginza)

530 政 9
▶せい，しょう
▷まつりごと

政治	せいじ politics
政治家	せいじか politician
政府	せいふ government
政局	せいきょく political situation
行政	ぎょうせい administration
◇ 政*権	せいけん administration e.g., クリントン政権
歴 *摂政	せっしょう regent

| 歴 政 | まつりごと state affairs |

531 治 8
▶じ，ち
▷おさ（める），おさ（まる），なお（る），なお（す）

政治	せいじ politics
明治	めいじ the Meiji era
地方自治体	ちほうじちたい local government
治る	なおる heal, be cured, get better
◇ 治める	おさめる rule, govern

532 台 5
▶だい，たい

台所	だいどころ kitchen
台本	だいほん script, screenplay
台	だい base, stand
～台	～だい (counter for machines)
天文台	てんもんだい astronomical observatory
台風	たいふう typhoon

533 路 13
▶ろ
▷じ

道路	どうろ street, road
水路	すいろ waterway,
通路	つうろ passageway, walkway, aisle
十字路	じゅうじろ intersection, crossroads
路上	ろじょう on the road/street
歴 大路	おおじ main street cf. 大通り（おおどおり）rather than 大路 is used in modern Japanese.

534 戸 4
▶こ
▷と

| 戸 | と door |
| 雨戸 | あまど storm door, shutter |

| 戸外で | こがいで | outdoors, in the open air |
| ◇ 下戸 | げこ | teetotaler |

535 居 ▶きょ ▷い(る)
8

居間	いま	living room
◇ 居る	いる	be present, exist (used for humans/animals/etc.)
◇ 居座る	いすわる	stay on, remain (in office)
◇ 居直る	いなおる	take a threatening attitude
住居	じゅうきょ	dwelling, residence

- -

㉟

536 民 ▶みん ▷たみ
5

民主主義	みんしゅしゅぎ	democracy
国民	こくみん	people, nation
住民	じゅうみん	inhabitants, residents
人民	じんみん	the people, citizens
難民	なんみん	refugee
民間	みんかん	private (enterprise/company/etc.)
民族	みんぞく	people, ethnic group
歴 民	たみ	people

537 守 ▶しゅ, す ▷まも(る), もり
6

留守	るす	absence from home
◇ 留守*番電話	るすばんでんわ	answering machine
守る	まもる	protect, keep (a promise/etc.)
見守る	みまもる	keep an eye on
子守歌	こもりうた	lullaby
◇*保守的な	ほしゅてきな	conservative

538 宅 ▶たく
6

住宅	じゅうたく	house
住宅地	じゅうたくち	residential area
宅地	たくち	land for housing
自宅	じたく	one's own home
帰宅	きたく	cv. go home
◇ 宅*配便	たくはいびん	home delivery service

539 管 ▶かん ▷くだ
14

水道管	すいどうかん	water pipe
気管	きかん	trachea
管理	かんり	cv. manage
管理職	かんりしょく	manager, management
◇ 管	くだ	pipe, tube

540 官 ▶かん
8

外交官	がいこうかん	diplomat
半官半民	はんかんはんみん	semi-governmental
国務長官	こくむちょうかん	the Secretary of State (of the U.S.)
◇ 官*房長官	かんぼうちょうかん	the Chief Cabinet Secretary (of Japan)
◇*次官	じかん	secretary of a ministry

541 庁 ▶ちょう
5

県庁	けんちょう	prefectural office
官庁街	かんちょうがい	civic center, district where lots of government offices are located
文化庁	ぶんかちょう	the Cultural Affairs Agency
警察庁	けいさつちょう	the National Police Agency

◇ 警*視庁　けいしちょう　the Tokyo Metropolitan Police

◇ 気*象庁　きしょうちょう　the Meteorological Agency

542　庭　10　▶てい　▷にわ

庭　にわ　garden, yard, backyard, courtyard

家庭　かてい　one's home

校庭　こうてい　schoolyard, school ground

日本庭園　にほんていえん　Japanese garden

◇ 庭*球　ていきゅう　tennis

543　床　7　▶しょう　▷とこ, ゆか

床　ゆか　floor

床の間　とこのま　alcove in a Japanese-style room

床屋　とこや　barbershop

◇ 病床　びょうしょう　sickbed

544　庫　10　▶こ, く

金庫　きんこ　safe

書庫　しょこ　library, stack (room)

車庫　しゃこ　garage　cf. ガレージ is normally used.

文庫本　ぶんこぼん　pocket edition, paperback

◇ *冷*蔵庫　れいぞうこ　refrigerator

◇ *倉庫　そうこ　warehouse, storehouse

◇ *在庫　ざいこ　goods in stock, inventory

特 庫裏　くり　priests' living quarters at a Buddhist temple

545　廊　12　▶ろう

廊下　ろうか　hall, corridor

画廊　がろう　picture/art-gallery

歴 回廊　かいろう　corridor

546　郎　9　▶ろう

太郎　たろう　(male given name)　cf. *次郎/二郎(じろう), 三郎(さぶろう), 四郎(しろう), 五郎(ごろう)

新郎　しんろう　bridegroom　反 新*婦(しんぷ) bride

㊱

547　市　5　▶し　▷いち

市　し　city

ロサンゼルス市　ロサンゼルスし　(the City of) Los Angeles

ニューヨーク市　ニューヨークし　New York City

市長　しちょう　mayor

市民　しみん　citizen

市立　しりつ　municipal

市場　いちば　marketplace

市場　しじょう　(stock/etc.) market

548　区　4　▶く

区　く　ward　e.g., 千代田区(ちよだく), *港区(みなとく), 新宿区(しんじゅくく), *渋谷区(しぶやく)

区民　くみん　inhabitants of a ward

地区　ちく　district, area, zone

区分　くぶん　cv. divide, demarcate

区切る　くぎる　punctuate, divide

549 町 7 ▶ちょう ▷まち

町	ちょう　town　e.g., 人形町(にんぎょうちょう), *永田町(ながたちょう)
町民	ちょうみん　townspeople
町人	ちょうにん　townspeople (in Edo period)
町	まち　town
下町	したまち　(low-lying) down-town area
歴 室町時代	むろまちじだい　the Muromachi era

550 丁 2 ▶ちょう, てい

| 〜丁目 | 〜ちょうめ　〜 block (in the numbering system for addresses) |
| ◇ 丁字路 | ていじろ　T-intersection |

551 番 12 ▶ばん

〜番	〜ばん　number 〜
番地	ばんち　house number
番号	ばんごう　number
電話番号	でんわばんごう　telephone number
郵便番号	ゆうびんばんごう　zip/postal code
局番	きょくばん　area code
交番	こうばん　police box
当番	とうばん　person on duty, (be on) duty

552 郡 10 ▶ぐん

| 郡 | ぐん　county　e.g., カリフォルニア州オレンジ郡 |

553 州 6 ▶しゅう ▷す

州	しゅう　state
カリフォルニア州	カリフォルニアしゅう　(the State of) California
本州	ほんしゅう　Honshu, the largest of the four main islands of Japan
九州	きゅうしゅう　Kyushu, the southwestern island of the four main islands of Japan
◇ 中州	なかす　sandbank in a river

554 欧 8 ▶おう　1625　cf. 殴

欧州	おうしゅう　Europe
欧州共同体	おうしゅうきょうどうたい　the European Community
◇ 欧*米	おうべい　Europe and the U.S.
◇ 西欧*諸国	せいおうしょこく　Western European countries　cf. 西*洋*諸国 (せいようしょこく) Western countries

555 満 12 ▶まん ▷み(ちる), み(たす)

満足	まんぞく　cv. be satisfied/content; satisfaction, contentment
不満	ふまん　dissatisfaction
満員	まんいん　be full (as in trains/theaters/etc.)

───〈漢字の形に気をつけましょう・14〉───

365　80　557　1245
付　何　向　*伺

日付　　何を食べたいですか　　方向　　先生のお宅に*伺う
　　　　　　　　　　　　　　　　　　　　　　　　　　うかが

95

満点	まんてん perfect score (on a test)
円満な	えんまんな harmonious, peaceful
満たす	みたす fill, fulfill
満ちる	みちる become full

556 両 6 ▶りょう

両親	りょうしん father and mother, (both) parents
両手	りょうて both hands
両足	りょうあし both legs
両方	りょうほう both
両立	りょうりつ cv. coexist

557 向 6 ▶こう ▷む(く), む(ける), む(かう), む(こう)

方向	ほうこう direction
向上	こうじょう cv. improve, become better
意向	いこう intention
向かう	むかう proceed, face (toward)
向く	むく face, turn, tend (toward), suit (one's preference)
◇*振り向く	ふりむく turn to
向き	むき direction
～向きの	～むきの for ～, suitable for ～
向ける	むける turn something (to)
向こう	むこう opposite side

子供向けの　こどもむけの　for children

558 周 8 ▶しゅう ▷まわ(り)

一周	いっしゅう cv. go around once/one lap
半周	はんしゅう cv. go half-way around, go half a lap
百周年	ひゃくしゅうねん 100th anniversary
◇ 円周	えんしゅう circumference
周り	まわり surroundings

③⑦

559 独 9 ▶どく ▷ひと(り)

独身	どくしん single, unmarried
独立	どくりつ cv. become independent
独学	どくがく cv. study by oneself
独特の/な	どくとくの/な peculiar to, characteristic of
日独関係	にちどくかんけい relations between Japan and Germany
独り	ひとり alone, solitary
独り立ちする	ひとりだちする be independent
独り言	ひとりごと talking to oneself

560 狭 9 ▶きょう ▷せま(い), せば(める), せば(まる)

狭い	せまい narrow, small (room/etc.)

〈漢字の形に気をつけましょう・15〉

14　350　308　558
円　同　用　周

一万円　同じやり方　使用法　地*球を一周する
　　　　　　　　　　　　　　　ち きゅう

96

◇ 狭める　　　せばめる　narrow, contract, reduce (the width)

◇ 狭まる　　　せばまる　become narrow, contract

◇ 狭心*症　　　きょうしんしょう　angina pectoris

561　肉　▶にく
6

牛肉　　　　ぎゅうにく　beef

◇ *豚肉　　　ぶたにく　pork

肉　　　　　にく　meat, flesh

肉屋　　　　にくや　butcher (shop)

肉体　　　　にくたい　the body, the flesh

562　米　▶べい，まい
6　　　　　▷こめ

米　　　　　こめ　rice

新米　　　　しんまい　new rice, novice

白米　　　　はくまい　polished rice

米国　　　　べいこく　the United States

日米関係　　にちべいかんけい　relations between Japan and the U.S.

北米　　　　ほくべい　North America

南米　　　　なんべい　South America

563　類　▶るい　　　　　　　　529
18　　　　　　　　　　　　　cf. 数

種類　　　　しゅるい　kind, type, sort

親類　　　　しんるい　relative, kin

人類　　　　じんるい　mankind

人類学　　　じんるいがく　anthropology

書類　　　　しょるい　papers, documents

分類　　　　ぶんるい　cv. classify

564　種　▶しゅ
14　　　　　▷たね

種類　　　　しゅるい　kind, type, sort

一種の　　　いっしゅの　a kind/sort of

人種　　　　じんしゅ　human race

種　　　　　たね　seed

不安の種　　ふあんのたね　cause of unease

565　科　▶か　　　　　　　　240
9　　　　　　　　　　　　　cf. 料

科学　　　　かがく　science

学科　　　　がっか　subject of study

理科　　　　りか　science (as a school subject) cf. 社会 (しゃかい) social studies (as a school subject)

科目　　　　かもく　subject, course (of study)

教科書　　　きょうかしょ　textbook

外科　　　　げか　surgery

内科　　　　ないか　internal medicine

566　芸　▶げい　　　　　　　1665
7　　　　　　　　　　　　　cf. 芳

芸術　　　　げいじゅつ　art

◇ 民芸*品　　みんげいひん　folk craft

◇ 文芸*批*評　ぶんげいひひょう　literary criticism

〈「〜科学」の例〉

自然科学（しぜんかがく）　　natural science

社会科学（しゃかいかがく）　　social science

人文科学（じんぶんかがく）　　humanities

◇ 工芸	こうげい industrial arts

入荷	にゅうか *cv.vi.* arrive

---

567 草 9 ▶そう ▷くさ

草	くさ grass, plants
草原	そうげん grassy plain, grass-lands
雑草	ざっそう weeds
草案	そうあん (rough) draft

568 芝 6 ▷しば   860 cf. 乏

芝生	△しばふ lawn, plot of grass
芝	しば lawn
人工芝	じんこうしば artificial turf
芝居	しばい (stage) play; *cv.* put on an act

569 葉 12 ▶よう   1653 ▷は   cf. 棄

言葉	ことば word, language
葉書	はがき postcard
葉	は leaf, foliage
木の葉	このは tree leaves
落ち葉	おちば fallen leaves
千葉県	ちばけん Chiba Prefecture
◇ 青葉	あおば green foliage
◇*紅葉	こうよう autumn/colored leaves
◇*紅葉	△もみじ maple tree, autumn/colored leaves

570 荷 10 ▶か   80 357 ▷に   cf. 何 符

荷物	にもつ luggage
重荷	おもに burden
出荷	しゅっか *cv.vt.* ship/forward (goods)

571 預 13 ▶よ ▷あず(ける), あず(かる)

預ける	あずける leave in someone's care, deposit, entrust
預かる	あずかる receive for safe-keeping, take care of
預金	よきん *cv.* deposit

572 頼 16 ▶らい ▷たの(む), たよ(る), たの(もしい)

頼む	たのむ ask (a favor), request
頼る	たよる rely on
◇*信頼	しんらい *cv.* trust
◇*依頼	いらい *cv.* ask, request
◇ 頼もしい	たのもしい reliable, dependable

573 顔 18 ▶がん ▷かお

顔	かお face
顔色	かおいろ complexion, a look
新顔	しんがお newcomer
◇ 笑顔	△えがお smiling face
◇*素顔	すがお face without makeup
◇*童顔	どうがん childlike face
◇ 顔面	がんめん face

574 産 11 ▶さん ▷う(む), う(まれる), うぶ

産業	さんぎょう industry
水産業	すいさんぎょう marine products industry
生産	せいさん *cv.* produce
生産物	せいさんぶつ product

産地	さんち	producing area/center
出産	しゅっさん	cv. give birth, be delivered
共産主義	きょうさんしゅぎ	communism
不動産	ふどうさん	real estate
◇ 原産国	げんさんこく	the country where the good is produced
産む	うむ	give birth to
(お)土産	△(お)みやげ	souvenir
◇ 産声	うぶごえ	the first cry of a new-born baby
◇ 産湯	うぶゆ	bath for a newborn baby

575 玉 5 ▶ぎょく ▷たま

玉子	たまご	egg
十円玉	じゅうえんだま	10-yen coin
◇ 玉	たま	gem, jewel, ball
歴 玉	ぎょく	jewel

576 宝 8 ▶ほう ▷たから

宝石	ほうせき	precious stone, gem
国宝	こくほう	national treasure
宝物	たからもの, ほうもつ	treasure
宝	たから	treasure

577 王 4 ▶おう

王国	おうこく	kingdom
王	おう	king
王子	おうじ	prince
王女	おうじょ	princess
女王	じょおう	queen
◇ 王*様	おうさま	king
法王	ほうおう	pope

| ローマ法王 | ローマほうおう | the Pope |

578 現 11 ▶げん ▷あらわ(れる), あらわ(す)

現代	げんだい	modern, contemporary; modern times, the present age
◇ 現*在	げんざい	present, current
表現	ひょうげん	cv. express
現金	げんきん	cash
◇*実現	じつげん	cv. realize
現れる	あらわれる	appear, come out, emerge
◇ 現す	あらわす	show, reveal

579 皇 9 ▶こう, おう

天皇	てんのう	(Japanese) emperor
皇居	こうきょ	imperial palace
皇室	こうしつ	imperial family
皇位	こうい	imperial throne
◇ 皇*帝	こうてい	emperor
歴 法皇	ほうおう	ex-emperor who has become a monk

580 聖 13 ▶せい

聖書	せいしょ	the Bible
聖人	せいじん	saint
◇*神聖な	しんせいな	sacred
聖母マリア	せいぼマリア	the Virgin Mary

581 望 11 ▶ぼう, もう ▷のぞ(む)

要望	ようぼう	cv. demand, request
◇*失望	しつぼう	cv. be disappointed
◇*希望	きぼう	hope, wish; cv. hope, wish

◇ *志望校 しぼうこう the school of one's choice

望む のぞむ hope, wish

望み のぞみ hope

◇ 本望 ほんもう full satisfaction

582 亡 3 ▶ぼう，もう
▷な(い)

死亡 しぼう *cv.* die

死亡者 しぼうしゃ the dead, the deceased

◇ *亡命 ぼうめい *cv.* flee (from) one's own country (for a political reason)

◇ 金の亡者 かねのもうじゃ money-mad

◇ 亡くなる なくなる pass away

③⑨

583 未 5 ▶み
1768
cf. 朱

未来 みらい future

未婚の みこんの unmarried

未知の みちの unknown

未亡人 みぼうじん widow

未明 みめい early dawn, before daybreak

◇ 前代未聞の ぜんだいみもんの unheard-of, unprecedented

584 末 5 ▶まつ，ばつ
▷すえ

週末 しゅうまつ weekend

月末 げつまつ end of the month

年末 ねんまつ end of the year

末っ子 すえっこ youngest child

㊙ 末子 ばっし，まっし youngest child

585 申 5 ▶しん
1816
▷もう(す) cf. 甲

申し上げる もうしあげる say, tell (humble)

申し入れ もうしいれ offer, proposal

◇ 答申 とうしん report (of a committee); *cv.* submit a report

586 神 9 ▶しん，じん
1299
▷かみ，かん，こう cf. 紳

神 かみ god

神風 かみかぜ kamikaze, divine wind

神社 じんじゃ shrine

神話 しんわ myth, mythology

神父 しんぷ Catholic priest, Father

◇ 神主 かんぬし Shinto priest

㊥ 神楽 かぐら *kagura* (sacred music and dancing of Shinto)

㊙ 神々しい こうごうしい divine, holy

587 存 6 ▶そん，ぞん

存在 そんざい *cv.* exist

生存 せいぞん *cv.* exist, survive

生存者 せいぞんしゃ survivor

共存 きょうぞん *cv.* coexist

ご存知だ ごぞんじだ know (honorific)

存じる ぞんじる know (humble)

588 在 6 ▶ざい
▷あ(る)

存在 そんざい *cv.* exist

現在 げんざい present, current

在日外国人 ざいにちがいこくじん foreigners residing in Japan

在学 ざいがく *cv.* be in school, be enrolled (at)

| 不在だ | ふざいだ　be away, be absent |
| 在る | ある　exist |

589 禅 13　▶ぜん

座禅	ざぜん　Zen meditation (in a cross-legged position)
禅寺	ぜんでら　Zen temple
◇ 禅*宗	ぜんしゅう　Zen sect
◇ 禅*僧	ぜんそう　Zen priest/monk

590 弾 12　▶だん　▷ひ(く), はず(む), たま

弾	たま　bullet
弾薬	だんやく　ammunition
弾頭	だんとう　warhead
◇ *核弾頭	かくだんとう　nuclear warhead
◇ *爆弾	ばくだん　bomb
弾力	だんりょく　elasticity
◇ 弾む	はずむ　bounce, rebound
◇ 弾く	ひく　play (a piano/guitar/etc.)

591 丸 3　▶がん　▷まる, まる(い), まる(める)

丸い	まるい　round
丸太	まるた　log
丸	まる　circle, ball, whole
丸める	まるめる　make round
弾丸	だんがん　bullet

592 弓 3　▶きゅう　▷ゆみ

| 弓 | ゆみ　bow |
| ◇ 弓道 | きゅうどう　Japanese archery |

593 矢 5　▶し　▷や

矢	や　arrow
弓矢	ゆみや　bow and arrow
◇ 一矢を*報いる	いっしをむくいる　retort, retaliate

594 失 5　▶しつ　▷うしな(う)

失業	しつぎょう　cv. lose one's job, be out of work
◇ 失*恋	しつれん　cv. be unlucky in love, have a broken heart
失望	しつぼう　cv. be disappointed
失神	しっしん　cv. faint, lose consciousness
◇ 失*敗	しっぱい　cv. fail
◇ 失*礼な	しつれいな　impolite
失う	うしなう　lose
見失う	みうしなう　lose sight of, lose one's way

⑩

595 夫 4　▶ふ, ふう　▷おっと

| 夫 | おっと　husband |

〈漢字の形に気をつけましょう・16〉

462	593	594	595
天	矢	失	夫

いい天気　　弓と矢　　失業者　　妻と夫

～夫人	～ふじん　Mrs. ～
夫婦	ふうふ　husband and wife, married couple
工夫	くふう　cv. devise, work out (a plan)

596　妻　8 ▶さい ▷つま　788 cf. 毒

妻	つま　wife
妻子	さいし　wife and child(ren)
～夫妻	～ふさい　Mr. and Mrs. ～
◇*良妻*賢母	りょうさいけんぼ　being a good wife and wise mother

597　婦　11 ▶ふ

夫婦	ふうふ　husband and wife, married couple
主婦	しゅふ　housewife
婦人服	ふじんふく　women's clothes
婦長	ふちょう　head nurse

598　姓　8 ▶せい，しょう

姓	せい　surname, last name
同姓	どうせい　same surname
夫婦別姓	ふうふべっせい　use of different surnames by a married couple
◇*旧姓	きゅうせい　one's maiden name
歴 百姓	ひゃくしょう　farmer

599　嫁　13 ▶か ▷よめ，とつ(ぐ)　1232 cf. 稼

花嫁	はなよめ　bride
嫁	よめ　bride
◇*責*任転嫁	せきにんてんか　cv. shift the responsibility (for something on someone)
◇ 嫁ぐ	とつぐ　get married

600　婿　12 ▶せい ▷むこ

花婿	はなむこ　bridegroom
◇ 婿*養子	むこようし　son-in-law who has married into the family
◇ 女婿	じょせい　son-in-law

601　娘　10 ▷むすめ

| 娘 | むすめ　(my) daughter, young woman |

602　良　7 ▶りょう ▷よ(い)

良い	よい　good
最良の	さいりょうの　best
消化不良	しょうかふりょう　indigestion
不良	ふりょう　delinquent
◇ 不良*品	ふりょうひん　defective product
良心	りょうしん　conscience
◇ 野良犬	△のらいぬ　ownerless/stray dog

603　飾　13 ▶しょく ▷かざ(る)

飾る	かざる　decorate, adorn
着飾る	きかざる　dress up
◇*修飾	しゅうしょく　cv. modify (in grammar)
◇*装飾*品	そうしょくひん　ornament, decoration

604　飯　12 ▶はん ▷めし

ご飯	ごはん　cooked rice, meal, food
夕飯	ゆうはん　dinner
赤飯	せきはん　rice cooked with adzuki beans

飯　　　めし　cooked rice, meal, food
　　　　cf. めし is a somewhat rough
　　　　expression.

605 坂
7
　▶はん　　　　　　987
　▷さか　　　cf. 板
坂　　　　さか　slope
◇ 登坂　　　とうはん, とはん　cv. go up a
　　　　slope

606 皆
9
　▶かい
　▷みな
皆さん　　　みなさん　everybody
◇ 皆勤　　　かいきん　perfect attendance
　　　　(at work); cv. have perfect
　　　　attendance
◇ 皆無　　　かいむ　nonexistent

- -
⑪

607 階
12
　▶かい
階段　　　かいだん　stairs
〜階　　　〜かい　〜 floor
階級　　　かいきゅう　social class

608 段
9
　▶だん　　　　　　622
　　　　cf. 暇
階段　　　かいだん　stairs
段　　　　だん　steps
石段　　　いしだん　flight of stone steps
段階　　　だんかい　stage (in a project/
　　　　etc.)
手段　　　しゅだん　means, measure
◇ 一段と　　いちだんと　further, even more

609 役
7
　▶やく, えき
役所　　　やくしょ　government office
役人　　　やくにん　government official

役員　　　やくいん　official, executive
役者　　　やくしゃ　actor
役目　　　やくめ　duty, function
主役　　　しゅやく　star (in a play)
役に立つ　やくにたつ　useful
◇ 役*割　　やくわり　role, part
◇ *兵役　　へいえき　military service

610 殺
10
　▶さつ, さい, せつ
　▷ころ(す)
殺す　　　ころす　kill
人殺し　　ひとごろし　murder, murderer
自殺　　　じさつ　cv. commit suicide
暗殺　　　あんさつ　cv. assassinate
殺人　　　さつじん　murder
◇ 相殺　　　そうさい　cv. compensate
歴 殺生　　せっしょう　cv. destroy/take
　　　　life

611 設
11
　▶せつ
　▷もう(ける)
施設　　　しせつ　facility
設立　　　せつりつ　cv. establish
新設校　　しんせつこう　newly-estab-
　　　　lished school
設置　　　せっち　cv. establish
◇ 設ける　　もうける　establish, provide

612 施
9
　▶し, せ
　▷ほどこ(す)
施設　　　しせつ　facility
施行　　　しこう　cv. enforce, put in force
◇ *実施　　じっし　cv. put into practice
◇ 施工　　　せこう　cv. construct, carry out
　a construction project
◇ 施す　　　ほどこす　give, give alms

613　備　12
▶び
▷そな（える），そな（わる）

準備	じゅんび	*cv.* prepare
設備	せつび	facilities
予備の	よびの	reserve
備考	びこう	notes, remarks
◇ *軍備	ぐんび	armaments, military preparedness
◇ 整備	せいび	*cv.* service (an airplane), fix (a machine), fit out (a ship), provide (facility/equipment/etc.)
◇ 備える	そなえる	prepare for, be furnished/equipped with

614　準　13
▶じゅん

準備	じゅんび	*cv.* prepare
水準	すいじゅん	level, standard
◇ *基準	きじゅん	standard
◇ *規準	きじゅん	criterion, standard
準決勝	じゅんけっしょう	semifinal game

615　率　11
▶そつ，りつ　306
▷ひき（いる）　cf. 卒

成長率	せいちょうりつ	(economic) growth rate
出生率	しゅっしょうりつ，しゅっせいりつ	birthrate
率	りつ	rate
倍率	ばいりつ	degree of magnification

効率	こうりつ	efficiency
能率	のうりつ	efficiency
率直な	そっちょくな	straightforward, frank
軽率な	けいそつな	rash, hasty, careless, thoughtless
◇ 率いる	ひきいる	lead, command

616　演　14
▶えん

講演	こうえん	lecture; *cv.* give a lecture
公演	こうえん	public performance; *cv.* perform in public
出演	しゅつえん	*cv.* appear (in a movie/play/etc.)
上演	じょうえん	*cv.* put (a play) on the stage, present (a drama)
演技	えんぎ	performance; *cv.* act, perform
演習	えんしゅう	seminar
◇ 演*奏	えんそう	musical performance; *cv.* give a musical performance
演じる	えんじる	perform

617　絵　12
▶かい，え

絵	え	painting, drawing
絵本	えほん	picture book
◇ 絵画	かいが	painting

〈漢字の形に気をつけましょう・17〉

153　旅　322　族　612　施

家族旅行　フレックスタイムを実施する

618 給 12 ▶きゅう

給料	きゅうりょう	salary
月給	げっきゅう	monthly salary
供給	きょうきゅう	*cv.* supply

反 *需要(じゅよう) demand

㊷

619 声 7 ▶せい，しょう
▷こえ，こわ

声	こえ	voice
音声	おんせい	audio, sound, voice
声明	せいめい	statement
共同声明	きょうどうせいめい	joint statement, joint communique
◇ 声色	こわいろ	voice impersonation
特 大音声	だいおんじょう	very loud voice

620 音 9 ▶おん，いん
▷おと，ね

発音	はつおん	*cv.* pronounce
足音	あしおと	sound of steps
物音	ものおと	(unidentified) sound
音	おと	sound
母音	ぼいん	vowel
子音	しいん	consonant
本音	ほんね	real intention

反 *建て前（たてまえ）formal principle/policy, professed position

621 昨 9 ▶さく
137
cf. 作

昨年	さくねん	last year
昨日	さくじつ，△きのう	yesterday
一昨日	いっさくじつ	the day before yesterday
一昨年	いっさくねん	the year before last

622 暇 13 ▶か
▷ひま
608
cf. 段

暇な	ひまな	not busy, have time, free
暇つぶし	ひまつぶし	killing time
暇	ひま	free time
休暇	きゅうか	vacation
◇ *余暇	よか	leisure, spare time

623 由 5 ▶ゆ，ゆう，ゆい
▷よし

理由	りゆう	reason
自由	じゆう	freedom, liberty
不自由な	ふじゆうな	inconvenient, uncomfortable, handicapped
由来	ゆらい	origin
◇ 由*緒ある	ゆいしょある	be of a noble family, historic
◇ ～の由	～のよし	I heard that ～ (used in letters)

⟨漢字の形に気をつけましょう・18⟩

585 申   623 由   1816 *甲

申し上げる   理由を言う   *甲*乙つけがたい
こう　おつ

624 油 8	▶ゆ 1254 ▷あぶら cf. 抽

石油	せきゆ oil
原油	げんゆ crude oil
油田	ゆでん oil field
油	あぶら oil
油絵	あぶらえ oil painting

625 曲 6	▶きょく ▷ま(がる)，ま(げる)

曲	きょく music, tune
作曲	さっきょく cv. compose music
名曲	めいきょく famous tune/music
曲がる	まがる make a turn, bend
◇ 曲がり*角	まがりかど corner (of a street), turning point
◇ 曲*線	きょくせん curve

626 農 13	▶のう 847 cf. 震

農業	のうぎょう agriculture, farming
農村	のうそん farming village
農家	のうか farm, farming family
農民	のうみん farmer
農産物	のうさんぶつ agricultural product
農薬	のうやく agricultural chemical
農協	のうきょう agricultural cooperative

627 濃 16	▶のう ▷こ(い)

| 濃い | こい dark (color), strong (coffee/tea/etc.), dense (fog) |
| 濃度 | のうど density, thickness cf. 人口*密度 (じんこうみつど) population density |

◇ 濃*霧　のうむ　dense fog

628 豊 13	▶ほう ▷ゆた(か)

豊かな	ゆたかな abundant, rich
豊富な	ほうふな abundant, rich
豊作	ほうさく good harvest
◇ 豊*漁	ほうりょう good catch of fish

629 富 12	▶ふ，ふう ▷と(む)，とみ

豊富な	ほうふな abundant, rich
◇ 富*士山	ふじさん Mt. Fuji
富	とみ wealth
◇ 富む	とむ be rich
歴 富*貴	ふうき riches and honors

㊸

630 典 8	▶てん

| 古典 | こてん classics |
| 百科事典 | ひゃっかじてん encyclopedia |

631 興 16	▶きょう，こう ▷おこ(る)，おこ(す)

興味	きょうみ interest cf. 関心(かんしん) interest, concern
◇ *即興	そっきょう improvisation
◇ 興*奮	こうふん cv. get excited
◇ 興る	おこる arise

632 己 3	▶こ，き ▷おのれ

自己中心的な	じこちゅうしんてきな egocentric
自己	じこ ego, self
利己的な	りこてきな selfish

◇ 知己　　　　　ちき　acquaintance

◇ 己　　　　　　おのれ　oneself

633　記　10
▶き
▷しる(す)

日記　　　　　にっき　diary

記事　　　　　きじ　article

記者　　　　　きしゃ　journalist

記号　　　　　きごう　sign, mark, symbol

暗記　　　　　あんき　*cv.* memorize

◇ 記*憶　　　　きおく　*cv.* memorize; memory

◇ 記す　　　　しるす　write down

634　紀　9
▶き

20世紀　　　　にじっせいき，にじゅっせいき　twentieth century

紀元前　　　　きげんぜん　B.C.

歴 紀行文　　　きこうぶん　account of a journey

635　組　11
▶そ
▷く(む)，くみ　　　　1924
cf. 且

組み立てる　　くみたてる　assemble

組み合わせ/組合せ　くみあわせ　combination

労働組合　　　ろうどうくみあい　labor union

◇ 組長　　　　くみちょう　head of a gang

◇ 組*織　　　　そしき　organization; *cv.* organize, set up

636　素　10
▶そ，す

水素　　　　　すいそ　hydrogen

元素　　　　　げんそ　chemical element

質素な　　　　しっそな　simple, plain

素質　　　　　そしつ　quality, nature, make-up

素直な　　　　すなおな　gentle, docile, obedient

素晴らしい　　すばらしい　splendid, wonderful

素人　　　　　△しろうと　amateur, layman

◇ 素*肌　　　　すはだ　bare skin (without make-up/clothes)

637　麦　7
▶ばく
▷むぎ

小麦　　　　　こむぎ　wheat

大麦　　　　　おおむぎ　barley

麦　　　　　　むぎ　wheat, barley, rye, oats

麦茶　　　　　むぎちゃ　barley tea

◇ 麦*畑　　　　むぎばたけ　wheat field

然 麦*芽　　　　ばくが　malt

638　責　11
▶せき
▷せ(める)

責任　　　　　せきにん　responsibility

責務　　　　　せきむ　duty, job

◇ 責める　　　せめる　blame

〈漢字の形に気をつけましょう・19〉

437　636　637　788
表　素　麦　*毒

本の表紙　　　素質がある　　　米と麦　　　アルコール中*毒
　　　　　　　　　　　　　　　　　　　　　　　　　　ちゅうどく

639 任 6 ▶にん ▷まか(せる)，まか(す)

責任	せきにん	responsibility
主任	しゅにん	person in charge, assistant manager, head of a team
就任	しゅうにん	cv. assume a post
後任の	こうにんの	succeeding (president/etc.)
任務	にんむ	duty, office, mission
一任	いちにん	cv. leave (a matter) entirely (to a person)
任意に	にんいに	voluntarily, by one's own choice
◇ 任*期	にんき	term of office
◇ 任*命	にんめい	cv. appoint
任せる	まかせる	entrust

640 信 9 ▶しん

信じる	しんじる	believe
信者	しんじゃ	believer (of a religion)
自信	じしん	(self-)confidence
通信	つうしん	communication; cv. communicate
信用	しんよう	cv. trust
不信	ふしん	distrust
信号	しんごう	traffic signal

㊹

641 徒 10 ▶と

生徒	せいと	pupil
キリスト教徒	キリストきょうと	Christian
仏教徒	ぶっきょうと	Buddhist
イスラム教徒	イスラムきょうと	Muslim

642 従 10 ▶じゅう，しょう，じゅ ▷したが(う)，したが(える)

従来の	じゅうらいの	conventional
従業員	じゅうぎょういん	employee/worker (of a factory/store/etc.) cf. 社員 (しゃいん) member/employee (of a company)
服従	ふくじゅう	cv. obey
◇ 従*順な	じゅうじゅんな	obedient
◇ 従事	じゅうじ	cv. engage in
従う	したがう	obey, comply with, follow
従える	したがえる	be attended by, conquer
歴 従〜位	じゅ〜い	rank in the Japanese medieval office system given to nobles/lords
特 従容として	しょうようとして	calmly, with composure/serenity

643 得 11 ▶とく ▷え(る)，う(る)

得意な/の	とくいな/の	good, strong, favorite (subject)
得意	とくい	strong point, forte, pride
得	とく	gain, advantage
損得	そんとく	loss and gain
得点	とくてん	points (gained)
所得	しょとく	income
得る	える，うる	gain, acquire
やむを得ない	やむをえない	inevitable
◇ 心得る	こころえる	understand, recognize

644 徳 14 ▶とく

道徳	どうとく	morality, morals
人徳	じんとく	one's natural virtue
徳川時代	とくがわじだい	the Tokugawa era

645 聴 17 ▶ちょう ▷き(く)

聴講	ちょうこう	*cv.* audit (a course)
聴講生	ちょうこうせい	auditing student
聴解	ちょうかい	listening comprehension
公聴会	こうちょうかい	public hearing
聴覚	ちょうかく	sense of hearing
◇ *視聴率	しちょうりつ	audience rating
◇ *視聴者	しちょうしゃ	TV viewer
◇ 聴*衆	ちょうしゅう	audience
◇ 事*情聴取	じじょうちょうしゅ	investigative inquiry (by the police)
◇ 聴く	きく	listen, hear

646 舟 6 ▶しゅう ▷ふね, ふな

舟	ふね	boat
小舟	こぶね	small boat
◇ 舟遊び	ふなあそび	boating
歴 雪舟	せっしゅう	(name of a famous Japanese painter in the medieval period)

647 船 11 ▶せん ▷ふね, ふな

船	ふね	vessel, ship
風船	ふうせん	(toy) balloon
客船	きゃくせん	passenger ship
船員	せんいん	sailor, crew
船長	せんちょう	captain
船室	せんしつ	cabin (of a ship)
船旅	ふなたび	voyage
船便	ふなびん	surface mail cf. 航空便(こうくうびん) air mail

648 般 10 ▶はん

一般的な	いっぱんてきな	common, ordinary
一般の	いっぱんの	general, ordinary
一般化	いっぱんか	*cv.* generalize
全般的に	ぜんぱんてきに	generally, at large
◇ *諸般の事*情により	しょはんのじじょうにより	for various reasons

649 航 10 ▶こう

航空便	こうくうびん	air mail
航空機	こうくうき	aircraft
◇ 航空*券	こうくうけん	airline ticket
航海	こうかい	voyage; *cv.* sail, make a voyage
航路	こうろ	route, line, service
◇ *巡航ミサイル	じゅんこうミサイル	cruise missile

650 億 15 ▶おく

| 一億 | いちおく | 100 million |

651 憶 16 ▶おく

| 記憶 | きおく | *cv.* memorize; memory |

652 漫 14 ▶まん

漫画	まんが	cartoon, comics
漫然と	まんぜんと	aimlessly
◇ *散漫な	さんまんな	aimless, vague
◇ 漫*才	まんざい	Japanese comic dialogue

㊸

653 14

慢

▶まん

自慢	じまん *cv.* boast, self-praise; (one's) pride and joy
慢性の	まんせいの chronic
◇*我慢	がまん *cv.* endure, bear
◇*怠慢	たいまん negligence

654 11

情

▶じょう，せい
▷なさけ

感情	かんじょう emotion, feeling
感情的な	かんじょうてきな emotional
同情	どうじょう *cv.* sympathize
友情	ゆうじょう friendship
苦情	くじょう complaint
情	じょう emotion, sympathy
無情の	むじょうの unfortunate, heartless
事情	じじょう circumstances, situation
◇*実情	じつじょう actual situation, reality
◇ 風情	ふぜい charm, good taste
◇ 情	なさけ sympathy, empathy

655 14

慣

▶かん
▷な(れる)，な(らす)

慣れる	なれる get used to
見慣れた	みなれた familiar
習慣	しゅうかん custom, practice, habit
慣習	かんしゅう rules and conventions
◇ 慣*例	かんれい custom, convention

656 7

快

▶かい
▷こころよ(い)

快適な	かいてきな comfortable, pleasant
快晴	かいせい clear sky, fine weather
全快	ぜんかい *cv.* recover from an illness completely
快速(電車)	かいそく(でんしゃ) rapid train
◇*愉快な	ゆかいな joyful, pleasant, delightful
◇ 快い	こころよい pleasant

657 14

適

▶てき

適当な	てきとうな appropriate, suitable
適度な	てきどな adequate
適切な	てきせつな appropriate
適用	てきよう *cv.* apply (a rule)
◇ 適*材適所	てきざいてきしょ (put) the right person in the right post/place
適する	てきする be suitable for

〈漢字の形に気をつけましょう・20〉

| 657 | 1256 | 1504 | 658 | 684 |
| 適 | *摘 | *滴 | 敵 | *商 |

適当な人　　*摘出手術　　一*滴、二*滴、三*滴　　敵と味方
　　　　　　てきしゅつ　　いってき　にてき　さんてき

米国通*商 代表部
つうしょう

658 敵 15
- ▶てき
- ▷かたき

敵	てき enemy	反味方 (みかた) ally, friend
強敵	きょうてき tough enemy	
敵意	てきい hostility	
敵対	てきたい *cv.* oppose	
不敵な	ふてきな fearless	
◇ 敵	かたき enemy	

659 欠 4
- ▶けつ
- ▷か(ける), か(く)

欠席	けっせき *cv.* be absent (from school/etc.)
欠員	けついん vacancy (in the staff)
◇ 欠ける	かける lack
◇ 欠く	かく lack

660 次 6
- ▶じ, し
- ▷つ(ぐ), つぎ

次の	つぎの following, next
次男	じなん second son
目次	もくじ table of contents
◇ 〜次第	〜しだい as soon as 〜, depending on 〜
◇ 次いで	subsequently
◇ 〜に次ぐ	〜につぐ rank next to 〜, follow 〜

661 姿 9
- ▶し
- ▷すがた

姿	すがた figure, appearance
後ろ姿	うしろすがた back view (of a person)
◇ 姿*勢	しせい posture, stance
◇ *容姿	ようし face and figure, appearance

662 冷 7
- ▶れい
- ▷つめ(たい), ひ(える), ひ(や), ひ(やす), さ(める), さ(ます)

冷たい	つめたい cold cf. 冷たい is used for things cold to the touch, whereas 寒い is used for air temperature.
冷える	ひえる become cold
冷やす	ひやす chill, cool
冷戦	れいせん cold war
冷水	れいすい cold water
冷静な	れいせいな calm, cool(-headed)
◇ 冷*蔵庫	れいぞうこ refrigerator
冷やかす	ひやかす tease, poke fun at
冷める	さめる cool off
冷ます	さます cool

㊻

663 句 5
- ▶く

文句	もんく grumbling, complaint, words
語句	ごく words and phrases

664 旬 6
- ▶じゅん

上旬	じょうじゅん the first ten days of a month
中旬	ちゅうじゅん the middle ten days of a month
下旬	げじゅん the last ten days of a month
初旬	しょじゅん (during) the first ten days of a month

665 保 9
- ▶ほ
- ▷たも(つ)

保証人	ほしょうにん guarantor
保証	ほしょう *cv.* guarantee

保存	ほぞん　*cv.* preserve, conserve	
◇ 保*険	ほけん　insurance	
◇ 保*健	ほけん　health care	
◇ 保*障	ほしょう　*cv.* secure	
◇ 保*育園	ほいくえん　nursery school	
保つ	たもつ　maintain, keep (warmth/relationship/etc.)	

666　証　12　▶しょう

証明	しょうめい　*cv.* prove
証人	しょうにん　witness
証言	しょうげん　*cv.* testify, give evidence
◇ 証*拠	しょうこ　evidence

667　許　11　▶きょ　▷ゆる(す)

許可	きょか　*cv.* allow, permit
特許	とっきょ　patent
◇ 許*容	きょよう　*cv.* allow, permit
◇ *免許	めんきょ　license
許す	ゆるす　allow, permit, forgive

668　認　14　▶にん　▷みと(める)

認める	みとめる　prove, allow, admit
認識	にんしき　*cv.* recognize, understand, perceive
公認の	こうにんの　officially recognized, authorized, certified
◇ *確認	かくにん　*cv.* confirm

669　課　15　▶か

課長	かちょう　section chief, manager
課	か　section, department

人事課	じんじか　personnel department
経理課	けいりか　accounting department
第〜課	だい〜か　section 〜, lesson 〜
課題	かだい　assignment, task
日課	にっか　daily work
課する	かする　impose (a tax/duty/etc.)

670　税　12　▶ぜい

税金	ぜいきん　tax
関税	かんぜい　customs
税関	ぜいかん　customs, customs house
所得税	しょとくぜい　income tax
無税	むぜい　tax-free
課税	かぜい　*cv.* impose a tax
◇ *免税	めんぜい　tax exemption; *cv.* make (a product/etc.) exempt from tax

671　程　12　▶てい　▷ほど　　　　1657　cf. 呈

程度	ていど　degree, extent
課程	かてい　course, program (of a school)
過程	かてい　process
日程	にってい　schedule
程々に	ほどほどに　moderately

672　実　8　▶じつ　▷み，みの(る)

事実	じじつ　fact
真実	しんじつ　truth
口実	こうじつ　excuse
実習	じっしゅう　*cv.* practice

実感	じっかん	*cv.* realize, experience personally
実行	じっこう	*cv.* put into practice, carry out
実力	じつりょく	actual ability, potential
実物	じつぶつ	the real thing
実際に	じっさいに	as a matter of fact, actually
実用的な	じつようてきな	practical
実は	じつは	actually, to tell the truth
◇ 実*例	じつれい	example
◇ 実に	じつに	surely, really
◇ 果実酒	かじつしゅ	fruit wine
◇ 実	み	fruit
◇ 実る	みのる	bear fruit

673 美 9 ▶び ▷うつく(しい)

美人	びじん	beautiful woman
美術館	びじゅつかん	art museum
美学	びがく	aesthetics
美しい	うつくしい	pretty, beautiful

㊼

674 差 10 ▶さ ▷さ(す)

差	さ	difference
時差	じさ	time difference
時差ボケ	じさボケ	jet lag
差別	さべつ	*cv.* discriminate
交差点	こうさてん	intersection
差す	さす	shine into/upon, stream in, fill (a vase with water), hold (an umbrella) over one's head
差し上げる	さしあげる	give (humble)
差し引く	さしひく	deduct, take away
物差し	ものさし	rule, measure
◇ 差し支える △さしつかえる		interfere

675 養 15 ▶よう ▷やしな(う)

休養	きゅうよう	*cv.* rest
教養	きょうよう	*cv.* culture
養子	ようし	adopted child
養育	よういく	*cv.* nurture
◇ 養分	ようぶん	nourishment
養う	やしなう	foster, support

676 善 12 ▶ぜん ▷よ(い)

善意	ぜんい	good intentions
善	ぜん	good, goodness, virtue
善良な	ぜんりょうな	good(-natured), honest
親善	しんぜん	friendship
善悪	ぜんあく	good and evil
◇ *改善	かいぜん	*cv.* improve, make better
◇ 善い	よい	good

677 様 14 ▶よう ▷さま

多様性	たようせい	diversity
多様化	たようか	diversification (of lifestyles/needs/etc.); *cv.* be diversified cf. 多角化(たかくか) diversification (of business operations)
多様な	たような	diversified
同様の	どうようの	same
様子	ようす	situation, appearance, aspect
神様	かみさま	God, gods
〜様	〜さま	Mr./Ms. 〜 (mainly used in writing)

678 植 12

▶しょく
▷う（える），う（わる）

植物	しょくぶつ plants 反動物（どうぶつ） animals
植民地	しょくみんち colony
植える	うえる plant (a tree/etc.)
田植(え)	たうえ transplanting of rice shoots

679 極 12

▶きょく，ごく
▷きわ（める），きわ（まる），きわ（み）

北極	ほっきょく the North Pole
南極	なんきょく the South Pole
極東	きょくとう the Far East
極端な	きょくたんな extreme
◇ 見極める	みきわめる ascertain, make sure
◇ 極まる	きわまる reach an extreme
◇ 極み	きわみ height, apex
◇ 極*秘	ごくひ top secret

680 端 14

▶たん
▷はし，は，はた

極端な	きょくたんな extreme
先端技術	せんたんぎじゅつ advanced technology
◇*異端	いたん heresy, heterodoxy
端	はし end, edge
端数	はすう fraction
半端な	はんぱな fractional
◇ 中*途半端な	ちゅうとはんぱな incomplete, halfway
道端	みちばた roadside

681 需 14

▶じゅ

需要	じゅよう demand 反供給（きょうきゅう） cv. supply

需給	じゅきゅう supply and demand
特需	とくじゅ special procurement
◇ 必需*品	ひつじゅひん necessities
◇*軍需*品	ぐんじゅひん munitions, war supplies
◇*軍需産業	ぐんじゅさんぎょう war industry

682 器 15

▶き
▷うつわ

楽器	がっき musical instrument
食器	しょっき tableware
受話器	じゅわき telephone receiver
器用な	きような skillful, tactful
不器用な	ぶきような awkward
◇ 器*具	きぐ appliances, utensils, tools
◇ 器	うつわ container

683 品 9

▶ひん
▷しな

品質	ひんしつ quality (of a product)
部品	ぶひん part
◇ 日用品	にちようひん daily necessities
◇ 薬品	やくひん medicine, drug, chemical
◇ 洋品店	ようひんてん Western-style apparel shop
品物	しなもの merchandise, commodity
◇ 品	しな goods, article
手品	てじな magic (show)
上品な	じょうひんな refined, elegant, graceful
下品な	げひんな gross, vulgar
品	ひん grace, elegance, dignity

684 商 11 ▶しょう ▷あきな(う)

商品	しょうひん	merchandise, commodity
商業	しょうぎょう	commerce
商人	しょうにん	merchant
商売	しょうばい	business; *cv.* engage in business
商社	しょうしゃ	trading firm
商店	しょうてん	shop, store, firm
◇ 商い	あきない	dealing, business

㊽

685 袋 11 ▶たい ▷ふくろ

袋	ふくろ	sack, bag
紙袋	かみぶくろ	paper bag
手袋	てぶくろ	glove
◇ 袋小路	ふくろこうじ	blind alley
特 郵袋	ゆうたい	mailbag

686 製 14 ▶せい

日本製	にほんせい	made in Japan
製品	せいひん	(manufactured) product
製作	せいさく	*cv.* produce
製鉄	せいてつ	iron manufacturing
製鉄所	せいてつしょ, せいてつじょ	ironworks

687 制 8 ▶せい

制度	せいど	system
制作	せいさく	*cv.* produce
強制	きょうせい	*cv.* compel, force
強制労働	きょうせいろうどう	forced labor
税制	ぜいせい	taxation system

688 誕 15 ▶たん

誕生日	たんじょうび	birthday
誕生	たんじょう	*cv.* be born; birth

689 延 8 ▶えん ▷の(びる), の(べる), の(ばす)

延期	えんき	*cv.* postpone
延長	えんちょう	*cv.* extend (time)
延びる	のびる	be postponed, be prolonged
延ばす	のばす	postpone, prolong, lengthen
引き延ばす	ひきのばす	draw/stretch out, put off (an appointment/payment/etc.)
◇ 延べる	のべる	lay out (a futon), make (a bed)

690 期 12 ▶き, ご

前期	ぜんき	first semester
後期	こうき	second semester
学期	がっき	semester, term
期間	きかん	period of time
短期大学	たんきだいがく	junior college
定期的に	ていきてきに	regularly
短期的な	たんきてきな	short-term
中期的な	ちゅうきてきな	medium-term
長期的な	ちょうきてきな	long-term
画期的な	かっきてきな	epoch-making
◇ 定期*券	ていきけん	pass (for riding a train/bus/etc.), season ticket
◇ 予期	よき	*cv.* anticipate
◇ 最期	さいご	the last moment of one's life

691 基 11
▶き
▷もと，もとい　cf. 墓　1156

基本	きほん	basis, foundation, ABCs
基金	ききん	foundation
基地	きち	(military) base
基礎	きそ	foundation, basis
基づく	もとづく	be based on
◇ 基	もと，もとい	foundation

692 礎 18
▶そ
▷いしずえ

基礎	きそ	foundation, basis
◇ 礎	いしずえ	cornerstone

693 疑 14
▶ぎ
▷うたが(う)

疑う	うたがう	doubt, be suspicious of, distrust
疑い	うたがい	doubt, suspicion
疑問	ぎもん	question, doubt
◇ 質疑*応答	しつぎおうとう	questions and answers
◇ 疑*念	ぎねん	doubt, suspicion
◇*容疑者	ようぎしゃ	suspect
◇*容疑	ようぎ	suspicion
◇ 疑*惑	ぎわく	suspicion
◇ 疑*獄	ぎごく	scandal

694 紹 11
▶しょう

紹介	しょうかい	cv. introduce, present
自己紹介	じこしょうかい	cv. introduce oneself

695 介 4
▶かい

紹介	しょうかい	cv. introduce, present
介入	かいにゅう	cv. intervene
介在	かいざい	cv. stand/come between
魚介類	ぎょかいるい	marine products, seafood

696 招 8
▶しょう
▷まね(く)

招待	しょうたい	cv. invite
招く	まねく	invite
◇ 手招き	てまねき	cv. beckon

49

697 委 8
▶い

委員会	いいんかい	committee
委員	いいん	member of a committee
◇ 委*託	いたく	cv. entrust, consign

〈漢字の形に気をつけましょう・21〉

694	696	867	1691
紹	招	*昭	*召

人を紹介する　　人を家に招待する　　*昭和20年　　*召し上がる
しょうわ　　め

698

季
8
▶き

季節	きせつ	season
季節風	きせつふう	monsoon
四季	しき	four seasons

699
節
13
▶せつ，せち
▷ふし

季節	きせつ	season
調節	ちょうせつ	cv. adjust
使節	しせつ	mission, envoy
節約	せつやく	cv. save (electricity/water/time/etc.)
関節	かんせつ	joint
お節料理	おせちりょうり	special dinner for the New Year
◇ 節	ふし	knot, joint (in a bamboo shaft)

700
即
7
▶そく

即興	そっきょう	improvisation
即時に	そくじに	instantly, immediately
即座に	そくざに	immediately

701
企
6
▶き
▷くわだ(てる)

| 企業 | きぎょう | corporation |
| 大企業 | だいきぎょう | large enterprises |

中小企業	ちゅうしょうきぎょう	medium and small enterprises
企画	きかく	cv. plan
◇ 企てる	くわだてる	plan, scheme, attempt, try, undertake
◇ 企て	くわだて	plan, scheme, project

702
歯
12
▶し
▷は

歯	は	tooth
虫歯	むしば	decayed tooth, cavity
前歯	まえば	front tooth
歯医者	はいしゃ	dentist
歯車	はぐるま	gear
歯科医	しかい	dentist

703
歳
13
▶さい，せい

〜歳	〜さい	〜 years old
歳出	さいしゅつ	expenditure
歳入	さいにゅう	revenue
歳末大売出し	さいまつおおうりだし	big year-end sale
万歳	ばんざい	Long live (the emperor/king/etc.)
二十歳	△はたち	twenty years old
◇ お歳*暮	おせいぼ	year-end gift

704
歴
14
▶れき
1720
cf. 暦

| 歴史 | れきし | history |

〈漢字の形に気をつけましょう・22〉

697　　　698　　　1171
委　　　季　　　*秀

予算委員会　　季節　　*優*秀な学生
　　　　　　　　　　　　ゆうしゅう

学歴	がくれき　(one's) educational history, academic background
職歴	しょくれき　(one's) record of employment
経歴	けいれき　personal history
前歴	ぜんれき　(one's) past record

705 **史** 5　▶し

歴史	れきし　history
日本史	にほんし　Japanese history
世界史	せかいし　world history
文学史	ぶんがくし　history of literature

706 **央** 5　▶おう

| 中央 | ちゅうおう　center |

㊿

707 **非** 8　▶ひ

非常口	ひじょうぐち　emergency exit
非公開の	ひこうかいの　private, closed to the public, unpublished
非人道的な	ひじんどうてきな　inhuman
非合法的な	ひごうほうてきな　illegal
非合法な	ひごうほうな　illegal
非公式の	ひこうしきの　informal

708 **常** 11　▶じょう　▷つね, とこ

日常会話	にちじょうかいわ　daily conversation
日常生活	にちじょうせいかつ　daily life
正常な	せいじょうな　normal
◇ *異常な	いじょうな　unusual, abnormal
通常の	つうじょうの　usual, ordinary
非常の	ひじょうの　emergency
非常口	ひじょうぐち　emergency exit
常識	じょうしき　common sense
常に	つねに　always
◇ 常夏の国	とこなつのくに　land of everlasting summer

709 **堂** 11　▶どう

食堂	しょくどう　restaurant
本堂	ほんどう　main hall of a temple
国会議事堂	こっかいぎじどう　the Diet Building

710 **党** 10　▶とう

自民党	じみんとう　the Liberal Democratic Party, LDP
民主党	みんしゅとう　the Democratic Party
共和党	きょうわとう　the Republican Party
保守党	ほしゅとう　the Conservative Party

〈代表的な日本の政党〉

自民党(じみんとう)	社会党(しゃかいとう)	共産党(きょうさんとう)
民社党(みんしゃとう)	公明党(こうめいとう)	新生党(しんせいとう)
日本新党(にほんしんとう)		

労働党	ろうどうとう	the Labor Party
政党	せいとう	political party
◇ *与党	よとう	ruling party
野党	やとう	opposition party
党首	とうしゅ	head of a political party

711 賞 15 ▶しょう

ノーベル賞	ノーベルしょう	Nobel Prize cf. アカデミー賞 Academy Award, グラミー賞 Grammy Award
賞	しょう	prize
賞品	しょうひん	prize
賞金	しょうきん	prize money
受賞者	じゅしょうしゃ	prize winner

712 償 17 ▶しょう ▷つぐな(う)

代償	だいしょう	price, return, reward
◇ *賠償金	ばいしょうきん	indemnity
◇ 損*害*賠償	そんがいばいしょう	indemnity, reparation
◇ 償う	つぐなう	atone for, expiate
◇ 償い	つぐない	atonement, expiation

713 与 3 ▶よ ▷あた(える)

与党	よとう	ruling party
与える	あたえる	give, provide
◇ 給与	きゅうよ	salary
◇ 供与	きょうよ	cv. offer
◇ 関与	かんよ	cv. relate oneself to

714 券 8 ▶けん

定期券	ていきけん	pass (for riding a train/bus/etc.), season ticket
回数券	かいすうけん	ticket book (for train/bus/etc.)
入場券	にゅうじょうけん	admission ticket
証券会社	しょうけんがいしゃ	securities firm
旅券	りょけん	passport

715 巻 9 ▶かん ▷ま(く), まき

第～巻	だい～かん	volume no. ～
上巻	じょうかん	vol. 1
中巻	ちゅうかん	vol. 2 (in a 3-volume set)
下巻	げかん	vol. 2 (in a 2-volume set), vol. 3 (in a 3-volume set)
巻く	まく	curl, wind
葉巻	はまき	cigar
寝巻き	ねまき	pajamas cf. パジャマ, rather than 寝巻き, is used in modern Japanese.
◇ 絵巻物	えまきもの	picture scroll

716 角 7 ▶かく ▷かど, つの

角	かど	corner
街角	まちかど	on the street
角度	かくど	angle
直角	ちょっかく	right angle
三角形	さんかくけい	triangle
三角関係	さんかくかんけい	love triangle
方角	ほうがく	direction
◇ 角	つの	horn, antler

51

717 負 9 ▶ふ ▷ま(ける), ま(かす), お(う)

負ける	まける	lose (a game)
勝負	しょうぶ	winning and losing; cv. have a match/contest

自負	じふ　self-confidence, pride; cv. be self-confident
◇ 負*担	ふたん　burden; cv. bear, shoulder, carry
負う	おう　take (responsibility)

718
11
敗　▶はい
　▷やぶ(れる)

失敗	しっぱい　cv. fail
敗戦	はいせん　defeat in a war
敗者	はいしゃ　loser
勝敗	しょうはい　victory or defeat
敗れる	やぶれる　be defeated

719
7
貝　▷かい

| 貝 | かい　shellfish |
| ◇ 貝*殻 | かいがら　shell |

720
8
具　▶ぐ

家具	かぐ　furniture
道具	どうぐ　tool
具体的な	ぐたいてきな　concrete, specific
具合	ぐあい　condition

721
12
散　▶さん
　▷ち(る), ち(らす), ち(らかす), ち(らかる)

散歩	さんぽ　walk, cv. take a walk
解散	かいさん　cv. break up, dissolve
散文	さんぶん　prose
散漫な	さんまんな　loose (lecture/thinking/etc.), distracted (attention)
散る	ちる　scatter, fall (as in blossoms/leaves/paper/etc.)
◇ 散らかす	ちらかす　scatter about, put in disorder

722
9
故　▶こ
　▷ゆえ

交通事故	こうつうじこ　traffic accident
事故	じこ　accident
故国	ここく　homeland, native country
故意に	こいに　intentionally, purposefully
故に	ゆえに　therefore

723
8
放　▶ほう
　▷はな(す), はな(つ), はな(れる)

放送	ほうそう　cv. broadcast
解放	かいほう　cv. liberate
開放	かいほう　cv. throw (a door) open, open to the public
放火	ほうか　cv. set on fire

〈いろいろな形の言い方〉

三角形(さんかくけい)　　四角形(しかくけい)　　五角形(ごかくけい)

正方形(せいほうけい)　　長方形(ちょうほうけい)　　ひし形(ひしがた)　　円(えん)

直方体(ちょくほうたい)　　立方体(りっぽうたい)　　*球(きゅう)

放置　ほうち *cv.* abandon (a car/bicycle/etc.) on a street

放す　はなす let go, release

放れる　はなれる leave, be separated

◊ 放つ　はなつ shoot, emit

724
敷
15
▶ふ
▷し(く)

敷石　しきいし paving stone, flagstone

屋敷　やしき estate, premises, mansion

敷地　しきち site, ground

敷く　しく pave, cover, spread (a futon/mat/etc.)

◊ 敷設　ふせつ *cv.* lay (a pipe), construct (a railroad)

725
致
10
▶ち
▷いた(す)

一致　いっち *cv.* agree, be consistent

合致　がっち *cv.* agree, be consistent

致死量　ちしりょう lethal dose

◊ 致*命*傷　ちめいしょう fatal wound

◊ 致す　いたす bring about

(52)

726
改
7
▶かい
▷あらた(める), あらた(まる)

改良　かいりょう *cv.* improve

改正　かいせい *cv.* revise, amend

改善　かいぜん *cv.* make better

改めて　あらためて newly, again, formally

◊ 改める　あらためる revise, change, renew

727
配
10
▶はい
▷くば(る)

心配　しんぱい *cv.* worry

支配　しはい *cv.* conquer, rule

配達　はいたつ *cv.* deliver

配る　くばる distribute, deliver

728
酔
11
▶すい
▷よ(う)

酔う　よう get drunk

酔っ払い　よっぱらい drunk

◊ *麻酔　ますい anesthesia

729
針
10
▶しん
▷はり

方針　ほうしん policy, guidelines

針路　しんろ course, direction (of a ship/airplane/etc.) cf. 進路(しんろ) course, direction (in general)

針　はり needle

◊ 針金　はりがね wire

730
録
16
▶ろく

録音　ろくおん *cv.* record (speech/sound/etc.)

録画　ろくが *cv.* record on videotape

記録　きろく *cv.* record

◊ 付録　ふろく supplement

731
緑
14
▶りょく, ろく
▷みどり

緑　みどり green

緑色　みどりいろ green

新緑　しんりょく fresh verdure

緑地　りょくち green zone

葉緑素　ようりょくそ chlorophyll

(特) 緑青　ろくしょう copper/green rust, patina

732 縁 15	▶えん ▷ふち		
	縁	えん	fate, karma relation
◇	因縁	いんねん	cause
◇	縁*側	えんがわ	veranda
◇	縁	ふち	edge

733 納 10	▶のう，なっ，な，なん，とう ▷おさ(める)，おさ(まる)		
	納得	なっとく	cv. understand, give one's consent to
	納税	のうぜい	cv. pay a tax
	納める	おさめる	pay, supply, store
◇	納屋	なや	barn, shed cf.*倉庫（そうこ）warehouse, storehouse
◇	出納	すいとう	receipts and disbursements
◇	出納係	すいとうがかり	cashier, teller
◇	納戸	なんど	closet

734 絶 12	▶ぜつ ▷た(える)，た(やす)，た(つ)		
	絶対に	ぜったいに	definitely
	絶望	ぜつぼう	cv. despair
	絶望的な	ぜつぼうてきな	hopeless
	絶大な	ぜつだいな	full/total (support)
◇	*根絶	こんぜつ	cv. exterminate, eradicate
◇	絶*滅	ぜつめつ	cv. be extinct
◇	絶えず	たえず	continuously, incessantly, all the time
◇	絶える	たえる	cease, die
◇	絶やす	たやす	run out of, exhaust
◇	絶つ	たつ	stop (drinking/smoking/etc.)

735 総 14	▶そう 1000 cf. 統		
	総合的な	そうごうてきな	comprehensive
	総計	そうけい	grand total; cv. total
	総会	そうかい	general assembly
	国民総生産	こくみんそうせいさん	gross national product
◇	総理大*臣	そうりだいじん	prime minister

736 為 9	▶い		
	行為	こうい	act, deed, behavior, conduct
	人為的な	じんいてきな	artificial
◇	無作為	むさくい	random (sampling)
◇	為政者	いせいしゃ	statesman
	為替相場	△かわせそうば	exchange rate
	為替レート	△かわせレート	exchange rate
	為替	△かわせ	currency

737 老 6	▶ろう ▷ふ(ける)，お(いる)		
	老人	ろうじん	old person
	長老	ちょうろう	elder (of a village/etc.)
	老子	ろうし	Lao-tse
◇	老ける	ふける	grow old (in terms of appearance)
◇	老いる	おいる	grow old

738 孝 7	▶こう		
	親孝行	おやこうこう	filial piety
	親不孝	おやふこう	disrespect to one's parents

⑤

739　才　3　▶さい

～才	～さい　～ years old　cf. 歳（さい）, rather than 才, is normally used.
天才	てんさい　genius
才能	さいのう　talent
多才な	たさいな　versatile (person)

740　材　7　▶ざい

材料	ざいりょう　material
教材	きょうざい　teaching material
取材	しゅざい　cv. gather material, collect data
題材	だいざい　theme
材木	ざいもく　lumber, timber
木材	もくざい　wood
新素材	しんそざい　new materials

741　財　10　▶ざい, さい

財産	ざいさん　estate, assets, property
財政	ざいせい　finance
財界	ざいかい　business world
財団	ざいだん　foundation
ロックフェラー財団	ロックフェラーざいだん the Rockefeller Foundation　cf. 国際交流基金（こくさいこうりゅうききん）the Japan Foundation
文化財	ぶんかざい　cultural asset
◇ 財*布	さいふ　purse, wallet

742　貯　12　▶ちょ

貯金	ちょきん　savings, deposit; cv.vi. save money
貯水池	ちょすいち　reservoir
◇ 貯*蔵	ちょぞう　cv. store

743　蓄　13　▶ちく　　1274 cf. 畜

貯蓄	ちょちく　savings; cv.vi. save money
備蓄	びちく　cv. store/save/reserve (something for an emergency)
◇ 蓄*積	ちくせき　cv. accumulate

744　氏　4　▶し　▷うじ

氏名	しめい　name (used for people)
～氏	～し　Mr./Ms. ～
歴 氏神	うじがみ　guardian god (of a village)

745　底　8　▶てい　▷そこ

海底	かいてい　bottom of the sea
◇ *根底	こんてい　bottom (in an abstract sense)
底	そこ　bottom
底値	そこね　bottom price

746　抵　8　▶てい

抵抗	ていこう　cv. resist
大抵	たいてい　usually
◇ 抵当	ていとう　mortgage
◇ 抵*触	ていしょく　cv. conflict (with the law)

747　抗　7　▶こう　　1928 cf. 坑

抵抗	ていこう　cv. resist
反抗	はんこう　cv. oppose, disobey
反抗的な	はんこうてきな　defiant

抗議　　　　こうぎ　cv. protest

抗争　　　　こうそう　rivalry, war

◇　抗ガン*剤　こうガンざい　anti-cancer drug

748
接
11
　▶せつ
　▷つ(ぐ)

直接　　　　ちょくせつ　direct

間接的に　　かんせつてきに　indirectly

面接　　　　めんせつ　cv. give an interview

接近　　　　せっきん　cv. approach

接続　　　　せつぞく　cv. connect

接待　　　　せったい　cv. entertain (usually for a business client)

◇　接ぐ　　　つぐ　connect

749
換
12
　▶かん
　▷か(える), か(わる)

乗り換える　　のりかえる　transfer (to another train/bus/etc.)

交換　　　　こうかん　cv. exchange, replace

変換　　　　へんかん　cv. change, convert

転換期　　　てんかんき　turning point, transition

換気　　　　かんき　cv. ventilate

換算　　　　かんさん, かんざん　cv. convert (from one currency to another)

㊼

750
条
7
　▶じょう

条約　　　　じょうやく　treaty

条文　　　　じょうぶん　text (of a constitution/law/treaty/etc.)

第〜条　　　だい〜じょう　article 〜

◇*憲法第九条　けんぽうだいきゅうじょう
　　Article 9 of the (Japanese) Constitution

条件　　　　じょうけん　condition

信条　　　　しんじょう　creed

751
契
9
　▶けい
　▷ちぎ(る)

契約　　　　けいやく　contract, agreement;
　　cv. enter into/sign a contract

◇　契機　　　けいき　opportunity, (serve as an) impetus

歴　契る　　　ちぎる　pledge (one's love/etc.)

752
喫
12
　▶きつ

喫茶店　　　きっさてん　coffee shop

◇　喫*煙　　　きつえん　smoking; cv. smoke

◇　満喫　　　まんきつ　cv. enjoy fully

753
潔
15
　▶けつ
　▷いさぎよ(い)

清潔な　　　せいけつな　clean, neat

不潔な　　　ふけつな　unclean, dirty, filthy

潔白　　　　けっぱく　innocence

◇　潔い　　　いさぎよい　good (loser), honorable (death)

754
清
11
　▶せい, しょう
　▷きよ(い), きよ(まる), きよ(める)

清潔な　　　せいけつな　clean, neat

清書　　　　せいしょ　cv. write a clean copy

清算　　　　せいさん　cv. liquidate, settle, clear (a debt), atone for

◇　清涼飲料(水)　せいりょういんりょう(すい)
　　refreshing beverage, soft drink

◇　清水　　　△しみず　spring water

清水寺　　　きよみずでら　Kiyomizu Temple (in Kyoto)

◇　清い　　　きよい　pure

◇　清める　　きよめる　purify

特　六*根清*浄　ろっこんしょうじょう　be completely purified

755 士 3 ▶し

会計士	かいけいし	licensed accountant
税理士	ぜいりし	licensed tax accountant
代議士	だいぎし	Diet member
学士	がくし	bachelor's degree, university/college graduate
学士号	がくしごう	bachelor's degree
◇ 弁*護士	べんごし	lawyer
歴*武士	ぶし	warrior (in medieval Japan), samurai

756 志 7 ▶し ▷こころざ(す)，こころざし

意志	いし	will, desire
◇ 有志	ゆうし	those interested, volunteer
◇ 同志	どうし	comrades, like-minded people
◇ 志向	しこう	orientation, inclination; cv. intend
志す	こころざす	aspire
志	こころざし	will, aspiration

757 恩 10 ▶おん

恩	おん	kindness, favor, debt of gratitude
恩人	おんじん	benefactor, patron
恩返し	おんがえし	repay a person's kindness
恩知らず	おんしらず	ungrateful person
恩給	おんきゅう	pension
◇ 恩*師	おんし	mentor

758 忠 8 ▶ちゅう

cf. 患 1367

忠実な	ちゅうじつな	faithful, loyal

◇ 忠*告	ちゅうこく	cv. advise, warn
◇ 忠*誠	ちゅうせい	loyalty

759 恐 10 ▶きょう ▷おそ(れる)，おそ(ろしい)

恐ろしい	おそろしい	terrible, frightening
恐れる	おそれる	fear
◇ 恐*縮	きょうしゅく	cv. feel obliged, be very grateful, be sorry
◇ 恐*怖	きょうふ	fear, terror
◇ 恐*慌	きょうこう	panic (in the stock market/etc.)

⑤⑤

760 翻 18 ▶ほん ▷ひるがえ(す)，ひるがえ(る)

翻訳	ほんやく	cv. translate
◇ 翻案	ほんあん	adaptation (from a play/novel/etc.)
◇ 翻意	ほんい	change one's mind
◇ 翻す	ひるがえす	turn aside/around quickly, change (one's mind)
◇ 翻る	ひるがえる	flutter

761 訳 11 ▶やく ▷わけ

通訳	つうやく	interpreter; cv. interpret
訳	やく	translation
英訳	えいやく	English translation; cv. translate into English
和訳	わやく	Japanese translation; cv. translate into Japanese
訳者	やくしゃ	translator
訳す	やくす	translate
訳	わけ	reason
言い訳	いいわけ	apology
申し訳	もうしわけ	apology
申し訳ない	もうしわけない	be very sorry, apologize for

762 尺 4 ▶しゃく

尺度	しゃくど	measure
尺	しゃく	*shaku* (unit of length, approx. 30.3 cm)

763 釈 11 ▶しゃく

解釈	かいしゃく	interpretation; *cv.* interpret
注釈	ちゅうしゃく	annotation, commentary; *cv.* annotate, comment
釈明	しゃくめい	*cv.* apologize
釈放	しゃくほう	*cv.* release (a suspect/etc.)
◊ 保釈	ほしゃく	*cv.* release on bail

764 択 7 ▶たく

選択	せんたく	*cv.* select, choose
選択科目	せんたくかもく	elective (subject)
二者択一	にしゃたくいつ	either-or alternative
◊*採択	さいたく	*cv.* adopt (a bill/act/etc.)

765 描 11 ▶びょう ▷えが(く)

描写	びょうしゃ	*cv.* describe
心理描写	しんりびょうしゃ	psychological description
描く	えがく	describe, draw, paint, sketch

766 拝 8 ▶はい ▷おが(む)

拝見	はいけん	*cv.* see, have a look at (humble)
参拝	さんぱい	*cv.* go and worship (at a shrine/temple)
参拝者	さんぱいしゃ	visitor (to a shrine/temple)
◊*礼拝	れいはい	church services; *cv.* worship
◊ 拝*啓	はいけい	Dear Sir/Madam (opening word for letters)
拝む	おがむ	pray, venerate, implore

767 提 12 ▶てい ▷さ(げる) 1852 1670 cf. 堤 是

提案	ていあん	*cv.* propose
提出	ていしゅつ	*cv.* present, submit
前提	ぜんてい	presuppositon
◊ 提供	ていきょう	*cv.* offer, supply
◊ 提げる	さげる	carry in one's hand

768 拡 8 ▶かく

拡大	かくだい	*cv.* expand, magnify
拡散	かくさん	*cv.* diffuse
拡声器	かくせいき	loudspeaker
◊ 拡*張	かくちょう	*cv.* extend, expand
◊ 拡*充	かくじゅう	*cv.* expand, enlarge, amplify

769 抜 7 ▶ばつ ▷ぬ(く), ぬ(ける), ぬ(かす), ぬ(かる)

抜群の	ばつぐんの	outstanding
選抜	せんばつ	*cv.* select, pick out
抜く	ぬく	pull out, surpass

�56

770 振 10 ▶しん ▷ふ(る), ふ(るう)

振動	しんどう	vibration; *cv.* vibrate, swing, oscillate
三振	さんしん	*cv.* be struck out
◊ 振興	しんこう	*cv.* promote

振る　　　　ふる　wave, shake

振り返る　　ふりかえる　look back, turn one's head

◇ 振る*舞う　ふるまう　behave

◇ 振り*仮名 △ふりがな　*kana* that are used to show the reading of *kanji*

---

771 打 ▶だ
5　　▷う(つ)

打つ　　　　うつ　hit, strike

打ち合わせ　うちあわせ　previous arrangement

◇ 打ち消す　うちけす　deny

打算的な　　ださんてき　calculating, selfish

打開　　　　だかい　*cv.* achieve a breakthrough, resolve (a situation)

◇ 打*撃　　　だげき　blow, shock

---

772 折 ▶せつ
7　　▷お(る)，おり，お(れる)

折る　　　　おる　fold, bend, break

折り紙　　　おりがみ　origami, paper for origami

◇ 折　　　　おり　occasion

◇ 右折　　　うせつ　*cv.* turn right

◇ 左折　　　させつ　*cv.* turn left

◇ 折半　　　せっぱん　*cv.* divide into halves

---

773 採 ▶さい
11　　▷と(る)

採用　　　　さいよう　*cv.* employ, adopt

採決　　　　さいけつ　*cv.* vote, take a vote

採集　　　　さいしゅう　*cv.* collect (plants/butterflies/etc.)

採算　　　　さいさん　profit

採点　　　　さいてん　*cv.* grade

採る　　　　とる　accept, employ, collect

---

774 菜 ▶さい
11　　▷な

野菜　　　　やさい　vegetable

菜食主義　　さいしょくしゅぎ　vegetarianism

菜園　　　　さいえん　vegetable garden

山菜　　　　さんさい　edible wild plants

菜の花　　　なのはな　rape blossoms

◇ 青菜　　　あおな　greens

---

775 指 ▶し
9　　▷ゆび，さ(す)

指　　　　　ゆび　finger

親指　　　　おやゆび　thumb　cf. 人差し指 (ひとさしゆび)，中指(なかゆび)，薬指(くすりゆび)，小指(こゆび)

指輪　　　　ゆびわ　(finger) ring

指導　　　　しどう　*cv.* lead, guide, instruct

指導員　　　しどういん　instructor

指名　　　　しめい　*cv.* nominate

指定席　　　していせき　reserved seat (in a train)　cf. 予約席(よやくせき) reserved seat (in a restaurant)

◇ 指*示　　　しじ　directions, instructions; *cv.* direct, instruct

指す　　　　さす　point

目指す　　　めざす　aim at

---

776 揮 ▶き
12

指揮者　　　しきしゃ　conductor (of an orchestra)

指揮　　　　しき　*cv.* conduct, command

発揮　　　　はっき　*cv.* exhibit/display (one's power/potential/etc.)

---

777 輝 ▶き
15　　▷かがや(く)

輝かしい　　かがやかしい　splendid, glorious

輝く	かがやく	glisten
輝き	かがやき	brilliancy, light, sparkle
特 光輝	こうき	brilliancy, luster

778 軍 9 ▶ぐん

軍隊	ぐんたい	military, army
◇*陸軍	りくぐん	army
空軍	くうぐん	air force
海軍	かいぐん	navy
軍人	ぐんじん	soldier
軍	ぐん	military, troops
十字軍	じゅうじぐん	crusade
軍国主義	ぐんこくしゅぎ	militarism

779 隊 12 ▶たい

軍隊	ぐんたい	military, army
部隊	ぶたい	squad
隊	たい	squad
隊長	たいちょう	squad chief

⑤⑦

780 衛 16 ▶えい

自衛隊	じえいたい	the Self-Defense Forces (of Japan)
衛星	えいせい	satellite
衛生	えいせい	hygiene, sanitation

781 防 7 ▶ぼう ▷ふせ(ぐ)

防衛	ぼうえい	cv. defend
防衛庁	ぼうえいちょう	the Defense Agency (of Japan)
国防省	こくぼうしょう	the Department of Defense

国防総省	こくぼうそうしょう	the Department of Defense (of the U.S.)
防止	ぼうし	cv. prevent, hold in check
予防	よぼう	cv. prevent, hold in check
消防車	しょうぼうしゃ	fire engine
◇ 防火*訓練	ぼうかくんれん	fire prevention drill
防ぐ	ふせぐ	prevent

782 坊 7 ▶ぼう, ぼっ

お坊さん	おぼうさん	Buddhist priest
坊主	ぼうず	Buddhist priest, shaved head, boy
赤ん坊	あかんぼう	baby
坊ちゃん	ぼっちゃん	(your/his/her) son, boy (honorific)
坊や	ぼうや	(your/his/her) son, boy (honorific)
朝寝坊	あさねぼう	late riser; cv. oversleep

783 訪 11 ▶ほう ▷たず(ねる), おとず(れる)

訪問	ほうもん	cv. visit
訪米	ほうべい	cv. visit the U.S.
訪ねる	たずねる	visit
◇ 訪れる	おとずれる	visit (a place)

784 妨 7 ▶ぼう ▷さまた(げる)

| 妨害 | ぼうがい | cv. interfere, interrupt |
| ◇ 妨げる | さまたげる | interfere |

785 害 10 ▶がい

| 公害 | こうがい | environmental pollution |

水害	すいがい	flood, flood damage
損害	そんがい	damage
利害	りがい	interest
◇ *被害	ひがい	damage

786 割 12 ▶かつ ▷わ（る），わり，わ（れる），さ（く）

割る	わる	divide, break (a glass/egg/etc.)
割合	わりあい	ratio
割引	わりびき	discount
二割引き	にわりびき	20-percent discount
時間割	じかんわり	class schedule
役割	やくわり	role
割り算	わりざん	division (in mathematics)
分割	ぶんかつ	cv. divide
◇ 割く	さく	spare (time/money/etc.) for someone/something

787 憲 16 ▶けん

憲法	けんぽう	constitution
憲法改正	けんぽうかいせい	revision of the consitition
改憲	かいけん	revision of the constitution
違憲	いけん	unconstitutional
◇ 立憲政治	りっけんせいじ	constitutional government
◇ 立憲*君主制	りっけんくんしゅせい	constitutional monarchy

788 毒 8 ▶どく
596
cf. 妻

毒	どく	poison
中毒	ちゅうどく	poisoning
食中毒	しょくちゅうどく	food poisoning

消毒	しょうどく	cv. disinfect
有毒な	ゆうどくな	poisonous
気の毒な	きのどくな	pitiable, unfortunate

789 危 6 ▶き ▷あぶ（ない），あや（うい），あや（ぶむ）

危ない	あぶない	dangerous
危険な	きけんな	dangerous
危機	きき	crisis
石油危機	せきゆきき	oil crisis, oil shock
危害	きがい	harm
◇ 危急の	ききゅうの	urgent
㊞ 危▲惧	きぐ	cv. worry
◇ 危うい	あやうい	dangerous
◇ 危ぶむ	あやぶむ	doubt (the success of)

790 険 11 ▶けん ▷けわ（しい）

危険な	きけんな	dangerous
保険	ほけん	insurance
険悪な	けんあくな	hostile
◇ *陰険な	いんけんな	treacherous, underhanded
◇ 険しい	けわしい	steep, stern

791 剣 10 ▶けん ▷つるぎ

真剣な	しんけんな	serious
剣道	けんどう	kendō, swordmanship
◇ 剣	つるぎ	sword

129

792	検 12	▶けん

点検	てんけん cv. examine
◇ 検*討	けんとう cv. examine, consider
検定	けんてい official approval (of a school textbook/etc.)
検証	けんしょう cv. probe
検察庁	けんさつちょう public prosecutor's office
検事	けんじ public prosecutor

793	験 18	▶けん, げん

経験	けいけん cv. experience
体験	たいけん cv. experience
◇*試験	しけん examination; cv. experiment, test
実験	じっけん cv. experiment
受験	じゅけん cv. take an exam
特 験	げん affect (of a prayer/etc.), omen

794	騒 18	▶そう ▷さわ(ぐ)

騒ぐ	さわぐ be noisy, make a fuss
騒がしい	さわがしい noisy, boisterous
大騒ぎ	おおさわぎ uproar, big fuss
騒音	そうおん noise
騒々しい	そうぞうしい clumsy
◇ 物騒な	ぶっそうな dangerous, frightening, unsettled

795	試 13	▶し ▷ため(す), こころ(みる)

試験	しけん examination; cv. experiment, test
試合	しあい match, game
試食	ししょく cv. try/taste (food)

試運転	しうんてん test/trial run; cv. make a test/trial run
試す	ためす try
◇ 試みる	こころみる try

796	式 6	▶しき

結婚式	けっこんしき wedding ceremony
入学式	にゅうがくしき (school) entrance ceremony
卒業式	そつぎょうしき commencement/graduation ceremony
正式に	せいしきに formally
公式の	こうしきの official
方式	ほうしき system, method
形式	けいしき form, formality
方程式	ほうていしき equation

797	専 9	▶せん ▷もっぱ(ら)

専門	せんもん major, area of expertise
専門家	せんもんか expert
専任の	せんにんの full-time (lecturer/instructor/etc.)
専制政治	せんせいせいじ autocracy
バス専用レーン	バスせんようレーン (exclusive) bus lane
◇ 専ら	もっぱら mainly, mostly

798	博 12	▶はく, ばく

博士	はくし, △はかせ Ph.D., Doctor
博士課程	はくしかてい, △はかせかてい Ph.D. program
博士号	はくしごう, △はかせごう Ph.D.
博物館	はくぶつかん museum

万博	ばんぱく　world's fair cf. This is an abbreviation of 万国博*覧会(ばんこくはくらんかい).
㊙ ▲賭博	とばく　gambling

799 **16** 薄　▶はく　1684
▷うす(い), うす(める), cf. 簿 うす(まる), うす(ら ぐ), うす(れる)

薄い	うすい　light (color), weak (coffee/tea/etc.), thin (book/paper/etc.)
薄暗い	うすぐらい　dim, gloomy
薄める	うすめる　make thin
薄利多売	はくりたばい　(gaining profit by) selling a lot with a small profit margin on each item
◇ 薄情な	はくじょうな　heartless, cold-hearted
◇ *精神薄弱	せいしんはくじゃく　mental weakness, feeble mindedness, low intelligence

800 **13** 夢　▶む
▷ゆめ

夢	ゆめ　dream
悪夢	あくむ　nightmare, bad dream
夢中になる	むちゅうになる　be fascinated with, be crazy about

801 **12** 葬　▶そう
▷ほうむ(る)

葬式	そうしき　funeral
◇ 葬*儀	そうぎ　funeral
火葬	かそう　cremation; cv. cremate
土葬	どそう　interment, burial; cv. bury
◇ *副葬品	ふくそうひん　items buried with the dead
◇ 葬る	ほうむる　bury

802 **13** 蒸　▶じょう
▷む(す), む(れる), む(らす)

蒸気	じょうき　steam
蒸気船	じょうきせん　steamship
水蒸気	すいじょうき　steam
蒸し暑い	むしあつい　muggy hot
◇ 蒸す	むす　steam
◇ 蒸れる	むれる　become stuffy
◇ 蒸らす	むらす　steam (rice/etc.)

⑤⑨

803 **15** 確　▶かく
▷たし(か), たし(かめる)

正確な	せいかくな　exact
確実な	かくじつな　certain
確率	かくりつ　probability
確信	かくしん　cv. believe firmly, be confident
確かな	たしかな　certain
確かめる	たしかめる　make sure

804 **15** 権　▶けん, ごん

権利	けんり　right
人権	じんけん　human rights
特権	とっけん　special privilege
権力	けんりょく　power, authority
主権	しゅけん　sovereignty
三権分立	さんけんぶんりつ　separation of powers
有権者	ゆうけんしゃ　voter
㊙ 権化	ごんげ　incarnation

805 観 18 ▶かん

観光	かんこう　sightseeing; *cv.* go sightseeing
観客	かんきゃく　spectator, audience
観点	かんてん　point of view
外観	がいかん　appearance
主観的	しゅかんてき　subjective
客観的	きゃっかんてき　objective
楽観的	らっかんてき　optimistic
悲観的	ひかんてき　pessimistic
人生観	じんせいかん　one's view of life
世界観	せかいかん　one's view of the world

806 視 11 ▶し

無視	むし　*cv.* ignore
重視	じゅうし　*cv.* attach importance to
視野	しや　range of vision, scope
視界	しかい　field of vision
視力	しりょく　eyesight, vision
近視	きんし　near-sighted
視察	しさつ　*cv.* visit to observe/inspect
◇*監視	かんし　*cv.* watch, keep a watch on

807 規 11 ▶き

規則	きそく　rule, regulation
規則的な	きそくてきな　regular
不規則な	ふきそくな　irregular
規定	きてい　rules, regulations; *cv.* prescribe, stipulate
定規	じょうぎ　ruler

| 規準 | きじゅん　criterion, standard |

808 則 9 ▶そく

規則	きそく　rule, regulation
法則	ほうそく　law
原則	げんそく　principle
変則的な	へんそくてきな　irregular
校則	こうそく　school regulations
会則	かいそく　regulations of a society

809 側 11 ▶そく ▷かわ

右側	みぎがわ　right-hand side
左側	ひだりがわ　left-hand side
反対側	はんたいがわ　opposite side
両側	りょうがわ　both sides
側面	そくめん　side
側近	そっきん　close associate

810 測 12 ▶そく ▷はか(る)

予測	よそく　*cv.* forecast, predict
観測	かんそく　*cv.* observe
測定	そくてい　*cv.* measure
測る	はかる　measure

811 例 8 ▶れい ▷たと(える)

例	れい　example
前例	ぜんれい　precedent
例外	れいがい　exception
特例	とくれい　exception
例年	れいねん　every year, average year

| 例えば | たとえば　for example |
| 例える | たとえる　liken |

⁸¹² **列** ▶れつ
6

列	れつ　row/line (of people/cars/etc.)
列車	れっしゃ　train
夜行列車	やこうれっしゃ　overnight train
日本列島	にほんれっとう　the Japanese Archipelago
◇ 行列	ぎょうれつ　line, queue; *cv.* line/queue up

⁸¹³ **殊** ▶しゅ　▷こと
10

| 特殊な | とくしゅな　special, peculiar |
| ◇ 殊に | ことに　especially, in particular |

⑥⓪

⁸¹⁴ **示** ▶じ, し　▷しめ(す)
5

指示	しじ　directions, instructions; *cv.* direct, instruct
明示	めいじ　*cv.* point out, clarify
暗示	あんじ　*cv.* suggest
公示	こうじ　*cv.* announce publicly
◇ *掲示	けいじ　notice; *cv.* put up (a notice)
◇ *掲示*板	けいじばん　bulletin board

| ◇ 示*唆 | しさ　*cv.* suggest |
| 示す | しめす　show |

⁸¹⁵ **禁** ▶きん
13

禁止	きんし　*cv.* prohibit
立入禁止	たちいりきんし　No Trespassing
発禁	はっきん　ban
禁じる	きんじる　forbid, prohibit
◇ 禁*煙	きんえん　*cv.* give up smoking; No Smoking

⁸¹⁶ **宗** ▶しゅう, そう
8

宗教	しゅうきょう　religion
改宗	かいしゅう　*cv.* be converted
特 宗家	そうけ　the head family, the originator (of a sect)

⁸¹⁷ **完** ▶かん
7

完成	かんせい　*cv.* complete
未完成の	みかんせいの　incomplete
完全な	かんぜんな　complete
完敗	かんぱい　*cv.* be totally defeated

〈漢字の形に気をつけましょう・23〉

⁷¹⁸ 敗　⁷¹⁹ 貝　⁸⁰⁸ 則　⁸⁰⁹ 側　⁸¹⁰ 測

失敗と成功　　海岸で貝を拾う　　規則を守る　　右側を歩く

水質を測定する

818 了 2 ▶りょう

終了	しゅうりょう cv. finish, complete
完了	かんりょう cv. complete
任期満了	にんきまんりょう expiration of a term of office
了解	りょうかい cv. understand, approve, consent

819 承 8 ▶しょう ▷うけたまわ(る)

承認	しょうにん cv. approve
承知	しょうち cv. be aware of, consent
◊ 了承	りょうしょう cv. acknowledge
◊ 伝承	でんしょう oral tradition; cv. transmit by word of mouth
◊ 承る	うけたまわる hear, be told (humble)

820 浮 10 ▶ふ ▷う(く), う(かれる), う(かぶ), う(かべる)

浮く	うく float
浮世絵	うきよえ ukiyoe
浮力	ふりょく buoyancy
浮気	△うわき extramarital affair
◊ 浮かぶ	うかぶ float, rise to the surface, think of
◊ 浮かべる	うかべる set afloat, appear

821 乳 8 ▶にゅう ▷ちち, ち

牛乳	ぎゅうにゅう milk
母乳	ぼにゅう mother's milk
◊ 乳首	ちくび nipple
◊ 乳母車	△うばぐるま baby carriage
◊ 乳	ちち milk

822 礼 5 ▶れい, らい 984 cf. 札

お礼	おれい gratitude, thanks
失礼な	しつれいな impolite
無礼な	ぶれいな rude
礼拝	れいはい, らいはい cv. worship
◊ 礼*儀	れいぎ etiquette, formality

823 祈 8 ▶き ▷いの(る)

祈る	いのる pray
お祈り	おいのり prayer
◊ 祈*願	きがん cv. pray

824 祖 9 ▶そ

祖父	そふ grandfather cf. お祖父さん (▲おじいさん) (polite)
祖母	そぼ grandmother cf. お祖母さん (▲おばあさん) (polite)
祖先	そせん ancestor
先祖	せんぞ ancestry

61

825 査 9 ▶さ

| 調査 | ちょうさ cv. investigate |
| 検査 | けんさ cv. examine |

826 助 7 ▶じょ ▷たす(ける), たす(かる), すけ

助ける	たすける help, assist, rescue
助かる	たすかる be helped/saved/rescued
助け合う	たすけあう help each other
助手	じょしゅ assistant
助言	じょげん cv. advise; suggestion

助力	じょりょく assistance, aid
助教授	じょきょうじゅ associate professor
◇ *援助	えんじょ *cv.* help, assist, aid
◇ 助六	すけろく name of a famous character in Kabuki drama

827 努 7 ▶ど ▷つと(める) 255 1871 cf. 怒 奴

努力	どりょく effort, endeavor; *cv.* make efforts
努力家	どりょくか hard worker
◇ 努める	つとめる exert oneself, make efforts

828 収 5 ▶しゅう ▷おさ(める), おさ(まる)

収入	しゅうにゅう income
買収	ばいしゅう *cv.* buy up, purchase, bribe
貿易収支	ぼうえきしゅうし trade balance
◇ 収*益	しゅうえき profit
◇ 収*容	しゅうよう *cv.* accomodate
◇ 収支決算	しゅうしけっさん settlement of accounts
◇ 収める	おさめる obtain (profit/good result/etc.)
◇ 収まる	おさまる settle down, calm down

829 状 7 ▶じょう

状態	じょうたい situation, state of affairs
現状	げんじょう present circumstances
招待状	しょうたいじょう invitation
お礼状	おれいじょう thank-you letter

830 将 10 ▶しょう

将来	しょうらい the future; in the future
将軍	しょうぐん shogun, general
◇ 将校	しょうこう officer
◇ 将*棋	しょうぎ *shōgi*, Japanese chess

831 奨 13 ▶しょう

奨学金	しょうがくきん scholarship
奨学生	しょうがくせい student on a scholarship
奨励	しょうれい *cv.* encourage, promote

832 励 7 ▶れい ▷はげ(む), はげ(ます)

奨励	しょうれい *cv.* encourage, promote
◇ 励行	れいこう *cv.* practice constantly
励む	はげむ do diligently
励み	はげみ encouragement
励ます	はげます encourage

833 陸 11 ▶りく

大陸	たいりく continent
陸	りく land
陸地	りくち land
上陸	じょうりく *cv.* land
陸軍	りくぐん army

834 陽 12 ▶よう

| 太陽 | たいよう the sun |
| 陽気な | ようきな cheerful |

◇ 陽光　　　　ようこう　sunshine

◇ 陽子　　　　ようし　proton

835 傷 13　　▶しょう
　　　　　　　▷きず，いた(む)，いた(める)

傷　　　　　　きず　injury, cut

無傷の　　　　むきずの　uninjured

負傷　　　　　ふしょう　*cv.* be injured, be wounded

重傷　　　　　じゅうしょう　serious injury

軽傷　　　　　けいしょう　slight injury

死傷者　　　　ししょうしゃ　casualty

傷害事件　　　しょうがいじけん　incident involving injury

◇ 中傷　　　　ちゅうしょう　*cv.* slander, slur

傷む　　　　　いたむ　be damaged, be worn out

⑥②

836 湯 12　　▶とう
　　　　　　　▷ゆ

湯　　　　　　ゆ　hot water

湯ぶね　　　　ゆぶね　bathtub

湯元　　　　　ゆもと　source of a hot spring

茶の湯　　　　ちゃのゆ　the tea ceremony

湯気　　　　　ゆげ　steam

湯飲み　　　　ゆのみ　cup (for drinking tea)

◇ *熱湯　　　　ねっとう　boiling water

◇ 湯治　　　　とうじ　hot-spring cure; *cv.* bathe in a hot spring as a remedy

837 混 11　　▶こん　　　　1859
　　　　　　　▷ま(じる)，ま(ざ る)，ま(ぜる)　cf. 昆

混雑　　　　　こんざつ　*cv.* be crowded, be congested

◇ 混*乱　　　　こんらん　*cv.* be confused, be thrown into confusion

◇ 混合　　　　こんごう　*cv.* mix

◇ 混同　　　　こんどう　*cv.* confound, confuse, mix

混ぜる　　　　まぜる　mix

かき混ぜる　　かきまぜる　mix

838 湿 12　　▶しつ
　　　　　　　▷しめ(る)，しめ(す)

湿度　　　　　しつど　humidity

湿気　　　　　しっけ　moisture, humidity

◇ 湿*布　　　　しっぷ　compress; *cv.* apply a compress

◇ 湿る　　　　しめる　become damp

839 温 12　　▶おん
　　　　　　　▷あたた(か)，あたた(かい)，あたた(まる)，あたた(める)

温度　　　　　おんど　temperature

気温　　　　　きおん　air temperature

水温　　　　　すいおん　water temperature

体温　　　　　たいおん　body temperature

温室　　　　　おんしつ　greenhouse

温和な　　　　おんわな　gentle

〈漢字の形に気をつけましょう・24〉

　　335　　834　　836　　1481　　835
　　場　　陽　　湯　　*揚　　傷

入場券　太陽と月　茶の湯　気持ちが高*揚する　重傷を負う
　　　　　　　　　　　　　こう　よう

| 温かい | あたたかい　warm　cf. 温かい is used for things warm to the touch, whereas 暖かい is used for air temperature. |
| 温める | あたためる　warm (up) something |

840　泉　9
▶せん
▷いずみ

| 温泉 | おんせん　hot spring |
| ◇ 泉 | いずみ　spring |

841　線　15
▶せん

線	せん　line
直線	ちょくせん　straight line
曲線	きょくせん　curve
下線	かせん　underline
地平線	ちへいせん　horizon
水平線	すいへいせん　horizon
線路	せんろ　railway line/track
電線	でんせん　electric wire
無線	むせん　radio, wireless
内線	ないせん　extension (of a telephone)
◇ 赤外線	せきがいせん　infrared light, infrared ray

842　雪　11
▶せつ
▷ゆき

雪	ゆき　snow
初雪	はつゆき　the first snowfall of the year
雪祭	ゆきまつり　snow festival
大雪	おおゆき　heavy snow
新雪	しんせつ　fresh snow
◇ *積雪	せきせつ　pile of snow
◇ *除雪	じょせつ　cv. remove snow
◇ 吹雪	△ふぶき　snowstorm

843　雷　13
▶らい
▷かみなり

雷	かみなり　thunder
雷雨	らいう　thunderstorm
雷鳴	らいめい　thunder
落雷	らくらい　lightning strike
◇ 地雷	じらい　(land) mine
◇ 魚雷	ぎょらい　torpedo

844　雲　12
▶うん
▷くも

雲	くも　cloud
雨雲	あまぐも　rain cloud
◇ 暗雲	あんうん　dark clouds
歴 出雲大社	▲いずもたいしゃ　Izumo Shrine

845　霧　19
▶む
▷きり

霧	きり　fog
霧雨	きりさめ　drizzle
濃霧	のうむ　dense fog

846　露　20
▶ろ, ろう
▷つゆ

露店	ろてん　street stall
◇ 露天風*呂	ろてんぶろ　open-air bath
◇ 露天	ろてん　open air
露出	ろしゅつ　exposure; *cv.* expose
◇ *暴露	ばくろ　*cv.* reveal, expose
◇ *披露*宴	ひろうえん　wedding reception
◇ 露	つゆ　dew
◇ 夜露	よつゆ　evening dew

| 847 | 震 | ▶しん | 626 |
| 15 | | ▷ふる(う), ふる(える) cf.農 | |

地震	じしん	earthquake
震度	しんど	seismic intensity
		e.g., 震度5の地震 earthquake of the 5th degree on the Japanese seismic scale
震動	しんどう	tremor, vibration
◇ 震*源	しんげん	epicenter
震える	ふるえる	tremble
震う	ふるう	shake

63

| 848 | 厚 | ▶こう |
| 9 | | ▷あつ(い) |

厚い	あつい	thick
厚かましい	あつかましい	shameless, brazenfaced
厚生省	こうせいしょう	the Ministry of Health and Welfare

| 849 | 宴 | ▶えん |
| 10 | | |

| 宴会 | えんかい | dinner party, banquet |
| ◇ 酒宴 | しゅえん | banquet |

| 850 | 宣 | ▶せん | 1658 |
| 9 | | | cf.宜 |

宣言	せんげん	cv. declare
独立宣言	どくりつせんげん	declaration of independence
宣伝	せんでん	propaganda, publicity; cv. propagate, publicize
◇ 宣教*師	せんきょうし	missionary

| 851 | 各 | ▶かく |
| 6 | | ▷おのおの |

| 世界各国 | せかいかっこく | many countries (around the world) |

各地	かくち	each area, many places
各種の	かくしゅの	every kind of, all sorts of
各自	かくじ	each person, individually
◇ 各々	おのおの	each, everyone

| 852 | 格 | ▶かく, こう |
| 10 | | |

性格	せいかく	personality
価格	かかく	price
合格	ごうかく	cv. pass (an examination)
人格	じんかく	personality, character
格好	かっこう	shape, form, figure
同格の	どうかくの	equal (in rank)
本格的な	ほんかくてきな	full-scale
◇ 格別な/の	かくべつな/の	particular, special, exceptional
◇ 格子	こうし	lattice, grille

| 853 | 資 | ▶し |
| 13 | | |

資源	しげん	resources
資本	しほん	capital
資金	しきん	funds
資格	しかく	qualification
物資	ぶっし	goods

| 854 | 源 | ▶げん |
| 13 | | ▷みなもと |

資源	しげん	resources
起源	きげん	origin
財源	ざいげん	source of revenue
歴 源氏物語	げんじものがたり	The Tale of Genji
◇ 源	みなもと	source, origin

855
貴
12
▶き
▷とうと(い), たっと(い),
　とうと(ぶ), たっと(ぶ)

貴重な　きちょうな　valuable, precious
貴重品　きちょうひん　valuables
貴族　きぞく　nobleman, the nobility
◇ 貴い　とうとい, たっとい　noble
◇ 貴ぶ　とうとぶ, たっとぶ　respect

856
賃
13
▶ちん

家賃　やちん　rent (for an apartment/house)
運賃　うんちん　fare
賃金　ちんぎん　wage
賃上げ　ちんあげ　wage hike

857
貨
11
▶か

通貨　つうか　currency
外貨　がいか　foreign currency
金貨　きんか　gold coin
貨物　かもつ　freight

858
費
12
▶ひ
▷つい(やす), つい(える)

費用　ひよう　cost, expense
経費　けいひ　cost, expense
人件費　じんけんひ　cost of labor
旅費　りょひ　traveling expenses
生活費　せいかつひ　cost of living
食費　しょくひ　food expenses
◇ 光"熱費　こうねつひ　heating and lighting expenses
◇ 費やす　ついやす　spend, waste, use up
◇ 費える　ついえる　be used up

64

859
貧
11
▶ひん, びん
▷まず(しい)

貧乏な　びんぼうな　poor
貧富の差　ひんぷのさ　disparity in wealth
◇ 貧困　ひんこん　poverty
◇ 貧弱な　ひんじゃくな　poor, scanty
貧しい　まずしい　poor

860
乏
5
▶ぼう
▷とぼ(しい)
568
cf. 芝

貧乏な　びんぼうな　poor
欠乏　けつぼう　shortage; cv. lack, run short of
◇ 乏しい　とぼしい　poor, scarce

861
額
18
▶がく
▷ひたい

額　がく　picture frame, framed picture, amount of money
金額　きんがく　amount of money
総額　そうがく　total amount
半額　はんがく　half price
差額　さがく　difference, balance
◇ 額　ひたい　forehead

862
願
19
▶がん
▷ねが(う)

お願い　おねがい　request
願う　ねがう　desire
願書　がんしょ　application (form)
志願者　しがんしゃ　applicant

863
塾
14
▶じゅく

(学習)塾　(がくしゅう)じゅく　private prep school attended after regular school hours

◇ *慶*応義塾大学　けいおうぎじゅくだいがく
　　　　　　　　　　Keio University

864
15 熟 ▶じゅく
　　　▷う(れる)

未熟な	みじゅくな	immature, inexperienced
成熟	せいじゅく	cv. mature
熟す	じゅくす	ripen
熟語	じゅくご	idiom, kanji compound

◇ 熟れる　うれる　ripen

865
13 勢 ▶せい
　　　▷いきお(い)

大勢	おおぜい	a lot of people
大勢	たいせい	general tendency
勢力	せいりょく	power, influence
情勢	じょうせい	situation
国勢調査	こくせいちょうさ	national census

◇ 勢い　いきおい　power, force

866
15 熱 ▶ねつ
　　　▷あつ(い)

熱い	あつい	hot cf. 熱い is used for things hot to the touch, whereas 暑い is used for air temperature.
熱	ねつ	heat, fever
高熱	こうねつ	high fever
熱湯	ねっとう	boiling water
情熱	じょうねつ	enthusiasm, passion
熱中	ねっちゅう	cv. be crazy about
熱心な	ねっしんな	earnest

867
9 昭 ▶しょう

| 昭和 | しょうわ | Shōwa (imperial era, 1926-1989) |

868
13 照 ▶しょう
　　　▷て(る), て(らす), て(れる)

対照的に	たいしょうてきに	in contrast
参照	さんしょう	cv. refer to
照明	しょうめい	lighting

◇ 東照宮　とうしょうぐう　Toshogu Shrine (the shrine in Nikko where the first shogun is enshrined)

| 照る | てる | shine (used for the sun) |
| 照れる | てれる | feel embarrassed |

869
15 黙 ▶もく
　　　▷だま(る)

| 黙る | だまる | become silent, say nothing |

◇ *沈黙　ちんもく　silence; cv. become/fall silent

| 黙認 | もくにん | cv. permit tacitly |

◇ 黙*秘権　もくひけん　the right of silence

◇ 黙殺　もくさつ　cv. ignore, take no notice of

870
16 燃 ▶ねん
　　　▷も(える), も(やす), も(す)

燃える	もえる	vi. burn
燃やす	もやす	vt. burn
燃料	ねんりょう	fuel

◇ 可燃性の　かねんせいの　flammable

◇ 不燃性の　ふねんせいの　nonflammable

65

871
6 灯 ▶とう
　　　▷ひ

cf. ▲燈 is the old kanji for 灯.

| 灯台 | とうだい | lighthouse |

◇ 点灯　てんとう　cv. turn a light on

◇ 灯　ひ　light

872 畑 9

▷はたけ，はた

畑	はたけ field, vegetable field, orchard
みかん畑	みかんばたけ *mikan* orchard
田畑	たはた the fields, rice paddies and vegetable fields

873 災 7

▶さい　　　　1803
▷わざわ(い)　cf. 炎

災害	さいがい disaster, accident
災難	さいなん misfortune, mishap
火災	かさい fire
天災	てんさい natural disaster
人災	じんさい disaster caused by human neglect
関東大震災	かんとうだいしんさい the great earthquake that struck the Kanto area in 1923
◊ 災い	わざわい misfortune; *cv.* cause misfortune

874 灰 6

▶かい
▷はい

灰	はい ash
◊ 灰*皿	はいざら ashtray
火山灰	かざんばい volcanic ash
灰色	はいいろ gray
◊ 石灰	せっかい chemical lime
◊ 石灰岩	せっかいがん limestone

875 炭 9

▶たん
▷すみ

石炭	せきたん coal
◊ 炭素	たんそ carbon
◊ 二*酸化炭素	にさんかたんそ carbon dioxide
◊ 炭*酸(ガス)	たんさん(ガス) carbonic acid (gas)
◊ 炭	すみ charcoal

876 鉱 13

▶こう

炭鉱	たんこう coal mine
鉱山	こうざん mine
鉱業	こうぎょう mining
◊ 鉱物	こうぶつ mineral

877 精 14

▶せい，しょう

精神	せいしん spirit, mind
◊ 精力	せいりょく energy
◊ 精子	せいし spermatozoon cf. *卵子(らんし) ovum
◊ 筆不精	ふでぶしょう someone who doesn't write letters often
◊ 精進	しょうじん *cv.* devote oneself
◊ 精進料理	しょうじんりょうり vegetarian food (served at a temple)

878 請 15

▶せい，しん
▷こ(う)，う(ける)

申請書	しんせいしょ application form (for a grant/permission/etc.)
要請	ようせい *cv.* request
◊ 下請け	したうけ subcontract
◊ 普請	ふしん construction; *cv.* build, construct
◊ 請う	こう ask for (help/assistance/etc.)

879 育 8

▶いく
▷そだ(つ)，そだ(てる)

| 教育 | きょういく education; *cv.* educate |
| 体育 | たいいく physical education |

発育	はついく growth (of an animal)
生育	せいいく growth (of a plant)
育つ	そだつ grow
育てる	そだてる bring up, raise (a child)

880 絹 13
▶けん
▷きぬ

| 絹 | きぬ silk |
| ◇ 人絹 | じんけん artificial silk |

881 綿 14
▶めん
▷わた

綿	わた, めん cotton
木綿	△もめん cotton
◇ 綿糸	めんし cotton thread
◇ 海綿	かいめん sponge
◇ 綿*密な	めんみつな detailed (plan/schedule/etc.)

882 織 18
▶しょく, しき 512
▷お(る) cf. 識

組織	そしき organization; cv. organize, set up
◇ 織物	おりもの textiles
◇ 織る	おる weave
特 織機	しょっき loom

883 編 15
▶へん
▷あ(む)

編集	へんしゅう cv. edit
編集長	へんしゅうちょう chief editor
短編小説	たんぺんしょうせつ short novel
編む	あむ knit
手編みの	てあみの hand-knit
編み物	あみもの knitting

⑥⑥

884 縮 17
▶しゅく
▷ちぢ(む), ちぢ(まる), ちぢ(める), ちぢ(れる), ちぢ(らす)

縮む	ちぢむ shrink, become short
縮める	ちぢめる shorten
◇ 縮れる	ちぢれる be frizzled, be wavy, curl
◇ 縮れ毛	ちぢれげ curly hair
縮小	しゅくしょう cv. reduce
短縮	たんしゅく cv. reduce (time)
縮図	しゅくず reduced drawing
軍縮	ぐんしゅく disarmament, arms reduction
◇ *伸縮自在	しんしゅくじざい elastic

〈漢字の形に気をつけましょう・25〉

47 281 754 877 878
青　晴　清　精　請

青春時代　今日は快晴だ　清潔なキッチン　精神的なダメージ　申請書

885 **績** ▶せき
17

成績	せいせき	results, grades, performance
成績表	せいせきひょう	school transcript, report card
業績	ぎょうせき	work, achievement, business performance
実績	じっせき	actual results
◇ 功績	こうせき	meritorious service
◇*紡績	ぼうせき	spinning

886 **積** ▶せき
16　　　▷つ(む), つ(もる)

積む	つむ	load, pile up
積もる	つもる	accumulate (as in snow/dust/etc.)
積極的な	せっきょくてきな	positive (attitude/etc.), active 反消極的な(しょうきょくてきな) negative (attitude/etc.), passive
面積	めんせき	area, square measure
体積	たいせき	volume, capacity, cubic measure
◇*容積	ようせき	volume, capacity
◇ 見積(も)り	みつもり	estimate

887 **布** ▶ふ
5　　　▷ぬの

毛布	もうふ	blanket
布	ぬの	cloth
分布	ぶんぷ	cv.vi. distribute

| 配布 | はいふ | cv.vt. distribute |
| 公布 | こうふ | cv. promulgate, make public |

888 **希** ▶き
7

| 希望 | きぼう | hope, wish; cv. hope, wish |
| 希少価値 | きしょうかち | scarcity value |

889 **衣** ▶い
6　　　▷ころも

衣食住	いしょくじゅう	food, clothing, and shelter
衣類	いるい	clothing
◇ 法衣	ほうい	vestment, clerical dress, canonicals
◇ 衣	ころも	clothes, robe, gown

890 **依** ▶い, え
8

依存	いそん, いぞん	cv. depend on
依頼	いらい	cv. request
◇ 依然として	いぜんとして	still, as ever
特 帰依	きえ	cv. become a believer (in a religion)

891 **報** ▶ほう
12　　　▷むく(いる)　　cf. 執 1823

報告	ほうこく	cv. report
天気予報	てんきよほう	weather forecast
情報	じょうほう	information

〈漢字の形に気をつけましょう・26〉

| 638 | 885 | 886 | 1249 | 1506 |
| 責 | 績 | 積 | *債 | *漬 |

責任を果たす　テストの成績　積極的に仕事をする　*債権　*漬物
　　　　　　　　　　　　　　　　　　　　　　さいけん　つけもの

143

電報	でんぽう telegram
報道機関	ほうどうきかん the news media, the press
報道	ほうどう news, information, report; *cv.* inform, report
◇ 報復	ほうふく retaliation; *cv.* retaliate
◇ 報*酬	ほうしゅう reward, remuneration
◇ 報い	むくい reward
◇ 報いる	むくいる reward

892
7 告 ▶こく ▷つ(げる)

報告	ほうこく *cv.* report
告白	こくはく *cv.* confess
◇ 告*訴	こくそ *cv.* enter a complaint, take legal action
◇ 告発	こくはつ *cv.* indict, prosecute, charge (a person for a crime), accuse
◇ 申告	しんこく *cv.* declare
◇ 告げる	つげる tell, anounce

893
6 吉 ▶きち, きつ

吉日	きちじつ, きつじつ lucky day
◇ 吉報	きっぽう good news
◇ 不吉な	ふきつな ill-omened, ominous, unlucky
◇ 吉田	▲よしだ (surname)

- -

⑥⑦

894
8 幸 ▶こう ▷さいわ(い), さち, しあわ(せ)

幸福	こうふく happiness
不幸	ふこう misery, unhappiness
幸運	こううん good fortune
幸せ	しあわせ happiness

幸	さち happiness, fortune
◇ 海の幸	うみのさち products of the sea
◇ 幸い	さいわい fortunately; happiness, good luck/fortune; *cv.* cause good fortune

895
13 福 ▶ふく

幸福	こうふく happiness
福祉	ふくし welfare, well-being
◇ *祝福	しゅくふく blessing; *cv.* bless
◇ 福音書	ふくいんしょ the Gospels

896
8 祉 ▶し

福祉	ふくし welfare, well-being
社会福祉	しゃかいふくし social/public welfare
福祉国家	ふくしこっか welfare state

897
12 幅 ▶ふく ▷はば

幅	はば width
大幅な	おおはばな big (fall/raise/cut/etc.)
◇ 振幅	しんぷく amplitude (of a swing)

898
11 副 ▶ふく

副社長	ふくしゃちょう vice president (of a company)
副業	ふくぎょう side business
副産物	ふくさんぶつ by-product
副作用	ふくさよう side effect
副題	ふくだい subtitle

899 判 7 ▶はん，ばん

判断	はんだん	cv. judge
◇*裁判	さいばん	trial, hearing
判事	はんじ	judge
判決	はんけつ	judgment, judicial decision
公判	こうはん	trial, hearing
◇ 判明	はんめい	cv. become clear, be ascertained
判(子)	はん(こ)	seal

900 断 11 ▶だん ▷た(つ)，ことわ(る)

判断	はんだん	cv. judge
決断	けつだん	cv. decide/determine (to do something)
油断	ゆだん	cv. be careless, be off one's guard
断定	だんてい	cv. conclude
横断歩道	おうだんほどう	pedestrian crossing
横断	おうだん	cv. cross, go across
断水	だんすい	stoppage of the water supply; cv. the water supply is cut off
◇ 断*念	だんねん	cv. give up
断る	ことわる	decline, refuse, give notice
◇ 断つ	たつ	cut off

901 継 13 ▶けい ▷つ(ぐ)

継続	けいぞく	cv. continue
後継者	こうけいしゃ	successor
衛星中継	えいせいちゅうけい	satellite broadcasting
継ぐ	つぐ	inherit, succeed to
受け継ぐ	うけつぐ	succeed, take over (another's business/etc.)

902 繰 19 ▷く(る)

繰り返す	くりかえす	repeat
引っ繰り返す	ひっくりかえす	turn upside down, overturn, upset, tip over
引っ繰り返る	ひっくりかえる	topple over, fall on one's back, be upset

903 燥 17 ▶そう

1485
cf. 操

乾燥	かんそう	cv. dry up, dry out
乾燥機	かんそうき	clothes dryer
◇ 乾燥地*帯	かんそうちたい	dry area

904 乾 11 ▶かん ▷かわ(く)，かわ(かす)

乾燥	かんそう	cv. dry up, dry out
乾電池	かんでんち	dry cell batery
◇ 乾*杯	かんぱい	cv. drink a toast; "Cheers!"
乾く	かわく	become dry, dry out

905 江 6 ▶こう ▷え

江戸	えど	Edo (the old name for Tokyo)
入り江	いりえ	inlet
◇ 江ノ島	えのしま	Enoshima (an island near Kamakura)
◇*揚子江	ようすこう	the Yangtze River

906 液 11 ▶えき

液体	えきたい	liquid cf. 固体(こたい) solid, 気体(きたい) gas
液化	えきか	cv. liquefy
◇▲唾液	だえき	saliva

907 汚 6

▶お
▷けが(す)，けが(れる)，けが(らわしい)，よご(す)，よご(れる)，きたな(い)

汚染	おせん	cv. pollute, contaminate
大気汚染	たいきおせん	air pollution
汚職	おしょく	corruption
◇ 汚名	おめい	stigma, dishonor
◇ 汚点	おてん	stain
汚い	きたない	dirty
汚す	よごす	stain, taint, dirty
汚れる	よごれる	get dirty, become soiled, be polluted/contaminated
◇ 汚す	けがす	dishonor, disgrace
◇ 汚れた	けがれた	filthy, impure

908 染 9

▶せん
▷そ(める)，そ(まる)，し(みる)，し(み)

汚染	おせん	cv. pollute, contaminate
大気汚染	たいきおせん	air pollution
伝染病	でんせんびょう	contagious disease
感染	かんせん	cv. be infected
◇ 染色	せんしょく	cv. dye
染める	そめる	dye
染み	しみ	stain
染みる	しみる	permeate, stain, soak into

909 港 12

▶こう
▷みなと

空港	くうこう	airport
◇ 横*浜港	よこはまこう	the port of Yokohama
港	みなと	harbor, port

910 湾 12

▶わん

港町	みなとまち	port town
東京湾	とうきょうわん	Tokyo Bay
湾	わん	bay, gulf
◇ 台湾	たいわん	Taiwan

911 浜 10

▶ひん
▷はま

横浜	よこはま	Yokohama (port city near Tokyo)
◇ 浜*辺	はまべ	beach, seashore
◇ 海浜公園	かいひんこうえん	seashore park

912 沖 7

▶ちゅう
▷おき

| 沖 | おき | offshore, open sea |
| ◇ 沖積*層 | ちゅうせきそう | alluvial bed |

913 波 8

▶は
▷なみ

波	なみ	wave
電波	でんぱ	radio wave
短波	たんぱ	shortwave (radio), short wavelength
波長	はちょう	wavelength

914 漁 14

▶ぎょ，りょう

漁業	ぎょぎょう	fishing industry
漁船	ぎょせん	fishing boat
漁村	ぎょそん	fishing village
漁場	ぎょじょう	fishing ground/spot
漁民	ぎょみん	fishermen
漁	りょう	fishing
◇ 漁*師	りょうし	fisherman

915 鯨 19	▶げい ▷くじら		
	鯨	くじら	whale
◇	鯨油	げいゆ	whale oil
◇	鯨肉	げいにく	whale meat
◇	白鯨	はくげい	*Moby Dick*
◇	*捕鯨船	ほげいせん	whaler

916 鮮 17	▶せん ▷あざ(やか)		
	新鮮な	しんせんな	fresh
	鮮魚	せんぎょ	fresh fish
	鮮度	せんど	freshness
	鮮明な	せんめいな	clear, distinct
◇	朝鮮半島	ちょうせんはんとう	the Korean Peninsula
	鮮やかな	あざやかな	vivid, bright, brilliant

917 洋 9	▶よう		
	太平洋	たいへいよう	the Pacific Ocean
	大西洋	たいせいよう	the Atlantic Ocean
	海洋	かいよう	ocean
	西洋	せいよう	the West
	東洋	とうよう	the East
	洋書	ようしょ	foreign/Western book

⑥⑨

918 卸 9	▷おろ(す)，おろし		
	卸売(り)	おろしうり	wholesale
	卸値	おろしね	wholesale price
	卸売物価	おろしうりぶっか	wholesale prices
	卸す	おろす	sell wholesale

919 御 12	▶ぎょ，ご ▷おん		
	御飯	ごはん	(cooked) rice, meal
	京都御所	きょうとごしょ	Kyoto Imperial Palace
◇	御礼	おんれい	gratitude, thanks
◇	制御	せいぎょ	*cv.* control

920 缶 6	▶かん		
	空き缶	あきかん	empty can
	缶ビール	かんビール	canned beer

921 益 10	▶えき，やく		
	利益	りえき	profit
	収益	しゅうえき	profit
	有益な	ゆうえきな	useful
	無益な	むえきな	useless, futile
	公益	こうえき	the public interest/good
◇	公益法人	こうえきほうじん	nonprofit organization, public corporation
◇	ご利益	ごりやく	divine assistance

922 盛 11	▶せい，じょう ▷も(る)，さか(ん)，さか(る)		
	盛大な	せいだいな	grand, magnificent
◇	*繁盛	はんじょう	*cv.* prosper, flourish
◇	盛り*込む	もりこむ	include
◇	盛る	もる	heap up, fill up (a bowl with rice)
◇	盛んな	さかんな	prosperous, energetic
◇	花盛り	はなざかり	in full bloom, at its best

147

923 13 ▶めい

同盟国	どうめいこく	allied nations
国際連盟	こくさいれんめい	the League of Nations
連盟	れんめい	league
加盟	かめい	cv. join (a league/federation/etc.)
◇ 盟主	めいしゅ	leader of a league/federation/etc.
◇ 盟約	めいやく	pledge

 924 13 ▶えん ▷しお

塩	しお	salt
塩分	えんぶん	salt content
食塩	しょくえん	table salt
塩水	しおみず, えんすい	salt water, brine

925 監 15 ▶かん

監督	かんとく	(film) director, manager (of a team); cv. supervise
監視	かんし	cv. watch, keep a watch on
◇ 監禁	かんきん	cv. imprison, confine
◇ 監査	かんさ	inspection; cv. inspect

 926 13 ▶とく

監督	かんとく	(film) director, manager (of a team); cv. supervise
◇ 督*促	とくそく	cv. demand/urge payment of a debt
◇ 家督	かとく	headship of a family

927 皿 5 ▷さら

皿	さら	plate, dish, saucer
皿洗い	さらあらい	dishwashing
灰皿	はいざら	ashtray

928 血 6 ▶けつ ▷ち

血	ち	blood
血液	けつえき	blood
血管	けっかん	blood vessel
出血	しゅっけつ	cv. bleed
輸血	ゆけつ	cv. give a blood transfusion
◇ 血*圧	けつあつ	blood pressure
◇ 高血*圧	こうけつあつ	high blood pressure
◇ *献血	けんけつ	cv. donate/give blood
◇ 流血	りゅうけつ	bloodshed

⑦⓪

 929 10 ▶きゅう, ぐう, く ▷みや

明治神宮	めいじじんぐう	Meiji Shrine
◇ 宮*殿	きゅうでん	palace cf. バッキンガム宮殿, ベルサイユ宮殿
◇ 子宮	しきゅう	uterus, womb
◇ お宮参り	おみやまいり	visit to a shrine
◇ 宮内庁	くないちょう	the Imperial Household Agency

930 営 12 ▶えい ▷いとな(む)

経営	けいえい	management; cv. manage, run
経営者	けいえいしゃ	manager
運営	うんえい	cv. manage, operate

営業　　　えいぎょう　business; *cv.* conduct business

◇ 非営利団体　ひえいりだんたい　nonprofit organization

◇ 公営ギャンブル　こうえいギャンブル　publicly operated gambling

◇ 営む　　　いとなむ　operate

931 辞 13　▶じ　▷や(める)

辞書　　　じしょ　dictionary

辞職　　　じしょく　*cv.* resign (from a job)

辞表　　　じひょう　letter of resignation

お世辞　　おせじ　flattery

辞める　　やめる　resign

932 乱 7　▶らん　▷みだ(れる)，みだ(す)

混乱　　　こんらん　*cv.* be confused, be thrown into confusion

反乱　　　はんらん　rebellion

内乱　　　ないらん　civil war

◇ 乱　　　らん　rebellion

◇ 乱筆　　らんぴつ　hasty handwriting

◇ 乱れる　みだれる　go out of order, be confused

933 求 7　▶きゅう　▷もと(める)

要求　　　ようきゅう　*cv.* demand, request

請求　　　せいきゅう　*cv.* claim, bill

求人　　　きゅうじん　help wanted (ad), job vacancy

求職　　　きゅうしょく　*cv.* look for a job

◇ 探求　　たんきゅう　*cv.* search for, pursue

求める　　もとめる　demand, request, seek

934 救 11　▶きゅう　▷すく(う)

救急車　　きゅうきゅうしゃ　ambulance

救助　　　きゅうじょ　*cv.* rescue

◇ 救*命具　きゅうめいぐ　life preserver

救う　　　すくう　help, rescue

935 球 11　▶きゅう　▷たま

野球　　　やきゅう　baseball

(野)球場　(や)きゅうじょう　baseball stadium

地球　　　ちきゅう　the earth

電球　　　でんきゅう　electric bulb

気球　　　ききゅう　balloon

◇ 球　　　たま　ball

936 儀 15　▶ぎ

礼儀　　　れいぎ　courtesy, decorum

礼儀正しい　れいぎただしい　courteous, polite

行儀　　　ぎょうぎ　manners

儀式　　　ぎしき　ceremony

地球儀　　ちきゅうぎ　(terrestrial) globe

937 犠 17　▶ぎ

犠牲　　　ぎせい　sacrifice, victim

犠牲者　　ぎせいしゃ　victim

938 牲 9　▶せい

犠牲　　　ぎせい　sacrifice, victim

犠牲者　　ぎせいしゃ　victim

939 象 12 ▶しょう, ぞう ⑦

対象	たいしょう subject (of investigation), object (of study), target (of criticism)
現象	げんしょう phenomenon
気象庁	きしょうちょう the Meteorological Agency
◇ 気象学	きしょうがく meteorology
象	ぞう elephant

940 像 14 ▶ぞう

想像	そうぞう cv. imagine
現像	げんぞう (film) development; cv. develop (a film)
映像	えいぞう picture, image
仏像	ぶつぞう statue/image of Buddha
自画像	じがぞう self-portrait

941 免 8 ▶めん
▷まぬか(れる)

免許	めんきょ permission, license
免税	めんぜい tax exemption; cv. make (a product/etc.) exempt from tax
免税店	めんぜいてん duty-free shop
◇ 免れる	まぬかれる exempt

942 城 9 ▶じょう
▷しろ

城	しろ castle
江戸城	えどじょう Edo Castle
城下町	じょうかまち castle town
歴 城主	じょうしゅ castle lord

943 誠 13 ▶せい
▷まこと

誠実な	せいじつな sincere
誠意	せいい sincerity
◇ 誠に	まことに truly

944 詳 13 ▶しょう
▷くわ(しい)

詳しい	くわしい detailed
詳細な	しょうさいな detailed
◇ 詳報	しょうほう detailed report

945 詩 13 ▶し

詩	し poetry, poem
詩人	しじん poet
詩集	ししゅう collection of poems
漢詩	かんし Chinese poem/poetry
◇ 詩歌	△しいか, しか poetry

946 討 10 ▶とう
▷う(つ)

討論	とうろん debate, discussion; cv.vi. debate, discuss
検討	けんとう cv. examine, consider
◇ 討議	とうぎ discussion, deliberation; cv.vi. discuss, deliberate, hold a discussion
◇ 討つ	うつ attack, defeat

947 謝 17 ▶しゃ
▷あやま(る)

謝る	あやまる apologize
感謝	かんしゃ cv. thank
◇ 謝*罪	しゃざい cv. apologize
◇ 謝礼	しゃれい remuneration, honorarium

◇ 新*陳代謝　しんちんたいしゃ　metabolism; *cv.* metabolize

948 評 12　▶ひょう

評判　　ひょうばん　reputation

評価　　ひょうか　*cv.* evaluate, appraise

◇ *批評　ひひょう　criticism; *cv.* criticize

◇ 論評　ろんぴょう　comment, criticism; *cv.* comment, criticize

◇ 書評　しょひょう　book review

949 誤 14　▶ご　⑦2 1329 1929
▷あやま(る)　cf. 娯呉

誤解　　ごかい　*cv.* misunderstand

◇ 誤報　ごほう　erroneous report/information

◇ 誤算　ごさん　miscalculation; *cv.* miscalculate

◇ 誤植　ごしょく　misprint

誤り　　あやまり　mistake, error

見誤る　みあやまる　fail to recognize, mistake (for someone/something else)

950 誇 13　▶こ
▷ほこ(る)

誇大広告　こだいこうこく　exaggerated advertisement

◇ 誇*張　こちょう　*cv.* exaggerate, overstate

誇り　　ほこり　pride

951 訓 10　▶くん

訓練　　くんれん　training; *cv. vt.* train

教訓　　きょうくん　teachings, precept, lesson, moral

訓読み　くんよみ　Japanese reading of a *kanji*

952 順 12　▶じゅん

順番　　じゅんばん　order, turn

順位　　じゅんい　ranking, standing

順序　　じゅんじょ　order, procedure

順　　　じゅん　order, sequence

道順　　みちじゅん　route, course

順調な　じゅんちょうな　smooth, favorable, satisfactory

◇ 順(々)に　じゅん(じゅん)に　in order, by turns

953 序 7　▶じょ

順序　　じゅんじょ　order, procedure

秩序　　ちつじょ　(public/world/etc.) order

序列　　じょれつ　ranking, grade

年功序列　ねんこうじょれつ　seniority system

序文　　じょぶん　preface, foreword

序論　　じょろん　introduction, first chapter (of a book/article/etc.)

◇ 序曲　じょきょく　overture, prelude

954 秩 10　▶ちつ

秩序　　ちつじょ　(public/world/etc.) order

955 矛 5　▶む
▷ほこ

矛盾　　むじゅん　contradiction

◇ 矛先　ほこさき　spearhead, aim of an attack

特 矛　　ほこ　halberd

956 盾 9

▶じゅん
▷たて

矛盾	むじゅん contradiction
矛盾した	むじゅんした contradictory
矛盾している	むじゅんしている be contradictory
◇ 後ろ盾	うしろだて supporter, backer, support, backing
◇ 盾	たて shield

957 掃 11

▶そう
▷は(く)

掃除	そうじ *cv.* clean
一掃	いっそう *cv.* sweep away, stamp out
掃く	はく sweep

958 除 10

▶じょ, じ
▷のぞ(く)

掃除	そうじ *cv.* clean
取り除く	とりのぞく remove
免除	めんじょ *cv.vt.* exempt
除外	じょがい *cv.* exclude
除名	じょめい *cv.* expel (from a club), remove a name from a list
解除	かいじょ *cv.* lift (a ban/siege/ etc.)

959 余 7

▶よ
▷あま(る)

余る	あまる be left over
余り	あまり remainder, surplus
余分な	よぶんな surplus, remaining
余計な	よけいな unwanted, uncalled-for
余地	よち room (for doubt/discussion/etc.)
余波	よは aftereffect, aftermath
◇ 余*裕	よゆう leeway, spare (time/money/etc.)
◇ 余*命	よめい rest of one's life, one's remaining days

73

960 途 10

▶と

途中	とちゅう on the way, midway
中途半端な	ちゅうとはんぱな incomplete, halfway
開発途上国	かいはつとじょうこく developing countries
前途	ぜんと one's future
途絶える	とだえる stop, cease
◇ ～した途端に	～したとたんに just as, the moment that

961 込 5

▷こ(む), こ(める)

込む	こむ be crowded cf. 混む may also be used.
飛び込む	とびこむ dive, plunge into
引っ込む	ひっこむ retire, withdraw
申し込む	もうしこむ apply

〈漢字の形に気をつけましょう・27〉

403	953	955	1310
予	序	矛	*柔

予約する　順序　矛盾　*柔道
　　　　　　　　　　　じゅうどう

払い込む　はらいこむ　pay (into an account)

申(し)込み　もうしこみ　application

人込み　ひとごみ　crowd, throng, crowded place

見込み　みこみ　prospects, outlook, estimate

込める　こめる　load (a gun), include

962 辺 5　▶へん　▷あた(り)，べ

この辺り　このあたり　this neighborhood, around here

この辺　このへん　this neighborhood, around here

近辺　きんぺん　neighborhood, vicinity

周辺　しゅうへん　environs, periphery

底辺　ていへん　base, bottom

海辺　うみべ　beach, seashore

水辺　みずべ　shore

◇ 辺*境地　へんきょうち　frontier

963 述 8　▶じゅつ　▷の(べる)

述べる　のべる　state

記述　きじゅつ　cv. describe

口述試験　こうじゅつしけん　oral examination

◇ 述語　じゅつご　predicate

◇ 上述の　じょうじゅつの　above-mentioned

964 迫 8　▶はく　▷せま(る)

迫る　せまる　press someone to do something, approach

迫力　はくりょく　force, power, impressiveness

迫害　はくがい　cv. persecute

切迫した　せっぱくした　pressing, imminent

965 造 10　▶ぞう　▷つく(る)

造船　ぞうせん　shipbuilding

製造　せいぞう　cv. manufacture

製造業　せいぞうぎょう　manufacturing

改造　かいぞう　cv. remodel

木造の　もくぞうの　wooden

人造湖　じんぞうこ　manmade lake

造る　つくる　make, build

966 追 9　▶つい　▷お(う)

追いかける　おいかける　chase, pursue

追いつく　おいつく　catch up with, overtake

◇ 追い*越す　おいこす　pass, get ahead of, outstrip

追う　おう　chase, pursue, drive away

追い風　おいかぜ　tail wind

追加　ついか　cv. add, supplement

〈漢字の形に気をつけましょう・28〉

134　597　957
帰　婦　掃

家に帰る　夫婦　掃除をする

| 追求 | ついきゅう *cv.* pursue |
| 追放 | ついほう *cv.* drive away, banish, purge |

967 師 10
▶し

教師	きょうし teacher
家庭教師	かていきょうし home tutor
医師	いし doctor
◇ 師*匠	ししょう master (in contrast to disciples)
◇ 師走	△しわす December

968 桜 10
▶おう
▷さくら
1887
cf. 楼

桜	さくら cherry tree
◇ 八重桜	やえざくら double-flowered cherry tree
◇ 桜花	おうか cherry blossoms

969 梅 10
▶ばい
▷うめ

梅	うめ *ume*, Japanese apricot
梅酒	うめしゅ *ume* wine
梅干(し)	うめぼし pickled *ume*
◇ 白梅	はくばい *ume* tree with white blossoms
◇ *紅梅	こうばい *ume* tree with pink blossoms
梅園	ばいえん *ume* tree orchard
梅雨	△つゆ, ばいう rainy season (in June)
梅雨前線	ばいうぜんせん warm front of early summer rain

970 松 8
▶しょう
▷まつ

松	まつ pine tree
松林	まつばやし pine woods
◇ 松島	まつしま Matsushima (scenic coastal area near Sendai)
◇ 松竹梅	しょうちくばい pine, bamboo, and *ume* (typical decorations at a celebration)

971 桃 10
▶とう
▷もも

桃	もも peach tree
桃色	ももいろ pink
特 桜桃	おうとう cherry
特 桃源*郷	とうげんきょう paradise

⑦④

972 枝 8
▶し
▷えだ

枝	えだ branch
小枝	こえだ twig
枝葉	えだは branches and leaves, small details
◇ 枝葉末節	しようまっせつ small details

973 株 10
▷かぶ

株式会社	かぶしきがいしゃ joint-stock corporation
株式	かぶしき stock, share
株券	かぶけん stock certificate
株主	かぶぬし stockholder
株主総会	かぶぬしそうかい stockholders' meeting
株	かぶ stock, share, tree stump
切り株	きりかぶ tree stump, (grain) stubble

974 根 10 ▶こん ▷ね

屋根	やね	roof
根	ね	root
根強い	ねづよい	deep-rooted
大根	だいこん	Japanese radish
根本的な	こんぽんてきな	fundamental, thorough
根気	こんき	perseverance, patience

975 限 9 ▶げん ▷かぎ(る)

制限	せいげん	cv. restrict, limit
限度	げんど	limit, limitation (quantity)
限界	げんかい	limit, limitation (ability/capacity/etc.)
期限	きげん	deadline, time limit
権限	けんげん	authority, competence
無限の	むげんの	unlimited, endless, infinite
◊ 有限の	ゆうげんの	limited, finite
限る	かぎる	limit

976 眼 11 ▶がん, げん ▷まなこ

主眼	しゅがん	chief aim, main purpose
◊ 眼球	がんきゅう	eyeball
特 開眼	かいげん	cv. be spiritually enlightened, be initiated into the mysteries of an art
特 眼	まなこ	eye
◊ 血眼になって	ちまなこになって	frantically

977 睡 13 ▶すい

睡眠	すいみん	sleep
睡眠不足	すいみんぶそく	lack of sleep
熟睡	じゅくすい	cv. have a sound/deep sleep

978 眠 10 ▶みん ▷ねむ(る), ねむ(い)

睡眠	すいみん	sleep
◊ 安眠	あんみん	cv. have a good/sound sleep
◊ 冬眠	とうみん	cv. hibernate
◊ 不眠*症	ふみんしょう	insomnia
眠る	ねむる	sleep
居眠り	いねむり	doze, nap
眠い	ねむい	sleepy

979 瞬 18 ▶しゅん ▷またた(く)

瞬間	しゅんかん	moment
瞬時に	しゅんじに	instantaneously
◊ 一瞬	いっしゅん	momentarily
◊ 瞬き	またたき	twinkling cf. 輝き(かがやき) glittering

980 隣 16 ▶りん ▷とな(る), となり

隣の	となりの	neighboring
隣人	りんじん	neighbor
◊ 隣国	りんごく	neighboring country
◊ 近隣*諸国	きんりんしょこく	neighboring countries
◊ 隣り合う	となりあう	be next door to each other, adjacent, adjoining

981 舞 15 ▶ぶ ▷ま(う), まい

舞台	ぶたい	stage
お見舞い	おみまい	inquiry after a person's health

◇ 見舞う　　みまう　inquire after a person's health

◇ 舞う　　まう　dance

◇ 舞　　まい　dancing

- -

名札　　なふだ　name tag

982 **枚** ▶まい
8　　　　　　1273
　　　　　　cf. 牧 ⑦⑤

～枚　　～まい　(counter for thin, flat objects)

枚数　　まいすう　number of sheets (of paper/etc.)

985 **析** ▶せき
8

分析　　ぶんせき　cv. analyze

◇ 解析　　かいせき　cv. analyze (used in mathematics)

◇ 析出　　せきしゅつ　cv. educe, extract

983 **杯** ▶はい
8　　　▷さかずき

～杯　　～はい/ぱい/ばい　～ glass/cup of　cf. 1杯(いっぱい), 2杯(にはい), 3杯(さんばい)

乾杯　　かんぱい　cv. drink a toast; "Cheers!"

◇*祝杯　　しゅくはい　toast

◇ 杯　　さかずき　sake cup, goblet

986 **核** ▶かく
10

核戦争　　かくせんそう　nuclear war

核エネルギー　かくエネルギー　nuclear energy

核燃料　　かくねんりょう　nuclear fuel

◇ 核*兵器　　かくへいき　nuclear weapons

◇ 核*廃*棄物　かくはいきぶつ　nuclear waste

◇ 原子核　　げんしかく　(atomic) nucleus

◇ 核　　かく　nucleus, core

核家族　　かくかぞく　nuclear family

核心　　かくしん　core, kernel

結核　　けっかく　tuberculosis

984 **札** ▶さつ
5　　　▷ふだ　　822
　　　　　　cf. 礼

千円札　　せんえんさつ　1,000-yen bill

札　　さつ　paper money, bill, slip of paper

札束　　さつたば　roll of bills

改札口　　かいさつぐち　ticket gate

表札　　ひょうさつ　nameplate (of a house)

◇*競争入札　きょうそうにゅうさつ　public tender, competitive bidding

987 **板** ▶はん, ばん
8　　　▷いた　　605
　　　　　　cf. 坂

黒板　　こくばん　blackboard

板　　いた　board

◇ 合板　　ごうはん, ごうばん　plywood

◇*甲板　　かんぱん　deck (of a ship)

┌─〈漢字の形に気をつけましょう・29〉────

822　　984　　1881
礼　　札　　*孔

お礼を言う　　千円札　　鼻*孔
　　　　　　　　　　び　こう

156

988 棒 12	▶ぼう	
	鉄棒	てつぼう iron bar/rod, horizontal bar
	棒	ぼう stick, rod, club
◇	棒グラフ	ぼうグラフ bar graph

989 柄 9	▶へい ▷がら，え	
	柄	がら pattern, design
	人柄	ひとがら character, personality
◇	家柄	いえがら social standing of a family
	横柄な	おうへいな arrogant
◇	柄	え handle, grip

990 柱 9	▶ちゅう ▷はしら	
	電柱	でんちゅう telephone/utility pole
	柱	はしら pillar
	大黒柱	だいこくばしら the main pillar (of a house), breadwinner for a family

991 構 14	▶こう ▷かま(える)，かま(う)	
	構造	こうぞう structure
	構成	こうせい composition, organization; cv. form, compose
	構想	こうそう cv. plan, plot
	機構	きこう organization
	心構え	こころがまえ mental attitude, mental readiness
	構える	かまえる set up (an office/store/etc.)
	構う	かまう mind, care about

992 再 6	▶さい，さ ▷ふたた(び)	
	再婚	さいこん cv. remarry
	再会	さいかい cv. meet again
	再開	さいかい cv. reopen, resume
	再編成	さいへんせい cv. reorganize, restructure
◇	再三	さいさん many times
	再来週	さらいしゅう the week after next
	再び	ふたたび again

993 黄 11	▶こう，おう ▷き，こ	
	黄色	きいろ yellow
	黄身	きみ egg yolk
◇	黄*河	こうが Hwang Ho, the Yellow River
◇	黄熱病	おうねつびょう yellow fever
◇	*硫黄	△いおう sulfur
◇	黄金	おうごん，こがね gold

994 兵 7	▶へい，ひょう	
	核兵器	かくへいき nuclear weapon
	兵器	へいき weapon
	兵士	へいし soldier
	兵役	へいえき military service
歴	兵*糧	ひょうろう (military) provisions

995 靴 13	▶か ▷くつ	
	靴	くつ shoes
	靴屋	くつや shoe store
	革靴	かわぐつ leather shoes

靴下	くつした	socks
特 軍靴	ぐんか	army boots

996 革 9
▶かく
▷かわ

革命	かくめい	revolution
革新	かくしん	cv. reform, renovate
技術革新	ぎじゅつかくしん	technological innovation
改革	かいかく	cv. reform, reorganize
変革	へんかく	cv. reform, innovate
◇*皮革製品	ひかくせいひん	leather goods
革	かわ	leather

997 命 8
▶めい, みょう
▷いのち

革命	かくめい	revolution
生命	せいめい	life
生命保険	せいめいほけん	life insurance
◇ 人命	じんめい	life
運命	うんめい	fate
使命	しめい	mission
任命	にんめい	cv. appoint, nominate
命令	めいれい	order; cv.vi. order, give orders
◇*寿命	じゅみょう	life span
命	いのち	life

998 令 5
▶れい

命令	めいれい	order; cv.vi. order, give orders
法令	ほうれい	law
政令	せいれい	government/cabinet ordinance

999 領 14
▶りょう

大統領	だいとうりょう	president (of a country)
領事	りょうじ	consul
総領事	そうりょうじ	consul general
領土	りょうど	territory (of a nation)
◇ 領地	りょうち	feudal estate
◇ 領主	りょうしゅ	feudal lord
領収書	りょうしゅうしょ	receipt
要領	ようりょう	point, gist, knack
◇ 横領	おうりょう	cv. usurp, misappropriate, embezzle

1000 統 12
▶とう
▷す(べる)
735
cf. 総

大統領	だいとうりょう	president (of a country)
統治	とうち	cv. reign, rule
統制経済	とうせいけいざい	controlled economy
統一	とういつ	cv. unify
統合	とうごう	cv. unite, combine, put together
伝統	でんとう	tradition
統計	とうけい	statistics
特 統べる	すべる	govern

1001 補 12
▶ほ
▷おぎな(う)
1049
cf. 捕

補助金	ほじょきん	subsidy
補助	ほじょ	cv. assist, help
補給	ほきゅう	cv. supply, replenish
補習	ほしゅう	supplementary class/lesson
補正	ほせい	revised/supplementary (budget/etc.); cv. revise, supplement (a budget/etc.)

◇ 補*充　　ほじゅう　cv. fill a vacancy, replenish, supplement

補う　　おぎなう　make up for, supplement, complement

1002 佐 ▶さ
7

補佐官　ほさかん　(presidential) aide

補佐　　ほさ　assistant aide; cv. assist, aid

◇ 大佐　たいさ　colonel

歴 佐*幕　さばく　supporting the Shogunate government

1003 臣 ▶しん，じん
7

大臣　　だいじん　(government) minister

総理大臣　そうりだいじん　prime minister

歴 臣民　しんみん　subjects (in contrast to royalty)

⑦⑦

1004 巨 ▶きょ
5

巨大な　きょだいな　gigantic

◇ 巨人　きょじん　giant, Yomiuri Giants (a professional baseball team)

1005 拒 ▶きょ
8　　　▷こば(む)

拒否　　きょひ　cv. reject, veto

◇ 拒絶　きょぜつ　cv. refuse, reject

◇ 拒む　こばむ　refuse, decline

1006 否 ▶ひ
7　　　▷いな

否定　　ひてい　cv. deny, negate

否認　　ひにん　cv. deny, repudiate

否決　　ひけつ　cv. vote down, reject

賛否　　さんぴ　approval or disapproval, yes or no

◇ 否めない　いなめない　undeniable

1007 距 ▶きょ
12

距離　　きょり　distance

1008 離 ▶り
19　　　▷はな(れる)，はな(す)

距離　　きょり　distance

離婚　　りこん　cv. get divorced

離陸　　りりく　cv. take off (from the ground)

◇ 離反　りはん　cv. secede, break away from

離れる　はなれる　be separated/apart

切り離す　きりはなす　cut off, sever

1009 推 ▶すい
11　　　▷お(す)

推理小説　すいりしょうせつ　detective story

推理　　すいり　cv. reason, deduct, detect

推論　　すいろん　cv. reason, infer, induce, deduce

推測　　すいそく　cv. surmise, suppose

推定　　すいてい　cv. presume, assume, infer

類推　　るいすい　cv. analogize

推進　　すいしん　cv. promote, propel, push forward

◇ 推し量る　おしはかる　guess, conjecture

1010 哲 ▶てつ
10

哲学　　てつがく　philosophy

哲学者　てつがくしゃ　philosopher

1011 掲 11 ▶けい ▷かか(げる)

掲示板	けいじばん	bulletin board
掲示	けいじ	notice; *cv.* put up (a notice)
◇ 掲*載	けいさい	*cv.* publish, carry an article
◇ 掲げる	かかげる	hoist (a flag), hang out (a sign/notice/etc.)

1012 抱 8 ▶ほう ▷だ(く), いだ(く), かか(える)

抱く	だく	hug, hold in one's arms
抱く	いだく	embrace, harbor (hope/ambition/etc.)
抱える	かかえる	carry in one's arms, employ
介抱	かいほう	*cv.* nurse, care for
◇ 抱負	ほうふ	ambition, aspiration
◇ 抱*擁	ほうよう	*cv.* embrace, hug, hold in one's arms

1013 包 5 ▶ほう ▷つつ(む)

包む	つつむ	wrap
包み紙	つつみがみ	wrapping paper
小包	こづつみ	parcel
◇ 包*容力	ほうようりょく	broadmindedness, tolerance
◇ 包丁	ほうちょう	kitchen knife
◇ 包*装紙	ほうそうし	wrapping paper

1014 均 7 ▶きん

平均	へいきん	average, mean; *cv.* even
均等に	きんとうに	equally
◇ 均一価格	きんいつかかく	uniform price

⑦⑧

1015 射 10 ▶しゃ ▷い(る) 947 cf. 謝

注射	ちゅうしゃ	injection, inoculation; *cv.* inject, give a shot
発射	はっしゃ	*cv.* launch, fire
反射	はんしゃ	*cv.* reflect
◇ 射殺	しゃさつ	*cv.* shoot someone dead
◇ 放射能	ほうしゃのう	radioactivity
◇ 射る	いる	shoot

1016 占 5 ▶せん ▷し(める), うらな(う)

占領	せんりょう	*cv.* occupy (another country/territory)
独占	どくせん	*cv.* monopolize, keep a thing to oneself
◇ *寡占市場	かせんしじょう	oligopolistic market
買い占める	かいしめる	buy up (all the goods), corner a market
占める	しめる	occupy
◇ 占う	うらなう	tell fortunes

〈漢字の形に気をつけましょう・30〉

1013	1012	1629	1630	1631	1632
包	抱	*泡	*胞	*砲	*飽
包丁	介抱する	気*泡	細*胞	大*砲	*飽和状態
		き ほう	さい ぼう	たい ほう	ほう わ じょうたい

160

1017 況 8 ▶きょう

不況	ふきょう	recession, depression
好況	こうきょう	brisk market, prosperity 反 不況(ふきょう)
状況/情況	じょうきょう	condition, situation cf. 状態(じょうたい) state
実況放送	じっきょうほうそう	on-the-spot broadcasting

1018 祝 9 ▶しゅく, しゅう ▷いわ(う)

お祝い	おいわい	celebration
結婚祝い	けっこんいわい	wedding celebration, wedding present
◇ 祝う	いわう	celebrate
祝日	しゅくじつ	national holiday
祝電	しゅくでん	telegram of congratulations
祝辞	しゅくじ	congratulatory address, speech
◇ 祝儀	しゅうぎ	gratuity

1019 賀 12 ▶が

年賀状	ねんがじょう	New Year's card
祝賀会	しゅくがかい	celebration, congratulatory banquet
◇ 志賀高原	しがこうげん	Shigakogen (famous resort area in Nagano Prefecture)

1020 競 20 ▶きょう, けい ▷きそ(う), せ(る)

競争	きょうそう	cv. compete, contest
競走	きょうそう	cv. run in a race
競売	きょうばい	auction; cv. sell by auction
競馬	けいば	horse racing
◇ 競う	きそう	compete
◇ 競る	せる	compete

1021 景 12 ▶けい

景気	けいき	business conditions
不景気	ふけいき	economic depression/recession
不景気な	ふけいきな	gloomy, cheerless
風景	ふうけい	landscape, scenery
光景	こうけい	scene
景色	△けしき	scenery

1022 影 15 ▶えい ▷かげ

影響	えいきょう	influence, effect; cv.vi. influence, affect
影	かげ	shadow, silhouette, figure
◇ 面影	おもかげ	visage, face, looks, image

1023 響 20 ▶きょう ▷ひび(く)

影響	えいきょう	influence, effect; cv.vi. influence, affect
反響	はんきょう	cv. echo, resound, reverberate
音響効果	おんきょうこうか	sound effect
交響曲	こうきょうきょく	symphony
響く	ひびく	echo, resound, affect

1024 郷 11 ▶きょう, ごう

故郷	こきょう	hometown, birthplace
◇ 郷土	きょうど	native province
歴 近郷	きんごう	neighboring villages

㊴

| 1025 | 里 7 | ▶り |
| | | ▷さと |

里　　　　さと　village, one's parents' home

◇　〜里　　　〜り　〜*ri* (unit of distance, approx. 3.9 km)

◇　海里　　　かいり　nautical mile

| 1026 | 童 12 | ▶どう |
| | | ▷わらべ |

童話　　　どうわ　fairy tale

童心　　　どうしん　child's mind

◇　*児童　　　じどう　pupil (in primary school), child, juvenile

特　童　　　わらべ　child

◇　童歌　　　わらべうた　children's song

| 1027 | 章 11 | ▶しょう |

文章　　　ぶんしょう　composition, writing, sentence

章　　　　しょう　chapter

第〜章　　だい〜しょう　chapter 〜

| 1028 | 障 14 | ▶しょう |
| | | ▷さわ(る) |

故障　　　こしょう　breakdown, failure, trouble; *cv.* break down, fail, be out of order

障害　　　しょうがい　obstacle, impediment

保障　　　ほしょう　*cv.* secure

支障　　　ししょう　hindrance, obstacle, problem

◇　障子　　　しょうじ　sliding paper door

◇　障る　　　さわる　harm, hurt

| 1029 | 壁 16 | ▶へき |
| | | ▷かべ |

壁　　　　かべ　wall

壁紙　　　かべがみ　wallpaper

壁画　　　へきが　fresco, mural

障壁　　　しょうへき　barrier

| 1030 | 卓 8 | ▶たく |

食卓　　　しょくたく　dining table

卓球　　　たっきゅう　ping-pong

電卓　　　でんたく　calculator

◇　卓*越した　たくえつした　excellent, eminent, superb

| 1031 | 著 11 | ▶ちょ |
| | | ▷あらわ(す), いちじる(しい) |

cf. 署　1316

著者　　　ちょしゃ　author, writer

著書　　　ちょしょ　(literary) work

名著　　　めいちょ　famous/great book

著名な　　ちょめいな　well-known, distinguished

著作権　　ちょさくけん　copyright

◇　*顕著な　けんちょな　remarkable

◇　著しい　いちじるしい　remarkable

◇　著す　　あらわす　write

| 1032 | 諸 15 | ▶しょ |

アジア諸国　アジアしょこく　Asian countries

◇　マリアナ諸島　マリアナしょとう　the Mariana Islands

| 1033 | 緒 14 | ▶しょ, ちょ |
| | | ▷お |

一緒に　　いっしょに　(together) with

| 情緒 | じょうちょ　emotion, feeling |
| ◇ *鼻緒 | はなお　*geta* strap |

| **1034** | 鏡 | ▶きょう |
| 19 | | ▷かがみ |

鏡	かがみ　mirror
望遠鏡	ぼうえんきょう　telescope
眼鏡	△めがね　eyeglasses

⑳

| **1035** | 環 | ▶かん |
| 17 | | |

| 環境 | かんきょう　environment |
| 環状線 | かんじょうせん　loop line |

| **1036** | 境 | ▶きょう，けい |
| 14 | | ▷さかい |

環境	かんきょう　environment
国境	こっきょう　border
境界	きょうかい　boundary, border
◇ 境	さかい　boundary
◇ 境目	さかいめ　borderline
◇ 境内	けいだい　precinct (of a temple/shrine)

| **1037** | 破 | ▶は |
| 10 | | ▷やぶ(る)，やぶ(れる) |

| 環境破壊 | かんきょうはかい　destruction of the environment |

破産	はさん　bankruptcy; *cv.* go bankrupt　cf. While 倒産 is used for bankruptcy of a company, 破産 is used for bankruptcy of a family or individual.
破る	やぶる　break (a promise/rule/etc.), tear (paper/clothing/etc.), defeat
見破る	みやぶる　see through (a plot), see (into someone's heart)
破く	やぶく　tear (paper)
破れる	やぶれる　be torn, be defeated

| **1038** | 壊 | ▶かい |
| 16 | | ▷こわ(す)，こわ(れる) |

環境破壊	かんきょうはかい　destruction of the environment
破壊	はかい　*cv.* destroy
壊す	こわす　break
壊れる	こわれる　be broken
◇ *崩壊	ほうかい　*cv.* collapse

| **1039** | 激 | ▶げき |
| 16 | | ▷はげ(しい) |

激しい	はげしい　fierce, intense
急激な	きゅうげきな　intense, drastic
過激な	かげきな　radical
◇ 過激*派	かげきは　radicals, extremists
激増	げきぞう　*cv.* increase sharply
感激	かんげき　*cv.* be moved (emotionally)
激動	げきどう　*cv.* shake violently, be thrown into turmoil

〈漢字の形に気をつけましょう・31〉

291	1020	1034	1036
意	競	鏡	境
意見	競争	三面鏡	国境

◇ 激流　　　げきりゅう　swift current, rapid stream, torrent

1040 攻 7
▶こう
▷せ(める)　　　cf. 功 378

攻撃　　　こうげき　cv. attack
◇ 専攻　　　せんこう　cv. major (in a subject)
◇ 攻める　　せめる　attack

1041 撃 15
▶げき
▷う(つ)

攻撃　　　こうげき　cv. attack
反撃　　　はんげき　counterattack; cv. make a counterattack
打撃　　　だげき　blow, shock
目撃者　　もくげきしゃ　eyewitness
◇ 撃つ　　　うつ　fire, shoot

1042 襲 22
▶しゅう
▷おそ(う)

世襲の　　せしゅうの　hereditary
襲撃　　　しゅうげき　cv. raid, attack
襲う　　　おそう　raid, attack

1043 暴 15
▶ぼう, ばく
▷あば(く), あば(れる)

暴力　　　ぼうりょく　violence
暴力団　　ぼうりょくだん　organized group of gangsters
乱暴な　　らんぼうな　violent, rude, unruly
暴風雨　　ぼうふうう　violent storm
暴走族　　ぼうそうぞく　motorcycle gang, hot rodders
◇ 暴徒　　　ぼうと　rioters, mob, insurgents
暴れる　　あばれる　act violently
◇ 暴露　　　ばくろ　cv. bring to light
◇ 暴く　　　あばく　bring to light

1044 爆 19
▶ばく

爆発　　　ばくはつ　cv. explode
爆撃　　　ばくげき　cv. bomb
爆破　　　ばくは　cv. blow up
爆弾　　　ばくだん　bomb
原爆　　　げんばく　atomic bomb
◇ *被爆者　ひばくしゃ　victims of the atomic bomb

1045 煙 13
▶えん
▷けむ(る), けむり, けむ(い)

煙　　　　けむり　smoke
煙い　　　けむい　smoky
喫煙　　　きつえん　cv. smoke; smoking
禁煙　　　きんえん　cv. give up smoking; No Smoking
◇ 黒煙　　　こくえん　black smoke
◇ 煙*突　　えんとつ　chimney, smokestack

1046 犯 5
▶はん
▷おか(す)

犯罪　　　はんざい　crime
犯罪者　　はんざいしゃ　criminal, offender
犯人　　　はんにん　criminal
犯行　　　はんこう　crime
共犯者　　きょうはんしゃ　accomplice
防犯カメラ　ぼうはんカメラ　surveillance camera
犯す　　　おかす　commit (a crime), violate (the law), rape

1047 罪 13
▶ざい
▷つみ　　　cf. 罰 1317

犯罪　　　はんざい　crime
有罪　　　ゆうざい　guilty

無罪	むざい	not guilty
罪	つみ	crime, sin, guilt

1048 逮 11 ▶たい 1054 cf. 康

逮捕	たいほ	cv. arrest
逮捕状	たいほじょう	arrest warrant

1049 捕 10 ▶ほ 1001 ▷と(らえる), と(らわ cf. 補 れる), と(る), つか (まえる), つか(まる)

逮捕	たいほ	cv. arrest
捕鯨船	ほげいせん	whaling ship
◇▲拿捕	だほ	cv. capture (a ship)
捕る	とる	catch
捕まえる	つかまえる	catch
捕まる	つかまる	be caught
◇ 捕らえる	とらえる	catch

1050 担 8 ▶たん 1344 ▷かつ(ぐ), にな(う) cf. 胆

担当	たんとう	cv. be in charge
担任の先生	たんにんのせんせい	home-room teacher
負担	ふたん	cv. bear (expenses/responsibility/etc.); burden, responsibility
担保	たんぽ	security, mortgage, guarantee
◇ 担ぐ	かつぐ	carry on one's shoulder, bear, shoulder
◇ 担う	になう	bear/shoulder (responsibility)

1051 批 7 ▶ひ

批判	ひはん	criticism; cv. criticize
批判的な	ひはんてきな	critical

文芸批評	ぶんげいひひょう	literary criticism

1052 刑 6 ▶けい 509 cf. 形

死刑	しけい	capital punishment
刑法	けいほう	criminal law
刑事	けいじ	(police) detective; criminal (case/liability/etc.)
◇ 刑*罰	けいばつ	punishment, penalty
◇ 刑	けい	punishment, penalty, sentence
◇ 刑務所	けいむしょ	prison

1053 健 11 ▶けん ▷すこ(やか)

健康	けんこう	health
保健	ほけん	health
◇ 健在	けんざい	healthy
◇ 健勝	けんしょう	healthy
◇*穏健な	おんけんな	moderate
◇ 健やかな	すこやかな	healthy

1054 康 11 ▶こう 1048 cf. 逮

健康	けんこう	health
健康な	けんこうな	healthy
不健康な	ふけんこうな	unhealthy
◇ 小康	しょうこう	(temporary) lull, breathing space

1055 建 9 ▶けん, こん ▷た(てる), た(つ)

建物	たてもの	building
〜階建て	〜かいだて	〜-story (building)
建てる	たてる	build
建前	たてまえ	formal principle/policy, professed position 反 本音 (ほんね) real intention

建設	けんせつ	cv. construct, build
◇ 建立	こんりゅう	cv. build

1056 築 16
▶ちく
▷きず(く)

新築の	しんちくの	newly-constructed
改築	かいちく	cv. rebuild
◇ 建築	けんちく	architecture, construction; cv. build, construct
◇ 建築家	けんちくか	architect
◇ 築く	きずく	build
㊧ 築山	△つきやま	small artificial hill (in a landscape garden)

1057 策 12
▶さく

政策	せいさく	policy
対策	たいさく	measure, countermeasure

⑧②

1058 籍 20
▶せき

国籍	こくせき	nationality
本籍	ほんせき	one's domicile, legal residence
籍	せき	census register
◇ 在籍	ざいせき	cv. be enrolled/registered (at a school)
◇ 除籍	じょせき	cv. remove from a register
◇ 書籍	しょせき	books

1059 筋 12
▶きん
▷すじ

筋肉	きんにく	muscle
筋道	すじみち	thread of an argument
筋	すじ	storyline

◇ 筋書	すじがき	synopsis, outline, plan

1060 箱 15
▷はこ

本箱	ほんばこ	bookcase
箱	はこ	box, case
◇ 箱根	はこね	Hakone (scenic spot near Mt. Fuji)

1061 範 15
▶はん

範囲	はんい	scope, range, sphere
◇ 広範な	こうはんな	extensive
◇ 規範	きはん	norm, criterion

1062 囲 7
▶い
▷かこ(む)，かこ(う)

範囲	はんい	scope, range, limits, sphere
周囲の	しゅういの	the surrounding ~
囲む	かこむ	surround, enclose
◇ 包囲	ほうい	cv. encircle, besiege

1063 雰 12
▶ふん

雰囲気	ふんいき	atmosphere (of a party/etc.)

1064 井 4
▶せい，しょう
▷い

井戸	いど	well
天井	てんじょう	ceiling
◇ 軽井*沢	かるいざわ	Karuizawa (summer resort area northwest of Tokyo)
㊧ 市井の人	しせいのひと	a man in the street, the common people

1065 帯 10	▶たい ▷お(びる)，おび		

熱帯雨林　ねったいうりん　tropical rain-forest

熱帯　　　ねったい　Torrid Zone

温帯　　　おんたい　Temperate Zone

寒帯　　　かんたい　Frigid Zone

熱帯の　　ねったいの　tropical

安全地帯　あんぜんちたい　safety zone

包帯　　　ほうたい　bandage

◇ 世帯　　せたい　household

◇ 帯　　　おび　sash (for kimono)

◇ 帯びる　おびる　wear

1066 帝 9	▶てい		

帝国主義　ていこくしゅぎ　imperialism

皇帝　　　こうてい　emperor　cf. 天皇(てんのう) (Japanese) emperor

◇ ローマ帝国　ローマていこく　the Roman Empire

◇ 帝政　　ていせい　imperial rule

◇ カール大帝　カールたいてい　Emperor Charlemagne

1067 締 15	▶てい ▷し(まる)，し(める)		

締(め)切り　しめきり　deadline, closing date

◇ 条約の締結　じょうやくのていけつ　conclusion of a treaty

◇ 取締役　とりしまりやく　executive director (of a company)

◇ 締める　しめる　tighten, tie

◇ 金融引(き)締め　きんゆうひきしめ　financial tightening

- -

83

1068 純 10	▶じゅん	1918 cf. 屯

単純な　　たんじゅんな　simple

純金　　　じゅんきん　pure gold

純毛　　　じゅんもう　pure/100-percent wool

純文学　　じゅんぶんがく　pure literature

純日本風の　じゅんにほんふうの　classical Japanese style

純情な　　じゅんじょうな　pure in heart

◇ 純益　　じゅんえき　net profit

1069 粋 10	▶すい	510 cf. 枠

純粋な　　じゅんすいな　pure, genuine

◇ 粋人　　すいじん　person of refined taste

1070 迷 9	▶めい ▷まよ(う)	

迷う　　　まよう　get lost, be unable to decide

迷子　　　△まいご　lost child

迷路　　　めいろ　maze

迷信　　　めいしん　superstition

〈漢字の形に気をつけましょう・32〉

510　　　1069　　　1550
枠　　　粋　　　*砕

窓枠　　　純粋な人　　　岩を*砕く
　　　　　　　　　　　　　くだ

◇ 低迷　　ていめい　*cv.* be in a slump

1071 **惑** 12 ▶わく ▷まど(う)

迷惑　　めいわく　trouble, inconvenience; *cv.* be troubled/annoyed

迷惑な　めいわくな　annoying

当惑　　とうわく　*cv.* be puzzled

困惑　　こんわく　*cv.* be embarrassed

思惑　　おもわく　intention, expectation

惑星　　わくせい　planet

戸惑う　とまどう　be bewildered/flustered

◇ 惑う　　まどう　go astray, be misguided/tempted

1072 **域** 11 ▶いき

地域　　ちいき　region, area, zone

領域　　りょういき　territory, domain

◇ 区域　　くいき　zone, district

◇ 流域　　りゅういき　(river) basin, valley

◇ 聖域　　せいいき　sacred precincts, sanctuary

1073 **越** 12 ▶えつ ▷こ(す), こ(える)

引っ越し　ひっこし　moving (to a new house)

引っ越す　ひっこす　move (to a new house)

乗り越す　のりこす　ride past

越える　　こえる　exceed, go over

◇ 超越　　ちょうえつ　*cv.* transcend

◇ 越権行為　えっけんこうい　overstepping one's authority

1074 **超** 12 ▶ちょう ▷こ(える), こ(す)

超大国　　ちょうたいこく　superpower

超満員　　ちょうまんいん　overcrowded, overflowing (with people)

超音速　　ちょうおんそく　supersonic speed

超過　　ちょうか　*cv.* exceed

超える　こえる　exceed, go over

1075 **赴** 9 ▶ふ ▷おもむ(く)

赴任　　ふにん　*cv.* take up a new post

単身赴任　たんしんふにん　*cv.* take up a post in a distant place, leaving one's family behind

◇ 赴く　　おもむく　proceed, go

⑧④

1076 **更** 7 ▶こう ▷さら, ふ(ける), ふ(かす)

変更　　へんこう　*cv.* change, alter

更衣室　こういしつ　dressing room, locker room

┌─〈漢字の形に気をつけましょう・33〉─

431	1071	1072	942	430	1333	1500
感	惑	域	城	減	*威	*滅

不安を感じる　　迷惑をかける　　地域社会　　名古屋城　　減少する

日本史の権*威　　ローマ帝国の*滅亡
　　　　けん　い　　　　　　　めつぼう

更新	こうしん　*cv.* renew, establish a new record
更に	さらに　furthermore
◇ 夜更かし	よふかし　*cv.* stay up late at night
◇ 更ける	ふける　grow dark

1077　恵　10
▶けい，え
▷めぐ(む)

恩恵	おんけい　favor, benefit
知恵	ちえ　wisdom, intelligence
恵まれている	めぐまれている　be blessed with
◇ 恵む	めぐむ　bestow a favor, bless
◇ 恵み	めぐみ　blessing

1078　恋　10
▶れん
▷こ(う)，こい，こい(しい)　　cf. 変 222

恋人	こいびと　boyfriend, girlfriend, lover
恋心	こいごころ　love
恋	こい　(romantic) love
恋しい	こいしい　dearest, beloved
恋愛	れんあい　love

1079　愛　13
▶あい

恋愛	れんあい　love
愛	あい　love
愛情	あいじょう　love, affection

| 愛国心 | あいこくしん　patriotic sentiment, patriotism |
| 愛読書 | あいどくしょ　favorite book |

1080　互　4
▶ご
▷たが(い)

お互いに	おたがいに　mutually
相互理解	そうごりかい　mutual understanding
交互に	こうごに　alternately

1081　涙　10
▶るい
▷なみだ　　cf. 戻 1201

涙	なみだ　teardrop, tears
◇ 涙声	なみだごえ　tearful voice
◇ 感涙	かんるい　tears (of strong emotion)

1082　房　8
▶ぼう
▷ふさ

冷房	れいぼう　air conditioning
暖房	だんぼう　heating; *cv.* heat (a room)
文房具	ぶんぼうぐ　stationery
官房長官	かんぼうちょうかん　chief secretary of the cabinet
◇ 女房	にょうぼう　one's wife
◇ 乳房	ちぶさ　breasts
◇ 房	ふさ　bunch, cluster, tassel, tuft

〈漢字の形に気をつけましょう・34〉

| 更 1076 | 便 227 | 使 199 | ＊吏 1883 |

予定を変更する　　便利な辞書　　パソコンを使う　　官＊吏
　　　　　　　　　　　　　　　　　　　　　　　　　かん　り

1083 雇 12 ▶こ ▷やと(う)

雇用制度	こようせいど	employment system
雇用	こよう	employment; *cv.* employ
解雇	かいこ	*cv.* fire (an employee) cf. 首にする(くびにする) fire, 首になる(くびになる) be fired
雇用主	こようぬし	employer
雇用者	こようしゃ	employee
雇う	やとう	employ, hire

1084 肩 8 ▶けん ▷かた

肩	かた	shoulder
肩書き	かたがき	(one's) title
肩代わり	かたがわり	shoulder (someone's debt)
肩身が狭い	かたみがせまい	feel ashamed
◇ 肩章	けんしょう	epaulet

1085 背 9 ▶はい ▷せ, せい, そむ(く), そむ(ける)

背中	せなか	back
背	せ	back
背	せ, せい	height
背広	せびろ	suit
背景	はいけい	background, setting
背後	はいご	back, rear

◇ 背信行為	はいしんこうい	betrayal, breach of trust
◇ 背く	そむく	disobey, betray, revolt
◇ 背ける	そむける	avert (one's eyes from), turn (one's face) away

1086 胸 10 ▶きょう ▷むね, むな

胸	むね	chest, breast
胸毛	むなげ	chest hair
胸囲	きょうい	girth of the chest
◇ 胸中	きょうちゅう	inner feeling
◇ 度胸	どきょう	courage, bravery, guts

1087 腰 13 ▶よう ▷こし

腰	こし	lower back, waist, hips
物腰	ものごし	demeanor
本腰を入れる	ほんごしをいれる	set about (a task) in earnest
◇ 腰痛	ようつう	backache, pain in the lower back, lumbago

1088 腹 13 ▶ふく ▷はら

空腹な	くうふくな	hungry
◇ 立腹	りっぷく	*cv.* get angry
◇ 腹が立つ	はらがたつ	get angry
◇ 腹	はら	stomach, belly
◇ お腹	▲おなか	stomach

〈漢字の形に気をつけましょう・35〉

798	797	1077	1856
博	専	恵	*穂

大学院の博士課程　　専門は文学です　　恩恵を受ける　　麦の*穂
　　　　　　　　　　　　　　　　　　　　　　　　　　　　ほ

1089 豚 11	▶とん ▷ぶた	52 cf. 家
	豚	ぶた pig, hog
	豚肉	ぶたにく pork
◇	豚カツ	とんカツ pork cutlet
◇	養豚	ようとん hog/pig raising

85

1090 届 8	▷とど(ける), とど(く)	
	欠席届	けっせきとどけ report of absence (from school)
	欠勤届	けっきんとどけ report of absence (from work)
	届ける	とどける report, notify, send
	届け先	とどけさき where to report, receiver's address
	届く	とどく be delivered, reach, arrive

1091 属 12	▶ぞく	
	属す(る)	ぞくす(る) belong to (an organization/etc.), be affiliated with
	所属	しょぞく cv. belong to (an organization/etc.), be affiliated
◇	金属	きんぞく metal
◇	属性	ぞくせい attributes, properties

1092 展 10	▶てん	
	発展	はってん cv. develop
	発展途上国	はってんとじょうこく developing countries
	展示	てんじ cv. exhibit
	展望	てんぼう view, prospect
	展開	てんかい cv. develop, unfold

1093 殿 13	▶でん, てん ▷との, どの	
	宮殿	きゅうでん palace
◇	御殿	ごてん palace
◇	殿下	でんか His/Her Highness
◇	皇太子殿下	こうたいしでんか His Imperial Highness the Crown Prince
◇	殿様	とのさま feudal lord
◇	〜殿	〜どの Mr./Ms. 〜 (used in official documents/etc.)

1094 凍 10	▶とう ▷こお(る), こご(える)	
	凍る	こおる freeze, be frozen
	冷凍食品	れいとうしょくひん frozen food
	凍結	とうけつ cv. be frozen, freeze (assets/etc.)
◇	凍傷	とうしょう frostbite
◇	凍死	とうし cv. freeze to death
◇	凍える	こごえる be frozen/chilled

1095 氷 5	▶ひょう ▷こおり, ひ	
	氷	こおり ice
	氷山	ひょうざん iceberg
◇	氷*河	ひょうが glacier
◇	流氷	りゅうひょう ice floe
◇	氷点下	ひょうてんか below the freezing point
特	氷室	ひむろ icehouse

1096 永 5	▶えい ▷なが(い)	
	永住	えいじゅう cv. reside permanently
	永遠に	えいえんに eternally

◇ 永眠　　　　えいみん　*cv.* sleep eternally, die

◇ 永続　　　　えいぞく　*cv.* continue forever/ perpetually

永い　　　　ながい　long (time)

◇ 永田町　　　ながたちょう　Nagatacho (the area in Tokyo where the Diet Building is located)

1097
3
久　▶きゅう，く
　　▷ひさ(しい)

久しぶりに　ひさしぶりに　after a long time

永久に　　　えいきゅうに　permanently, eternally, perpetually

◇ 持久力　　　じきゅうりょく　endurance, tenacity

特 久遠　　　くおん　eternity, time immemorial

1098
3
及　▶きゅう
　　▷およ(ぶ)，およ(び)，およ(ぼ
　　　す)

普及　　　　ふきゅう　*cv.* come into wide use, spread

◇ 言及　　　　げんきゅう　*cv.* refer to, mention

及ぶ　　　　およぶ　reach, extend to, amount to

及び　　　　および　and (formal expression)

及ぼす　　　およぼす　exert (influence on)

1099
5
幼　▶よう　　　　　　1814
　　▷おさな(い)　cf. 幻

幼稚園　　　ようちえん　kindergarten

幼稚な　　　ようちな　childish, infantile, unrefined

◇ 幼い　　　　おさない　very young, childish, infantile

1100
13
稚　▶ち　　　　　　　1297
　　　　　　　　　　cf. 維

幼稚園　　　ようちえん　kindergarten

幼稚な　　　ようちな　childish, infantile, unrefined

- -
⑧⑥

1101
11
移　▶い
　　▷うつ(る)，うつ(す)

移民　　　　いみん　immigrant; *cv.* immigrate

移住　　　　いじゅう　*cv.* immigrate

移動　　　　いどう　*cv.* move (from one place to another)

移転　　　　いてん　*cv.vi.* move (as in an office/school/etc.)

移植　　　　いしょく　*cv.* transplant

移る　　　　うつる　*vi.* move

移す　　　　うつす　*vt.* move

1102
10
秘　▶ひ
　　▷ひ(める)

秘密　　　　ひみつ　secret

秘書　　　　ひしょ　secretary

神秘的な　　しんぴてきな　mysterious, mystical

◇ 極秘　　　　ごくひ　top secret

◇ 秘められた　ひめられた　hidden, secret

1103
11
密　▶みつ

秘密　　　　ひみつ　secret

密輸　　　　みつゆ　*cv.* smuggle

人口密度　　じんこうみつど　population density

精密な　　　せいみつな　precise, detailed, minute

密接な　　　みっせつな　close

親密な　　　しんみつな　close, intimate

1104
10
骨　▶こつ
　　▷ほね

骨　　　　　ほね　bone

骨折	こっせつ　*cv.* break a bone; bone fracture
◇ 鉄骨	てっこつ　steel frame
◇ 骨子	こっし　outlines

1105　胃　▶い
9

| 胃 | い　stomach |
| 胃がん | いがん　stomach cancer |

1106　腸　▶ちょう
13

腸	ちょう　intestines, bowels
胃腸	いちょう　stomach and intestines
◇ 小腸	しょうちょう　small intestine
◇ 大腸	だいちょう　large intestine

1107　肝　▶かん
7　　　**▷きも**

肝心な	かんじんな　main, essential
肝臓	かんぞう　liver
◇ 肝	きも　liver, guts

1108　臓　▶ぞう
19

心臓	しんぞう　heart
肝臓	かんぞう　liver
内臓	ないぞう　internal organs, viscera
臓器	ぞうき　internal organs, viscera

1109　脳　▶のう
11

脳	のう　brain
洗脳	せんのう　*cv.* brainwash
脳卒中	のうそっちゅう　cerebral hemorrhage

| 首脳会談 | しゅのうかいだん　summit conference |
| ◇ 頭脳 | ずのう　brain |

1110　悩　▶のう
10　　　**▷なや(む)，なや(ます)**

悩み	なやみ　trouble, worry, agony, anguish
伸び悩む	のびなやむ　fail to make progress
悩ます	なやます　annoy, pester, harass
◇ 苦悩	くのう　*cv.* suffer, be distressed/afflicted
◇ 悩殺	のうさつ　*cv.* enchant, captivate

1111　蔵　▶ぞう
15　　　**▷くら**

冷蔵庫	れいぞうこ　refrigerator
貯蔵	ちょぞう　*cv.* store, reserve
蔵書	ぞうしょ　(one's personal) library
蔵	くら　storehouse, warehouse
大蔵省	おおくらしょう　the Ministry of Finance
大蔵大臣	おおくらだいじん　the Finance Minister
蔵相	ぞうしょう　the Finance Minister

1112　倉　▶そう
10　　　**▷くら**

| 倉庫 | そうこ　warehouse |
| ◇ 倉 | くら　storehouse, warehouse |

1113　創　▶そう
12

創造性	そうぞうせい　creativity
創造	そうぞう　*cv.* create
創作	そうさく　*cv.* create

創立　　　　そうりつ　*cv.* establish, found

独創的な　　どくそうてきな　original, creative

◇ 創価学会　そうかがっかい　Soka Gakkai (a Buddhist sect)

1114　看　9　▶かん

看護婦　　　かんごふ　nurse

看病　　　　かんびょう　nursing

看板　　　　かんばん　signboard, sign

◇ 看守　　　かんしゅ　prison guard

◇ 看破　　　かんぱ　see through, detect

1115　護　20　▶ご

看護婦　　　かんごふ　nurse

弁護士　　　べんごし　lawyer

弁護　　　　べんご　*cv.* defend, plead, speak for

保護　　　　ほご　*cv.* protect, preserve

◇ 護衛　　　ごえい　bodyguard, escort; *cv.* guard, escort

1116　弁　5　▶べん

弁護士　　　べんごし　lawyer

弁解　　　　べんかい　*cv.* explain, justify, excuse

答弁　　　　とうべん　*cv.* reply, answer (at an assembly)

関西弁　　　かんさいべん　Kansai dialect/accent

弁当　　　　べんとう　box lunch

駅弁　　　　えきべん　box lunch sold at a train station

1117　念　8　▶ねん

信念　　　　しんねん　belief, faith, conviction

理念　　　　りねん　idea

念頭に　　　ねんとうに　in mind

念入りに　　ねんいりに　with special care, thoroughly

記念　　　　きねん　*cv.* commemorate

記念日　　　きねんび　memorial day, anniversary

1118　息　10　▶そく　▷いき　　1285　cf. 臭

休息　　　　きゅうそく　*cv.* rest, take a rest

利息　　　　りそく　interest (on a loan)

◇ 消息　　　しょうそく　news, information, contact

息子　　　　△むすこ　son

息　　　　　いき　breath

◇ 息吹　　　△いぶき　a breath (of spring), an emanation (of youth)

1119　応　7　▶おう

反応　　　　はんのう　*cv.* react

応答　　　　おうとう　answer

質疑応答　　しつぎおうとう　questions and answers

応用　　　　おうよう　*cv.* apply

応接間　　　おうせつま　reception room, living room

1120　寄　11　▶き　▷よ(る), よ(せる)　　1292　cf. 奇

寄る　　　　よる　approach, draw near, drop in

近寄る　　　ちかよる　draw near, approach

立ち寄る　　たちよる　drop in, stop at

最寄りの　△もよりの　nearest, nearby

寄付　きふ　cv. contribute, donate

寄付金　きふきん　contribution, dona-
tion, gift of money

◇ 寄生　きせい　cv. be parisitic (on a
tree/animal/etc.)

寄せる　よせる　bring near, gather
together

1121 突 8

▶とつ
▷つ(く)

突然　とつぜん　suddenly

突入　とつにゅう　cv. storm (a building), rush (into a strike)

◇ 突破　とっぱ　cv. break through

突く　つく　poke

突き当たり　つきあたり　the end of a
street/hall/etc.

突き当たる　つきあたる　come to the end
of a street, run/bump against

突っ込む　つっこむ　thrust into, pierce

1122 穴 5

▶けつ
▷あな

穴　あな　hole

落とし穴　おとしあな　pitfall

囲*洞穴　どうけつ　cave

- -

⑧⑧

1123 容 10

▶よう
1501
cf. 溶

美容院　びよういん　beauty parlor

美容　びよう　beauty

内容　ないよう　contents

容器　ようき　container

容量　ようりょう　volume, capacity

受容　じゅよう　cv. accept, take in

◇ 形容詞　けいようし　adjective

1124 欲 11

▶よく
▷ほっ(する)，ほ(しい)

食欲　しょくよく　appetite

性欲　せいよく　sexual desire, sex
drive

欲望　よくぼう　desire, craving

欲　よく　desire

無欲な　むよくな　free from avarice,
unselfish

欲しい　ほしい　want

◇ 欲する　ほっする　want

1125 裕 12

▶ゆう

余裕　よゆう　leeway, spare (time/
money/etc.)

裕福な　ゆうふくな　wealthy

1126 浴 10

▶よく
▷あ(びる)，あ(びせる)

入浴　にゅうよく　cv. take a bath

浴室　よくしつ　bathroom

海水浴　かいすいよく　sea bathing

日光浴　にっこうよく　sun bathing

浴衣　△ゆかた　yukata (cotton kimono
for the summer)

浴びる　あびる　be bathed in, take (a
shower)

◇ 浴びせる　あびせる　pour over, douse,
bombard (with criticism/ques-
tions/etc.)

1127 河 8

▶か
▷かわ

運河　うんが　canal

河　かわ　river

銀河　ぎんが　the Milky Way

黄河　こうが　Hwang Ho, the Yel-
low River

◇ 河川　かせん　rivers

◇ 河原　　△かわら　dry riverbed

1128 沿 8
▶えん
▷そ(う)

～に沿って　～にそって　along (the coast/river/etc.)

川沿いの　かわぞいの　along the river

沿岸　えんがん　(on/along) the coast/shore

沿線　えんせん　along a train line

1129 沈 7
▶ちん
▷しず(む)，しず(める)

沈没　ちんぼつ　cv. sink

◇ 沈着冷静な　ちんちゃくれいせいな　composed, calm

沈む　しずむ　sink

1130 没 7
▶ぼつ

沈没　ちんぼつ　cv. sink

没落　ぼつらく　downfall, ruin (of a family/etc.); cv. be ruined/bankrupt

没収　ぼっしゅう　cv. confiscate

◇ 出没　しゅつぼつ　cv. appear frequently

1131 添 11
▶てん
▷そ(える)，そ(う)

付き添う　つきそう　attend on, accompany

◇ 添える　そえる　add, attach

◇ 添加物　てんかぶつ　additive

◇ 添*削　てんさく　cv. correct, revise

1132 歓 15
▶かん
1615 cf. 勧

歓迎　かんげい　cv. welcome

歓待　かんたい　cv. give a cordial reception

歓声　かんせい　shout of joy, cheer

◇ 歓楽街　かんらくがい　entertainment district, red-light district

1133 迎 7
▶げい
▷むか(える)

歓迎　かんげい　cv. welcome

送迎バス　そうげいバス　shuttle bus

出迎える　でむかえる　go out to greet (someone at the front door/station/etc.)

迎えに行く　むかえにいく　go to meet someone (at the airport/etc.), pick up

迎合　げいごう　cv. get along easily with others

⑧⑨

1134 仰 6
▶ぎょう，こう
▷あお(ぐ)，おお(せ)

信仰　しんこう　religious conviction/faith

◇ 仰向け　あおむけ　facing upward
反 うつ*伏せ(うつぶせ) facing downward

〈漢字の形に気をつけましょう・36〉

1133	1134	1264	1135	1136	918
迎	仰	*抑	卵	印	卸

ホテルの送迎バス　　信仰を捨てる　　核の*抑止 力　　カエルの卵
　　　　　　　　　　　　　　　　　　よく し りょく

印刷する　　卸値

◇ 仰ぐ　あおぐ　look up at, ask for (advice/support/etc.)

◇ 仰天　ぎょうてん　*cv.* be astonished

◇ 仰せ　おおせ　your wish (honorific)

1135 卵 7
▶らん
▷たまご

卵　たまご　egg　cf. 玉子焼き(たまごやき) fried egg

◇ 卵子　らんし　ovum　cf. 精子 (せいし) spermatozoon

㊛ 卵*巣　らんそう　ovary

1136 印 6
▶いん
▷しるし

印刷　いんさつ　*cv.* print

印象　いんしょう　impression

◇ 調印　ちょういん　*cv.* sign (a treaty/contract/etc.)

◇ 印税　いんぜい　royalty (on a book)

矢印　やじるし　(directional) arrow

目印　めじるし　mark, landmark

印　しるし　mark, sign

1137 刷 8
▶さつ
▷す(る)

印刷　いんさつ　*cv.* print

印刷物　いんさつぶつ　printed matter

刷新　さっしん　*cv.* reform

刷る　する　print

1138 刊 5
▶かん

週刊誌　しゅうかんし　weekly magazine

朝刊　ちょうかん　morning edition (of a newspaper)

夕刊　ゆうかん　evening edition (of a newspaper)

新刊書　しんかんしょ　new publication

1139 刻 8
▶こく
▷きざ(む)

深刻な　しんこくな　grave, serious

時刻　じこく　time

◇ *彫刻　ちょうこく　sculpture; *cv.* sculpt, carve, engrave

刻む　きざむ　cut, chop up, engrave

1140 劇 15
▶げき

劇　げき　drama, play

演劇　えんげき　drama, play, theatrical performance

歌劇　かげき　opera

劇場　げきじょう　theater

喜劇　きげき　comedy

悲劇　ひげき　tragedy, tragical event

◇ 劇的な　げきてきな　dramatic

◇ 劇薬　げきやく　powerful drug, poison

1141 仮 6
▶か, け
▷かり

仮定　かてい　*cv.* suppose, assume

仮説　かせつ　hypothesis

仮面　かめん　mask

平仮名　△ひらがな　*hiragana*

仮の　かりの　provisional, tentative, temporary

◇ 仮病　けびょう　faked illness

1142 版 8
▶はん

出版　しゅっぱん　*cv.* publish

出版社　しゅっぱんしゃ　publisher, publishing company

版権	はんけん copyright
初版	しょはん first edition
改訂版	かいていばん revised edition
版画	はんが woodblock print

1143 片 4

▶へん
▷かた

破片	はへん fragment, splinter
断片的な	だんぺんてきな fragmentary
◊ 断片	だんぺん fragment
片道	かたみち one-way (ticket) cf. 一方通行（いっぽうつうこう）one-way traffic
片手	かたて one hand/arm
片仮名	△かたかな katakana
片付く	かたづく be put in order, be settled, be finished, be married
片付ける	かたづける put in order, tidy (up), put away, finish, marry off
◊ 片寄る	かたよる lean to, incline toward

⑨⓪

1144 皮 5

▶ひ
▷かわ

皮	かわ skin, hide, leather, bark, rind
毛皮	けがわ fur
皮革製品	ひかくせいひん fur and leather goods
皮肉	ひにく irony, sarcasm
◊ 皮相的な	ひそうてきな superficial

1145 被 10

▶ひ
▷こうむ(る)

被害	ひがい damage, harm, injury
被害者	ひがいしゃ victim
被告	ひこく defendant
◊ 被選挙権	ひせんきょけん eligibility
◊ 被る	こうむる suffer

1146 彼 8

▶ひ
▷かれ，かの

彼	かれ he, boyfriend
彼女	かのじょ she, girlfriend
◊ 彼岸	ひがん equinoctial week

1147 徹 15

▶てつ

徹夜	てつや cv. stay up all night
徹底的に	てっていてきに thoroughly
冷徹な	れいてつな cool-headed
◊ *貫徹	かんてつ cv. accomplish, carry out

1148 徴 14

▶ちょう

象徴	しょうちょう symbol; cv. symbolize
特徴	とくちょう special feature, distinguishing characteristic
◊ 徴*候	ちょうこう sign, indication, symptom

〈漢字の形に気をつけましょう・37〉

1144	913	1037	1145	1146	1468
皮	波	破	被	彼	*披

皮革製品　電波　環境破壊　被害を受ける　お彼岸　*披露宴
ひろうえん

| 徴兵 | ちょうへい (military) draft, conscription; *cv.* conscript, draft |
| ◇ 徴税 | ちょうぜい tax collection; *cv.* collect taxes |

1149 微 13 ▶び

微妙な	びみょうな delicate, subtle
微笑	びしょう *cv.* smile
微熱	びねつ slight fever
微生物	びせいぶつ microbe, micro-organism

1150 妙 7 ▶みょう

微妙な	びみょうな delicate, subtle
◇*奇妙な	きみょうな strange, curious, odd
◇ 妙な	みょうな strange, curious, odd
◇ 妙案	みょうあん excellent idea, bright idea
◇ 絶妙な	ぜつみょうな exquisite, superb
◇ 神妙な	しんみょうな solemn
◇*巧妙な	こうみょうな tactful

1151 秒 9 ▶びょう

| ～秒 | ～びょう ～ second(s) |

1152 砂 9 ▶さ, しゃ ▷すな

砂	すな sand
砂浜	すなはま sandy beach
砂時計	すなどけい hourglass
砂利	△じゃり gravel
土砂	どしゃ earth and sand
土砂降り	どしゃぶり downpour

◇ 土砂*崩れ	どしゃくずれ landslide
◇ 砂金	さきん gold dust
◇ 砂*糖	さとう sugar
◇ 砂*漠	さばく desert
◇ 砂*丘	さきゅう sand hill, dune

1153 劣 6 ▶れつ ▷おと(る)

劣等感	れっとうかん inferiority complex
劣等生	れっとうせい poor student
◇*優劣	ゆうれつ superior or inferior, relative merit
◇ 劣勢	れっせい numerical inferiority (as in a war/etc.)
◇ 劣る	おとる be inferior

⑨①

1154 勇 9 ▶ゆう ▷いさ(む)

勇気	ゆうき courage
◇ 勇退	ゆうたい *cv.* retire voluntarily
◇ 勇ましい	いさましい brave, courageous, valiant

1155 募 12 ▶ぼ ▷つの(る) 1660 cf. 寡

募集	ぼしゅう *cv.* recruit
応募	おうぼ *cv.* apply for
応募者	おうぼしゃ applicant
募金運動	ぼきんうんどう fund-raising campaign
公募	こうぼ *cv.* advertise (for someone to fill a post)
◇ 募る	つのる recruit, invite (donations), raise (funds), grow intense

1156 墓 13 ▶ぼ ▷はか 691 cf. 基

墓	はか	grave
墓参り	はかまいり	visit a grave
墓石	はかいし, ぼせき	gravestone
墓地	ぼち	cemetery
◊ 墓穴を掘る	ぼけつをほる	dig one's own grave, bring about one's own ruin

1157 幕 13 ▶まく, ばく

幕	まく	(stage) curtain, act (of a play)
開幕	かいまく	beginning of a performance/event; cv. (an event) begins
閉幕	へいまく	end of a performance/event; cv. (an event) ends
字幕	じまく	subtitle
◊ 内幕	うちまく	behind-the-scenes story
◊ 幕府	ばくふ	the Shogunate government

1158 暮 14 ▶ぼ ▷く(れる), く(らす)

暮らす	くらす	live
一人暮らし	ひとりぐらし	living alone
夕暮れ	ゆうぐれ	twilight, evening
暮れる	くれる	grow dark
お歳暮	おせいぼ	year-end gift

1159 漠 13 ▶ばく

砂漠	さばく	desert
漠然としている	ばくぜんとしている	vague, obscure

1160 模 14 ▶も, ぼ

規模	きぼ	scale
大規模な	だいきぼな	large-scale
◊ 模*型	もけい	model
模範	もはん	model, example
模造品	もぞうひん	imitation
模様	もよう	pattern, figure, design, appearance, look

1161 概 14 ▶がい

概念	がいねん	concept
概要	がいよう	outline
◊ 概*略	がいりゃく	outline
概算	がいさん	rough estimate; cv. make a rough estimate
概論	がいろん	introduction, outline
◊ 大概	たいがい	mainly, generally

1162 既 10 ▶き ▷すで(に)

既に	すでに	already
既成事実	きせいじじつ	accomplished fact

〈漢字の形に気をつけましょう・38〉

1159	1160	1546
漠	模	*膜
砂漠	大規模な調査	油の*膜 まく

既成概念	きせいがいねん　preconceived idea
既製服	きせいふく　ready-made clothes
既婚の	きこんの　married
既存の	きそんの　existing

1163　**裁**　12

▶さい
▷た(つ), さば(く)

裁判	さいばん　trial, hearing
裁判官	さいばんかん　judge
裁判所	さいばんしょ　law court
独裁者	どくさいしゃ　dictator
総裁	そうさい　president, general director
裁く	さばく　judge, decide (a case)
洋裁	ようさい　(Western-style) dressmaking
◇ 裁つ	たつ　cut (cloth/leather/etc.)

1164　**我**　7

▶が
▷われ, わ

我々	われわれ　we
我が国	わがくに　our country
自我	じが　self, ego
無我夢中で	むがむちゅうで　desperately

1165　**武**　8

▶ぶ
▷む

武器	ぶき　weapon, arms
武力	ぶりょく　military force
武道	ぶどう　martial arts
歴 武士	ぶし　warrior (in medieval Japan), samurai
歴 武者	むしゃ　warrior

⑨2

1166　**輩**　15

▶はい

先輩	せんぱい　one's senior (at school/work/etc.)
後輩	こうはい　one's junior (at school/work/etc.)
年輩の	ねんぱいの　elderly

1167　**俳**　10

▶はい

俳優	はいゆう　actor
俳句	はいく　haiku, Japanese short poem consisting of 17 syllables
俳人	はいじん　haiku poet

1168　**優**　17

▶ゆう　　　　　　1829
▷やさ(しい),　　cf. 憂
　すぐ(れる)

| 俳優 | はいゆう　actor |
| 女優 | じょゆう　actress |

〈漢字の形に気をつけましょう・39〉

796　　377　　1164　　1165　　1163　　1821　　1307
式　成　我　武　裁　*栽　*載

結婚式　　手術が成功する　　我々　　武士　　裁判

草花を*栽培する　　論文が掲*載される
　　　　さいばい　　　　けい さい

優勝　ゆうしょう　*cv.* win a championship

優先　ゆうせん　*cv.* take precedence/priority, give priority

◇ 優*秀な　ゆうしゅうな　excellent

◇ 優れた　すぐれた　excellent

優しい　やさしい　gentle, tender, kind-hearted

1169
6
仲
▶ちゅう
▷なか　　　1246
cf. 伸

仲がいい　なかがいい　be on good terms

仲　なか　relation

仲人　△なこうど　go-between, match-maker

◇ 仲介　ちゅうかい　*cv.* mediate

◇ 仲裁　ちゅうさい　arbitration, mediation; *cv.* arbitrate, mediate

1170
9
促
▶そく
▷うなが(す)

促進　そくしん　*cv.* promote

◇ *催促　さいそく　*cv.* press (a person for), urge (a person to do)

◇ 促成*栽*培　そくせいさいばい　artificially accelerated growth

◇ 促す　うながす　urge (a person to do something)

1171
7
秀
▶しゅう
▷ひい(でる)

優秀な　ゆうしゅうな　excellent

秀才　しゅうさい　brilliant/bright student

◇ 秀でる　ひいでる　excel

1172
7
似
▶じ
▷に(る)

似ている　にている　resemble

似顔絵　にがおえ　portrait

似合う　にあう　go well (with)

類似品　るいじひん　imitation

◇ 疑似体験　ぎじたいけん　simulated experience

1173
13
傾
▶けい
▷かたむ(く), かたむ(ける)

傾向　けいこう　tendency, trend

◇ 傾*斜　けいしゃ　inclination, slant, slope; *cv.* slant, slope

◇ 傾倒　けいとう　*cv.* respect (the master of an art/leader of a movement/etc.)

◇ 傾く　かたむく　lean, incline

1174
10
候
▶こう
▷そうろう　　　1876
cf. 侯

気候　きこう　weather, climate

天候　てんこう　weather

候補者　こうほしゃ　candidate

立候補　りっこうほ　*cv.* run in an election　cf. 出馬(しゅつば)　*cv.* stand as a candidate (for the election)

◇ 居候　いそうろう　freeloader

◇ 候文　そうろうぶん　*sōrō*-style writing (formal writing style in the Edo period)

〈「仲〜」の表現〉

・仲がいい ⟷ 仲が悪い　　・仲が良くなる ⟷ 仲が悪くなる

・けんかする ⟷ 仲直りする　　・AとBは仲良しだ　　・仲間

1175 修 10	▶しゅう，しゅ ▷おさ（める），おさ（まる）

修理	しゅうり　*cv.* repair
修正	しゅうせい　*cv.* amend, revise, correct, retouch
修了	しゅうりょう　*cv.* complete
修了証	しゅうりょうしょう　certificate of completion of a course
研修	けんしゅう　study and training; *cv.* be trained
◇ 修める	おさめる　master
◇ 修行	しゅぎょう　(religious/artistic/ etc.) training; *cv.* train oneself

1176 偏 11	▶へん ▷かたよ（る）

偏見	へんけん　prejudice, bias
偏食	へんしょく　*cv.* have an unbalanced diet
偏差値	へんさち　deviation value/ score
偏る	かたよる　lean, incline

- (93)

1177 遍 12	▶へん

| 普遍的な | ふへんてきな　universal |
| ◇ 遍歴 | へんれき　wandering, travel, pilgrimage |

1178 遇 12	▶ぐう

待遇	たいぐう　treatment, pay
優遇	ゆうぐう　*cv.* treat someone well, give favorable treatment to
◇ 冷遇	れいぐう　*cv.* treat someone coldly, give a cold reception

1179 遺 15	▶い，ゆい 　　　　　　1214 cf. 遣

遺伝	いでん　heredity; *cv.* be inherited
遺産	いさん　an inheritance, estate
遺族	いぞく　family of the deceased
遺体	いたい　corpse
遺言	ゆいごん　will, last wishes

1180 貢 10	▶こう，く ▷みつ（ぐ）

貢献	こうけん　*cv.* contribute, serve
◇ 貢ぐ	みつぐ　send tribute, give financial aid to
◇ 貢ぎ物	みつぎもの　tribute
歴 年貢	ねんぐ　annual tribute

1181 献 13	▶けん，こん

貢献	こうけん　*cv.* contribute, serve
献金	けんきん　gift of money, contribution
献血	けんけつ　*cv.* donate/give blood
文献	ぶんけん　literature, bibliography
◇ 献立	こんだて　menu

1182 僚 14	▶りょう

同僚	どうりょう　colleague, co-worker
官僚	かんりょう　bureaucrat
官僚制度	かんりょうせいど　bureaucracy
◇ *閣僚	かくりょう　cabinet member

1183 寮 15	▶りょう

| 寮 | りょう　dormitory |

学生寮	がくせいりょう student dormitory
社員寮	しゃいんりょう company dormitory
独身寮	どくしんりょう dormitory for single men or women
寮長	りょうちょう dormitory director
寮生	りょうせい students living in a dormitory

1184
11 帳 ▶ちょう

電話帳	でんわちょう telephone directory
手帳	てちょう (pocket) notebook
通帳	つうちょう bankbook, passbook
帳消し	ちょうけし cancellation of a debt

1185
11 張 ▶ちょう
▷は(る)

緊張	きんちょう cv. be nervous
主張	しゅちょう cv. assert, insist, emphasize
出張	しゅっちょう business trip; cv. make a business trip
出張所	しゅっちょうじょ branch office
拡張	かくちょう cv. extend, expand
引っ張る	ひっぱる pull, draw, drag
見張る	みはる keep watch
張る	はる spread (a net/paper/etc.), stretch (a rope), paste (a poster/paper/etc.)

張り切る	はりきる be full of pep, be enthusiastic
欲張り	よくばり greedy person, avarice, greed
欲張りな	よくばりな greedy

1186
15 緊 ▶きん
1711
cf. 紫

緊張	きんちょう cv. be nervous
緊急の	きんきゅうの urgent
緊密な	きんみつな close
緊迫	きんぱく cv. be tense/under pressure

1187
16 繁 ▶はん

繁栄	はんえい cv. prosper (used for nations/civilizations/etc.)
繁盛	はんじょう cv. prosper (used for business)
◇ 繁*華街	はんかがい busy shopping area

1188
9 栄 ▶えい
▷さか(える), は(え), は(える)

繁栄	はんえい cv. prosper (used for nations/civilizations/etc.)
栄養	えいよう nutrition
◇ 栄光	えいこう glory
◇ 栄える	さかえる thrive, prosper
◇ 栄えある	はえある honorable
◇ 栄える	はえる shine, be bright

〈漢字の形に気をつけましょう・40〉

1182 僚 **1183** 寮 **1362** *療

会社の同僚　大学の寮　病気の治*療のために入院する
ちりょう

1189 挙 10 ▶きょ ▷あ(げる)，あ(がる)

選挙	せんきょ	election; *cv.* elect
挙手	きょしゅ	*cv.* raise one's hand
検挙	けんきょ	*cv.* arrest
歴 挙兵	きょへい	*cv.* raise an army
◇ 一挙に	いっきょに	at a stroke, at once
◇ 挙げる	あげる	raise, enumerate, arrest

1190 厳 17 ▶げん，ごん ▷おごそ(か)，きび(しい)

厳しい	きびしい	strict, severe
厳重な	げんじゅうな	strict, rigid
厳格な	げんかくな	strict, stern
厳禁	げんきん	*cv.* be strictly prohibited
◇ 尊厳	そんげん	dignity
◇ *威厳	いげん	dignity, stateliness
◇ 厳かな	おごそかな	solemn, grave
◇ *荘厳な	そうごんな	sublime, majestic, impressive

1191 派 9 ▶は
94
1353
cf. 脈

派閥	はばつ	faction
右派	うは	right-wing faction
左派	さは	left-wing faction
～派	～は	～ faction
宗派	しゅうは	religious sect
特派員	とくはいん	correspondent
派出所	はしゅつじょ	police box
派手な	はでな	showy, flashy 反地味な (じみな) plain, sober
立派な	りっぱな	fine, splendid, admirable, magnificent

◇ 派*遣	はけん	*cv.* dispatch

1192 閥 14 ▶ばつ

派閥	はばつ	faction
財閥	ざいばつ	*zaibatsu*, financial combine/group/clique
◇ 軍閥	ぐんばつ	militarists, military clique

1193 閣 14 ▶かく

内閣	ないかく	cabinet
閣議	かくぎ	cabinet meeting
閣僚	かくりょう	cabinet member
組閣	そかく	*cv.* form a cabinet
◇ 金閣寺	きんかくじ	Kinkakuji Temple, Temple of the Golden Pavillion

1194 衆 12 ▶しゅう，しゅ
52
cf. 家

公衆電話	こうしゅうでんわ	pay phone
大衆文化	たいしゅうぶんか	popular culture
アメリカ合衆国	アメリカがっしゅうこく	the United States of America
民衆	みんしゅう	the people, the masses
歴 衆生	しゅじょう	mankind, the world (in Buddhism)

1195 略 11 ▶りゃく

省略	しょうりゃく	*cv.* omit, abbreviate
略す	りゃくす	omit, abbreviate
略語	りゃくご	abbreviation
略歴	りゃくれき	brief personal history

略式の りゃくしきの informal
反 正式の(せいしきの) formal
cf. 公式の(こうしきの) official,
非公式の(ひこうしきの) unoffi-
cial, private

戦略 せんりゃく strategy

1196 異 11 ▶い ▷こと

異常な いじょうな unusual, abnormal
反 正常な(せいじょうな) nor-
mal, usual

異質の/な いしつの/な heterogeneous
反 同質の/な(どうしつの/な)
homogeneous

異国 いこく foreign country

異民族 いみんぞく other tribe, other
ethnic group

異教徒 いきょうと heathen, pagan

異議 いぎ objection

突然変異 とつぜんへんい mutation

異なる ことなる be different

1197 圧 5 ▶あつ

圧力 あつりょく pressure

気圧 きあつ atmospheric pressure;
air pressure

高気圧 こうきあつ high atmospheric
pressure

低気圧 ていきあつ low atmospheric
pressure

◊ 圧縮 あっしゅく cv. compress,
press, condense, constrict

◊ 圧迫 あっぱく cv. oppress

◊ *抑圧 よくあつ cv. suppress

圧倒的に あっとうてきに overwhelming-
ly

1198 至 6 ▶し ▷いた(る)

至急 しきゅう urgently

◊ 夏至 げし summer solstice

◊ 冬至 とうじ winter solstice

◊ 必至の ひっしの inevitable

◊ 至る いたる arrive, lead to

1199 票 11 ▶ひょう

投票 とうひょう cv. vote

開票 かいひょう cv. count votes,
open ballot boxes

得票率 とくひょうりつ percentage of
votes obtained

票 ひょう vote, ballot, slip of
paper

1200 標 15 ▶ひょう

目標 もくひょう goal

標準的な ひょうじゅんてきな standard

標準語 ひょうじゅんご standard lan-
guage

◊ 標語 ひょうご motto, slogan

◊ 標本 ひょうほん specimen

◊ 道路標識 どうろひょうしき traffic sign

第 4 水準

(Level 4)

1201−1420

(95)

1201 戻 7
▶れい 1081
▷もど(す), もど(る) cf. 涙

戻る もどる return, go back
後戻り あともどり *cv.* go/turn back
戻す もどす pay/give back, vomit
差し戻す さしもどす send back, remand (a case)
◊ 返戻 へんれい *cv.* give back, return

1202 丘 5
▶きゅう
▷おか

丘 おか hill cf. *Oka* can be written as 岡, but this is not a *Jōyō Kanji.*
自由が丘 じゆうがおか Jiyugaoka (an area in Tokyo)
砂丘 さきゅう sand hill, dune

1203 匹 4
▶ひつ
▷ひき

～匹 ～ひき/びき/ぴき (counter for animals) cf. 一匹(いっぴき), 二匹(にひき), 三匹(さんびき)
匹敵 ひってき *cv.* be a match for

1204 司 5
▶し

司会 しかい emcee, chairperson (of a conference/etc.); *cv.* chair (a conference/etc.)
上司 じょうし (one's) boss
司法 しほう judiciary

1205 詞 12
▶し

歌詞 かし lyrics, words to a song
品詞 ひんし part of speech

1206 訂 9
▶てい

訂正 ていせい *cv.* correct
改訂 かいてい *cv.* revise

1207 訴 12
▶そ
▷うった(える)

訴える うったえる sue, appeal
訴訟 そしょう lawsuit
起訴 きそ *cv.* prosecute, charge
告訴 こくそ *cv.* accuse, sue, lodge a complaint
勝訴 しょうそ *cv.* win a suit/case
敗訴 はいそ *cv.* lose a suit/case

1208 訟 11
▶しょう

訴訟 そしょう lawsuit

1209 譲 20
▶じょう
▷ゆず(る)

譲る ゆずる yield, transfer
親譲りの おやゆずりの inherited from a parent
譲歩 じょうほ *cv.* compromise, concede
譲渡 じょうと *cv.* hand over, transfer

〈いろいろな品詞〉

名詞(めいし) noun　動詞(どうし) verb　形容詞(けいようし) adjective
副詞(ふくし) adverb　代名詞(だいめいし) pronoun

歴 割譲　　かつじょう　*cv.* cede (territory)

1210 購 17　▶こう

購読	こうどく　*cv.* subscribe
購読料	こうどくりょう　subscription rate
購買力	こうばいりょく　purchasing power
購入	こうにゅう　*cv.* purchase

⑼⑹

1211 廷 7　▶てい

法廷	ほうてい　law court
開廷	かいてい　*cv.* open a court
出廷	しゅってい　*cv.* appear in court
宮廷	きゅうてい　imperial palace

1212 処 5　▶しょ

対処	たいしょ　*cv.* cope with
処理	しょり　*cv.* treat, deal with
処分	しょぶん　*cv.* dispose of, deal with, punish
処置	しょち　treatment, measures; *cv.* deal with, take measures
処女	しょじょ　virgin

1213 拠 8　▶きょ，こ

| 証拠 | しょうこ　evidence |

根拠	こんきょ　basis, grounds
拠点	きょてん　base, position
準拠	じゅんきょ　*cv.* conform to (guidelines/standards/etc.)

1214 遣 13　▶けん　▷つか(う)，つか(わす)

派遣	はけん　*cv.* dispatch
小遣い	こづかい　pocket money
仮名遣い	△かなづかい　*kana* usage
言葉遣い	ことばづかい　wording, phraseology
遣わす	つかわす　send, dispatch, give

1215 還 16　▶かん

返還	へんかん　*cv.* return
生還	せいかん　*cv.* come back alive
還元	かんげん　*cv.* restore, return (the company's profits to the consumers)

1216 逐 10　▶ちく

逐語訳	ちくごやく　word-for-word/literal translation
逐一	ちくいち　one by one, in detail
逐次	ちくじ　one after another, one by one
◇*駆逐	くちく　*cv.* expel, drive away

〈漢字の形に気をつけましょう・41〉

1209	495	991	1210	1499
譲	講	構	購	*溝
譲歩する	講義をする	流通機構	家を購入する	*溝を*掘る

みぞ　ほ

1217 遂 12 ▶すい
▷と(げる)

遂行	すいこう *cv.* carry out, execute, accomplish
自殺未遂	じさつみすい attempted suicide
やり遂げる	やりとげる carry out, go through with

1218 墜 15 ▶つい
1693
cf. 堕

墜落	ついらく *cv.* fall, crash (used for aircraft)
撃墜	げきつい *cv.* shoot down (a plane)
失墜	しっつい *cv.* lose (prestige/credit/etc.)

1219 悔 9 ▶かい
▷く(いる), く(やむ), くや(しい)

後悔	こうかい *cv.* regret
悔しい	くやしい feel bitter/vexed
悔やむ	くやむ repent, regret, be sorry for
◇ 悔いる	くいる repent, regret

1220 慎 13 ▶しん
▷つつし(む)

| 慎重な | しんちょうな cautious |
| 慎む | つつしむ be discreet, refrain from |

1221 頻 17 ▶ひん

頻繁に	ひんぱんに frequently
頻発	ひんぱつ *cv.* occur frequently
頻出	ひんしゅつ *cv.* appear frequently
頻度	ひんど frequency

1222 項 12 ▶こう

事項	じこう matters, items
項目	こうもく item, heading
条項	じょうこう article, clause, provision
要項	ようこう guidelines/handbook (on applying to a school/etc.)

1223 販 11 ▶はん

販売	はんばい *cv.* sell, market, deal in
自動販売機	じどうはんばいき vending machine
市販	しはん *cv.* market
販路	はんろ market (for goods), outlet

1224 贈 18 ▶ぞう, そう
▷おく(る)

| 贈(り)物 | おくりもの gift |

〈漢字の形に気をつけましょう・42〉

1213	1212	1211	542	689	688
拠	処	廷	庭	延	誕

証拠を提出する　　適切な処置　　法廷に出る　　日本庭園

延長戦　　誕生日

贈る	おくる　give a present
贈与税	ぞうよぜい　gift tax
贈答品	ぞうとうひん　gift
寄贈	きそう，きぞう　*cv.* give a present, donate

1225 **賄** 13
▶わい
▷まかな（う）

賄賂	わいろ　bribe
贈賄	ぞうわい　giving a bribe, bribery
収賄	しゅうわい　accepting a bribe, bribery
贈収賄事件	ぞうしゅうわいじけん　bribery case
賄う	まかなう　cover the cost of, provide (meals/etc.)

1226 **賂** 13
▶ろ

cf. 賂 is not a *Jōyō Kanji*, but it has been included in this text.

| 賄賂 | わいろ　bribe |

1227 **賢** 16
▶けん
▷かしこ（い）

賢明な	けんめいな　wise, intelligent
賢人会議	けんじんかいぎ　wise people's forum
良妻賢母	りょうさいけんぼ　good wife and wise mother
賢い	かしこい　wise

1228 **堅** 12
▶けん
▷かた（い）

堅い	かたい　firm, hard, solid
堅固な	けんごな　strong, solid
堅実な	けんじつな　reliable, sound, solid
中堅企業	ちゅうけんきぎょう　medium-sized company
堅持	けんじ　*cv.* hold fast to, adhere to

1229 **臨** 18
▶りん
▷のぞ（む）

臨時の	りんじの　temporary, extraordinary
臨時国会	りんじこっかい　extraordinary session of the Diet
臨床心理学	りんしょうしんりがく　clinical psychology
臨終	りんじゅう　one's last moments, one's death
臨む	のぞむ　face (the ocean/a tough situation/etc.)

1230 **幹** 13
▶かん
▷みき

新幹線	しんかんせん　the *Shinkansen*, Japan's bullet train
幹部	かんぶ　managing staff, executive members, key officers
幹事長	かんじちょう　secretary-general/executive secretary (of a party)
根幹	こんかん　basis, root, nucleus
語幹	ごかん　stem of a word

〈漢字の形に気をつけましょう・43〉

1179　1214　1215　1035
遺　遣　還　環

遺伝の法則　　自衛隊の海外派遣　　領土を返還する　　環境破壊

| 幹 | みき | tree trunk, important part |

1231 稿 15 ▶こう　　83 313　cf. 高橋

原稿	げんこう	manuscript
草稿	そうこう	rough draft
投稿	とうこう	cv. contribute (to a magazine/newspaper/etc.)

1232 稼 15 ▶か　▷かせ(ぐ)　52 599　cf. 家嫁

稼ぐ	かせぐ	earn money
稼ぎ	かせぎ	earnings, income
稼働	かどう	cv. work, operate

1233 稲 14 ▶とう　▷いね, いな

稲	いね	rice plant
稲作	いなさく	rice growing
◇ 水稲	すいとう	paddy rice
◇ 早稲田大学	わせだだいがく	Waseda University

1234 穏 16 ▶おん　▷おだ(やか)

穏やかな	おだやかな	gentle, calm, peaceful
平穏な	へいおんな	peaceful
穏和な	おんわな	gentle
安穏な	あんのんな	easy and peaceful

1235 隠 14 ▶いん　▷かく(す), かく(れる)

隠す	かくす	hide, conceal
隠れる	かくれる	hide
隠居	いんきょ	a person retired from public life; cv. retire from public life

1236 隔 13 ▶かく　▷へだ(てる), へだ(たる)

間隔	かんかく	space, interval
隔離	かくり	cv. isolate, quarantine
隔てる	へだてる	separate, partition off
隔たる	へだたる	be distant from, be isolated/estranged

1237 融 16 ▶ゆう

金融	きんゆう	finance, financing
金融機関	きんゆうきかん	financial institution
融資	ゆうし	cv.vi. finance, loan, furnish funds
融通がきく	ゆうずうがきく	flexible
融通	ゆうずう	cv. lend (money)
融合	ゆうごう	cv. fuse, merge
核融合	かくゆうごう	nuclear fusion

〈漢字の形に気をつけましょう・44〉

1216 逐　1217 遂　1218 墜　1693 *堕

逐語訳　任務を遂行する　旅客機が墜落する　*堕落した生活
だらく

1238　邸　8	▶てい		

首相官邸	しゅしょうかんてい　official residence of the prime minister
私邸	してい　private residence (in contrast to official residence)
公邸	こうてい　official residence
邸宅	ていたく　residence

1239　隅　12　　▶ぐう　　▷すみ

隅	すみ　corner
隅田川	すみだがわ　Sumida River
◇ 一隅	いちぐう　corner, nook

1240　偶　11　　▶ぐう

偶然	ぐうぜん　by chance, by coincidence
偶発的な	ぐうはつてきな　accidental
偶数	ぐうすう　even number 反*奇数(きすう)　odd number
配偶者	はいぐうしゃ　spouse
偶像	ぐうぞう　idol, icon

99

1241　僕　14　　▶ぼく

僕	ぼく　I (in masculine speech)
◇ 下僕	げぼく　manservant
◇ 従僕	じゅうぼく　servant

1242　偉　12　　▶い　　▷えら(い)

偉大な	いだいな　great, grand
偉人	いじん　great person
偉い	えらい　great

1243　俗　9　　▶ぞく　　1126　cf. 浴

俗語	ぞくご　slang
風俗	ふうぞく　public morals, manners, customs
民俗学	みんぞくがく　folklore

1244　侵　9　　▶しん　　▷おか(す)　　1496　cf. 浸

侵略	しんりゃく　cv. invade, commit act of aggression
侵入	しんにゅう　cv. invade
侵害	しんがい　cv. infringe
侵攻	しんこう　cv. invade
侵す	おかす　invade, violate, infringe on

1245　伺　7　　▶し　　▷うかが(う)

| 伺う | うかがう　visit, ask, inquire (humble) |
| 歴 伺候 | しこう　cv. attend (one's lord), make a courtesy call |

〈漢字の形に気をつけましょう・45〉

74 母　164 毎　454 海　969 梅　1219 悔　1801 *侮

父と母　毎日　青い海　梅の花　悔しい思いをする　人を*侮*辱する
ぶじょく

1246 伸 7	▶しん ▷の(びる), 　の(ばす)	585 1169 cf. 申 仲

伸びる	のびる	be stretched, be prolonged, be extended
伸ばす	のばす	stretch, prolong, extend
追伸	ついしん	P.S.
屈伸	くっしん	bending and stretching

1247 倣 10	▶ほう ▷なら(う)	

模倣	もほう	cv. imitate
例に倣って	れいにならって	following the example

1248 催 13	▶さい ▷もよお(す)	

開催	かいさい	cv. hold (an event)
主催	しゅさい	cv. sponsor, promote
主催者	しゅさいしゃ	sponsor, promoter
催す	もよおす	hold (an event), feel (sleepy/cold/etc.)
催し物	もよおしもの	entertainment, special event
催眠術	さいみんじゅつ	hypnotism
◊ 催涙ガス	さいるいガス	tear gas

1249 債 13	▶さい	886 638 cf. 積 責

国債	こくさい	goverment bond

社債	しゃさい	bond, debenture
債券	さいけん	bond
債権(者)	さいけん(しゃ)	credit(or)
債務(者)	さいむ(しゃ)	debt(or)
負債	ふさい	debt, liabilities

1250 併 8	▶へい ▷あわ(せる)	

合併	がっぺい	cv. form a merger
併用	へいよう	cv. use together, use two things at the same time
併発	へいはつ	cv. have complications (from surgery/a disease/etc.)
併せる	あわせる	put together, combine

1251 圏 12	▶けん	

首都圏	しゅとけん	metropolitan area
共産圏	きょうさんけん	the Communist bloc
北極圏	ほっきょくけん	the Arctic Circle
南極圏	なんきょくけん	the Antarctic Circle
大気圏	たいきけん	the atmosphere

1252 宇 6	▶う	

宇宙	うちゅう	the universe, space

〈漢字の形に気をつけましょう・46〉

238	433	853	1227
質	貿	資	賢

質問をする　　外国との貿易　　教員の資格　　賢明なやり方

1253 宙 8 ▶ちゅう

| 宇宙 | うちゅう | the universe, space |
| 宙返り | ちゅうがえり | somersault |

1254 抽 8 ▶ちゅう　624 cf. 油

抽象的な	ちゅうしょうてきな	abstract
抽出	ちゅうしゅつ	cv. extract, sample
抽選	ちゅうせん	lottery, drawing of lots; cv. draw lots, ballot

1255 拍 8 ▶はく，ひょう

拍手	はくしゅ	cv. clap one's hands, applaud
拍車	はくしゃ	spur
◇*脈拍	みゃくはく	pulse
拍子	ひょうし	tempo, time, chance, the moment

1256 摘 14 ▶てき ▷つ(む)

指摘	してき	cv. point out
摘出	てきしゅつ	cv. extract, take out, remove
摘発	てきはつ	cv. expose, unmask
摘む	つむ	pick (flowers/berries/etc.)
茶摘み	ちゃつみ	tea picking

1257 握 12 ▶あく ▷にぎ(る)

握手	あくしゅ	cv. shake hands
握力	あくりょく	grasping power, grip
◇*掌握	しょうあく	cv. hold, command, seize
握る	にぎる	grip, grasp, take hold of

1258 探 11 ▶たん ▷さぐ(る)，さが(す)

探す	さがす	look for
探る	さぐる	grope for, search
探求	たんきゅう	cv. investigate
探知器	たんちき	detector

1259 掘 11 ▶くつ ▷ほ(る)　349 cf. 屈

掘る	ほる	dig
発掘	はっくつ	cv. excavate
採掘	さいくつ	cv. mine

1260 堀 11 ▷ほり　349 cf. 屈

堀	ほり	moat
内堀	うちぼり	inner moat
外堀	そとぼり	outer moat
◇*釣堀	つりぼり	fishing pond

〈漢字の形に気をつけましょう・47〉

1178　　1239　　1240
遇　隅　偶

社員の待遇　部屋の隅　街で偶然友達に会った

1261 埋 10	▶まい ▷う(める), う(まる), う(もれる)	
埋める	うめる	bury, fill up
埋立地	うめたてち	reclaimed land
埋もれる	うもれる	be buried, sink into obscurity
埋葬	まいそう	cv. bury (a dead person)
埋没	まいぼつ	cv. be buried
埋蔵金	まいぞうきん	money buried in the ground

⑩

1262 排 11	▶はい	
排気ガス	はいきガス	exhaust gas
排水	はいすい	drainage; cv.vi. drain
排他的な	はいたてきな	exclusive
排日運動	はいにちうんどう	anti-Japanese movement

1263 拓 8	▶たく	
開拓	かいたく	cv. open up, bring (land) under cultivation
開拓者	かいたくしゃ	settler, pioneer
干拓	かんたく	cv. reclaim land by drainage
特 拓本	たくほん	rubbing (of an inscription)

1264 抑 7	▶よく ▷おさ(える)	1854 cf. 柳
抑制	よくせい	cv. control, restrain, suppress
抑圧	よくあつ	cv. oppress, suppress
抑止力	よくしりょく	deterrent
抑える	おさえる	hold down

1265 拐 8	▶かい	
誘拐	ゆうかい	cv. kidnap

1266 扱 6	▷あつか(う)	
扱う	あつかう	handle, deal with
取り扱う	とりあつかう	deal in, handle
取扱注意	とりあつかいちゅうい	Handle with Care

1267 撮 15	▶さつ ▷と(る)	439 cf. 最
撮影	さつえい	cv. make a film, take a picture
撮影所	さつえいじょ	film studio
撮る	とる	take (a picture)

1268 挑 9	▶ちょう ▷いど(む)	
挑戦	ちょうせん	cv. challenge
挑戦者	ちょうせんしゃ	challenger
挑発	ちょうはつ	cv. arouse, excite

〈漢字の形に気をつけましょう・48〉

307 業	1241 僕	1489 *撲
大企業と中小企業	*君と僕 きみ	打*撲傷 だ ぼくしょう

196

挑発的な	ちょうはつてきな provocative, suggestive
挑む	いどむ challenge, defy

1269 6 兆 ▶ちょう
▷きざ(す)，きざ(し)

一兆円	いっちょうえん one trillion yen cf. 一億円（いちおくえん）one hundred million yen
前兆	ぜんちょう omen, sign
兆し	きざし sign, symptoms, indication

1270 12 援 ▶えん

援助	えんじょ cv. aid, assist
応援	おうえん cv. cheer, aid, support
声援	せいえん shout of encouragement; cv. cheer, encourage
援軍	えんぐん reinforcements
後援会	こうえんかい group supporting a politician, fan club

1271 15 緩 ▶かん
▷ゆる(い)，ゆる(やか)，ゆる(む)，ゆる(める)

緩和	かんわ cv. relieve, ease, relax
規制緩和	きせいかんわ deregulation, relaxation of restrictions
緩やかな	ゆるやかな loose, slack
緩い	ゆるい loose, gentle
緩める	ゆるめる loosen, relieve, relax, slacken

⑩

1272 3 丈 ▶じょう
▷たけ

大丈夫	だいじょうぶ all right, okay, safe
丈夫な	じょうぶな strong, durable, robust
◇ 背丈	せたけ one's height

1273 8 牧 ▶ぼく
▷まき　cf. 枚 982

牧場	ぼくじょう stock farm, ranch, pasture
牧草	ぼくそう grass, pasture, meadow
放牧	ほうぼく cv. pasture, graze
遊牧	ゆうぼく nomadism
牧師	ぼくし clergyman, minister
◇ 牧場	まきば pasture

1274 10 畜 ▶ちく　cf. 蓄 743

家畜	かちく livestock, domestic animal
牧畜業	ぼくちくぎょう stock farming

1275 6 充 ▶じゅう
▷あ(てる)

充電	じゅうでん cv. charge/recharge (electricity)
充実した	じゅうじつした full, complete, satisfying

〈漢字の形に気をつけましょう・49〉

385	1242	110	1865
違	偉	遠	*猿

規則に違反する　　偉大な人物　　遠心力　　類人*猿
るいじん えん

充満	じゅうまん　*cv.* be full of (poisonous gas/etc.)
充足	じゅうそく　*cv.* suffice
充血	じゅうけつ　*cv.* be bloodshot, be congested
拡充	かくじゅう　*cv.* expand, enlarge, amplify
充てる	あてる　assign, use, allot

1276 玄 5　▶げん

玄関	げんかん　front door/entrance, porch
玄米	げんまい　brown rice
玄人	△くろうと　expert, professional, specialist　cf. 素人（△しろうと）amateur

1277 豪 14　▶ごう　52 cf. 家

豪雨	ごうう　heavy rainfall, torrential downpour
豪遊	ごうゆう　*cv.* go on an extravagant spree
◇ 豪*華な	ごうかな　luxurious, magnificent
豪勢な	ごうせいな　luxurious, grand
豪州	ごうしゅう　Australia

1278 盲 8　▶もう

| 盲人 | もうじん　blind person, the blind |
| 色盲 | しきもう　color blind |

文盲	もんもう　illiterate
盲目の	もうもくの　blind
盲点	もうてん　blind spot

1279 帽 12　▶ぼう　1669 cf. 冒

| 帽子 | ぼうし　hat, cap |

1280 昇 8　▶しょう　1915 ▷のぼ(る)　cf. 升

上昇	じょうしょう　*cv.* rise, ascend
昇進	しょうしん　*cv.* be promoted
昇格	しょうかく　*cv.* be promoted (to an upper rank)
昇給	しょうきゅう　*cv.* get a pay raise
昇る	のぼる　rise

⑩

1281 曇 16　▶どん　▷くも(る)

曇り	くもり　cloudy
曇る	くもる　get cloudy
曇天	どんてん　cloudy

1282 糧 18　▶りょう，ろう　▷かて

食糧	しょくりょう　food, provisions
歴 兵糧	ひょうろう　military provisions
◇ 日々の糧	ひびのかて　one's daily bread

〈漢字の形に気をつけましょう・50〉

312　339　1270　1271
授　暖　援　緩

つまらない授業　　暖房　　海外経済援助　　規制緩和

1283 糖 16 ▶とう

砂糖	さとう	sugar
糖分	とうぶん	sugar content

1284 粧 12 ▶しょう

化粧	けしょう	cv. make up, put on make up
化粧品	けしょうひん	cosmetics
化粧室	けしょうしつ	dressing room, lavatory

1285 臭 9 ▶しゅう 1118 ▷くさ(い) cf. 息

臭い	くさい	smelly, suspicious (-looking)
悪臭	あくしゅう	bad smell, offensive odor

1286 鼻 14 ▶び ▷はな

鼻	はな	nose
鼻血	はなぢ	nosebleed
特 鼻*孔	びこう	nostril

1287 憩 16 ▶けい 392 ▷いこ(い)，いこ(う) cf. 想

休憩	きゅうけい	rest, break; cv. rest, have a break
休憩時間	きゅうけいじかん	recess, intermission

憩い	いこい	rest
憩う	いこう	rest

1288 舌 6 ▶ぜつ ▷した

舌	した	tongue
二枚舌	にまいじた	forked tongue, duplicity
舌打ち	したうち	cv. click one's tongue
舌戦	ぜっせん	verbal warfare, heated discussion
弁舌	べんぜつ	eloquence
毒舌	どくぜつ	malicious words, venomous tongue

1289 君 7 ▶くん ▷きみ

君	きみ	you, ruler
君主	くんしゅ	monarch, sovereign
立憲君主制	りっけんくんしゅせい	constitutional monarchy
君臨	くんりん	cv. reign over (a country)

1290 含 7 ▶がん ▷ふく(む)，ふく(める)

含む	ふくむ	contain, include, hold (in one's mouth)
含める	ふくめる	include
含有量	がんゆうりょう	amount contained
含蓄	がんちく	implication

〈漢字の形に気をつけましょう・51〉

87 大　　320 文　　1272 丈

大きい家　　文学と歴史　　丈夫な体

⑩

1291	叫 6	▶きょう 828 ▷さけ(ぶ) cf. 収

叫ぶ	さけぶ shout, cry out
叫び声	さけびごえ scream
絶叫	ぜっきょう *cv.* scream

1292	奇 8	▶き 1120 cf. 寄

好奇心	こうきしん curiosity
奇妙な	きみょうな strange, curious, odd
奇数	きすう odd number 反 偶数 (ぐうすう) even number

1293	崎 11	▷さき

| 長崎 | ながさき Nagasaki (a city on the western coast of Kyushu) |
| 宮崎 | みやざき Miyazaki (a city on the eastern coast of Kyushu) |

1294	峡 9	▶きょう 560 cf. 狭

| 海峡 | かいきょう strait, channel |
| ドーバー海峡 | ドーバーかいきょう the Strait of Dover |

1295	紅 9	▶こう, く ▷べに, くれない

| 紅茶 | こうちゃ black tea |

紅葉	こうよう autumn/colored leaves
紅葉	△もみじ maple tree, autumn/colored leaves
真紅の	しんくの scarlet
口紅	くちべに lipstick
◇ 紅	くれない crimson

1296	繊 17	▶せん 882 cf. 織

繊維	せんい fiber, textile
繊維工業	せんいこうぎょう textile industry
合成繊維	ごうせいせんい synthetic fiber
化学繊維	かがくせんい synthetic fiber cf. *abbr.* 化繊(かせん)
繊細な	せんさいな delicate, fine

1297	維 14	▶い 81 1100 cf. 誰 稚

維持	いじ *cv.* maintain, sustain
維持費	いじひ maintenance costs
歴 明治維新	めいじいしん the Meiji Restoration

1298	紛 10	▶ふん 1557 ▷まぎ(れる), まぎ(らす), cf. 粉 まぎ(らわす), まぎ(らわしい)

| 国境紛争 | こっきょうふんそう border dispute |

〈漢字の形に気をつけましょう・52〉

532	892	893	1006	1288	1289	1290
台	告	吉	否	舌	君	含

台所　報告をする　大安吉日　犯行を否認する　毒舌家

君と僕　ボーナスを含めて年収一千万円

内紛	ないふん internal trouble/strife
紛失	ふんしつ *cv.* lose (an object)
紛れる	まぎれる be mistaken (for), be mixed with
紛らす	まぎらす divert, distract
紛らわしい	まぎらわしい easily confused, hard to distinguish

1299 紳 11 ▶しん 586 cf. 神

紳士	しんし gentleman
紳士服	しんしふく men's clothing
紳士協定	しんしきょうてい gentlemen's agreement

1300 縦 16 ▶じゅう ▷たて

縦の	たての vertical
縦線	たてせん vertical line
縦断	じゅうだん *cv.* travel across
◇ *操縦	そうじゅう *cv.* steer

⑩

1301 索 10 ▶さく

索引	さくいん index
思索	しさく *cv.* contemplate
◇ *捜索	そうさく *cv.* search/look for
探索	たんさく *cv.* search/look for

1302 累 11 ▶るい

累積赤字	るいせきあかじ cumulative deficit
累積債務	るいせきさいむ cumulative debts
累進課税	るいしんかぜい progressive/graduated taxation
累計	るいけい (sum) total; *cv.* total

1303 畳 12 ▶じょう 1924 ▷たた(む), たたみ cf. 且

畳	たたみ *tatami*, Japanese straw mat
四畳半	よじょうはん four-and-a-half-mat room
折り畳み式	おりたたみしき collapsible
畳む	たたむ fold up

1304 翼 17 ▶よく ▷つばさ

右翼	うよく the right wing, rightist
左翼	さよく the left wing, leftist
翼	つばさ wing

1305 裸 13 ▶ら ▷はだか

裸	はだか nude, naked
◇ 裸足	▲はだし barefoot
裸婦	らふ nude woman
裸体画	らたいが nude picture

1306 軌 9 ▶き

| 軌道 | きどう orbit, (railroad) track, right lines |

1307 載 13 ▶さい ▷の(せる), の(る)

掲載	けいさい *cv.* publish, carry an article
積載	せきさい *cv.* load
載せる	のせる place (on), load, publish

1308 軟 11

▶なん
▷やわ(らか)，やわ(らかい)

軟らかい	やわらかい	soft
◇*柔軟な	じゅうなんな	flexible
軟弱な	なんじゃくな	weak, feeble
軟骨	なんこつ	cartilage
軟化	なんか	cv. become flexible

1309 硬 12

▶こう
▷かた(い)

硬い	かたい	hard, solid
硬貨	こうか	coin
硬度	こうど	(degree of) hardness
強硬な	きょうこうな	firm (attitude), strong
硬化	こうか	cv. stiffen, harden

1310 柔 9

▶じゅう，にゅう　　1855
▷やわ(らか)，　　cf. 桑
やわ(らかい)

柔らかい	やわらかい	soft, tender, gentle
柔軟な	じゅうなんな	pliant, supple, flexible
柔道	じゅうどう	judo
◇ 柔和な	にゅうわな	gentle, mild, tender, soft

----

⑩⑥

1311 炊 8

▶すい
▷た(く)

炊事	すいじ	cooking, kitchen work; cv. vi. do the cooking
自炊	じすい	cv. do one's own cooking
炊飯器	すいはんき	rice cooker
炊く	たく	cook (rice)

1312 冊 5

▶さつ，さく

～冊	～さつ	(counter for books)
別冊	べっさつ	separate volume
分冊	ぶんさつ	separate volume
◇ 短冊	たんざく	strip of fancy paper (for writing haiku/etc.)

1313 盤 15

▶ばん　　648
cf. 般

基盤	きばん	foundation, base
地盤	じばん	foundation, base, constituency, sphere of influence
円盤	えんばん	disk, UFO cf. "UFO" is usually written as UFO, and is read as *yūfō*.
終盤戦	しゅうばんせん	last stage (of a game/election campaign /etc.)

1314 盆 9

▶ぼん

(お)盆	(お)ぼん	the *Bon* Festival, tray
盆地	ぼんち	basin
◇ 盆*栽	ぼんさい	bonsai, potted dwarf tree

1315 煮 12

▶しゃ
▷に(る)，に(える)，に(やす)

煮る	にる	boil, cook
煮える	にえる	boil, be cooked
◇ 業を煮やす	ごうをにやす	become exasperated
◇ 煮*沸	しゃふつ	cv. boil

1316 署 13

▶しょ　　1031
cf. 著

署名	しょめい	cv. sign
警察署	けいさつしょ	police office
消防署	しょうぼうしょ	fire station

税務署　　ぜいむしょ　tax office

1317 罰 14　▶ばつ，ばち　cf. 罪 1047

罰　　　　ばつ　punishment
罰する　　ばっする　punish, chastise
罰金　　　ばっきん　fine
体罰　　　たいばつ　corporal/physical punishment
歴 罰　　　ばち　divine punishment, curse, retribution

1318 型 9　▶けい　▷かた

大型　　　おおがた　large (truck/machine/etc.)
中型　　　ちゅうがた　medium (truck/machine/etc.)
小型　　　こがた　small (truck/machine/etc.)
型　　　　かた　type, model
典型的な　てんけいてきな　typical
原型　　　げんけい　prototype
類型的な　るいけいてきな　stereotypical

1319 刺 8　▶し　▷さ(す)，さ(さる)

刺す　　　さす　pierce, stab
刺さる　　ささる　stick, pierce
刺し身　　さしみ　sliced raw fish
名刺　　　めいし　business card
風刺　　　ふうし　satire; cv. satirize

刺激　　　しげき　cv. stimulate, incite, irritate

1320 削 9　▶さく　▷けず(る)

削減　　　さくげん　cv. reduce
削除　　　さくじょ　cv. delete
削る　　　けずる　sharpen (a pencil), plane, curtail, cut down
◇*鉛筆削り　えんぴつけずり　pencil sharpener

1321 剰 11　▶じょう

過剰な　　かじょうな　excessive
余剰人員　よじょうじんいん　superflous personnel
剰余金　　じょうよきん　surplus (fund)

1322 垂 8　▶すい　▷た(れる)，た(らす)

垂直の　　すいちょくの　vertical, perpendicular
垂線　　　すいせん　perpendicular line
雨垂れ　　あまだれ　raindrops (from a tree/roof/etc.)
垂らす　　たらす　drip (as in sweat/saliva/etc.)

1323 華 10　▶か，け　▷はな

中華料理　ちゅうかりょうり　Chinese food

〈漢字の形に気をつけましょう・53〉

垂 郵 睡 *錘
1322　226　977　1942

垂線　郵便局　睡眠時間　*紡*錘
　　　　　　　　　　　　ぼう すい

203

中華思想	ちゅうかしそう the belief that China is the center of the world/civilization
中華人民共和国	ちゅうかじんみんきょうわこく People's Republic of China
中華民国	ちゅうかみんこく Republic of China
華道	かどう the Japanese art of flower arrangement
華やかな	はなやかな flowery, brilliant
歴 *香華	こうげ incense and flowers

1324 兼 10 ▶けん ▷か(ねる)

兼任	けんにん cv. hold two posts simultaneously
首相兼外相	しゅしょうけんがいしょう prime minister who is also the foreign minister
兼ねる	かねる double as

1325 嫌 13 ▶けん, げん ▷きら(う), いや cf. 嬢 1649

嫌いな	きらいな dislike
好き嫌い	すききらい likes and dislikes
嫌う	きらう dislike, hate
嫌悪感	けんおかん disgust
機嫌	きげん mood
嫌な	いやな disagreeable, unpleasant, disgusting

1326 尋 12 ▶じん ▷たず(ねる)

尋ねる	たずねる inquire
尋問	じんもん cv. question, examine
◊ 尋常な	じんじょうな ordinary

1327 寿 7 ▶じゅ ▷ことぶき

寿命	じゅみょう lifespan
長寿	ちょうじゅ longevity
◊ 寿	ことぶき congratulations, longevity
◊ 寿司	すし sushi

1328 闘 18 ▶とう ▷たたか(う)

戦闘	せんとう battle, combat
戦闘機	せんとうき fighter (plane)
階級闘争	かいきゅうとうそう class struggle
春闘	しゅんとう spring labor offensive
◊ 闘う	たたかう fight, struggle, battle

1329 娯 10 ▶ご cf. 誤 呉 949 1929

| 娯楽 | ごらく amusement, entertainment |

1330 妊 7 ▶にん

妊娠	にんしん cv. become pregnant
妊婦	にんぷ pregnant woman
◊ *避妊	ひにん contraception; cv. prevent conception, practice birth control

1331 娠 10 ▶しん

| 妊娠 | にんしん cv. become pregnant |
| 人工妊娠中絶 | じんこうにんしんちゅうぜつ abortion cf. 人工妊娠中絶 is very often abbreviated as 人工中絶. |

108

1332 妥 7 ▶だ cf. 受 安 269 84

| 妥協 | だきょう cv. compromise |

妥当な　　だとうな　proper, appropriate, adequate

妥結　　　だけつ　cv. come to terms, reach an agreement

1333 威 9	▶い

権威　　　けんい　authoritative figure, authority

威厳　　　いげん　dignity, stateliness

威信　　　いしん　prestige

威力　　　いりょく　destructive power

威張る　　いばる　be haughty, put on airs, boast

示威行動　じいこうどう　threatening action

◇ *脅威　　きょうい　threat

1334 戒 7	▶かい　　　　　511 ▷いまし(める)　cf. 械

十戒　　　じゅっかい　the Ten Commandments

戒律　　　かいりつ　(religious) precepts

警戒　　　けいかい　cv. be on one's guard, be cautious, watch out for

厳戒体制　げんかいたいせい　be on full alert

戒め　　　いましめ　admonition

1335 釣 11	▶ちょう ▷つ(る)

釣り　　　つり　fishing

釣る　　　つる　fish

釣(り)合い　つりあい　balance, proportion

釣り合う　つりあう　be balanced, be matched

お釣り　　おつり　change

◇ 釣果　　ちょうか　catch (of fish)

1336 鈴 13	▶れい, りん ▷すず

鈴　　　　すず　bell (that tinkles/jingles) cf. *鐘(かね) bell (like those used at a temple/church)

鈴虫　　　すずむし　bell cricket

鈴木　　　すずき　(surname)

風鈴　　　ふうりん　wind-bell

呼び鈴　　よびりん　doorbell

◇ 電鈴　　でんれい　electric bell

1337 鋼 16	▶こう ▷はがね

鉄鋼　　　てっこう　steel

鉄鋼業　　てっこうぎょう　steel industry

◇ 鋼　　　はがね　steel

1338 鎖 18	▶さ ▷くさり

連鎖反応　れんさはんのう　chain reaction

鎖　　　　くさり　chain

鎖国　　　さこく　cv. close the country

閉鎖　　　へいさ　cv. shut down, close down

〈漢字の形に気をつけましょう・54〉

84	269	1332	661
安	受	妥	姿

安心する　　受付　　妥協する　　姿を見せる

封鎖	ふうさ	cv. block off, blockade

1339 13
鉛
▶えん
▷なまり

鉛筆	えんぴつ	pencil
鉛	なまり	lead

1340 14
銅
▶どう

銅	どう	copper
銅像	どうぞう	bronze statue
銅メダル	どうメダル	bronze medal

⑩⑨

1341 10
胴
▶どう

胴	どう	trunk
胴体	どうたい	body, trunk, fuselage
胴上げ	どうあげ	cv. hoist shoulder-high
胴回り	どうまわり	girth

1342 12
腕
▶わん
▷うで
979
cf. 瞬

腕	うで	arm, skill, ability
腕時計	うでどけい	wristwatch
腕力	わんりょく	physical strength, force
手腕	しゅわん	ability

1343 9
肺
▶はい

肺	はい	lung
肺病	はいびょう	lung disease
肺結核	はいけっかく	pulmonary tuberculosis
◇ 肺*炎	はいえん	pneumonia

1344 9
胆
▶たん
1050
cf. 担

大胆な	だいたんな	bold, daring
落胆	らくたん	cv. be disappointed, be discouraged
◇ 胆石	たんせき	gallstone

1345 6
肌
▷はだ

肌寒い	はだざむい	chilly
肌	はだ	(human) skin, disposition, character, temperament
地肌	じはだ	bare skin (without make up), (the surface of) the ground
肌着	はだぎ	underwear
◇ 肌*触り	はだざわり	touch, feel

1346 10
飢
▶き
▷う(える)

飢餓	きが	hunger, starvation
飢える	うえる	starve

〈漢字の形に気をつけましょう・55〉

1086	1342	1630	1526
胸	腕	*胞	*陶
胸囲	腕力	細*胞 さい ぼう	*陶器 とう き

1347 15	餓	▶が

| 飢餓 | きが | hunger, starvation |
| 餓死 | がし | cv. starve to death |

1348 13	飼	▶し ▷か(う)

飼う	かう	raise/have/keep (animals)
飼い主	かいぬし	(pet) owner
羊飼い	ひつじかい	shepherd
飼育	しいく	cv. raise, breed
飼料	しりょう	feed, fodder

1349 6	旨	▶し ▷むね

要旨	ようし	gist
趣旨	しゅし	purport
論旨	ろんし	point of an argument
◊ 旨	むね	purport

1350 10	脂	▶し ▷あぶら

脂肪	しぼう	fat
脂	あぶら	fat
脂っこい	あぶらっこい	oily, fatty, greasy

1351 8	肪	▶ぼう

| 脂肪 | しぼう | fat |

1352 8	肥	▶ひ ▷こ(える), こえ, こ(やす), こ(やし)

肥料	ひりょう	fertilizer
肥満	ひまん	cv. grow fat
肥大化	ひだいか	cv. enlarge
◊ 肥える	こえる	grow fat, grow fertile
◊ 肥やす	こやす	fertilize
◊ 肥やし	こやし	manure, night soil
◊ 肥	こえ	manure, night soil

1353 10	脈	▶みゃく 1191 cf. 派

文脈	ぶんみゃく	context
人脈	じんみゃく	line of personal connections
脈	みゃく	pulse, pulsation, vein
動脈	どうみゃく	artery
静脈	じょうみゃく	vein
不整脈	ふせいみゃく	irregular pulse
山脈	さんみゃく	mountain range

1354 16	膨	▶ぼう ▷ふく(らむ), ふく(れる)

膨大な	ぼうだいな	enormous amount of
膨張	ぼうちょう	cv. expand, swell
膨らむ	ふくらむ	swell, expand
膨らます	ふくらます	blow up (a balloon)

1355 8	肢	▶し

| 選択肢 | せんたくし | choices, options |
| 四肢 | しし | the limbs |

1356 9	枯	▶こ ▷か(れる), か(らす)

枯れる	かれる	wither
枯れ葉	かれは	dead/withered leaf
枯れ木	かれき	dead/withered tree

◇ 栄枯盛*衰　えいこせいすい　ups and downs, rises and falls

1357 杉 7	▶すぎ
杉	すぎ　Japanese cedar
杉並木	すぎなみき　row of cedar trees
杉並区	すぎなみく　Suginami Ward (in Tokyo)

1358 彫 11	▶ちょう ▷ほ(る)
彫刻	ちょうこく　sculpture; cv. carve, engrave
彫金	ちょうきん　metal engraving
彫る	ほる　carve
木彫り	きぼり　wood carving
浮き彫り	うきぼり　relief

1359 髪 14	▶はつ ▷かみ
髪の毛	かみのけ　hair (on the head)
白髪の	はくはつの　gray-haired
白髪	△しらが　gray hair, white hair

1360 珍 9	▶ちん ▷めずら(しい)
珍しい	めずらしい　rare, unusual
珍品	ちんぴん　rarity
珍味	ちんみ　delicacy
珍客	ちんきゃく　welcome guest

111

1361 診 12	▶しん ▷み(る)
診察	しんさつ　medical examination; cv. examine (a patient)
診断	しんだん　cv. diagnose

検診	けんしん　medical examination; cv. examine (a person's) body
打診	だしん　cv. tap, sound out (a person on a matter)
往診	おうしん　(doctor's) house call; cv. make a house call
診る	みる　examine, diagnose

1362 療 17	▶りょう
治療	ちりょう　medical treatment, therapy; cv. treat, cure, remedy
医療費	いりょうひ　medical expenses
診療所	しんりょうじょ　clinic
療養所	りょうようじょ　sanitarium, nursing home

1363 症 10	▶しょう
症状	しょうじょう　symptom
病症	びょうしょう　condition of a disease/patient
不眠症	ふみんしょう　insomnia
自閉症	じへいしょう　autism
症候群	しょうこうぐん　syndrome

1364 癖 18	▶へき ▷くせ
癖	くせ　personal habit
◇ 盗癖	とうへき　propensity to steal, kleptomania
◇ 潔癖性の	けっぺきしょうの　fastidious about cleanliness

1365 避 16	▶ひ ▷さ(ける)
避難	ひなん　cv. take refuge
避妊	ひにん　contraception; cv. prevent conception, practice birth control
回避	かいひ　cv. avoid

不可避の　　ふかひの　unavoidable

避ける　　　さける　avoid

1366 恥 10　▶ち
▷は(じる), はじ, は(じらう), は(ずかしい)

恥ずかしい　はずかしい　be embarrassed, be ashamed

恥　　　　　はじ　shame, disgrace

恥じる　　　はじる　feel shame

恥じらう　　はじらう　be shy

◇▲羞恥心　　しゅうちしん　sense of shame, modesty

1367 患 11　▶かん
▷わずら(う)　　cf. 忠 758

患者　　　　かんじゃ　patient

患部　　　　かんぶ　affected/diseased part

◇ 長患い　　ながわずらい　long illness

1368 菌 11　▶きん

殺菌　　　　さっきん　cv. sterilize

無菌の　　　むきんの　germ-free, sterilized

菌　　　　　きん　germ, bacterium, fungus

細菌　　　　さいきん　bacterium, germ

1369 荘 9　▶そう

別荘　　　　べっそう　country villa, summer house

山荘　　　　さんそう　mountain villa/retreat

◇ 荘重な　　そうちょうな　solemn, grave

◇ 荘厳な　　そうごんな　solemn, majestic, impressive

1370 装 12　▶そう, しょう
▷よそお(う)

服装　　　　ふくそう　(style of) dress, clothes

変装　　　　へんそう　cv. disguise

武装　　　　ぶそう　armament; cv. arm

装飾　　　　そうしょく　ornament, decoration; cv. decorate

装置　　　　そうち　device, apparatus, equipment

◇ 衣装　　　いしょう　costume, (wedding) dress

◇ 装う　　　よそおう　wear, feign, pretend

1371 裂 12　▶れつ
▷さ(く), さ(ける)

分裂　　　　ぶんれつ　cv. break up, disunite

破裂　　　　はれつ　cv. burst, explode

決裂　　　　けつれつ　cv. break down (in negotiations)

裂く　　　　さく　vt. tear, split, rip

裂ける　　　さける　vi. tear, split, rip

裂け目　　　さけめ　split, crack

⑪⑫

1372 鈍 12　▶どん
▷にぶ(い), にぶ(る)

鈍感な　　　どんかんな　insensitive, dull

鈍い　　　　にぶい　dull, slow-moving, slow (to understand/learn)

鈍る　　　　にぶる　become dull

1373 鋭 15　▶えい
▷するど(い)

鋭い　　　　するどい　sharp

鋭利な　　　えいりな　sharp

最新鋭の　　さいしんえいの　newest and most powerful

鋭気　　　　えいき　spirit, energy

209

1374 克 7 ▶こく

克服	こくふく　cv. conquer, overcome
克明に	こくめいに　conscientiously, minutely, faithfully

1375 児 7 ▶じ, に

育児	いくじ　child care, nursing
産児制限	さんじせいげん　birth control
児童	じどう　pupil (in a primary school), child, juvenile
小児科	しょうにか　pediatrics

1376 旧 5 ▶きゅう

旧約聖書	きゅうやくせいしょ　the Old Testament　cf.新約聖書(しんやくせいしょ) the New Testament
旧式の	きゅうしきの　old-fashioned, outdated
新旧	しんきゅう　old and new
復旧工事	ふっきゅうこうじ　repair work

1377 慮 15 ▶りょ　1884 cf.虜

遠慮	えんりょ　cv. restrain, hesitate, show reserve
考慮	こうりょ　cv. consider, give consideration to
配慮	はいりょ　consideration, care, concern; cv. give consideration/attention
◇*憂慮	ゆうりょ　cv. be anxious/apprehensive/concerned, worry

1378 寧 14 ▶ねい

丁寧な	ていねいな　polite, careful

1379 寛 13 ▶かん

寛大な	かんだいな　broad-minded
寛容な	かんような　tolerant

1380 寂 11 ▶じゃく, せき ▷さび, さび(しい), さび(れる)

寂しい	さびしい　lonely
寂れる	さびれる　decline in prosperity
寂	さび　elegancy in simplicity
◇ 静寂	せいじゃく　silence, stillness
◇ 寂然とした	せきぜんとした, じゃくねんとした　lonesome, desolate

⑬

1381 孤 9 ▶こ　1447 cf.弧

孤独な	こどくな　lonely, solitary
孤立	こりつ　cv. be isolated
孤島	ことう　solitary island
孤児	こじ　orphan
孤児院	こじいん　orphanage

1382 触 13 ▶しょく ▷ふ(れる), さわ(る)　293 716 cf.解 角

触る	さわる　touch
触れる	ふれる　touch
接触	せっしょく　cv. touch, be in contact with
感触	かんしょく　touch, feel
抵触	ていしょく　cv. conflict (with the law)

1383 踊 14 ▶よう ▷おど(る), おど(り)

踊る	おどる　dance

踊り子　　　　おどりこ　dancer

◇ 日本舞踊　　にほんぶよう　Japanese dancing

1384 躍 21　▶やく
　　　　　　　▷おど（る）

活躍　　　　かつやく　cv. be active

暗躍　　　　あんやく　cv. be active behind the scenes

躍進　　　　やくしん　cv. advance by leaps and bounds

飛躍　　　　ひやく　cv. leap, jump, progress rapidly

躍動　　　　やくどう　cv. move lively

躍り出る　　おどりでる　appear heroically

1385 焦 12　▶しょう
　　　　　　　▷こ（げる），こ（がす），こ（がれる），あせ（る）

焦点　　　　しょうてん　focal point, focus

焦げる　　　こげる　become scorched

焦がす　　　こがす　burn, scorch, char

焦る　　　　あせる　be hasty, be impatient

◇ 焦がれる　こがれる　yearn for

1386 駐 15　▶ちゅう

駐車場　　　ちゅうしゃじょう　parking lot

駐日大使　　ちゅうにちたいし　Ambassador to Japan

1387 循 12　▶じゅん

悪循環　　　あくじゅんかん　vicious circle

血液循環　　けつえきじゅんかん　blood circulation

循環器　　　じゅんかんき　circulatory organ

1388 衝 15　▶しょう

衝突　　　　しょうとつ　cv. collide

衝撃　　　　しょうげき　shock

衝動的な　　しょうどうてきな　impulsive

折衝　　　　せっしょう　negotiation, adjustment; cv. negotiate

緩衝地帯　　かんしょうちたい　buffer zone

1389 征 8　▶せい

征服　　　　せいふく　cv. conquer

征服者　　　せいふくしゃ　conqueror

出征　　　　しゅっせい　cv. go to the front

1390 徐 10　▶じょ

徐々に　　　じょじょに　gradually, slowly

徐行　　　　じょこう　cv. drive slowly

1391 斜 11　▶しゃ
　　　　　　　▷なな（め）　　　　1920
　　　　　　　　　　　　　cf. 斗

斜面　　　　しゃめん　slope, slant

〈漢字の形に気をつけましょう・56〉

190　　1114　　956　　1387

着　看　盾　循

服を着る　　看護婦　　矛盾した考え　　悪循環

斜線	しゃせん	slanting line, slash
斜陽産業	しゃようさんぎょう	declining industry
斜め	ななめ	slanting, diagonal

⑭

1392 滑 13
▶かつ
▷すべ(る)，なめ(らか)

滑る	すべる	slide, slip
滑らかな	なめらかな	smooth
滑走	かっそう	*cv.* slide, roll
滑走路	かっそうろ	runway
円滑な	えんかつな	smooth

1393 潜 15
▶せん
▷ひそ(む)，もぐ(る)

潜水	せんすい	*cv.* dive, submerge
潜水夫	せんすいふ	diver
◇ 潜水*艦	せんすいかん	submarine
潜在的な	せんざいてきな	hidden, latent, potential
潜入	せんにゅう	*cv.* infiltrate
潜る	もぐる	dive, crawl into
潜む	ひそむ	lurk, be in hiding

1394 渇 11
▶かつ
▷かわ(く)

渇く	かわく	be thirsty, get dry
枯渇	こかつ	*cv.* run dry, run out, be exhausted
渇水	かっすい	drought, water shortage

渇望	かつぼう	*cv.* crave, long for

1395 沢 7
▶たく 761 762
▷さわ cf. 訳 尺

金沢	かなざわ	Kanazawa (the capital city of Ishikawa Prefecture)
沢田	さわだ	(surname)
沢	さわ	marsh, mountain stream
光沢	こうたく	luster
毛沢東	もうたくとう	Mao Tse-Tung
◇ *潤沢な	じゅんたくな	abundant
◇▲贅沢な	ぜいたくな	extravagant, luxurious

1396 洪 9
▶こう 418
cf. 供

洪水	こうずい	flood

1397 津 9
▶しん
▷つ

津波	つなみ	tsunami, tidal wave
津軽半島	つがるはんとう	Tsugaru Peninsula (the peninsula at the northern tip of Honshu)
◇ 興味津々	きょうみしんしん	very interested

1398 浪 10
▶ろう

浪費	ろうひ	*cv.* waste
浮浪者	ふろうしゃ	vagabond, tramp, hobo

〈漢字の形に気をつけましょう・57〉

959	958	1390	1391
余	除	徐	斜
余分なお金	除外する	徐々に増えてきた	山の斜面

浪人	ろうにん masterless samurai, student who has failed the university entrance examinations and will resit them the following year; *cv.* be forced to resit university examinations

1399
5   汁   ▶じゅう
     ▷しる

みそ汁	みそしる *miso* soup
汁	しる juice, sap, broth, soup
果汁	かじゅう fruit juice

1400
11   渋   ▶じゅう
     ▷しぶ，しぶ(い)，しぶ(る)

渋谷	しぶや Shibuya (an area in downtown Tokyo)
渋い	しぶい quiet and tasteful, glum, astringent
渋	しぶ astringent juice
渋る	しぶる be reluctant (to do), hesitate
◇ 渋*滞	じゅうたい *cv.* be delayed/congested; traffic jam
苦渋	くじゅう anguish
渋面	じゅうめん sour face, scowl

1401
11   淡   ▶たん
     ▷あわ(い)

淡い	あわい light, pale
淡路島	あわじしま Awaji Island (the largest island in the Seto Inland Sea)

冷淡な	れいたんな cold-hearted, cold
淡泊な	たんぱくな plain (food), aloof/indifferent (person)
濃淡	のうたん light and shade, shading
淡水	たんすい fresh water
淡水魚	たんすいぎょ freshwater fish

1402
13   滞   ▶たい
     ▷とどこお(る)

滞在	たいざい *cv.* stay
滞納	たいのう *cv.* default in payment, fail to keep up payment
渋滞	じゅうたい *cv.* be delayed/congested; traffic jam
沈滞	ちんたい *cv.* stagnate, become dull
滞る	とどこおる be left undone, fall into arrears

1403   肯   ▶こう   ⑴⑸
8   1085
                                  cf. 背

肯定	こうてい *cv.* affirm
◇ 首肯	しゅこう *cv.* agree, consent

1404
17   齢   ▶れい

年齢	ねんれい age
高齢者	こうれいしゃ aged person, the aged
高齢化社会	こうれいかしゃかい aged society

   〈漢字の形に気をつけましょう・58〉

    335   834   836   1394   1011   1434   1556
   場   陽   湯   渇   掲   *喝   *褐

   入場券   太陽と月   茶の湯   渇水の被害

   論文が掲載される   恐*喝   *褐色
                          きょう かつ   かっしょく

1405 履 15	▶り ▷は（く）
履歴書	りれきしょ resume
履行	りこう cv. fulfill, implement, perform (a contract)
草履	△ぞうり (Japanese) sandals
履く	はく wear/put on (shoes/pants/skirt/etc.)

1406 奮 16	▶ふん ▷ふる（う）
興奮	こうふん cv. be excited
奮起	ふんき cv. rouse oneself (to action), be inspired
◇ 奮発	ふんぱつ cv. exert oneself, make great efforts, splurge
◇ 奮い立つ	ふるいたつ be inspired

1407 奪 14	▶だつ ▷うば（う）
奪う	うばう snatch away, take by force
強奪	ごうだつ cv. seize, rob
略奪	りゃくだつ cv. plunder, pillage
奪回	だっかい cv. recapture, retake
争奪戦	そうだつせん competition/contest for (power/trophy/etc.)

1408 獲 16	▶かく ▷え（る）
獲得	かくとく cv. acquire, gain
捕獲	ほかく cv. catch (an animal/a big fish/etc.)
乱獲	らんかく cv. overfish, overhunt
漁獲高	ぎょかくだか catch of fish
獲物	えもの game, catch, trophy
◇ 獲る	える obtain, acquire, gain

1409 穫 18	▶かく
収穫	しゅうかく cv. harvest, crop
収穫高	しゅうかくだか crop, yield
収穫期	しゅうかくき harvest time

1410 猫 11	▶びょう ▷ねこ
猫	ねこ cat
山猫	やまねこ wildcat, lynx
◇ 愛猫家	あいびょうか cat lovers

1411 薦 16	▶せん ▷すす（める）
推薦状	すいせんじょう letter of recommendation
推薦	すいせん cv. recommend
推薦者	すいせんしゃ recommender
薦める	すすめる recommend

1412 廃 12	▶はい ▷すた（れる），すた（る）
廃止	はいし cv. abolish
廃人	はいじん disabled person
退廃的な	たいはいてきな decadent
◇ 廃れる	すたれる go out of fashion

1413 庶 11	▶しょ 332 333 cf. 席 度
庶民	しょみん common people
庶民的な	しょみんてきな common, popular
庶務	しょむ general affairs
庶務課	しょむか general affairs section

1414 麻 11	▶ま ▷あさ	
麻薬	まやく	drugs
大麻	たいま	marijuana
◇ 麻	あさ	hemp, flax, linen

1415 摩 15	▶ま cf. 歴 704	
摩擦	まさつ	friction; *cv.* create/feel/apply friction

1416 擦 17	▶さつ ▷す(る), す(れる)	
摩擦	まさつ	friction; *cv.* create/feel/apply friction
擦れる	すれる	rub, chafe
擦(り)傷	すりきず	abrasion, graze, scratch

1417 邪 8	▶じゃ cf. 雅 1638	
風邪	△かぜ	a cold
邪魔な	じゃまな	obstructive
邪魔	じゃま	interference, obstacle; *cv.* interrupt, disturb
邪道	じゃどう	evil ways, wrong course
邪教	じゃきょう	heretical religion

1418 魔 21	▶ま cf. 摩 1415	
邪魔な	じゃまな	obstructive
悪魔	あくま	devil
魔術	まじゅつ	magic
魔法	まほう	magic, witchcraft, sorcery

1419 魅 15	▶み	
魅力	みりょく	charm, appeal, fascination, attraction
魅力的な	みりょくてきな	fascinating
◇ 魅惑の	みわくの	fascinating, charming

1420 酸 14	▶さん ▷す(い)	
酸性雨	さんせいう	acid rain
酸性の	さんせいの	acid
酸素	さんそ	oxygen
酸化	さんか	*cv.vi.* oxidize
◇ 塩酸	えんさん	hydrochloric acid
酸っぱい	すっぱい	sour

〈漢字の形に気をつけましょう・59〉

704 歴	1720 *暦	1415 摩	1418 魔	1731 *磨	1414 麻

日本の歴史　太陽*暦　経済摩擦　仕事の邪魔をする　研*磨する　麻薬
　　　　　　たいよう れき　　　　　　　　　　　　　　　　　けん ま

第 5 水準

(Level 5)

1421−1832

1421 6	伏	▶ふく　⑪⑦ ▷ふ(せる), ふ(す)　829 cf. 状

うつ伏せになる	うつぶせになる	lie face down
伏せる	ふせる	lie on the ground
伏す	ふす	lie down (on the ground), prostrate oneself
起伏	きふく	ups and downs, undulations; cv. rise and fall
潜伏	せんぷく	cv. hide oneself, lie dormant
潜伏期間	せんぷくきかん	latent period
伏線	ふくせん	foreshadowing

1422 6	伐	▶ばつ　413 cf. 代

伐採	ばっさい	cv. cut/hew down, fell
殺伐とした	さつばつとした	deserted
征伐	せいばつ	cv. subjugate

1423 7	伴	▶はん, ばん ▷ともな(う)

伴う	ともなう	accompany, go with
◇ 伴*奏	ばんそう	accompaniment (of a piano/guitar/etc.); cv. play an accompaniment
同伴	どうはん	cv. accompany, go with
◇ 伴*侶	はんりょ	partner
◇ 言語*随伴行動	げんごずいはんこうどう	language-accompanying behavior

1424 9	俊	▶しゅん

| 俊才 | しゅんさい | brilliant person |
| ◇ 俊*敏な | しゅんびんな | swift |

1425 10	倹	▶けん　790 cf. 険

| 倹約 | けんやく | cv. be thrifty |

1426 10	俵	▶ひょう ▷たわら

土俵	どひょう	sumo ring
～俵	～ひょう/びょう/ぴょう	(counter for straw bags of rice)
俵	たわら	bale, straw bag
米俵	こめだわら	straw rice bag

1427 10	俸	▶ほう

年俸	ねんぽう	annual salary
俸給	ほうきゅう	salary
本俸	ほんぽう	basic salary

1428 11	偽	▶ぎ　736 ▷いつわ(る), にせ　cf. 為

偽物	にせもの	imitation, fake
偽札	にせさつ	counterfeit bills
偽の	にせの	false, forged, counterfeit
偽る	いつわる	deceive, feign
偽りの	いつわりの	counterfeit
偽名	ぎめい	false name
真偽	しんぎ	truth or falsehood
◇ *虚偽の	きょぎの	false

1429 12	傍	▶ぼう　748 ▷かたわ(ら)　cf. 接

傍聴	ぼうちょう	cv. attend/hear a trial
傍観	ぼうかん	cv. look on, watch (from the side)
傍線	ぼうせん	sideline (next to a word in vertical writing)

| 路傍 | ろぼう　roadside |
| 傍ら | かたわら　the side |

1430 僧 13　▶そう

僧	そう　Buddhist priest/monk
僧院	そういん　Buddhist monastery/convent
高僧	こうそう　high-ranking Buddhist priest
◇ 僧▲侶	そうりょ　Buddhist priest
◇ *尼僧	にそう　Buddist nun

1431 傑 13　▶けつ　　980　cf. 隣

傑作	けっさく　masterpiece
豪傑	ごうけつ　hero, daring man
傑物	けつぶつ　outstanding person

1432 吐 6　▶と　▷は(く)

吐く	はく　vomit, spit, give vent to
吐き気	はきけ　nausea, sickness
吐血	とけつ　cv. vomit blood
◇▲嘔吐	おうと　cv. vomit
吐露	とろ　cv. vent one's feelings

1433 唆 10　▶さ　　1424　▷そそのか(す)　cf. 俊

示唆	しさ　cv. suggest, hint at
教唆	きょうさ　cv. instigate
唆す	そそのかす　stir up, instigate, coax into

1434 喝 11　▶かつ

| 恐喝 | きょうかつ　cv. threaten, blackmail |

| 一喝 | いっかつ　cv. scold |

1435 喚 12　▶かん

証人喚問	しょうにんかんもん　testimony given at the Diet
喚声	かんせい　cry/shout of deep emotion (by a crowd)
◇ *召喚	しょうかん　cv. summon

1436 嘆 13　▶たん　　527　▷なげ(く), cf. 漢　なげ(かわしい)

感嘆	かんたん　cv. admire, be impressed
驚嘆	きょうたん　cv. be struck with admiration
嘆願	たんがん　cv. entreat
嘆息	たんそく　cv. sigh
嘆く	なげく　lament, deplore
嘆き	なげき　sorrow, grief
嘆かわしい	なげかわしい　sad, regrettable

1437 嘱 15　▶しょく

| 委嘱 | いしょく　cv. entrust (someone with a matter) |
| ◇ 嘱*託 | しょくたく　contract-based employee |

1438 塔 12　▶とう

| 五重の塔 | ごじゅうのとう　five-storied pagoda |
| 石塔 | せきとう　stone pagoda |

1439 塀 12　▶へい　　1250 1260　cf. 併 堀

| 塀 | へい　wall, fence |
| 板塀 | いたべい　wooden wall/fence |

1440	壇	▶だん，たん	1888 cf. 墳
16			

花壇	かだん	flower bed
演壇	えんだん	platform
壇上	だんじょう	on the platform
文壇	ぶんだん	the literary world
土壇場	どたんば	at the last moment

⑪

1441	如	▶じょ，にょ
6		

欠如	けつじょ	cv. vi. lack
突如	とつじょ	suddenly
如実に	にょじつに	realistically, vividly, graphically
歴 如来	にょらい	Buddha

1442	姻	▶いん
9		

婚姻届	こんいんとどけ	marriage registration
◇ 姻▲戚関係	いんせきかんけい	relation by marriage

1443	岐	▶き
7		

岐路に立つ	きろにたつ	stand at the turning point/crossroads
分岐点	ぶんきてん	junction, diverging point
多岐にわたる	たきにわたる	a variety of (topics)

1444	帆	▶はん ▷ほ	467 cf. 凡
6			

帆	ほ	sail
帆船	はんせん	sailing ship/boat
出帆	しゅっぱん	cv. sail, set sail
帆走	はんそう	cv. sail

1445	壮	▶そう	829 cf. 状
6			

壮大な	そうだいな	magnificent, grand
壮健な	そうけんな	very healthy

1446	弦	▶げん ▷つる
8		

弦	げん	string (on an instrument)
弦	つる	bowstring, string
上弦の月	じょうげんのつき	waxing crescent moon

1447	弧	▶こ	1381 cf. 狐
9			

弧	こ	arc
弧状の	こじょうの	arched
◇ *括弧	かっこ	parentheses

1448	径	▶けい
8		

直径	ちょっけい	diameter
半径	はんけい	radius

〈漢字の形に気をつけましょう・60〉

116	515	1448	1450
軽	経	径	怪

軽工業　　経済発展　　直径　　奇怪な事件

1449 衡 16 ▶こう

貿易不均衡	ぼうえきふきんこう	trade imbalance
均衡	きんこう	balance, equilibrium
平衡感覚	へいこうかんかく	sense of balance

1450 怪 8 ▶かい　▷あや(しい), あや(しむ)

怪しい	あやしい	suspicious, doubtful
怪しげな	あやしげな	suspicious, doubtful
怪しむ	あやしむ	suspect
怪物	かいぶつ	monster
怪談	かいだん	ghost story
奇怪な	きかいな	weird, mysterious, strange

1451 怖 8 ▶ふ　▷こわ(い)

怖い	こわい	be afraid of
怖がる	こわがる	be afraid of
恐怖	きょうふ	fear, horror, terror,
◊▲畏怖の念	いふのねん	awe, dread

1452 恨 9 ▶こん　▷うら(む), うら(めしい)　974 cf. 根

恨む	うらむ	bear a grudge, feel resentment
恨み	うらみ	grudge, resentment
恨めしい	うらめしい	reproachful, rueful
悔恨	かいこん	remorse, regret, repentance
遺恨	いこん	grudge, spite, enmity
痛恨の	つうこんの	deeply regrettable

1453 悦 10 ▶えつ

悦楽	えつらく	joy
喜悦	きえつ	cv. be full of joy

1454 悟 10 ▶ご　▷さと(る)

悟り	さとり	spiritual enlightenment
悟る	さとる	be enlightened spiritually, realize
覚悟	かくご	readiness of mind; cv. be prepared/determined
悟性	ごせい	reason

1455 惜 11 ▶せき　▷お(しい), お(しむ)

負け惜しみ	まけおしみ	a case of sour grapes
惜しむ	おしむ	regret, miss (having), be reluctant to part with
惜しい	おしい	regrettable
惜敗	せきはい	cv. lose a close game
愛惜	あいせき	cv. be loath to (part with), be reluctant to (separate)
愛惜の情	あいせきのじょう	sorrow of parting

1456 悼 11 ▶とう　▷いた(む)　1030 cf. 卓

追悼式	ついとうしき	memorial service
悼辞	とうじ	words of condolence
◊*哀悼の念	あいとうのねん	sorrow over someone's death
悼む	いたむ	mourn

1457 惨 11 ▶さん, ざん　▷みじ(め)

悲惨な	ひさんな	miserable, wretched
惨劇	さんげき	tragedy, tragic event

| 惨殺 | ざんさつ | cv. kill without mercy |
| 惨めな | みじめな | miserable |

1458 愉 12 ▶ゆ

| 愉快な | ゆかいな | pleasant, merry, cheerful |

1459 慌 12 ▶こう ▷あわ(てる), あわ(ただしい)

慌てる	あわてる	be in a hurry, be flustered, lose one's presence of mind
大慌て	おおあわて	great hurry
慌ただしい	あわただしい	busy, hurried
恐慌	きょうこう	panic (in the stock market/etc.)

1460 惰 12 ▶だ

| 惰性 | だせい | force of habit |
| ◇*怠惰な | たいだな | lazy |

1461 慨 13 ▶がい　1161 1162 cf. 概 既

感慨	かんがい	deep emotion
慨嘆	がいたん	cv. lament, deplore
◇*憤慨	ふんがい	cv. be indignant, resent

1462 憎 14 ▶ぞう ▷にく(む), にく(い), にく(らしい), にく(しみ)

憎しみ	にくしみ	hatred
憎らしい	にくらしい	hateful
憎い	にくい	hateful, horrible, repulsive
憎む	にくむ	hate
憎悪	ぞうお	hatred; cv. hate
愛憎	あいぞう	love and hatred

1463 懐 16 ▶かい　1038 ▷ふところ, なつ(かしい), なつ(かしむ), なつ(く), なつ(ける)　cf. 壊

懐中電灯	かいちゅうでんとう	flashlight
懐古趣味	かいこしゅみ	retrospection
述懐	じゅっかい	cv. speak reminiscently
懐かしい	なつかしい	dear old, fondly-remembered
懐かしむ	なつかしむ	yearn, feel a longing
懐く	なつく	get attached, be tamed
懐ける	なつける	tame
懐	ふところ	pocket (in a kimono)

1464 憾 16 ▶かん

| 遺憾に思う | いかんにおもう | feel sorry (formal) |

〈漢字の形に気をつけましょう・61〉

429　1224　1430　1462
増　贈　僧　憎

赤字が増大する　　蔵書を学校に寄贈する　　僧　　憎悪

1465 抄 ▶しょう ⑦ 1151 cf. 秒

抄訳 しょうやく abridged translation; *cv.* make an abridged translation

抄本 しょうほん abstract

抄録 しょうろく extract, summary; *cv.* extract, summarize

1466 扶 ▶ふ ⑦

扶養家族 ふようかぞく one's dependents

扶助 ふじょ assistance; *cv.* assist

1467 把 ▶は ⑦

把握 はあく *cv.* grasp (the meaning), get hold of (the subject)

把持 はじ *cv.* hold firm

〜把 〜わ/ば/ぱ (counter for bundles/bunches) cf. 一把(いちわ), 三把(さんば), 十把(じっぱ)

1468 披 ▶ひ ⑧ 1144 cf. 皮

披露宴 ひろうえん wedding reception

披露 ひろう *cv.* announce, introduce, advertize

1469 拘 ▶こう ⑧

拘束 こうそく *cv.* restrain a person; restriction, control

拘留 こうりゅう *cv.* detain, take someone into custody

拘置所 こうちしょ detention center, prison

1470 拙 ▶せつ ⑧

稚拙な ちせつな artless, naive

拙速な せっそくな hasty

拙劣な せつれつな badly-done, ill-managed, unskillful, blundering

◊ *巧拙 こうせつ skill, dexterity

1471 抹 ▶まつ ⑧

抹消 まっしょう *cv.* erase, cross out

抹殺 まっさつ *cv.* wipe out, deny (existence), kill

一抹の不安 いちまつのふあん slight anxiety

1472 括 ▶かつ ⑨

包括的な ほうかつてきな comprehensive, inclusive

括弧 かっこ parentheses

一括 いっかつ *cv.* lump together

1473 挟 ▶きょう ▷はさ(む), はさ(まる) ⑨

挟む はさむ put in/between

挟まる はさまる be caught in/between

挟撃 きょうげき *cv.* attack from both sides

〈漢字の形に気をつけましょう・62〉

1288 舌　178 話　517 活　1472 括

毒舌家　話題　日常生活　包括的なプラン

1474 9	拷	▶ごう
	拷問	ごうもん　*cv.* torture

1475 10	捜	▶そう ▷さが(す)
	捜査	そうさ　*cv.* (police/prosecutor's) investigation
	捜索	そうさく　*cv.* search
	捜す	さがす　seek, look for, search

1476 11	措	▶そ
	措置	そち　measure, step
	挙措	きょそ　movement, behavior

1477 11	掛	▷か(ける), か(かる), かかり　　371 cf. 街
	掛ける	かける　hang
	出掛ける	でかける　go out
	お出掛け	おでかけ　going out (honorific)
	見掛ける	みかける　see
	掛け算	かけざん　multiplication
	掛かる	かかる　be suspended
	掛	かかり　section cf. 係 is normally used.

1478 10	挿	▶そう ▷さ(す)　256 cf. 押
	挿入	そうにゅう　*cv.* insert

	挿話	そうわ　episode
	挿絵	さしえ　illustration
	挿す	さす　insert, put in

1479 11	控	▶こう ▷ひか(える)
	控除	こうじょ　*cv.* deduct
	控訴	こうそ　*cv.* appeal
	控室	ひかえしつ　waiting room
	控える	ひかえる　wait in another room, refrain, restrain
	控え	ひかえ　note, memorandum, duplicate

1480 11	据	▷す(える), す(わる)
	据える	すえる　put into position, set, place, lay, install
	据え置く	すえおく　leave something as it is, leave (a loan) unredeemed, defer (payment)
	目が据わる	めがすわる　have a fixed stare

⑳

1481 12	揚	▶よう ▷あ(げる), あ(がる)
	意気揚々と	いきようようと　triumphantly
	抑揚	よくよう　intonation
	揚げる	あげる　raise, hoist, fry
	荷揚げ	にあげ　unloading
	揚がる	あがる　go up, rise, be fried

〈漢字の形に気をつけましょう・63〉

428	182	1455	1476
昔	借	惜	措
今と昔	借金	惜敗する	措置

1482 摂 13 ▶せつ

摂取	せっしゅ	*cv.* take in/adopt (a foreign custom/etc.)
包摂	ほうせつ	*cv.* subsume
摂氏	せっし	centigrade, Celsius cf. 華氏(かし) Fahrenheit
歴 摂政	せっしょう	regent, regency

1483 搭 12 ▶とう

搭乗券	とうじょうけん	boarding pass
搭載	とうさい	*cv.* be armed with (missiles/etc.)

1484 搾 13 ▶さく ▷しぼ(る)

搾取	さくしゅ	*cv.* exploit
圧搾機	あっさくき	(hydraulic/etc.) press
搾る	しぼる	squeeze

1485 操 16 ▶そう ▷みさお, あやつ(る)　　902 903 cf. 繰 燥

操作	そうさ	*cv.* operate, manipulate, handle
操縦	そうじゅう	*cv.* steer, fly (an airplane)
体操	たいそう	gymnastics, stretching
節操	せっそう	chastity, integrity
操り人形	あやつりにんぎょう	puppet
操る	あやつる	handle
操	みさお	chastity, virginity

1486 携 13 ▶けい ▷たずさ(える), たずさ(わる)

携帯電話	けいたいでんわ	portable phone

技術提携	ぎじゅつていけい	technological cooperation
業務提携	ぎょうむていけい	business cooperation
携える	たずさえる	have/carry something with
携わる	たずさわる	have a hand in, be involved in, participate in

1487 搬 13 ▶はん　　648 cf. 般

運搬	うんぱん	*cv.* transport
搬入	はんにゅう	*cv.* carry/bring something in
搬出	はんしゅつ	*cv.* carry something out

1488 撤 15 ▶てつ　　1147 cf. 徹

撤回	てっかい	*cv. vt.* withdraw, take back
撤去	てっきょ	*cv. vt.* withdraw, remove, take away
撤退	てったい	*cv. vi.* withdraw, evacuate, pull out
撤兵	てっぺい	*cv.* withdraw troops, pull troops out

1489 撲 15 ▶ぼく

相撲	△すもう	sumo
打撲傷	だぼくしょう	bruise
撲殺	ぼくさつ	*cv.* beat to death
◇ 撲*滅	ぼくめつ	*cv.* exterminate

1490 擁 16 ▶よう

擁護	ようご	*cv.* protect, safeguard, defend
擁立	ようりつ	*cv.* have one's leader stand as a candidate
抱擁	ほうよう	*cv.* embrace

1491 汽 7 ▶き

汽船	きせん	steamship
汽車	きしゃ	train
◇ 汽*笛	きてき	whistle

1492 泌 8 ▶ひつ，ひ　　1102　cf. 秘

分泌	ぶんぴつ	cv. secrete
内分泌	ないぶんぴつ，ないぶんぴ	internal secretion
◇ 泌*尿器科	ひにょうきか	urology department

1493 泥 8 ▶でい　▷どろ

泥棒	どろぼう	thief, robber
泥	どろ	mud
泥沼	どろぬま	bog, quagmire, morass (of difficulties)
雲泥の差	うんでいのさ	completely different (in quality)
泥土	でいど	mud, muddy soil
拘泥	こうでい	cv. adhere/stick to

1494 沸 8 ▶ふつ　▷わ(く)，わ(かす)

沸く	わく	vi. be boiling, be ready (as in bath water)
沸かす	わかす	vt. heat up, boil
湯沸(かし)器	ゆわかしき	water heater
沸点	ふってん	boiling point
煮沸	しゃふつ	cv. vt. boil
◇ 沸*騰	ふっとう	cv. vi. boil

1495 浄 9 ▶じょう

浄化	じょうか	cv. purify, clean up
◇ 浄化*槽	じょうかそう	purification tank
清浄な	せいじょうな	clean and pure
不浄な	ふじょうな	unclean, impure

1496 浸 10 ▶しん　　1244　▷ひた(す)，ひた(る)　cf. 侵

水浸しになる	みずびたしになる	be inundated with water
浸す	ひたす	soak, moisten
浸る	ひたる	be immersed
浸水	しんすい	cv. be flooded/inundated
◇ 浸*透	しんとう	cv. penetrate, infiltrate, permeate

1497 涯 11 ▶がい

| 生涯 | しょうがい | one's life, one's lifetime |

1498 渦 12 ▶か　　284　▷うず　cf. 過

渦	うず	eddy, whirlpool, vortex
渦巻(き)	うずまき	eddy, whirlpool, vortex
渦巻く	うずまく	swirl, eddy
渦中の人	かちゅうのひと	the person concerned/involved

1499 溝 13 ▶こう　　495 991　▷みぞ　cf. 講 構

溝	みぞ	ditch, gutter
排水溝	はいすいこう	drainage
下水溝	げすいこう	sewer

1500 滅 13 ▶めつ　▷ほろ(びる)，ほろ(ぼす)

| 絶滅 | ぜつめつ | cv. become extinct |
| 消滅 | しょうめつ | cv. be extinguished, disappear |

滅亡	めつぼう	*cv.* perish, fall into ruin, die out
滅多に	めったに	seldom
◇*幻滅	げんめつ	*cv.* be disillusioned
滅びる	ほろびる	perish, fall into ruin, die out
滅ぼす	ほろぼす	ruin, destroy, overthrow, annihilate

1501　⑫1
溶 13　▶よう　1126
▷と(ける)，と(かす)，cf. 浴 と(く)

水溶液	すいようえき	solution
溶液	ようえき	solution
溶解	ようかい	*cv.* melt, dissolve
溶岩	ようがん	lava
溶ける	とける	*vi.* melt, dissolve
溶け込む	とけこむ	conform oneself to, blend into, melt into
溶かす	とかす	*vt.* melt, dissolve
溶く	とく	*vt.* melt, dissolve

1502
漏 14　▶ろう
▷も(る)，も(れる)，も(らす)

雨漏り	あまもり	leaking of rain (through the roof)
漏る	もる	leak
漏れる	もれる	leak
漏らす	もらす	reveal, divulge
漏電	ろうでん	*cv.* short circuit
◇*疎漏な	そろうな	careless

1503
漸 14　▶ぜん

| 漸次 | ぜんじ | gradually, step by step, little by little |
| 漸進的に | ぜんしんてきに | gradually |

1504
滴 14　▶てき
▷しずく，したた(る)

～滴	てき	(counter for drops)
水滴	すいてき	waterdrop
点滴	てんてき	intravenous drip
滴	しずく	drop
滴る	したたる	drip, drop, trickle
滴り	したたり	dripping, drop, trickle

1505
漆 14　▶しつ
▷うるし

漆器	しっき	lacquerware
漆黒	しっこく	jet black
漆	うるし	lacquer

1506
漬 14　▷つ(ける)，つ(かる)　886 638 cf. 積 責

漬物	つけもの	pickles
漬ける	つける	pickle, salt, soak, preserve
漬かる	つかる	be soaked in, be seasoned

1507
漂 14　▶ひょう　1199 ▷ただよ(う)　cf. 票

漂白	ひょうはく	*cv.* bleach
漂流	ひょうりゅう	*cv.* drift
漂着	ひょうちゃく	*cv.* drift ashore, be washed ashore
漂う	ただよう	drift, float

1508
潮 15　▶ちょう
▷しお

風潮	ふうちょう	the current of the times, tendency
満潮	まんちょう	full tide
干潮	かんちょう	low tide

潮流	ちょうりゅう　tide, current, trend, tendency
潮	しお　tide, current, seawater, brine
潮風	しおかぜ　sea breeze

1509 潤 15　▶じゅん　▷うるお(う), うるお(す), うる(む)

潤滑油	じゅんかつゆ　lubricating oil
潤滑に	じゅんかつに　smoothly
潤沢な	じゅんたくな　abundant (money/funds/etc.)
湿潤な	しつじゅんな　wet, damp, humid
潤色	じゅんしょく　cv. embellish, color
潤う	うるおう　be moistened, get wet, profit
潤い	うるおい　moisture
潤す	うるおす　wet, water, moisten, benefit/enrich (someone)
潤む	うるむ　be wet/emotional

1510 澄 15　▶ちょう　▷す(む), す(ます)

澄む	すむ　become clear, become tranquil
上澄み	うわずみ　top clear layer (of soup stock/a liquid/etc.)
澄ます	すます　look unconcerned/prim/indifferent
澄まし顔	すましがお　indifferent/unconcerned look
特 清澄な	せいちょうな　clear

1511 濁 16　▶だく　▷にご(る), にご(す)

濁る	にごる　be muddy, have a voiced sound
濁り	にごり　muddiness, turbidity
言葉を濁す	ことばをにごす　speak ambiguously

| 濁流 | だくりゅう　muddy stream |
| 濁音 | だくおん　sonant, voiced sound |

1512 濫 18　▶らん　925 cf. 監

濫伐	らんばつ　cv. cut down trees recklessly
職権濫用	しょっけんらんよう　cv. abuse power
濫費	らんぴ　waste, extravagance; cv. waste, dissipate, squander
◇▲氾濫	はんらん　cv. inundate, overflow, flood

1513 狂 7　▶きょう　▷くる(う), くる(おしい)

熱狂的な	ねっきょうてきな　enthusiastic, fervent
狂気	きょうき　madness, insanity
狂人	きょうじん　madman, lunatic
狂言	きょうげん　*kyōgen* (Japanese comic play), made-up affair, sham
狂喜	きょうき　cv. be filled with great joy
狂う	くるう　go mad
狂おしい	くるおしい　mad/crazy (with love/grief/etc.)

1514 狩 9　▶しゅ　▷か(る), か(り)

狩り	かり　hunting
ぶどう狩り	ぶどうがり　picking grapes
狩る	かる　hunt
狩猟	しゅりょう　hunting, shooting; cv.vi. hunt

1515 猟 11　▶りょう

| 猟師 | りょうし　hunter |
| 猟犬 | りょうけん　hound, hunting dog |

228

| 狩猟 | しゅりょう　hunting, shooting; cv.vi. hunt |
| ◇ 猟*銃 | りょうじゅう　hunting gun, shotgun |

1516　猛　11　▶もう

勇猛な	ゆうもうな　daring, valiant, brave
◇ *猛獣	もうじゅう　ferocious animal
◇ 猛*烈な	もうれつな　fierce, intense, violent

1517　猶　12　▶ゆう

| 猶予 | ゆうよ　cv. postpone, delay, grace |
| ◇ *執行猶予 | しっこうゆうよ　stay of execution, suspended sentence |

1518　獄　14　▶ごく

地獄	じごく　hell, inferno 反 天国 (てんごく) heaven, paradise
疑獄	ぎごく　scandal
監獄	かんごく　jail, prison
◇ 獄*舎	ごくしゃ　jail

1519　阻　8　▶そ　▷はば(む)

阻止	そし　cv. obstruct, stop, hamper, hinder
阻害	そがい　cv. obstruct, block, hamper, hinder
阻む	はばむ　obstruct, block, hamper, hinder

1520　附　8　▶ふ

| 附属 | ふぞく　attached to (as in a hospital attached to a university) cf. 付属 is more often used in modern Japanese. |

1521　陛　10　▶へい

| 陛下 | へいか　His/Her Majesty |

1522　陥　10　▶かん　▷おちい(る), おとしい(れる) 　1233 cf. 稲

欠陥	けっかん　defect, fault, flaw
陥落	かんらく　cv. fall, surrender
陥没	かんぼつ　cv. subside, sink, cave in
陥る	おちいる　fall into
陥れる	おとしいれる　entrap, capture

1523　陣　10　▶じん

陣痛	じんつう　labor pains
陣頭	じんとう　front, head
東側陣営	ひがしがわじんえい　Eastern/ communist camp
陣	じん　camp, formation, position

1524　陳　11　▶ちん

陳列	ちんれつ　cv. exhibit, display
陳謝	ちんしゃ　cv. apologize
◇ 陳*腐な	ちんぷな　old-fashioned, commonplace, trite, stale
陳情	ちんじょう　cv. petition

1525　陰　11　▶いん　▷かげ, かげ(る)

| 陰気な | いんきな　gloomy, melancholic 反 陽気な(ようきな) cheerful |
| 陰性 | いんせい　negative (in a medical test) 反 陽性(ようせい) positive (in a medical test) |

山陰地方	さんいんちほう	the San'in region (the Japan Sea-side of the western part of Honshu)
陰	かげ	shade, behind the scenes
日陰	ひかげ	shade
陰る	かげる	be shaded (by a cloud)
陰り	かげり	clouds (on one's happiness/business prospects/etc.)

1526　陶　11　▶とう

陶器	とうき	pottery, earthenware, ceramics
陶酔	とうすい	*cv.* be charmed/fascinated/intoxicated
◇ *薫陶	くんとう	tutelage, guidance, education

1527　旋　11　▶せん

旋律	せんりつ	melody
旋回	せんかい	*cv.* turn, circle, revolve
周旋	しゅうせん	mediation, good offices; *cv.* mediate

1528　旗　14　▶き　▷はた

国旗	こっき	national flag
校旗	こうき	school flag
◇ 旗*艦	きかん	flagship
旗	はた	flag
手旗	てばた	semaphore flag

旗色	はたいろ	tide/fortune/outlook/situation of war

1529　朴　6　▶ぼく

素朴な	そぼくな	unaffected
純朴な	じゅんぼくな	pure and unaffected

1530　枢　8　▶すう

中枢神経	ちゅうすうしんけい	the central nervous system
中枢	ちゅうすう	pivot, hub
枢密院	すうみついん	the Privy Council
◇ 枢*軸国	すうじくこく	the Axis powers cf. 連合国(れんごうこく) the Allied powers

1531　栓　10　▶せん

栓抜き	せんぬき	bottle opener
栓	せん	cork, bottle cap
消火栓	しょうかせん	fire hydrant

1532　桟　10　▶さん　223 cf. 残

桟橋	さんばし	pier, jetty

1533　棟　12　▶とう　▷むね, むな

病棟	びょうとう	hospital ward

〈漢字の形に気をつけましょう・64〉

153	612	1527	1528
旅	施	旋	旗

海外旅行　　新しい税制が実施される　　ピアノの旋律　　国旗

別棟　　べつむね　another building

棟　　　むね　ridge of a roof

〜棟　　〜むね　(counter for houses)

棟木　　むなぎ　ridgepole, rooftree

1534
棺
12　▶かん

出棺　　しゅっかん　cv. carry out a coffin from a house/temple

◇ 棺▴桶　かんおけ　coffin

1535
棋
12　▶き　　690　cf. 期

将棋　　しょうぎ　shōgi, Japanese chess

1536
棚
12　▷たな

棚　　　たな　shelf

戸棚　　とだな　cupboard, cabinet

棚上げにする　たなあげにする　put aside, suspend

1537
槽
15　▶そう　　1933　cf. 曹

浴槽　　よくそう　bathtub

水槽　　すいそう　aquarium, water tank

1538
欄
20　▶らん　　1509　cf. 潤

投書欄　とうしょらん　readers' column

欄外　　らんがい　margin

空欄　　くうらん　blank

欄干　　らんかん　banister, railing

1539
殉
10　▶じゅん　　664　cf. 旬

殉教　　じゅんきょう　cv. die a martyr

殉教者　じゅんきょうしゃ　martyr

殉死　　じゅんし　cv. kill oneself after the death of one's lord/master

殉職　　じゅんしょく　cv. die at one's post, be killed in the line of duty

1540
殖
12　▶しょく　　220 678
　▷ふ(える),　cf. 直 植
　ふ(やす)

養殖　　ようしょく　cv. breed, raise, cultivate

生殖器　せいしょくき　sexual/generative organ

利殖　　りしょく　moneymaking

殖産　　しょくさん　promotion of industry

殖やす　ふやす　vt. increase

殖える　ふえる　vi. increase

⑫⑬

1541
班
10　▶はん

班　　　はん　group

班長　　はんちょう　group leader

〈漢字の形に気をつけましょう・65〉

296　　1094　　1524　　1533　　1602
練　　凍　　陳　　棟　　*錬

発音の練習　冷凍食品　商品を陳列する　小児病棟　アルミ精*錬所
　　　　　　　　　　　　　　　　　　　　　　　　　　　せい れんじょ

1542　祥　10
▶しょう　　917　488
cf. 洋 羊

不祥事　　ふしょうじ　scandal

発祥(の)地　　はっしょう(の)ち　where something started, place of origin

清祥　　せいしょう　good and healthy

1543　禍　13
▶か　　284
cf. 過

禍根　　かこん　root of evil, source of trouble

禍福　　かふく　fortune and misfortune

1544　胎　9
▶たい

胎児　　たいじ　embryo

受胎　　じゅたい　cv. conceive (a child)

◇*堕胎　　だたい　abortion; cv. have an abortion cf. 人工中絶(じんこうちゅうぜつ), rather than 堕胎, is normally used.

1545　脚　11
▶きゃく, きゃ
▷あし

脚本　　きゃくほん　script, scenario

三脚　　さんきゃく　tripod

脚色　　きゃくしょく　cv. dramatize

脚光　　きゃっこう　footlight

脚立　　きゃたつ　stepladder

脚　　あし　leg

行脚　　あんぎゃ　pilgrimage; cv. make a pilgrimage

1546　膜　14
▶まく　　1159
cf. 漠

膜　　まく　membrane, film

◇細*胞膜　　さいぼうまく　cell membrane

◇*粘膜　　ねんまく　mucous membrane

◇*鼓膜　　こまく　eardrum

1547　騰　20
▶とう　　263　1937
cf. 勝 謄

高騰　　こうとう　steep rise (in prices); cv. soar, skyrocket

暴騰　　ぼうとう　sudden/sharp/abnormal rise (in prices); cv. rise suddenly

沸騰　　ふっとう　cv. vi. boil

騰貴　　とうき　rise/jump (in prices); cv. rise, go up

1548　眺　11
▶ちょう　　1269
▷なが(める)　cf. 兆

眺望　　ちょうぼう　view

眺め　　ながめ　view

眺める　　ながめる　gaze, watch

1549　矯　17
▶きょう　　313
▷た(める)　cf. 橋

矯正　　きょうせい　cv. correct (poor eyesight/crooked teeth/etc.), cure (a bad habit)

奇矯な　　ききょうな　eccentric

矯める　　ためる　correct, straighten

1550　砕　9
▶さい　　510　1069
▷くだ(く),　cf. 枠 粋
　くだ(ける)

砕く　　くだく　break, smash, crush

砕ける　　くだける　be broken

◇*粉砕　　ふんさい　cv. vt. crush, smash up

砕石　　さいせき　macadam

1551　硫　12
▶りゅう

硫酸　　りゅうさん　sulfuric acid

硫黄　　△いおう　sulfur

1552 硝 12 ▶しょう

硝酸	しょうさん	nitric acid
硝煙	しょうえん	powder smoke
硝石	しょうせき	saltpeter

1553 礁 17 ▶しょう

岩礁	がんしょう	(shore) reef
暗礁	あんしょう	reef, submerged rock
◇▲珊▲瑚礁	さんごしょう	coral reef

1554 称 10 ▶しょう

名称	めいしょう	name
愛称	あいしょう	nickname, term of endearment
称する	しょうする	call oneself ～, pretend, fein
自称	じしょう	self-professed, would-be; cv. pretend to be
称賛	しょうさん	cv. praise, applaud cf. *Shōsan* can also be written as 賞賛.

1555 襟 18 ▶きん ▷えり cf. 禁 815

襟	えり	collar
襟首	えりくび	nape
開襟シャツ	かいきんシャツ	open-necked shirt
胸襟を開く	きょうきんをひらく	open one's heart

1556 褐 13 ▶かつ

褐色の	かっしょくの	brown

1557 粉 10 ▶ふん ▷こな, こ cf. 紛 1298

小麦粉	こむぎこ	flour
パン粉	パンこ	bread crumbs
粉雪	こなゆき	powder snow
粉	こな	powder
粉末	ふんまつ	powder
粉砕	ふんさい	cv. vt. crush, smash up
粉飾	ふんしょく	cv. embellish

1558 粒 11 ▶りゅう ▷つぶ

粒	つぶ	grain, droplet
粒子	りゅうし	(atomic) particle, grain
◇▲顆粒	かりゅう	granule

1559 粘 11 ▶ねん ▷ねば(る)

粘着テープ	ねんちゃくテープ	adhesive tape
粘土	ねんど	clay
粘液	ねんえき	mucus
粘る	ねばる	be sticky, be tenacious, stay long
粘り	ねばり	stickiness
粘り強い	ねばりづよい	tenacious

1560 粗 11 ▶そ ▷あら(い)

粗大ゴミ	そだいゴミ	large/bulky garbage
粗末な	そまつな	coarse, simple, plain
粗野な	そやな	rustic, boorish, unrefined
粗い	あらい	coarse, rough
粗筋	あらすじ	outline

⑫

1561 糾 9 ▶きゅう

紛糾　ふんきゅう　*cv.* become entan-gled

糾弾　きゅうだん　*cv.* impeach

1562 紺 11 ▶こん

紺　こん　dark blue, navy blue

濃紺　のうこん　dark blue, navy blue

1563 紡 10 ▶ぼう
▷つむ(ぐ)

紡績業　ぼうせきぎょう　the spinning industry

混紡　こんぼう　mixed spinning

紡ぐ　つむぐ　spin, make yarn

1564 紋 10 ▶もん

波紋　はもん　ripple, sensation

指紋　しもん　fingerprint

紋章　もんしょう　crest

紋切り型の　もんきりがたの　convention-al, stereotyped, formal

1565 絞 12 ▶こう
▷しぼ(る)，し(める)，し(ま る)

絞る　しぼる　squeeze, wring, press

絞める　しめる　strangle

絞まる　しまる　feel choked

絞殺　こうさつ　*cv.* strangle to death

絞首刑　こうしゅけい　hanging

1566 綱 14 ▶こう
▷つな

横綱　よこづな　*yokozuna,* the grand-champion of sumo wrestling

綱　つな　rope, line

大綱　たいこう　general principles

綱領　こうりょう　party platform, general principles

◇　綱紀*粛正　こうきしゅくせい　enforce-ment of the law of the land

1567 網 14 ▶もう
▷あみ

網　あみ　net

網戸　あみど　screen door

◇　投網　△とあみ　casting net

通信網　つうしんもう　communications network

網膜　もうまく　retina

漁網　ぎょもう　fishing net

1568 縄 15 ▶じょう
▷なわ

沖縄　おきなわ　Okinawa

縄　なわ　rope, cord

縄張り　なわばり　territory, sphere of influence

〈漢字の形に気をつけましょう・66〉

1337	1566	1567
鋼	綱	網
鉄鋼業	党の綱領	通信網

縄文式土器　じょうもんしきどき　straw-rope pattern pottery

自縄自縛になる　じじょうじばくになる
lose one's freedom of action as a result of one's own actions

1569 縛 16	▶ばく ▷しば(る)
束縛	そくばく　cv. restrict, restrain, fetter, bind
捕縛	ほばく　cv. arrest
縛る	しばる　bind, tie, fasten, restrict, restrain

1570 緯 16	▶い
経緯	けいい　circumstances, background, details
緯度	いど　latitude　反経度(けいど) longitude
北緯	ほくい　north latitude
南緯	なんい　south latitude

1571 縫 16	▶ほう ▷ぬ(う)
裁縫	さいほう　sewing, needlework
縫製	ほうせい　cv. sew
縫合	ほうごう　cv. suture
縫う	ぬう　sew
縫い目	ぬいめ　seam, stitch

1572 繕 18	▶ぜん ▷つくろ(う)
修繕	しゅうぜん　cv. mend, repair
繕う	つくろう　repair, hem
繕い	つくろい　repairing, hemming

1573 舶 11	▶はく
船舶	せんぱく　vessel, ship

舶来の　はくらいの　foreign-made, imported

1574 託 10	▶たく
信託銀行	しんたくぎんこう　trust bank
委託	いたく　cv. entrust (someone with a matter); consignment
嘱託	しょくたく　contract-based employee
託宣	たくせん　oracle
託す	たくす　entrust (someone with something), commit to the care of
託児所	たくじしょ　public nursery

1575 詐 12	▶さ
詐称	さしょう　cv. make a false statement regarding one's educational background/age/name/etc.

◇ 詐*欺　さぎ　fraud, swindling

1576 詰 13	▶きつ　　　302 893 ▷つめ(る), つ(ま cf. 結 吉 る), つ(む)
缶詰	かんづめ　canned food
詰める	つめる　stuff, cram, pack into
見詰める	みつめる　stare/gaze at, fix one's eyes on
詰め込む	つめこむ　cram, load, squeeze into
詰め物	つめもの　stuffing, filling
詰まる	つまる　be stuffed/full/packed/blocked
行き詰まる	いきづまる　vi. come to a deadlock
詰む	つむ　be stuffed/full/packed/blocked
詰問	きつもん　cv. cross-examine, question closely
難詰	なんきつ　cv. blame

1577 該 13 ▶がい 986 cf. 核

該当する	がいとうする	relevant, applicable
当該の	とうがいの	concerned

1578 諾 15 ▶だく

承諾	しょうだく	cv. consent, agree
受諾	じゅだく	cv. accept
快諾	かいだく	cv. give ready consent
諾否	だくひ	acceptance or refusal

1579 諭 16 ▶ゆ ▷さと(す)

説諭	せつゆ	cv. admonish, reprove
教諭	きょうゆ	school teacher
諭旨免職	ゆしめんしょく	resignation done at the suggestion of one's superior
諭す	さとす	admonish, remonstrate, warn, counsel

1580 諮 16 ▶し ▷はか(る)

諮問機関	しもんきかん	advisory body
諮る	はかる	consult, ask for advice

⑫⑤

1581 謙 17 ▶けん 1325 1324 cf. 嫌 兼

謙譲の美徳	けんじょうのびとく	virtue of modesty/humility
◇ 謙*虚な	けんきょな	modest, humble
◇ 謙▲遜	けんそん	cv. be modest/humble

1582 謹 17 ▶きん ▷つつし(む) 525 cf. 勤

謹賀新年	きんがしんねん	Happy New Year
謹慎	きんしん	cv. conduct oneself with best behavior, confine oneself home in penitance
謹む	つつしむ	be discrete/prudent/modest

1583 譜 19 ▶ふ

楽譜	がくふ	score
譜面	ふめん	sheet music
系譜	けいふ	genealogy
年譜	ねんぷ	chronological history

1584 賊 13 ▶ぞく

海賊	かいぞく	pirate
海賊版	かいぞくばん	pirated edition
盗賊	とうぞく	burglar, robber
賊	ぞく	robber, rebel
賊軍	ぞくぐん	rebel army

1585 賦 15 ▶ふ

天賦の才	てんぷのさい	genius
賦役	ふえき	imposed labor
月賦	げっぷ	monthly installment

1586 跳 13 ▶ちょう ▷は(ねる), と(ぶ) 1269 cf. 兆

跳ぶ	とぶ	jump, leap
縄跳び	なわとび	rope skipping
跳ねる	はねる	leap, jump
跳躍	ちょうやく	cv. jump

1587 跡 13	▶せき ▷あと	
足跡	あしあと	footprint
足跡	そくせき	footprint, track
跡	あと	trace, ruins, remains
遺跡	いせき	ruins, remains
名所旧跡	めいしょきゅうせき	famous places and remains
追跡	ついせき	cv. chase, run after

1588 践 13	▶せん	223 cf. 残
実践	じっせん	cv. practice

1589 軸 12	▶じく	
軸	じく	pivot, spindle, axle, scroll
地軸	ちじく	earth's axis
車軸	しゃじく	axle
枢軸国	すうじくこく	the Axis powers cf. 連合国（れんごうこく）the Allied powers

1590 轄 17	▶かつ	
管轄	かんかつ	control, jurisdiction; cv. have jurisdiction/control
所轄官庁	しょかつかんちょう	the competent authorities
直轄領	ちょっかつりょう	districts under the direct control of the Shogunate government

1591 酌 10	▶しゃく ▷く（む）	
晩酌	ばんしゃく	cv. have a drink at supper
情状酌量	じょうじょうしゃくりょう making allowances in consideration of the circumstances	
◇*媒酌人	ばいしゃくにん	matchmaker

事情を酌む	じじょうをくむ	take someone's circumstances into consideration

1592 酢 12	▶さく ▷す	
酢	す	vinegar
酢の物	すのもの	vinegared dish
酢酸	さくさん	acetic acid

1593 酪 13	▶らく	
酪農	らくのう	dairy farming
酪製品	らくせいひん	dairy products

1594 酬 13	▶しゅう	
報酬	ほうしゅう	reward
応酬	おうしゅう	cv. exchange (heated words)

1595 酵 14	▶こう	
酵素	こうそ	enzyme
発酵	はっこう	cv. ferment
酵母（菌）	こうぼ（きん）	yeast

1596 酷 14	▶こく	
残酷な	ざんこくな	merciless, cruel
冷酷な	れいこくな	heartless, cruel
酷似	こくじ	cv. be very much like, be similar (in appearance)
酷使	こくし	cv. work someone very hard

1597 鉢 13	▶はち，はつ	
植木鉢	うえきばち	flower pot

鉢	はち bowl, pot, flower pot
◇▲托鉢	たくはつ religious mendicancy; cv. beg for alms

1598 銭 14
▶せん
▷ぜに cf. 残 223

銭湯	せんとう bathhouse
金銭の授受	きんせんのじゅじゅ giving and receiving of money
小銭	こぜに small change

1599 銃 14
▶じゅう cf. 統 充 1000 1275

銃	じゅう gun
小銃	しょうじゅう rifle
銃弾	じゅうだん bullet
銃声	じゅうせい the sound of a gunshot
銃刀法	じゅうとうほう gun and sword restriction law
◇▲拳銃	けんじゅう pistol, handgun

1600 銘 14
▶めい

銘柄	めいがら brand, name, issue
感銘を受ける	かんめいをうける be deeply impressed
銘記	めいき cv. bear in mind
銘々	めいめい each, each respectively

1601 鋳 15
▶ちゅう
▷い(る)

鋳造	ちゅうぞう cv. cast, mint
鋳る	いる cast
鋳物	いもの casting
鋳型	いがた mold, cast

1602 錬 16
▶れん

精錬所	せいれんじょ refinery, smelting works
錬金術	れんきんじゅつ alchemy
◇ 心身の*鍛錬	しんしんのたんれん training of body and mind
◇ 錬*磨	れんま cv. train, drill, practice

1603 錯 16
▶さく

錯覚	さっかく cv. hallucinate, mistake for somebody/something else
交錯	こうさく cv. intertwine/mingle with each other
試行錯誤	しこうさくご trial and error

1604 錠 16
▶じょう

手錠	てじょう handcuffs
錠前	じょうまえ lock
◇ 錠*剤	じょうざい tablet, pill

〈漢字の形に気をつけましょう・67〉

122	223	1532	1588	1598
浅	残	桟	践	銭
浅いところ	残念な結果	桟橋	理論と実践	銭湯

1605 鍛 17

▶たん
▷きた(える)

| 鍛える | きたえる train, drill, cultivate, forge |
| 心身の鍛錬 | しんしんのたんれん training of mind and body |

1606 鎮 18

▶ちん
▷しず(める)，しず(まる)

鎮圧	ちんあつ cv. suppress, repress, subjugate
鎮火	ちんか cv. be put out/extinguished
鎮座	ちんざ cv. be enshrined
鎮静	ちんせい cv. become calm, subside
◇ 鎮静*剤	ちんせいざい tranquilizer
重鎮	じゅうちん leader, leading figure
鎮める	しずめる calm, quiet, suppress, repress, quell
鎮まる	しずまる become quiet, calm down, be suppressed, be enshrined

1607 鐘 20

▶しょう
▷かね

教会の鐘	きょうかいのかね church bell
警鐘	けいしょう warning bell, warning
半鐘	はんしょう fire alarm

1608 鑑 23

▶かん
925 cf. 監

鑑賞	かんしょう cv. appreciate, enjoy
鑑定	かんてい cv. estimate, identify, judge, appraise
年鑑	ねんかん yearbook
図鑑	ずかん picture/illustrated book

1609 剖 10

▶ぼう

| 解剖 | かいぼう autopsy, dissection; cv. perform an autopsy, dissect |

1610 駄 14

▶だ

無駄な	むだな wasteful, useless, nothing
駄目な	だめな useless, vain, no good
駄作	ださく poor work, shoddy craftsmanship, (literary) trash
◇ 駄*菓子	だがし cheap sweets

1611 駆 14

▶く
▷か(ける)，か(る)

四輪駆動	よんりんくどう four-wheel drive
駆使	くし cv. use freely/as one pleases
駆逐	くちく cv. expel, drive away, exterminate
◇ 駆逐*艦	くちくかん destroyer
駆除	くじょ cv. exterminate, destroy
先駆者	せんくしゃ forerunner
駆ける	かける run, canter, gallop
駆り立てる	かりたてる drive, urge on

1612 刈 4

▷か(る)

稲刈り	いねかり rice harvesting
芝刈り	しばかり mowing
芝刈り機	しばかりき mower
刈る	かる mow, cut
刈り入れ	かりいれ reaping, harvesting

1613 剛 10

▶ごう

| 剛健な | ごうけんな sturdy, robust |

金剛力　こんごうりき　miraculous power

1614 劾 8　▶がい

弾劾　だんがい　*cv.* impeach

1615 勧 13　▶かん　1132
▷すす(める)　cf. 歓

勧誘　かんゆう　*cv.* invite, persuade, solicit, canvass

勧告　かんこく　*cv.* advise, counsel, recommend

第一勧業銀行　だいいちかんぎょうぎんこう The Dai-Ichi Kangyo Bank, Ltd.

勧奨　かんしょう　*cv.* advise, encourage, urge

勧める　すすめる　advise, encourage, urge

勧め　すすめ　recommendation

1616 却 7　▶きゃく

却下　きゃっか　*cv.* reject, turn down, dismiss

売却　ばいきゃく　*cv.* sell, sell off

退却　たいきゃく　*cv.* retreat, withdraw

1617 叙 9　▶じょ

叙述　じょじゅつ　*cv.* describe, narrate

叙景　じょけい　description of scenery

叙事詩　じょじし　epic poem

叙情詩　じょじょうし　lyric poem

叙*勲　じょくん　decoration, medal

1618 耐 9　▶たい
▷た(える)

耐久性　たいきゅうせい　endurance, durability

耐火構造　たいかこうぞう　fireproof structure

耐震構造　たいしんこうぞう　earthquake-proof structure

耐熱ガラス　たいねつガラス　heat-resistant glass

◇ *忍耐　にんたい　perseverance, patience, endurance; *cv.* persevere, be patient, endure

耐える　たえる　endure, bear, withstand

1619 彩 11　▶さい
▷いろど(る)

多彩な行事　たさいなぎょうじ　a variety of events

鮮やかな色彩　あざやかなしきさい bright color

彩色　さいしき　coloring

彩る　いろどる　color

彩り　いろどり　coloring, color scheme

1620 彰 14　▶しょう

表彰式　ひょうしょうしき　commendation/award ceremony

表彰状　ひょうしょうじょう　certificate of commendation, testimonial

表彰　ひょうしょう　*cv.* (officially) commend

⑫⑦

1621 邦 7　▶ほう

邦画　ほうが　Japanese film　反洋画 (ようが) foreign (Western) film, Western painting

邦楽　ほうがく　Japanese music

連邦政府　れんぽうせいふ　federal government

旧ソビエト連邦　きゅうソビエトれんぽう
the former Soviet Union/
U.S.S.R.　cf. *abbr.* 旧ソ連

本邦初公開　ほんぽうはつこうかい　first
appearance in this country

1622 敢 12 ▶かん

勇敢に　　ゆうかんに　bravely, heroically,
courageously

果敢に　　かかんに　boldly

敢然と　　かんぜんと　boldly, resolutely,
bravely, fearlessly

1623 欺 12 ▶ぎ ▷あざむ(く)

詐欺　　　さぎ　fraud, swindling

欺く　　　あざむく　deceive

1624 款 12 ▶かん

円借款　　えんしゃっかん　yen loan

定款　　　ていかん　articles of association, certificate of incorporation

1625 殴 8 ▶おう ▷なぐ(る)　554 548 cf.欧区

殴る　　　なぐる　beat, punch

殴打　　　おうだ　*cv.* give a blow, hit

1626 殻 11 ▶かく ▷から

貝殻　　　かいがら　seashell

殻　　　　から　shell, husk

地殻変動　ちかくへんどう　alteration of the earth's crust

甲殻類　　こうかくるい　crustaceans

1627 穀 14 ▶こく

穀物　　　こくもつ　grain, cereal, corn

雑穀　　　ざっこく　cereals

1628 朗 10 ▶ろう ▷ほが(らか)　546 cf.郎

朗読　　　ろうどく　*cv.* recite

朗報　　　ろうほう　good news, glad tidings

朗々と　　ろうろうと　sonorously, clearly

明朗な　　めいろうな　cheerful

朗らかな　ほがらかな　cheerful, bright

1629 泡 8 ▶ほう ▷あわ

泡　　　　あわ　foam, bubble, froth

泡立つ　　あわだつ　*vi.* froth, lather

水泡　　　すいほう　foam, bubble

気泡　　　きほう　airbubble, blowhole

発泡スチロール　はっぽうスチロール　Styrofoam

〈漢字の形に気をつけましょう・68〉

　　773　　1357　　1619　　1620

採　杉　彩　彰

新しい社員を採用する　杉の木　鮮やかな色彩　表彰状を授与する

1630 胞 9 ▶ほう

細胞	さいぼう	cell
胞子	ほうし	spore
同胞	どうほう	compatriot, fellow countryman

1631 砲 10 ▶ほう

大砲	たいほう	artillery gun, cannon
鉄砲	てっぽう	gun, rifle
砲撃	ほうげき	cv. bombard, fire at

1632 飽 13 ▶ほう ▷あ(きる), あ(かす)

飽きる	あきる	get tired of, be weary of, lose interest
飽きっぽい	あきっぽい	easily bored, fickle
暇に飽かして	ひまにあかして	being weary of staying home and doing nothing
飽和状態	ほうわじょうたい	saturation, completely full
飽食の時代	ほうしょくのじだい	an age of gluttony

1633 噴 15 ▶ふん ▷ふ(く)

噴水	ふんすい	fountain, jet of water
噴火	ふんか	(volcanic) eruption; cv. erupt
噴出	ふんしゅつ	cv. spew/gush/spurt out
噴射	ふんしゃ	cv. shoot out, spray
噴き出す	ふきだす	spurt out, burst into laughter

1634 憤 15 ▶ふん ▷いきどお(る)

憤慨	ふんがい	cv. be indignant, resent
発憤	はっぷん	cv. be roused, be stimulated
義憤	ぎふん	righteous indignation
憤る	いきどおる	get angry, resent, be indignant
憤り	いきどおり	resentment, indignation, anger

1635 准 10 ▶じゅん

批准	ひじゅん	cv. ratify
准将	じゅんしょう	brigadier general

1636 唯 11 ▶ゆい, い

唯一の	ゆいいつの	only, sole
唯物論	ゆいぶつろん	materialism (in philosophical terms) 反 唯心論 (ゆいしんろん) idealism, spiritualism cf. 物質主義 (ぶっしつしゅぎ) materialism (in terms of way of life), 精神主義 (せいしんしゅぎ) spiritualism
唯物史観	ゆいぶつしかん	historical materialism
唯々諾々として	いいだくだくとして	obediently, tamely, submissively

1637 雄 12 ▶ゆう ▷お, おす

英雄	えいゆう	hero
雄大な	ゆうだいな	magnificent, majestic, grand
雄	おす	male (for animals) 反 雌(めす) female
雄犬	おすいぬ	male dog
雄花	おばな	male flower

雄牛　　　おうし　ox

雄しべ　　おしべ　stamen

雄々しい　おおしい　brave

雄飛　　　ゆうひ　cv. do something great

1638 雅 13　▶が　　　　　　　　　1417 cf. 邪

優雅な　　ゆうがな　elegant, graceful, refined

風雅　　　ふうが　elegance, refined taste

雅楽　　　ががく　gagaku (Japanese ceremonial court music)

1639 雌 14　▶し　▷め, めす

雌　　　　めす　female (for animals) 反 雄(おす) male

雌犬　　　めすいぬ　female dog

雌花　　　めばな　female flower

雌牛　　　めうし　cow

雌しべ　　めしべ　pistil

雌雄　　　しゆう　male or female, superior or inferior

雌伏　　　しふく　cv. lie dormant, remain inactive 反 雄飛(ゆうひ) cv. do something great

1640 培 11　▶ばい　▷つちか(う)

培養基　　ばいようき　culture medium

培養液　　ばいようえき　culture liquid

◇ *栽培　　さいばい　cv. cultivate, grow

培う　　　つちかう　cultivate, nurture, breed, raise, grow

(128)

1641 陪 11　▶ばい

陪席　　　ばいせき　cv. sit with one's superior

◇ 陪*審員　ばいしんいん　juror, member of the jury

◇ 陪*審制度　ばいしんせいど　jury system

1642 賠 15　▶ばい

賠償金　　ばいしょうきん　indemnity, reparations

損害賠償　そんがいばいしょう　compensation for damages

1643 頂 11　▶ちょう　▷いただ(く), いただき

頂上　　　ちょうじょう　top, summit, peak

頂点　　　ちょうてん　climax, apex, vertex, zenith

絶頂　　　ぜっちょう　climax, height

頂く　　　いただく　be given, receive, eat, drink (humble)

頂　　　　いただき　top, summit, peak

〈漢字の形に気をつけましょう・69〉

　53　　1609　　158　　1640　　1641　　1642
　部　　剖　　倍　　培　　陪　　賠

部屋を片付ける　死体を解剖する　4倍ズーム　草花を栽培する

陪*審制度　賠償金
ばい しん

1644 頑 13　▶がん

頑張る	がんばる	try hard, not give up, persist
頑固な	がんこな	obstinate, stubborn
頑強な	がんきょうな	obstinate, stubborn
頑健な	がんけんな	very strong, robust, sturdy
頑丈な	がんじょうな	strong, sturdy

1645 頒 13　▶はん

頒布	はんぷ	cv. distribute, circulate
頒価	はんか	handling cost for a non-profit publication/mail-order product/etc.

1646 煩 13　▶はん, ぼん
▷わずら(う), わずら(わす)

煩雑な	はんざつな	troublesome
煩悩	ぼんのう	carnal desire, worldly passions, lust
煩わしい	わずらわしい	troublesome, annoying, cumbersome
煩わす	わずらわす	vt. trouble, bother, annoy
煩う	わずらう	have trouble, be troubled
思い煩う	おもいわずらう	worry, be annoyed

1647 顕 18　▶けん

顕微鏡	けんびきょう	microscope
顕著な	けんちょな	remarkable, significant

1648 顧 21　▶こ
▷かえり(みる)

顧問	こもん	consultant, advisor, counsellor, teacher in charge of a club
回顧	かいこ	cv. retrospect
顧慮	こりょ	cv. consider, regard
顧みる	かえりみる	look back on, reflect upon

1649 嬢 16　▶じょう

お嬢さん	おじょうさん	young lady, (your/his/her) daughter (honorific)
令嬢	れいじょう	(your/his/her) daughter

1650 壌 16　▶じょう

土壌	どじょう	soil

1651 醸 20　▶じょう
▷かも(す)

醸造酒	じょうぞうしゅ	alcoholic beverage made by fermentation
醸成	じょうせい	cv. brew, cause, bring about
醸し出す	かもしだす	brew, cause, bring about, arouse

1652 亭 9　▶てい　　481 cf. 停

料亭	りょうてい	traditional Japanese-style restaurant
亭主	ていしゅ	one's husband (vulgar expression), host of a tea ceremony

1653 棄 13　▶き　　569 cf. 葉

放棄	ほうき	cv. give up, abandon, relinquish
廃棄	はいき	cv. do away with, abolish, abandon, scrap
産業廃棄物	さんぎょうはいきぶつ	industrial waste
核廃棄物	かくはいきぶつ	nuclear waste

死体遺棄	したいいき	abandonment of a dead body
棄権	きけん	*cv.* abstain (from voting), withdraw (from a contest)
棄却	ききゃく	*cv.* reject, abandon, dismiss

1654 舎 8 ▶しゃ

校舎	こうしゃ	schoolhouse, school building
官舎	かんしゃ	official residence
宿舎	しゅくしゃ	lodgings, quarters
寄宿舎	きしゅくしゃ	dormitory
舎監	しゃかん	dormitory superintendent
田舎	△いなか	countryside, rural district, one's hometown

1655 傘 12 ▶さん　▷かさ

傘	かさ	umbrella, parasol
雨傘	あまがさ	umbrella
日傘	ひがさ	parasol, sunshade
傘下	さんか	under the umbrella/banner (of)
落下傘	らっかさん	parachute

1656 冠 9 ▶かん　▷かんむり

冠詞	かんし	(definite/indefinite) article
王冠	おうかん	crown
栄冠	えいかん	crown, laurels
冠	かんむり	crown, coronet

1657 呈 7 ▶てい　671 cf. 程

贈呈	ぞうてい	*cv.* present
進呈	しんてい	*cv.* present
露呈	ろてい	*cv.* be revealed

1658 宜 8 ▶ぎ　850 cf. 宣

便宜	べんぎ	convenience
適宜	てきぎ	properly, suitably, at one's (own) discretion

1659 宰 10 ▶さい　344 cf. 辛

宰相	さいしょう	prime minister
宰領	さいりょう	*cv.* organize, supervise, oversee
主宰	しゅさい	*cv.* preside over, supervise, run

1660 寡 14 ▶か　1155 cf. 募

寡占市場	かせんしじょう	oligopolistic market
寡黙な	かもくな	taciturn
寡婦	かふ	widow
多寡	たか	quantity

〈漢字の形に気をつけましょう・70〉

1325	1581	1209	1649	1650	1651
嫌	謙	譲	嬢	壌	醸

嫌悪感を持つ　　謙譲の美徳　　譲歩する　　隣のお嬢さん

土壌を改良する　　醸造酒

⑫⑨

1661 15

審 ▶しん

審判	しんぱん	umpire, judge
主審	しゅしん	chief umpire
副審	ふくしん	assistant umpire
審議	しんぎ	discussion (at a government assembly); cv. discuss
不審な	ふしんな	suspicious

1662 15

賓 ▶ひん

貴賓室	きひんしつ	VIP room
主賓	しゅひん	guest of honor
来賓	らいひん	guest/visitor (at an official ceremony)

1663 11

崩 ▶ほう ▷くず(れる)，くず(す)

崩壊	ほうかい	cv. collapse, disintegrate
崩御	ほうぎょ	cv. (the emperor) passes away
崩れる	くずれる	crumble, fall to pieces, collapse, break
山崩れ	やまくずれ	landslide
崩す	くずす	demolish, change/break (a large bill), write character in running style
㊟ 雪崩	△なだれ	snowslide, avalanche

1664 11

崇 ▶すう 816 cf. 宗

崇拝	すうはい	cv. worship, venerate, adore, admire
偶像崇拝	ぐうぞうすうはい	idolatry, idol worship
崇高な理念	すうこうなりねん	lofty/sublime idea

1665 7

芳 ▶ほう 566 ▷かんば(しい) cf. 芸

芳香	ほうこう	fragrance
芳しくない	かんばしくない	not good, poor, bad (performance/reputation/etc.)

1666 9

荒 ▶こう ▷あら(い)，あ(れる)，あ(らす)

荒れる	あれる	become rough, be ruined, rage, run wild, be stormy, be devastated
荒れ地	あれち	wasteland, barren land
大荒れ	おおあれ	raging storm/temper
荒らす	あらす	devastate, lay waste, damage
荒い	あらい	rude, wild rough, savage
荒波	あらなみ	raging waves, rough waters, heavy sea
荒々しい	あらあらしい	wild, fierce
荒廃	こうはい	cv. be devastated, go to ruin
荒天	こうてん	stormy weather
荒涼とした	こうりょうとした	desolate, dreary, deserted, inhospitable

1667 11

菓 ▶か 502 1862 cf. 果 巣

(お)菓子	(お)かし	candy, cake

1668 14

慕 ▶ぼ 1157 ▷した(う) cf. 幕

慕う	したう	admire, love dearly, yearn for, idolize
慕わしい	したわしい	dear, beloved
慕情	ぼじょう	longing, affection, love
敬慕	けいぼ	cv. admire
思慕	しぼ	cv. long for

1669 **冒** 9	▶ぼう 1279 ▷おか(す) cf. 帽
冒険	ぼうけん adventure; cv. have an adventure
冒頭	ぼうとう opening, beginning
感冒	かんぼう cold, catarrh
冒す	おかす take a risk, brave
冒される	おかされる be afflicted (by a disease)

1670 **是** 9	▶ぜ 767 cf. 提
是正	ぜせい cv. correct, rectify
是認	ぜにん cv. approve of, endorse
国是	こくぜ national policy
是非	ぜひ right or wrong, by all means, without fail

1671 **罷** 15	▶ひ
罷免	ひめん cv. dismiss

1672 **羅** 19	▶ら
羅列	られつ cv. list, enumerate
網羅	もうら cv. include/contain everything, cover all (the facts)
羅針盤	らしんばん cv. (magnetic) compass
◇*甲羅	こうら shell, carapace

1673 **窃** 9	▶せつ
窃盗	せっとう theft

1674 **窒** 11	▶ちつ
窒息	ちっそく cv. be suffocated/asphyxiated

| 室素 | ちっそ nitrogen |

1675 **窮** 15	▶きゅう ▷きわ(める), きわ(まる)
窮屈な	きゅうくつな narrow, tight
窮乏生活	きゅうぼうせいかつ impoverished life, life of austerity
窮状	きゅうじょう sorry plight, distress
困窮	こんきゅう cv. distress
窮極の	きゅうきょくの ultimate, final cf. Kyūkyoku-no is normally written as 究極の.
窮める	きわめる carry to extremes, bring to an end
窮まる	きわまる reach an extreme, come to an end

1676 **蛍** 11	▶けい ▷ほたる
蛍光灯	けいこうとう fluorescent lamp
蛍光*塗料	けいこうとりょう fluorescent paint
蛍	ほたる firefly

1677 **掌** 12	▶しょう
車掌	しゃしょう (train) conductor
掌中	しょうちゅう in one's hands
掌握	しょうあく cv. control, hold, come into power, command
職掌	しょくしょう duties
分掌	ぶんしょう cv. share work/tasks

1678 **奉** 8	▶ほう, ぶ ▷たてまつ(る)
社会奉仕	しゃかいほうし social services
信奉	しんぽう cv. believe in, follow, espouse
奉公人	ほうこうにん cv. servant of a family

247

奉納	ほうのう	*cv.* dedicate/offer (to the gods, Buddha)
歴 奉行	ぶぎょう	magistrate (in the Edo period)
歴 奉る	たてまつる	offer, present, revere (humble)

1679 奏 9

▶そう
▷かな(でる)

演奏	えんそう	musical performance; *cv.* give a musical performance
合奏	がっそう	*cv.* play in concert
伴奏	ばんそう	accompaniment (of a piano/guitar/etc.); *cv.* play an accompaniment
奏でる	かなでる	play (a string instrument)

1680 泰 10

▶たい

| 安泰だ | あんたいだ | be stable and secure |
| 泰然と | たいぜんと | composedly, calmly |

⑬

1681 笛 11

▶てき 1837
▷ふえ cf. 苗

笛	ふえ	flute, whistle
口笛	くちぶえ	whistle
警笛	けいてき	warning horn, alarm whistle
汽笛	きてき	steam whistle

1682 箇 14

▶か

| 箇条書き | かじょうがき | itemization |
| 箇所 | かしょ | place, part, point |

1683 篤 16

▶とく

危篤の	きとくの	dangerously/hopelessly ill cf. 重態の(じゅうたいの) in critical condition
篤実な	とくじつな	sincere, faithful
篤志家	とくしか	supporter, volunteer

1684 簿 19

▶ぼ 799
cf. 薄

名簿	めいぼ	name roster, list of members
帳簿	ちょうぼ	account book
簿記	ぼき	bookkeeping

1685 覇 19

▶は

覇権	はけん	hegemony
覇者	はしゃ	champion, ruler
制覇	せいは	*cv.* conquer, dominate, gain supremacy, win the championship
連覇	れんぱ	*cv.* win the championship consecutively

1686 覆 18

▶ふく
▷おお(う), くつがえ(す), くつがえ(る)

覆う	おおう	cover, conceal, spread over
覆い	おおい	covering, cover
覆す	くつがえす	overturn, overthrow
覆る	くつがえる	be overturned/overthrown
覆面	ふくめん	(cloth) mask
転覆	てんぷく	*cv.* overturn, capsize, overthrow

1687 13	零	▶れい

零細企業	れいさいきぎょう　small business
零下	れいか　below zero
零点	れいてん　zero (on a test)
零落	れいらく　cv. (a family/etc.) fall to a low position, go down in the world

1688 15	霊	▶れい，りょう ▷たま

霊	れい　spirit, soul
◇ 霊*魂	れいこん　spirit, soul
霊園	れいえん　cemetery
霊感	れいかん　inspiration, extra-sensory perception of the supernatural
霊長類	れいちょうるい　primates
◇ 霊▲柩車	れいきゅうしゃ　hearse
◇ *幽霊	ゆうれい　ghost
悪霊	あくりょう　evil spirit
死霊	しりょう　spirit of a dead person, ghost
御霊	みたま　the Holy Spirit

1689 17	霜	▶そう ▷しも

霜	しも　frost
初霜	はつしも　the first frost of the year
霜柱	しもばしら　frost columns
霜害	そうがい　frost damage

1690 11	啓	▶けい

| 拝啓 | はいけい　Dear Sir, Dear Madam (opening word for letters) |

自己啓発	じこけいはつ　self-enlightenment
神の啓示	かみのけいじ　revelation (by God)
◇ 啓▲蒙	けいもう　cv. enlighten

1691 5	召	▶しょう ▷め(す)

召集	しょうしゅう　cv. summon, conscript, draft
召集令状	しょうしゅうれいじょう　draft notice
召喚	しょうかん　cv. summon
召しあがる	めしあがる　eat, drink (honorific)
お召しになる	おめしになる　wear, have (a cold) (honorific)

1692 12	塁	▶るい

一塁	いちるい　first base
塁審	るいしん　base umpire
土塁	どるい　earthwork
塁	るい　fort, base (in baseball)

1693 12	堕	▶だ 1218 cf. 墜

| 堕落 | だらく　cv. become depraved, fall into decadence |
| 堕胎 | だたい　abortion; cv. have an abortion cf. 人工中絶 (じんこうちゅうぜつ), rather than 堕胎, is normally used. |

1694 13	塗	▶と ▷ぬ(る)

塗る	ぬる　paint
ペンキ塗り立て	ペンキぬりたて　freshly painted
塗料	とりょう　paints
塗装	とそう　cv. coat with paint

| 塗布 | とふ　*cv.* apply (paint/ointment/etc.) |

1695 墨 14　▶ぼく　▷すみ

墨絵	すみえ　ink drawing
墨	すみ　Indian/Chinese ink, ink stick
お墨付き	おすみつき　approval from a superior/influential person
墨汁	ぼくじゅう　Indian/Chinese ink
墨守	ぼくしゅ　*cv.* show strict adherence (to tradition/customs/etc.)

1696 妄 6　▶もう，ぼう

妄想	もうそう　wild fantasy, delusion; *cv.* be deluded
妄信	もうしん　*cv.* accept blindly
妄言	もうげん，ぼうげん　reckless remark, thoughtless words

1697 忌 7　▶き　▷い(む)，い(まわしい)

忌避	きひ　*cv.* evade, shirk
禁忌	きんき　taboo
忌中	きちゅう　in mourning
忌む	いむ　abhor, detest, have a taboo against
忌まわしい	いまわしい　abominable, disgusting, offensive

1698 怠 9　▶たい　▷おこた(る)，なま(ける)

怠慢	たいまん　negligence, neglect, procrastination
怠惰な	たいだな　lazy, idle
怠ける	なまける　be idle/lazy
怠け者	なまけもの　idler, lazybones
怠る	おこたる　be negligent/idle, neglect

1699 悠 11　▶ゆう

悠々と	ゆうゆうと　composedly, slowly, calmly
悠然と	ゆうぜんと　calmly, with perfect composure
悠長に	ゆうちょうに　leisurely, slowly
悠久の	ゆうきゅうの　eternal

1700 愁 13　▶しゅう　▷うれ(える)，うれ(い)

愁い	うれい　sorrow, sadness
愁える	うれえる　lament
愁傷	しゅうしょう　grief, deep sorrow
◇*哀愁	あいしゅう　sadness, sorrow
◇*憂愁	ゆうしゅう　melancholy, gloom

1701 愚 13　▶ぐ　▷おろ(か)

愚かな	おろかな　foolish, stupid, silly, witless
愚問	ぐもん　stupid question
愚鈍な	ぐどんな　stupid, silly
◇ 愚*痴	ぐち　idle complaint, grumbling

1702 慰 15　▶い　▷なぐさ(める)，なぐさ(む)

慰める	なぐさめる　console, comfort, amuse
慰め	なぐさめ　consolation
慰む	なぐさむ　amuse oneself, make a plaything of
慰み	なぐさみ　diversion, amusement
慰謝料	いしゃりょう　consolation money, compensation, damages
慰労	いろう　*cv.* acknowledge a person's services

慰留	いりゅう *cv.* persuade someone to stay in office, persuade someone not to resign
慰問	いもん *cv.* go to console
慰安旅行	いあんりょこう entertainment trip by the members of an office
自慰行為	じいこうい masturbation

1703 懲 18
▶ちょう　1148
▷こ(りる)，こ(らす)，cf. 徴
こ(らしめる)

懲役	ちょうえき penal servitude, imprisonment
懲罰	ちょうばつ punishment
懲戒免職	ちょうかいめんしょく disciplinary dismissal
懲らしめる	こらしめる chastise, punish, correct, discipline
懲らす	こらす chastise, punish, correct, discipline
懲りる	こりる learn one's lesson
性懲りもなく	しょうこりもなく obstinately

1704 架 9
▶か
▷か(ける)，か(かる)

十字架	じゅうじか cross
書架	しょか bookshelf, bookcase
架橋	かきょう bridge construction
架線工事	かせんこうじ wiring
架空の	かくうの fictitious, imaginary
架ける	かける construct/build (a bridge)
架かる	かかる be constructed/built
架け橋	かけはし bridge, go-between

1705 香 9
▶こう，きょう
▷か，かお(り)，かお(る)

香水	こうすい perfume, fragrance
線香	せんこう incense stick, mosquito coil
香気	こうき fragrance, perfume, aroma
香り	かおり scent, fragrance, odor, smell
香る	かおる smell sweet, be fragrant
色香	いろか the charms of a woman
移り香	うつりが lingering scent
特 香車	きょうしゃ lance (in Japanese chess)

1706 暫 15
▶ざん

暫定予算	ざんていよさん provisional budget
暫定政権	ざんていせいけん provisional government
暫時	ざんじ short while

1707 脅 10
▶きょう
▷おびや(かす)，おど(す)，おど(かす)

脅迫	きょうはく *cv.* intimidate, threat
脅威	きょうい threat, menace, danger to
脅す	おどす threaten, menace, intimidate
脅し	おどし threat, menace
脅かす	おどかす frighten, scare
脅かす	おびやかす threaten, menace

1708 烈 10
▶れつ　812
cf. 列

猛烈な	もうれつな fierce, intense, strong
壮烈な	そうれつな heroic, brave
烈風	れっぷう strong wind, gale
烈火	れっか raging fire

1709 15	**勲**	▶くん

勲章	くんしょう decoration, order, medal
叙勲式	じょくんしき decoration-conferring ceremony
勲功	くんこう distinguished services
最高殊勲選手	さいこうしゅくんせんしゅ most valuable player, MVP

1710 16	**薫**	▶くん ▷かお(る)

薫製	くんせい smoked product (such as smoked salmon/herring/etc.) cf. *Kunsei* can be written as 燻製, but 燻 is not a *Jōyō Kanji*.
薫り	かおり scent, fragrance
薫る	かおる smell sweet, be fragrant

1711 11	**紫**	▶し ▷むらさき	1186 cf. 緊

紫外線	しがいせん ultraviolet rays
紫	むらさき purple, violet

1712 14	**誓**	▶せい ▷ちか(う)

誓う	ちかう swear, promise, make an oath
誓い	ちかい oath, promise
誓約書	せいやくしょ written oath
宣誓	せんせい *cv.* take an oath, pledge

1713 13	**誉**	▶よ ▷ほま(れ)	1189 cf. 挙

名誉	めいよ honor, reputation
栄誉	えいよ honor, credit, distinction, glory
誉れ	ほまれ honor, glory

1714 11	**貫**	▶かん ▷つらぬ(く)

一貫性	いっかんせい consistency
一貫性がある	いっかんせいがある consistent
貫通	かんつう *cv.* pierce, penetrate, pass through
縦貫	じゅうかん *cv.* run right across, traverse the whole length
貫く	つらぬく pierce, penetrate, pass through, attain

1715 6	**匠**	▶しょう

意匠権	いしょうけん design right
巨匠	きょしょう great master
師匠	ししょう master, teacher

1716 10	**匿**	▶とく

匿名で	とくめいで anonymously
隠匿	いんとく *cv.* conceal, hide (stolen property/etc.)

1717 5	**囚**	▶しゅう	254 406 cf. 困 因

囚人	しゅうじん prisoner, convict
死刑囚	しけいしゅう condemned criminal

1718 12	**閑**	▶かん

閑静な	かんせいな quiet (neighborhood)

1719 15	**閲**	▶えつ

検閲	けんえつ *cv.* censor
校閲	こうえつ *cv.* read and correct, look over (a manuscript)

閲兵	えっぺい　*cv.* inspect/review the troops
◇ 閲*覧	えつらん　*cv.* peruse, inspect, read
◇ 閲*覧室	えつらんしつ　reading room

1720　暦　14　▶れき　▷こよみ　704　cf. 歴

西暦	せいれき　the Christian Era, Anno Domini, A.D.
太陽暦	たいようれき　the solar calendar
太陰暦	たいいんれき　the lunar calendar
新暦	しんれき　the new calendar, the solar calendar
旧暦	きゅうれき　the old calendar, the lunar calendar
還暦	かんれき　sixtieth birthday
暦	こよみ　calendar cf. カレンダー, rather than 暦, is used in modern Japanese.

⑬②

1721　厄　4　▶やく

厄介な	やっかいな　troublesome, burdensome, annoying
厄	やく　misfortune, disaster
災厄	さいやく　misfortune, disaster
厄年	やくどし　unlucky/bad year

1722　尼　5　▶に　▷あま

尼	あま　nun
尼寺	あまでら　nunnery
尼僧	にそう　nun
修道尼	しゅうどうに　nun

1723　尾　7　▶び　▷お

尾	お　tail
尾根	おね　mountain ridge
尾行	びこう　*cv.* tail, follow, shadow
首尾一貫した	しゅびいっかんした　consistent
語尾	ごび　word ending
末尾	まつび　close, end

1724　尿　7　▶にょう

糖尿病	とうにょうびょう　diabetes
尿	にょう　urine
放尿	ほうにょう　*cv.* urinate
尿意を催す	にょういをもよおす　have a desire to urinate
尿素	にょうそ　urea
夜尿症	やにょうしょう　enuresis

1725　層　14　▶そう　429　cf. 増

高層ビル	こうそうビル　skyscraper
断層	だんそう　dislocation, fault, gap
低所得層	ていしょとくそう　range of population with low income
一層	いっそう　even more, all the more
大層	たいそう　very (much), greatly

1726　尽　6　▶じん　▷つ(くす), つ(きる), つ(かす)

力を尽くす	ちからをつくす　make an effort, endeavor, do one's best
尽くす	つくす　render (service), exert (one's power/ability/etc.)
心尽くし	こころづくし　thoughtfulness

尽きる　つきる　run out, be spent/exhausted

愛想が尽きる　あいそがつきる　run out of patience with a person

無尽蔵の　むじんぞうの　inexhaustible

尽力　じんりょく　cv. make an effort, endeavor

1727 唐 10
▶とう
▷から

唐突な　とうとつな　abrupt, sudden

唐　とう　the Tang dynasty

唐草模様　からくさもよう　arabesque pattern

1728 庸 11
▶よう
cf. 粛 1824

中庸　ちゅうよう　moderation

凡庸な　ぼんような　mediocre, ordinary, common

1729 廉 13
▶れん
cf. 兼 1324

清廉潔白な　せいれんけっぱくな　honest, upright

破廉恥な　はれんちな　shameless, infamous

廉価　れんか　low price

廉売　れんばい　bargain sale

1730 腐 14
▶ふ
▷くさ(る), くさ(れる), くさ(らす)

豆腐　とうふ　tofu, soybean curd

腐敗　ふはい　cv. decay, rot, grow corrupt

腐心　ふしん　cv. worry, take pains

腐食　ふしょく　cv. corrode, erode, eat away

陳腐な　ちんぶな　old-fashioned, commonplace, trite, stale

腐る　くさる　rot, decay

腐れ縁　くされえん　unfortunate but inescapable relationship, fatal bond

ふて腐れる　ふてくされる　sulk

腐らす　くさらす　let rot/spoil, corrode

1731 磨 16
▶ま
▷みが(く)
cf. 歴 704

磨く　みがく　brush (one's teeth), shine (shoes/etc.)

歯磨き　はみがき　toothpaste, toothbrushing

磨き粉　みがきこ　polishing powder

研磨　けんま　cv. grind, polish

1732 慶 15
▶けい

慶応大学　けいおうだいがく　Keio University

慶事　けいじ　happy event

1733 扇 10
▶せん
▷おうぎ

扇風機　せんぷうき　electric fan

扇子　せんす　fan

扇状地　せんじょうち　(alluvial) fan

扇動　せんどう　cv. fan, agitate

扇　おうぎ　fan

1734 扉 12
▶ひ
▷とびら

扉　とびら　door, title page

門扉　もんぴ　door (of a gate)

開扉　かいひ　cv. open the door

1735 疫 9
▶えき, やく

疫病　えきびょう　epidemic

防疫	ぼうえき	prevention of epidemics
疫病神	やくびょうがみ	plague, a pest

1736 疾 10 ▶しつ

疾走	しっそう	*cv.* run at full speed, make a dash
疾患	しっかん	disease, ailment
疾病	しっぺい	disease, illness
悪疾	あくしつ	malignant disease

1737 痢 12 ▶り

下痢	げり	diarrhea
赤痢	せきり	dysentery

1738 痴 13 ▶ち

愚痴	ぐち	idle complaint, grumbling
痴漢	ちかん	molester of women, pervert
痴情	ちじょう	blind love, passion, jealousy
◇ 痴▲呆症	ちほうしょう	dementia

1739 癒 18 ▶ゆ

癒着	ゆちゃく	*cv.* adhere
治癒	ちゆ	*cv.vi.* heal, be cured

1740 虐 9 ▶ぎゃく　▷しいた(げる)

虐殺	ぎゃくさつ	*cv.* slaughter, massacre, butcher
虐待	ぎゃくたい	*cv.* treat cruelly, abuse
残虐な	ざんぎゃくな	cruel, brutal, heartless

虐げる	しいたげる	oppress, persecute, tyrannize

---

⑬③

1741 虚 11 ▶きょ，こ

謙虚な	けんきょな	modest, humble
虚偽	きょぎ	falsehood, lie, fallacy
空虚な	くうきょな	empty, vacant, hollow
虚無主義	きょむしゅぎ	Nihilism
虚空	こくう	air, space, sky

1742 膚 15 ▶ふ

皮膚	ひふ	skin
完膚なきまで	かんぷなきまで	(defeat the enemy) thoroughly

1743 巡 6 ▶じゅん　▷めぐ(る)

巡礼	じゅんれい	pilgrimage, pilgrim; *cv.* make a pilgrimage
巡査	じゅんさ	police officer
巡回	じゅんかい	*cv.* go around, patrol
巡視	じゅんし	*cv.* patrol, make an inspection
巡業	じゅんぎょう	provincial tour (by singer/theatrical group/etc.); *cv.* make a provincial tour
一巡	いちじゅん	*cv.* make a round
巡る	めぐる	travel around
巡り歩く	めぐりあるく	walk around, travel around
巡り合わせ	めぐりあわせ	fortunate, good/bad luck
お巡りさん	△おまわりさん	police officer

1744 6	**迅**	▶じん

迅速に　じんそくに　promptly, swiftly

◇▲獅子奮迅の努力　ししふんじんのどりょく　desperate effort

1745 8	**迭**	▶てつ　206 cf. 送

更迭　こうてつ　cv. make a switch (in the Cabinet/etc.)

1746 10	**透**	▶とう　1171 ▷す(く), す(かす), す(ける)　cf. 秀

透明の/な　とうめいの/な　transparent

透視　とうし　cv. see through, examine by fluoroscopy

透過性　とうかせい　permeability

浸透　しんとう　cv. penetrate

透かす　すかす　look through, hold up to the light

透かし　すかし　watermark, openwork

透ける　すける　be transparent

透き間　すきま　small opening/gap

透き通る　すきとおる　be transparent, be seen through

1747 10	**逝**	▶せい　772 ▷ゆ(く)　cf. 折

逝去　せいきょ　cv. pass away, die

急逝　きゅうせい　cv. pass away suddenly, die a sudden death

逝く　ゆく　pass away, die

1748 11	**逸**	▶いつ　941 cf. 免

逸話　いつわ　anecdote

逸品　いっぴん　excellent article

逸材　いつざい　person of talent, able person

逸脱　いつだつ　cv. deviate, depart

逸する　いっする　fail to catch, lose

1749 14	**遮**	▶しゃ ▷さえぎ(る)

遮断　しゃだん　cv. cut off, stop, interrupt (traffic/etc.)

遮断機　しゃだんき　railroad crossing gate

遮る　さえぎる　interrupt, obstruct, block, intercept

1750 14	**遭**	▶そう ▷あ(う)

遭難　そうなん　cv. meet with accident/disaster

遭遇　そうぐう　cv. encounter, meet

遭う　あう　meet

1751 15	**遵**	▶じゅん　479 cf. 尊

遵守　じゅんしゅ　cv. obey (the law)

遵法精神　じゅんぽうせいしん　law-abiding spirit

1752 10	**鬼**	▶き ▷おに

鬼ごっこ　おにごっこ　tag

鬼　おに　ogre, demon, devil

鬼才　きさい　genius

餓鬼　がき　hungry ghost, devil, brat

1753 13	**塊**	▶かい ▷かたまり

団塊の世代　だんかいのせだい　the Baby Boomers

山塊　さんかい　group of mountains

塊　かたまり　lump, mass

1754 魂 14 ▶こん ▷たましい

霊魂	れいこん soul, spirit
商魂	しょうこん commercial enthusiasm, salesmanship
魂胆	こんたん intrigue, plot
魂	たましい soul

1755 醜 17 ▶しゅう ▷みにく(い)

醜聞	しゅうぶん scandal, bad reputation
醜態	しゅうたい disgraceful behavior
美醜	びしゅう appearance, looks
醜悪な	しゅうあくな ugly, mean
醜い	みにくい ugly, bad-looking

1756 甚 9 ▶じん ▷はなは(だ), はなは(だしい)

甚大な	じんだいな serious, great, enormous
甚だ	はなはだ very, greatly
甚だしい	はなはだしい extreme, enormous, outrageous

1757 勘 11 ▶かん

勘定	かんじょう payment of a bill; cv. count, calculate
勘弁	かんべん cv. forgive, excuse, pardon
勘当	かんどう cv. disinherit, disown, renounce
勘違い	かんちがい misunderstanding, misinterpretation
勘	かん intuition

1758 堪 12 ▶かん ▷た(える)

| 堪える | たえる endure, bear, put up with |
| ◇ 堪*忍 | かんにん cv. forgive, excuse |

1759 某 9 ▶ぼう

某国	ぼうこく a certain country
某所	ぼうしょ somewhere, a certain place
某氏	ぼうし someone, a certain person
某ホテル	ぼうホテル a certain hotel

1760 媒 12 ▶ばい

媒酌人	ばいしゃくにん matchmaker, go-between
媒介	ばいかい cv. mediate, intervene, act as an agent
媒体	ばいたい medium
触媒	しょくばい catalyst

⑭

1761 謀 16 ▶ぼう, む ▷はか(る)

陰謀	いんぼう conspiracy, intrigue, plot
謀略	ぼうりゃく plot, scheme
首謀者	しゅぼうしゃ ring leader
無謀な	むぼうな reckless, thoughtless
謀反	むほん rebellion, insurrection
謀る	はかる attempt, plot, plan

1762 又 2 ▶また

| 又 | また moreover, again |
| 又は | または or |

1763 双 4

▶そう
▷ふた

双方向	そうほうこう	two-way (communication)
双方	そうほう	both parties, both sides
双子	ふたご	twin(s)
双葉	ふたば	seed leaf, bud

1764 貞 9

▶てい

貞操	ていそう	chastity, virtue, honor
貞節	ていせつ	chastity, faith
◇ 貞*淑な	ていしゅくな	chaste, virtuous

1765 偵 11

▶てい

偵察	ていさつ	cv. reconnoiter, scout
探偵	たんてい	detective
内偵	ないてい	cv. make private inquiries

1766 叔 8

▶しゅく

叔父	△おじ	uncle
叔母	△おば	aunt
歴 *伯叔	はくしゅく	uncles

1767 淑 11

▶しゅく

貞淑な	ていしゅくな	chaste, virtuous
淑女	しゅくじょ	lady
私淑	ししゅく	cv. look up to/model oneself after a person (though not directly studying under that person)

1768 朱 6

▶しゅ

583
cf. 未

朱色	しゅいろ	vermilion, cinnabar red
朱肉	しゅにく	vermilion inkpad
朱塗りの	しゅぬりの	painted in vermilion

1769 珠 10

▶しゅ

真珠	しんじゅ	pearl
珠玉	しゅぎょく	pearls and jewels, excellent/precious works
珠算	しゅざん	calculation on an abacus
数珠	△じゅず	(Buddhist) rosary

1770 卑 9

▶ひ
▷いや(しい), いや(しむ), いや(しめる)

卑屈な	ひくつな	mean, inferior, poor
卑近な例	ひきんなれい	familiar example
卑下	ひげ	cv. humble oneself
卑劣な	ひれつな	sneaky, mean, unfair
◇ 卑▲怯な	ひきょうな	unfair, cowardly
◇ 卑▲猥な	ひわいな	obscene, indecent
卑しい身分	いやしいみぶん	low (social) status/class
卑しむべき	いやしむべき	contemptible
卑しめる	いやしめる	despise, condemn, scorn, look down on

1771 碑 14

▶ひ

記念碑	きねんひ	monument
石碑	せきひ	stone monument
碑文	ひぶん	inscription (on a stone monument), epitaph
碑銘	ひめい	epitaph

1772 享 8 ▶きょう

享受	きょうじゅ　*cv.* enjoy, have, be given
享有	きょうゆう　*cv.* be given (talent/etc.) by nature
享楽	きょうらく　enjoyment
享楽主義	きょうらくしゅぎ　epicurism, hedonism

1773 郭 11 ▶かく

輪郭	りんかく　outline
外郭団体	がいかくだんたい　government-related institution
城郭	じょうかく　castle

1774 刃 3 ▶じん　441 ▷は　cf. 刀

かみそりの刃	かみそりのは　razor blade
刃物	はもの　cutlery, knives
両刃の	りょうばの　double-edged (blade)
白刃	はくじん　blade
自刃	じじん　*cv.* commit suicide with a sword
◇ *凶刃	きょうじん　a knife or other bladed weapon used to kill a person

1775 忍 7 ▶にん　▷しの(ぶ), しの(ばせる)

忍耐	にんたい　perseverance, patience, endurance; *cv.* persevere, be patient, endure
残忍な	ざんにんな　cruel, merciless
忍者	にんじゃ　*ninja*, spy warrior in feudal times
忍ぶ	しのぶ　bear, stand, endure
忍び足	しのびあし　stealthy steps
声を忍ばせる	こえをしのばせる　lower one's voice

1776 滋 12 ▶じ

滋養強壮	じようきょうそう　nutrition and health
滋味	じみ　tastiness, delicacy
◇ 滋賀県	▲しがけん　Shiga Prefecture

1777 磁 14 ▶じ

磁石	じしゃく　magnet, compass
磁気	じき　magnetism
磁器	じき　ceramics
陶磁器	とうじき　ceramic ware

1778 慈 13 ▶じ　▷いつく(しむ)

慈悲	じひ　mercy, charity
慈愛	じあい　affection, love
慈善事業	じぜんじぎょう　relief/charitable work
慈しむ	いつくしむ　love, be tender
慈しみ	いつくしみ　love, affection

1779 斉 8 ▶せい

| 一斉に | いっせいに　all together, simultaneously, all at once |
| ◇ 斉*唱 | せいしょう　*cv.* sing in chorus |

1780 剤 10 ▶ざい

洗剤	せんざい　detergent
錠剤	じょうざい　pill, tablet
消化剤	しょうかざい　digestive
薬剤師	やくざいし　pharmacist

⑬⑤

1781 斎 11	▶さい
書斎	しょさい study, library
斎場	さいじょう funeral hall

1782 耕 10	▶こう ▷たがや(す)
農耕	のうこう farming
耕地	こうち arable/cultivated land
耕作	こうさく *cv.* farm, till
耕す	たがやす till, plow, cultivate

1783 耗 10	▶もう，こう
消耗	しょうもう *cv.* consume/exhaust (energy)
摩耗	まもう *cv.* wear out
心神耗弱	しんしんこうじゃく weakening of the mind and body

1784 垣 9	▷かき
石垣	いしがき stone wall
垣根	かきね hedge, fence, boundary

| 1785 恒 9 | ▶こう |
| 恒久の | こうきゅうの permanent, eternal |

| 恒例 | こうれい usual practice, established custom |
| 恒常的に | こうじょうてきに constantly |

1786 巧 5	▶こう ▷たく(み)
巧妙な	こうみょうな clever, skillful
巧拙	こうせつ skill, dexterity
技巧	ぎこう technique, art
巧みに	たくみに skillfully, cleverly, ingeniously

1787 朽 6	▶きゅう ▷く(ちる)
不朽の名作	ふきゅうのめいさく immortal work
老朽化	ろうきゅうか *cv.* get old, become decrepit
朽ちる	くちる rot, decay, crumble
朽木	くちき decayed tree, rotten wood

1788 謡 16	▶よう ▷うたい，うた(う)
童謡	どうよう children's song
民謡	みんよう folk song
歌謡曲	かようきょく popular song
謡曲	ようきょく Noh song/chant
謡	うたい Noh chanting
謡う	うたう sing without accompaniment, chant

〈漢字の形に気をつけましょう・71〉

| 516 | 1779 | 1780 | 1781 |
| 済 | 斉 | 剤 | 斎 |

自由経済　一斉に走り出す　洗剤　書斎

1789 揺 12	▶よう ▷ゆ(れる), ゆ(る), ゆ(らぐ), ゆ(るぐ), ゆ(する), ゆ(さぶる), ゆ(すぶる)
揺りかご	ゆりかご cradle
揺れる	ゆれる vi. shake, sway, vibrate
揺れ	ゆれ shaking, tremor, jolting
揺する	ゆする vt. shake
揺さぶる	ゆさぶる vt. shake, rock
揺すぶる	ゆすぶる vt. shake, rock
揺らぐ	ゆらぐ vi. shake
揺るぐ	ゆるぐ vi. shake, sway
揺るぎない	ゆるぎない unshakable
動揺	どうよう cv. waver, be disturbed

1790 凝 16	▶ぎょう 693 ▷こ(る), こ(らす) cf. 疑
凝視	ぎょうし cv. gaze, stare
凝固	ぎょうこ cv.vi. congeal, solidify
凝結	ぎょうけつ cv.vi. congeal, solidify, freeze
凝る	こる grow stiff, clot, be particularly interested
凝り性	こりしょう fastidious, single-minded
目を凝らす	めをこらす look hard

1791 擬 17	▶ぎ 693 cf. 疑
擬人法	ぎじんほう personification
擬声語	ぎせいご onomatopoeic word
擬態語	ぎたいご mimesis, mimetic word
擬態	ぎたい mimesis
擬装	ぎそう cv. camouflage, disguise
模擬テスト	もぎテスト practice (entrance) examination

1792 随 12	▶ずい
随行	ずいこう cv. accompany, follow, attend
随員	ずいいん attendant, member of an entourage
随時	ずいじ any time, all times
随想録	ずいそうろく jottings, (occasional) essays
随筆	ずいひつ essay
随分	ずいぶん fairly
言語随伴行動	げんごずいはんこうどう language-accompanying behavior
追随	ついずい cv. catch up, follow
随意筋	ずいいきん voluntary muscle

1793 髄 19	▶ずい
骨髄	こつずい marrow
脳髄	のうずい brains
延髄	えんずい nerve bulb
心髄	しんずい essence, soul

1794 唇 10	▶しん ▷くちびる
唇	くちびる lip
口唇	こうしん lip

1795 辱 10	▶じょく ▷はずかし(める)
屈辱	くつじょく humiliation, disgrace
恥辱	ちじょく disgrace, dishonor, shame
雪辱を果たす	せつじょくをはたす avenge an insult, have one's revenge
◇*侮辱	ぶじょく cv. insult, put to shame, disgrace

| 辱める | はずかしめる　*vt.* humiliate, disgrace, violate, rape |
| 辱め | はずかしめ　humiliation, disgrace |

1796　幣　15　▶へい

紙幣	しへい　paper money, bill
貨幣	かへい　currency, money, coin
造幣局	ぞうへいきょく　mint, the Mint Bureau

1797　弊　15　▶へい

弊害	へいがい　ill effects, evil
疲弊	ひへい　*cv.* become impoverished/exhausted
旧弊	きゅうへい　old evil, conventional bad practices
弊社	へいしゃ　our company (humble)

1798　墾　16　▶こん

| 開墾 | かいこん　*cv.* cultivate, reclaim (land) |

1799　懇　17　▶こん　▷ねんご(ろ)

懇親会	こんしんかい　friendship party, social gathering
懇談会	こんだんかい　informal talk (with the prime minister/etc.)
懇切丁寧に	こんせつていねいに　kindly and thoroughly
懇ろに	ねんごろに　intimately, courteously

1800　敏　10　▶びん

敏感な	びんかんな　sensitive
敏速に	びんそくに　promptly, quickly
機敏な	きびんな　swift, quick
鋭敏な	えいびんな　sharp, sensitive

1801　侮　8　▶ぶ　▷あなど(る)　164　cf. 毎

侮辱	ぶじょく　*cv.* insult
軽侮	けいぶ　*cv.* despise, look down on
侮る	あなどる　despise, look down on
侮り	あなどり　despise, insult

1802　炉　8　▶ろ

原子炉	げんしろ　atomic reactor
暖炉	だんろ　fireplace, stove
溶鉱炉	ようこうろ　furnace
炉辺	ろへん　fireside

1803　炎　8　▶えん　▷ほのお　873　cf. 災

炎天下	えんてんか　under the burning sun
炎上	えんじょう　*cv.* be destroyed by fire, be burned down
火炎	かえん　flame
炎	ほのお　flame, fire

1804　哀　9　▶あい　▷あわ(れ), あわ(れむ)

哀れな	あわれな　piteous, pitiable, pathetic
哀れむ	あわれむ　pity, feel sympathy/compassion
哀れみ	あわれみ　pity, pathos, sorrow
悲哀	ひあい　grief, sadness, sorrow
哀愁	あいしゅう　sadness, sorrow, grief

哀願　　　　あいがん　*cv.* make an earnest request, entreat

1805　衰　10　▶すい　▷おとろ(える)

衰弱　　　　すいじゃく　*cv.* weaken, become feeble, be worn out

衰退　　　　すいたい　*cv.* decline, degenerate

老衰　　　　ろうすい　*cv.* become senile

盛衰　　　　せいすい　rise and fall, ups and down

衰える　　　おとろえる　become weak, lose vigor, waste away

衰え　　　　おとろえ　weakening, emaciation, decline

1806　衷　9　▶ちゅう

折衷案　　　せっちゅうあん　compromise plan

折衷主義　　せっちゅうしゅぎ　eclecticism

折衷　　　　せっちゅう　*cv.* blend, cross, compromise

1807　喪　12　▶そう　▷も

記憶喪失　　きおくそうしつ　amnesia

喪失　　　　そうしつ　*cv.* lose

喪服　　　　もふく　mourning dress

喪主　　　　もしゅ　chief mourner

喪中　　　　もちゅう　period of mourning

喪　　　　　も　mourning

1808　晶　12　▶しょう

結晶　　　　けっしょう　crystal, crystallization, fruit (of one's efforts/etc.); *cv.vi.* crystallize

水晶　　　　すいしょう　crystal

1809　唱　11　▶しょう　▷とな(える)

合唱　　　　がっしょう　*cv.* sing in chorus

唱歌　　　　しょうか　singing, songs

提唱　　　　ていしょう　*cv.* advocate

唱える　　　となえる　advocate, chant

1810　尚　8　▶しょう　　　557　cf. 向

高尚な　　　こうしょうな　noble

時期尚早　　じきしょうそう　premature, too early

1811　肖　7　▶しょう

肖像画　　　しょうぞうが　portrait

1812　凶　4　▶きょう

凶悪な　　　きょうあくな　terrible, evil

凶暴な　　　きょうぼうな　brutal

凶器　　　　きょうき　murder weapon

凶作　　　　きょうさく　poor harvest

吉凶　　　　きっきょう　fortunate or unfortunate, fortune

1813　丹　4　▶たん

丹念に　　　たんねんに　elaborately, laboriously, carefully

丹精込めて　たんせいこめて　laboriously, painstakingly

1814　幻　4　▶げん　　　1099　▷まぼろし　cf. 幼

幻想　　　　げんそう　fantasy, illusion, dream

幻覚　　　　げんかく　hallucination

幻滅　　　　げんめつ　*cv.* be disillusioned

| 幻 | まぼろし　phantom, illusion, hallucination |

1815 弔 4　▶ちょう　76　▷とむら(う)　cf. 弟

弔問外交	ちょうもんがいこう　diplomacy at a condolence call (by a head of state/etc.)
弔辞	ちょうじ　memorial address
弔電	ちょうでん　condolatory telegram
慶弔	けいちょう　congratulations and condolences
弔う	とむらう　mourn, condole, perform a Buddhist memorial service
弔い	とむらい　condolence, funeral, burial, mass for the dead

1816 甲 5　▶こう, かん　585　cf. 申

甲板	かんぱん　(ship's) deck
甲高い声	かんだかいこえ　high-pitched/shrill voice
手の甲	てのこう　back of the hand
装甲車	そうこうしゃ　armored car
甲殻類	こうかくるい　crustaceans
◊ 甲*乙つけがたい	こうおつつけがたい　be difficult to distinguish which is better
甲種	こうしゅ　A rank　cf. *乙種(おつしゅ) B rank, *丙種(へいしゅ) C rank

1817 斥 5　▶せき

| 排斥 | はいせき　cv. boycott, exclude |
| 斥候 | せっこう　scout, patrol (in medieval times) |

1818 亜 7　▶あ　114　cf. 悪

亜熱帯	あねったい　the subtropical zone
亜流	ありゅう　epigone
亜鉛	あえん　zinc

1819 奔 8　▶ほん

奔走	ほんそう　cv. make efforts
自由奔放な	じゆうほんぽうな　free and unrestrained, uninhibited
出奔	しゅっぽん　cv. abscond, run away, elope

1820 幽 9　▶ゆう

幽霊	ゆうれい　ghost
幽玄	ゆうげん　mystery, occult
幽閉	ゆうへい　cv. confine, shut up

137

1821 栽 10　▶さい

| 栽培 | さいばい　cv. grow, cultivate |
| 盆栽 | ぼんさい　bonsai, potted dwarf tree |

1822 瓶 11　▶びん

ビール瓶	ビールびん　bottle of beer
花瓶	かびん　vase
瓶詰	びんづめ　bottled

1823 執 11　▶しつ, しゅう　891 894　▷と(る)　cf. 報 幸

| 執務室 | しつむしつ　office (of a president/emperor/etc.) |
| 執筆 | しっぴつ　cv. write |

執行	しっこう	*cv.* execute, carry out
執行猶予	しっこうゆうよ	stay of execution, suspended sentence
確執	かくしつ	discord, feud
◇ 執▲拗な	しつような	obstinate, persistent
執念	しゅうねん	persistence, tenacity, devotion
執心	しゅうしん	*cv.* be infatuated (with a boy/girl)
執着	しゅうちゃく	*cv.* stick to, insist, be attached
執る	とる	do, handle

1824 **粛** **11** ▶しゅく   1728   cf. 庸

自粛	じしゅく	*cv.* voluntarily refrain, practice self-control
綱紀粛正	こうきしゅくせい	enforcement of official discipline
粛清	しゅくせい	*cv.* purge
静粛にする	せいしゅくにする	keep quiet
粛然と	しゅくぜんと	silently, quietly, solemnly

1825 **蛮** **12** ▶ばん

野蛮な	やばんな	barbarous, uncivilized, savage
野蛮人	やばんじん	barbarian, savage
南蛮人	なんばんじん	southern barbarians, Europeans sailing to Japan from the south between the 16th-18th centuries
蛮行	ばんこう	barbarous act, barbarity

1826 **疎** **12** ▶そ ▷うと(い), うと(む)

疎外	そがい	*cv.* alienate, shun, estrange
親疎	しんそ	closeness (in relations)
疎遠になる	そえんになる	become estranged
意思の疎通	いしのそつう	communication
疎い	うとい	unfamiliar; know little
疎む	うとむ	shun, neglect, estrange
疎ましい	うとましい	disagreeable, offensive

1827 **鼓** **13** ▶こ ▷つづみ

太鼓	たいこ	drum
鼓動	こどう	beat, pulsation
鼓舞	こぶ	*cv.* inspire (someone to greater efforts), encourage, cheer
鼓	つづみ	hand drum
舌鼓	したつづみ	eating with gusto

1828 **碁** **13** ▶ご   691   cf. 基

碁	ご	*go* (a board game)
囲碁	いご	*go* (a board game)
碁石	ごいし	*go* piece
碁盤	ごばん	*go* board

1829 **憂** **15** ▶ゆう   1168   ▷うれ(える), うれ(い), う(い)   cf. 優

憂慮	ゆうりょ	*cv.* be anxious/apprehensive/concerned, worry
一喜一憂	いっきいちゆう	*cv.* be alternately glad and sad, cannot put one's mind at ease
◇ 憂▲鬱な	ゆううつな	melancholic, gloomy
憂える	うれえる	be distressed/anxious, grieve
憂い	うれい	anxiety, distress, grief
憂き目をみる	うきめをみる	have a hard time of it

物憂い	ものうい	be melancholic, be gloomy

1830
15　舗　▶ほ

舗装	ほそう	*cv.* pave (a road/street/etc.)
舗装道路	ほそうどうろ	paved road, pavement
店舗	てんぽ	shop, store
◇ 老舗	▲しにせ	long-established store

1831
17　覧　▶らん

ご覧になる	ごらんになる	see, look (honorific)

閲覧	えつらん	*cv.* peruse, inspect, read
一覧表	いちらんひょう	list, table
展覧会	てんらんかい	exhibition, show

1832
19　麗　▶れい
**　　　▷うるわ(しい)**

華麗な	かれいな	splendid, magnificent, gorgeous
端麗な	たんれいな	graceful, sophisticated
麗人	れいじん	beautiful woman
美辞麗句	びじれいく	flowery words
麗しい	うるわしい	beautiful, pretty, lovely, fine

第6水準

(Level 6)

1833-1947

●自　然

1833 11	菊	▷きく
	菊	きく chrysanthemum
	白菊	しらぎく white chrysanthemum

1834 6	芋	▷いも
	芋	いも potato, sweet potato
	焼き芋	やきいも roasted sweet potato
	里芋	さといも taro

1835 8	芽	▶が ▷め
	芽が出る	めがでる bud, sprout
	芽	め bud, sprout
	新芽	しんめ bud, sprout
	発芽	はつが *cv.* germinate, bud, sprout
	麦芽	ばくが malt

1836 8	茎	▶けい ▷くき
	茎	くき stalk, stem
	歯茎	はぐき, しけい gums
	地下茎	ちかけい underground/subterranean stem

1837 8	苗	▶びょう　1681 ▷なえ, なわ　cf. 笛
	苗	なえ seedling, sapling, shoot
	苗木	なえぎ sapling, young tree
	苗代	なわしろ rice nursery
	種苗	しゅびょう seeds and saplings

1838 16	薪	▶しん ▷たきぎ
	薪	たきぎ firewood
	薪能	たきぎのう Noh performance beside a fire
	薪炭	しんたん firewood and charcoal, winter fuel
	薪水	しんすい firewood and water

1839 19	藻	▶そう　903 ▷も　cf. 燥
	藻	も waterweed, seaweed
	海藻	かいそう seaweed
	藻類	そうるい water weeds, seaweed

1840 8	茂	▶も ▷しげ(る)
	茂み	しげみ bush, thicket
	茂る	しげる grow thickly/luxuriantly
	繁茂	はんも *cv.* grow thickly/luxuriantly

1841 13	滝	▷たき
	滝	たき waterfall
◇	滝壺	たきつぼ waterfall basin

1842 8	沼	▶しょう ▷ぬま
	沼	ぬま swamp, marsh, bog
	沼地	ぬまち marshland
	湖沼	こしょう lakes and marshes
	沼沢地	しょうたくち marshland, swampy area

| 1843 11 | 渓 | ▶けい |

渓谷　けいこく　(steep-walled) valley, ravine, canyon

渓流　けいりゅう　mountain stream/ torrent

雪渓　せっけい　snowy valley/ravine

| 1844 9 | 洞 | ▶どう ▷ほら |

洞察力　どうさつりょく　insight, discernment

空洞　くうどう　hollow, cave

洞穴　どうけつ，ほらあな　cave

◇ 洞▲窟　どうくつ　cave, cavern

| 1845 19 | 瀬 | ▷せ |

浅瀬　あさせ　shallows, shoal

瀬　せ　rapids, shallows, shoal

立つ瀬がない　たつせがない　be put in an awkward position

瀬戸物　せともの　porcelain, china

| 1846 10 | 浦 | ▶ほ ▷うら |

三浦半島　みうらはんとう　Miura Peninsula

浦　うら　inlet, shore, bay

津々浦々　つつうらうら　throughout the country, far and wide

特 曲浦　きょくほ　bay with a winding shore

| 1847 15 | 潟 | ▷かた 836 cf. 湯 |

新潟　にいがた　Niigata

干潟　ひがた　tideland, tidal flats

| 1848 10 | 峰 | ▶ほう ▷みね |

峰　みね　peak, summit, top

後立山連峰　うしろたてやまれんぽう　the Ushirotateyama Mountains

霊峰　れいほう　sacred mountain

| 1849 9 | 峠 | ▷とうげ |

峠　とうげ　mountain pass, height

峠を越す　とうげをこす　cross a ridge, pass the critical point, be over the hump

| 1850 8 | 岬 | ▷みさき |

岬　みさき　cape

- (139)

| 1851 8 | 岳 | ▶がく ▷たけ |

山岳地帯　さんがくちたい　mountainous region

岳父　がくふ　the father of one's wife

北岳　きただけ　Kitadake (a peak in the Southern Alps)

| 1852 12 | 堤 | ▶てい ▷つつみ　767 1670 cf. 提 是 |

堤防　ていぼう　bank, embankment, dike, levee

防波堤　ぼうはてい　breakwater, seawall

堤　つつみ　bank, embankment, dike

| 1853 16 | 樹 | ▶じゅ |

街路樹　がいろじゅ　roadside trees

果樹園　かじゅえん　orchard

樹木	じゅもく　trees
樹林帯	じゅりんたい　forest
樹立	じゅりつ　*cv.* establish/set (a record/etc.)

1854 柳 9 ▶りゅう 1264 ▷やなぎ　cf. 抑

柳	やなぎ　willow
川柳	せんりゅう　*senryū*, satrical poem, witticism in verse
花柳界	かりゅうかい　the world of *geisha*

1855 桑 10 ▶そう 1310 ▷くわ　cf. 柔

桑	くわ　mulberry
桑畑	くわばたけ　mulberry field
桑園	そうえん　mulberry plantation

1856 穂 15 ▶すい 1077 ▷ほ　cf. 恵

穂	ほ　ear, head, spike
稲穂	いなほ　ear of a rice plant
穂状の	すいじょうの　ear-shaped

1857 畔 10 ▶はん

湖畔	こはん　lakeside

1858 暁 12 ▶ぎょう 218 ▷あかつき　cf. 焼

暁	あかつき　daybreak, dawn
早暁	そうぎょう　early dawn

1859 昆 8 ▶こん 837 cf. 混

昆虫	こんちゅう　insect
昆布	こんぶ　sea tangle, kelp

1860 蚊 10 ▷か

蚊	か　mosquito

1861 蛇 11 ▶じゃ, だ ▷へび

蛇	へび　snake
大蛇	だいじゃ　huge serpent
蛇腹	じゃばら　cornice, bellows
蛇口	じゃぐち　faucet, tap
蛇行	だこう　*cv.* wind its way (through), meander
長蛇の列	ちょうだのれつ　long line/queue
蛇足	だそく　superfluity, redundancy

1862 巣 11 ▶そう 1667 502 ▷す　cf. 菓 果

鳥の巣	とりのす　bird nest
巣箱	すばこ　birdhouse, beehive
巣立つ	すだつ　leave the nest, make one's own start in life
卵巣	らんそう　ovary
病巣	びょうそう　focus

1863 鶏 19 ▶けい ▷にわとり

鶏	にわとり　chicken, hen, cock, rooster
鶏卵	けいらん　(hen's) egg
養鶏場	ようけいじょう　poultry/chicken farm
闘鶏	とうけい　cockfight

1864 獣 16 ▶じゅう ▷けもの

野獣	やじゅう　wild beast
猛獣	もうじゅう　fierce animal

鳥獣	ちょうじゅう	birds and beasts
珍獣	ちんじゅう	rare animal
獣	けもの	animal, beast

1865 13 猿 ▶えん ▷さる cf. 遠 110

猿	さる	monkey, ape
野猿	やえん	wild monkey
類人猿	るいじんえん	anthropoid
犬猿の仲	けんえんのなか	be like cats and dogs, be on bad terms

1866 10 蚕 ▶さん ▷かいこ

蚕	かいこ	silkworm
養蚕業	ようさんぎょう	silk industry
蚕糸	さんし	silk thread
蚕食	さんしょく	cv. encroach, make inroads

1867 10 竜 ▶りゅう ▷たつ

竜	りゅう，たつ	dragon
竜頭蛇尾	りゅうとうだび	bright beginning and dull ending
竜巻	たつまき	tornado

●歴史・文学 ⑭

1868 10 姫 ▷ひめ

| 姫 | ひめ | princess |

1869 6 妃 ▶ひ

| 王妃 | おうひ | queen |
| 妃殿下 | ひでんか | Her Imperial Highness |

| ◇▲楊貴妃 | ようきひ | Yang Kuei-fei (a famous Chinese beauty of the Tang dynasty) |

1870 14 嫡 ▶ちゃく

| 嫡子 | ちゃくし | one's heir |

1871 5 奴 ▶ど cf. 努 827

奴隷	どれい	slave
農奴	のうど	serf
売国奴	ばいこくど	traitor to one's country

1872 16 隷 ▶れい cf. 逮 1048

奴隷	どれい	slave
隷属	れいぞく	cv. be subordinate to, follow orders
隷従	れいじゅう	cv. be subordinate to

1873 6 后 ▶こう

| 皇后 | こうごう | empress |
| 皇太后 | こうたいごう | empress dowager |

1874 8 騎 ▶き

騎士	きし	knight, cavalier
騎手	きしゅ	jockey, rider
騎馬民族	きばみんぞく	equestrian people

1875 17 爵 ▶しゃく

| 爵位 | しゃくい | title of nobility, peerage |
| 侯爵 | こうしゃく | marquis |

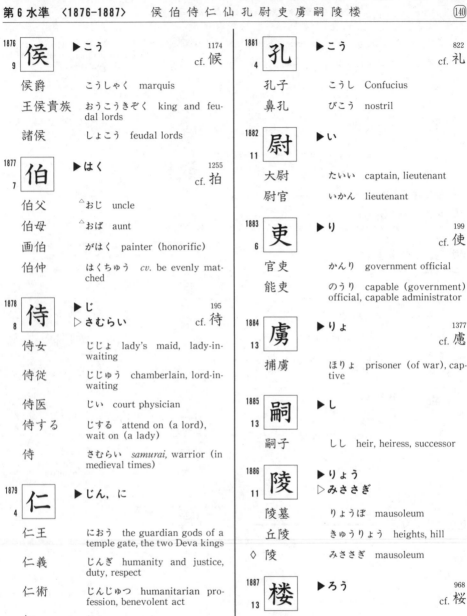

1876 侯 9　▶こう　1174　cf. 候

侯爵　こうしゃく　marquis
王侯貴族　おうこうきぞく　king and feudal lords
諸侯　しょこう　feudal lords

1877 伯 7　▶はく　1255　cf. 拍

伯父　△おじ　uncle
伯母　△おば　aunt
画伯　がはく　painter (honorific)
伯仲　はくちゅう　*cv.* be evenly matched

1878 侍 8　▶じ　▷さむらい　195　cf. 待

侍女　じじょ　lady's maid, lady-in-waiting
侍従　じじゅう　chamberlain, lord-in-waiting
侍医　じい　court physician
侍する　じする　attend on (a lord), wait on (a lady)
侍　さむらい　*samurai,* warrior (in medieval times)

1879 仁 4　▶じん, に

仁王　におう　the guardian gods of a temple gate, the two Deva kings
仁義　じんぎ　humanity and justice, duty, respect
仁術　じんじゅつ　humanitarian profession, benevolent act
仁　じん　compassion

1880 仙 5　▶せん

仙人　せんにん　hermit, wizard

1881 孔 4　▶こう　822　cf. 礼

孔子　こうし　Confucius
鼻孔　びこう　nostril

1882 尉 11　▶い

大尉　たいい　captain, lieutenant
尉官　いかん　lieutenant

1883 吏 6　▶り　199　cf. 使

官吏　かんり　government official
能吏　のうり　capable (government) official, capable administrator

1884 虜 13　▶りょ　1377　cf. 慮

捕虜　ほりょ　prisoner (of war), captive

1885 嗣 13　▶し

嗣子　しし　heir, heiress, successor

1886 陵 11　▶りょう　▷みささぎ

陵墓　りょうぼ　mausoleum
丘陵　きゅうりょう　heights, hill
◇ 陵　みささぎ　mausoleum

1887 楼 13　▶ろう　968　cf. 桜

楼閣　ろうかく　tower
鐘楼　しょうろう　belltower, belfry
望楼　ぼうろう　watch tower
◇▲妓楼　ぎろう　brothel

1888 15	墳	▶ふん	1633 1634 cf. 噴 憤

古墳	こふん tumulus, ancient tomb (mound)
墳墓	ふんぼ grave, tomb

1889 12	塚	▷つか	52 cf. 家

貝塚	かいづか shell mound
◇▲蟻塚	ありづか anthill
塚	つか mound, hillock, tumulus

1890 18	藩	▶はん	

藩	はん feudal domain/fief in the Tokugawa era
藩主	はんしゅ feudal lord in the Tokugawa era

⑭①

1891 16	儒	▶じゅ	681 cf. 需

儒教	じゅきょう Confucianism
儒学	じゅがく Confucianism
儒者	じゅしゃ Confucian

1892 22	艦	▶かん	925 cf. 監

軍艦	ぐんかん warship
戦艦	せんかん warship
艦隊	かんたい fleet, armada
◇ 艦*艇	かんてい naval vessels

1893 10	租	▶そ	635 cf. 組

租税	そぜい taxes

1894 9	帥	▶すい	967 cf. 師

統帥権	とうすいけん prerogative of supreme command
総帥	そうすい commander
元帥	げんすい marshal

1895 9	勅	▶ちょく	

勅語	ちょくご imperial rescript
勅使	ちょくし imperial envoy
勅令	ちょくれい imperial decree
◇*詔勅	しょうちょく imperial edict/ proclamation/rescript

1896 15	遷	▶せん	1215 cf. 還

変遷	へんせん change, transition; cv.vi. change
遷都	せんと transfer of the capital; cv.vi. transfer the capital

1897 11	赦	▶しゃ	46 cf. 赤

恩赦	おんしゃ pardon, amnesty
大赦	たいしゃ amnesty, general amnesty
赦免	しゃめん cv. pardon, remit a punishment, let someone off

1898 15	賜	▶し ▷たまわ(る)	434 335 cf. 易 場

賜る	たまわる be given, be honored with
下賜	かし cv. give (honorific)
恩賜	おんし gift from the emperor

1899 15	謁	▶えつ	1011 cf. 掲

拝謁	はいえつ cv. have an audience (with a noble person)

謁見	えっけん *cv.* have an audience (with a noble person)
謁する	えっする have an audience (with a noble person)

1900 **15** 窯 ▶よう 1674
▷かま cf. 室

| 窯業 | ようぎょう pottery industry |
| 窯 | かま kiln |

1901 **15** 戯 ▶ぎ 1741
▷たわむ(れる) cf. 虚

戯曲	ぎきょく drama, play
戯れる	たわむれる play, tease, joke, flirt
戯れ	たわむれ play, joke, fun, flirtation
◊ 戯作	▲げさく popular/lowbrow literature in the Edo period

1902 **11** 婆 ▶ば 913 661
cf. 波 姿

老婆	ろうば old woman
産婆	さんば midwife
◊ お婆さん	▲おばあさん old woman cf. お祖母さん (▲おばあさん) grandmother

1903 **19** 韻 ▶いん

韻	いん rhyme
韻律	いんりつ meter, rhythm
韻文	いんぶん verse
音韻	おんいん phoneme

1904 **7** 吟 ▶ぎん

| 吟味 | ぎんみ *cv.* select with care, examine, inquire into |
| 詩吟 | しぎん recitation/chanting of a Chinese poem |

吟詠	ぎんえい *cv.* recite/chant a Chinese poem

1905 **12** 詠 ▶えい
▷よ(む)

詠嘆の声	えいたんのこえ voice of admiration
朗詠	ろうえい *cv.* recite, chant (a poem)
詠む	よむ recite, chant (a poem)

1906 **12** 琴 ▶きん
▷こと

琴	こと *koto*, Japanese zither-like instrument
木琴	もっきん xylophone
心の琴線	こころのきんせん one's heart-strings

1907 **10** 宵 ▶しょう 1811
▷よい cf. 肖

| 宵 | よい early evening |
| 徹宵 | てっしょう overnight |

●特殊━━━━━━━━━ 142

1908 **1** 乙 ▶おつ

乙	おつ B
乙種	おつしゅ B rank cf. 甲種 (こうしゅ) A rank
甲乙つけがたい	こうおつつけがたい be difficult to distinguish which is better
乙女	△おとめ maiden, (young) girl, virgin

1909 **5** 丙 ▶へい

| 丙 | へい C |
| 丙種 | へいしゅ C rank |

274

1910 9	厘	▶りん
	～厘	～りん　～*rin*　(0.1 percent)

1911 7	壱	▶いち
	壱万円	いちまんえん　ten thousand yen

1912 6	弐	▶に　1165 cf. 武
	弐万円	にまんえん　twenty thousand yen

1913 8	坪	▷つぼ　351 cf. 平
	～坪	～つぼ　～*tsubo* (unit of area, approx. 3.3 m²)
	坪数	つぼすう　acreage, area
	建坪	たてつぼ　floor space

1914 4	斤	▶きん　772 cf. 折
	～斤	～きん　～*kin* (unit of weight, approx. 600 g)

1915 4	升	▶しょう　1280 ▷ます　cf. 昇
	～升	～しょう　～*shō* (unit of capacity, approx. 1.8 *l*)
	升	ます　measure, box (seat)
	升目	ますめ　measure

1916 4	匁	▷もんめ
	～匁	～もんめ　～*monme* (unit of weight, approx. 3.75 g)

1917 3	勺	▶しゃく　381 cf. 約
	～勺	～しゃく　～*shaku* (unit of capacity, approx. 818 *ml*)

1918 4	屯	▶とん　1068 cf. 純
	駐屯	ちゅうとん　*cv.* be stationed
	駐屯地	ちゅうとんち　post, army post, garrison

1919 10	隻	▶せき　224 cf. 集
	～隻	～せき　(counter for ships)

1920 4	斗	▶と　1391 cf. 斜
	～斗	～と　～*to* (unit of capacity, approx. 18*l*)
	北斗七星	ほくとしちせい　the Big Dipper

1921 5	凸	▶とつ
	凸レンズ	とつレンズ　convex lens

1922 5	凹	▶おう
	凹レンズ	おうレンズ　concave lens
	凹凸	おうとつ　unevenness, ruggedness, irregularity
	凸凹	△でこぼこ　unevenness, ruggedness, irregularity

1923 7	但	▷ただ(し)　1050 cf. 担
	但し	ただし　but, however
	但し書き	ただしがき　proviso

1924 5	且	▷か(つ)　635 cf. 組
	且つ	かつ　moreover, besides

1925 17	嚇	▶かく　46 cf. 赤
	威嚇	いかく　*cv.* menace, threat

275

1926 11	隆	▶りゅう

隆起　りゅうき　*cv.* rise, bulge, be elevated

興隆　こうりゅう　*cv.* rise, prosper, flourish

隆盛　りゅうせい　prosperity

1927 12	脹	▶ちょう

膨脹剤　ぼうちょうざい　inflating agent

1928 7	坑	▶こう　747　cf.抗

炭坑　たんこう　coal mine

坑道　こうどう　(coal) pit

廃坑　はいこう　abandoned mine

1929 7	呉	▶ご　949 1329　cf.誤娯

呉服　ごふく　kimono

呉服店　ごふくてん　kimono fabric shop

呉越同舟　ごえつどうしゅう　bitter enemies (placed by fate) in the same boat　cf. 呉 and 越 are two rival countries in ancient China.

1930 13	艇	▶てい　1211　cf.廷

競艇　きょうてい　motorboat race

艦艇　かんてい　naval vessels

⑭

1931 8	佳	▶か

佳作　かさく　honorable mention, fine work

佳人　かじん　beautiful woman

1932 12	痘	▶とう

天然痘　てんねんとう　smallpox

種痘　しゅとう　vaccination

1933 11	曹	▶そう　1537　cf.槽

法曹界　ほうそうかい　the judicial world

軍曹　ぐんそう　sergeant

1934 10	恭	▶きょう　419　▷うやうや(しい)　cf.共

恭順　きょうじゅん　submission, obedience

恭しく　うやうやしく　respectfully, reverently

1935 12	詔	▶しょう　694　▷みことのり　cf.紹

詔書　しょうしょ　imperial edict

詔勅　しょうちょく　imperial edict/proclamation/rescript

詔　みことのり　imperial edict

1936 15	褒	▶ほう　665　▷ほ(める)　cf.保

褒める　ほめる　praise

褒美　ほうび　prize, reward

1937 17	謄	▶とう　263 1547　cf.勝 謄

謄写版　とうしゃばん　mimeograph

戸籍謄本　こせきとうほん　certified copy of one's family register

1938 10	朕	▶ちん

朕　ちん　I (traditionally used by the emperor)

1939 10	畝	▷せ, うね
	畝	うね ridge, furrow, groove
	〜畝	〜せ 〜se (unit of area, approx. 0.091 a)

1940 10	翁	▶おう
	老翁	ろうおう old man

1941 10	逓	▶てい
	逓減	ていげん cv. decrease gradually, diminish successively
	逓信省	ていしんしょう Communication Ministry (of the prewar Japanese government)

1942 16	錘	▶すい 226 1322 ▷つむ cf. 郵 垂
	紡錘	ぼうすい spindle
	錘	つむ spindle

1943 14	銑	▶せん
	銑鉄	せんてつ pig iron

1944 13	塑	▶そ
	可塑性	かせい plasticity
	塑像	そぞう plastic image, clay figure/statue
	彫塑	ちょうそ carvings and sculptures

1945 13	虞	▷おそれ 1929 cf. 呉
	虞	おそれ fear, anxiety

1946 18	繭	▶けん ▷まゆ
	繭	まゆ cocoon
	繭糸	けんし silk thread

1947 19	璽	▶じ
	国璽	こくじ seal of state
	御璽	ぎょじ imperial seal

付　　録
(Appendices)

学習漢字一覧表
（List of *Kanji*）

第　1　水　準						250字

No.	漢字	No.	漢字	No.	漢字	No.	漢字	No.	漢字	No.	漢字
1	一	30	後	59	会	88	小	117	早	146	地
2	二	31	上	60	社	89	長	118	遅	147	鉄
3	三	32	下	61	電	90	短	119	暑	148	者
4	四	33	中	62	車	91	朝	120	寒	149	所
5	五	34	横	63	自	92	昼	121	深	150	外
6	六	35	右	64	動	93	夜	122	浅	151	国
7	七	36	左	65	転	94	晩	123	細	152	内
8	八	37	本	66	道	95	夕	124	太	153	旅
9	九	38	机	67	男	96	春	125	若	154	語
10	十	39	東	68	女	97	夏	126	忙	155	英
11	百	40	西	69	子	98	秋	127	寝	156	世
12	千	41	南	70	主	99	冬	128	起	157	界
13	万	42	北	71	奥	100	山	129	始	158	倍
14	円	43	方	72	私	101	川	130	終	159	半
15	人	44	白	73	父	102	石	131	食	160	全
16	日	45	黒	74	母	103	田	132	飲	161	間
17	月	46	赤	75	兄	104	多	133	来	162	回
18	火	47	青	76	弟	105	少	134	帰	163	週
19	水	48	先	77	姉	106	明	135	乗	164	毎
20	木	49	生	78	妹	107	暗	136	降	165	体
21	金	50	学	79	友	108	低	137	作	166	頭
22	土	51	校	80	何	109	近	138	休	167	口
23	曜	52	家	81	誰	110	遠	139	見	168	目
24	年	53	部	82	名	111	強	140	勉	169	耳
25	時	54	屋	83	高	112	弱	141	住	170	手
26	分	55	店	84	安	113	広	142	持	171	足
27	今	56	駅	85	新	114	悪	143	知	172	心
28	午	57	銀	86	古	115	重	144	酒	173	力
29	前	58	行	87	大	116	軽	145	茶	174	立

No.	漢字	No.	漢字	No.	漢字	No.	漢字	No.	漢字	No.	漢字	No.	漢字
175	座	188	買	201	習	214	教	227	便	240	料		
176	歩	189	払	202	思	215	開	228	局	241	理		
177	走	190	着	203	言	216	閉	229	病	242	真		
178	話	191	脱	204	通	217	止	230	院	243	紙		
179	聞	192	働	205	渡	218	焼	231	窓	244	好		
180	読	193	泳	206	送	219	消	232	雨	245	元		
181	書	194	写	207	泊	220	直	233	京	246	気		
182	借	195	待	208	覚	221	並	234	映	247	静		
183	貸	196	遊	209	忘	222	変	235	画	248	利		
184	返	197	呼	210	調	223	残	236	仕	249	親		
185	出	198	洗	211	続	224	集	237	事	250	切		
186	入	199	使	212	考	225	倒	238	質				
187	売	200	歌	213	答	226	郵	239	問				

第　２　水　準　　100字／計350字

No.	漢字	No.	漢字	No.	漢字	No.	漢字	No.	漢字	No.	漢字
251	笑	268	盗	285	捨	302	結	319	犬	336	県
252	泣	269	受	286	発	303	婚	320	文	337	府
253	喜	270	取	287	到	304	運	321	物	338	都
254	困	271	合	288	計	305	案	322	族	339	暖
255	怒	272	吸	289	定	306	卒	323	公	340	涼
256	押	273	拾	290	注	307	業	324	園	341	悲
257	引	274	誘	291	意	308	用	325	医	342	苦
258	死	275	疲	292	説	309	去	326	宿	343	楽
259	吹	276	比	293	解	310	趣	327	題	344	辛
260	咲	277	決	294	参	311	味	328	寺	345	甘
261	置	278	伝	295	加	312	授	329	図	346	痛
262	勝	279	流	296	練	313	橋	330	館	347	有
263	選	280	落	297	研	314	花	331	室	348	退
264	飛	281	晴	298	究	315	薬	332	席	349	屈
265	踏	282	投	299	連	316	色	333	度	350	同
266	進	283	逃	300	絡	317	服	334	機		
267	進	284	過	301	濯	318	客	335	場		

第　３　水　準　　　　850字／計1200字

No.	漢字	No.	漢字	No.	漢字	No.	漢字	No.	漢字	No.	漢字
351	平	385	違	419	共	453	湖	487	鳴	521	復
352	和	386	逆	420	以	454	海	488	羊	522	複
353	等	387	整	421	性	455	島	489	群	523	雑
354	第	388	務	422	不	456	岸	490	毛	524	誌
355	筆	389	省	423	必	457	岩	491	羽	525	勤
356	算	390	談	424	要	458	谷	492	翌	526	難
357	符	391	相	425	価	459	林	493	義	527	漢
358	簡	392	想	426	値	460	森	494	議	528	字
359	単	393	首	427	普	461	空	495	講	529	数
360	戦	394	身	428	昔	462	天	496	論	530	政
361	争	395	員	429	増	463	星	497	倫	531	治
362	反	396	損	430	減	464	光	498	輪	532	台
363	対	397	別	431	感	465	風	499	輸	533	路
364	村	398	特	432	留	466	虫	500	較	534	戸
365	付	399	点	433	貿	467	凡	501	効	535	居
366	団	400	無	434	易	468	冗	502	果	536	民
367	寸	401	然	435	量	469	個	503	郊	537	守
368	支	402	当	436	裏	470	固	504	交	538	宅
369	技	403	予	437	表	471	豆	505	渉	539	管
370	術	404	野	438	面	472	登	506	干	540	官
371	街	405	原	439	最	473	祭	507	汗	541	庁
372	封	406	因	440	初	474	際	508	軒	542	庭
373	筒	407	正	441	刀	475	察	509	形	543	床
374	竹	408	幾	442	号	476	警	510	枠	544	庫
375	替	409	系	443	労	477	驚	511	械	545	廊
376	賛	410	級	444	協	478	敬	512	識	546	郎
377	成	411	能	445	門	479	尊	513	職	547	市
378	功	412	可	446	関	480	導	514	就	548	区
379	工	413	代	447	係	481	停	515	経	549	町
380	的	414	化	448	孫	482	件	516	済	550	丁
381	約	415	他	449	系	483	牛	517	活	551	番
382	束	416	仏	450	懸	484	馬	518	法	552	郡
383	速	417	位	451	態	485	魚	519	律	553	州
384	達	418	供	452	池	486	鳥	520	往	554	欧

555 満	591 丸	627 濃	663 句	699 節	735 総
556 両	592 弓	628 豊	664 旬	700 即	736 為
557 向	593 矢	629 富	665 保	701 企	737 老
558 周	594 失	630 典	666 証	702 歯	738 孝
559 独	595 夫	631 興	667 許	703 歳	739 才
560 狭	596 妻	632 己	668 認	704 歴	740 材
561 肉	597 婦	633 記	669 課	705 史	741 財
562 米	598 姓	634 紀	670 税	706 央	742 貯
563 類	599 嫁	635 組	671 程	707 非	743 蓄
564 種	600 婿	636 素	672 実	708 常	744 氏
565 科	601 娘	637 麦	673 美	709 堂	745 底
566 芸	602 良	638 責	674 差	710 党	746 抵
567 草	603 飾	639 任	675 養	711 賞	747 抗
568 芝	604 飯	640 信	676 善	712 償	748 接
569 葉	605 坂	641 徒	677 様	713 与	749 換
570 荷	606 皆	642 従	678 植	714 券	750 条
571 預	607 階	643 得	679 極	715 巻	751 契
572 頼	608 段	644 徳	680 端	716 角	752 喫
573 顔	609 役	645 聴	681 需	717 負	753 潔
574 産	610 殺	646 舟	682 器	718 敗	754 清
575 玉	611 設	647 船	683 品	719 貝	755 士
576 宝	612 施	648 般	684 商	720 具	756 志
577 王	613 備	649 航	685 袋	721 散	757 恩
578 現	614 準	650 億	686 製	722 故	758 忠
579 皇	615 率	651 憶	687 制	723 放	759 恐
580 聖	616 演	652 漫	688 誕	724 敷	760 翻
581 望	617 絵	653 慢	689 延	725 致	761 訳
582 亡	618 給	654 情	690 期	726 改	762 尺
583 未	619 声	655 慣	691 基	727 配	763 釈
584 末	620 音	656 快	692 礎	728 酔	764 択
585 申	621 昨	657 適	693 疑	729 針	765 描
586 神	622 暇	658 敵	694 紹	730 録	766 拝
587 存	623 由	659 欠	695 介	731 緑	767 提
588 在	624 油	660 次	696 招	732 縁	768 拡
589 禅	625 曲	661 姿	697 委	733 納	769 抜
590 弾	626 農	662 冷	698 季	734 絶	770 振

771	打	807	規	843	雷	879	育	915	鯨	951	訓
772	折	808	則	844	雲	880	絹	916	鮮	952	順
773	採	809	側	845	霧	881	綿	917	洋	953	序
774	菜	810	測	846	露	882	織	918	卸	954	秩
775	指	811	例	847	震	883	編	919	御	955	矛
776	揮	812	列	848	厚	884	縮	920	缶	956	盾
777	輝	813	殊	849	宴	885	績	921	益	957	掃
778	軍	814	示	850	宣	886	積	922	盛	958	除
779	隊	815	禁	851	各	887	布	923	盟	959	余
780	衛	816	宗	852	格	888	希	924	塩	960	途
781	防	817	完	853	資	889	衣	925	監	961	込
782	坊	818	了	854	源	890	依	926	督	962	辺
783	訪	819	承	855	貴	891	報	927	皿	963	述
784	妨	820	浮	856	賃	892	告	928	血	964	迫
785	害	821	乳	857	貨	893	吉	929	宮	965	造
786	割	822	礼	858	費	894	幸	930	営	966	追
787	憲	823	祈	859	貧	895	福	931	辞	967	師
788	毒	824	祖	860	乏	896	祉	932	乱	968	桜
789	危	825	査	861	額	897	幅	933	求	969	梅
790	険	826	助	862	願	898	副	934	救	970	松
791	剣	827	努	863	塾	899	判	935	球	971	桃
792	検	828	収	864	熟	900	断	936	儀	972	枝
793	験	829	状	865	勢	901	継	937	犠	973	株
794	騒	830	将	866	熱	902	繰	938	牲	974	根
795	試	831	奨	867	昭	903	燥	939	象	975	限
796	式	832	励	868	照	904	乾	940	像	976	眼
797	専	833	陸	869	黙	905	江	941	免	977	睡
798	博	834	陽	870	燃	906	液	942	城	978	眠
799	薄	835	傷	871	灯	907	汚	943	誠	979	瞬
800	夢	836	湯	872	畑	908	染	944	詳	980	隣
801	葬	837	混	873	災	909	港	945	詩	981	舞
802	蒸	838	湿	874	灰	910	湾	946	討	982	枚
803	確	839	温	875	炭	911	浜	947	謝	983	杯
804	権	840	泉	876	鉱	912	沖	948	評	984	札
805	観	841	線	877	精	913	波	949	誤	985	析
806	視	842	雪	878	請	914	漁	950	誇	986	核

987	板	1023	響	1059	筋	1095	氷	1131	添	1167	俳
988	棒	1024	郷	1060	箱	1096	永	1132	歓	1168	優
989	柄	1025	里	1061	範	1097	久	1133	迎	1169	仲
990	柱	1026	童	1062	囲	1098	及	1134	仰	1170	促
991	構	1027	章	1063	零	1099	幼	1135	卵	1171	秀
992	再	1028	障	1064	井	1100	稚	1136	印	1172	似
993	黄	1029	壁	1065	帯	1101	移	1137	刷	1173	傾
994	兵	1030	卓	1066	帝	1102	秘	1138	刊	1174	候
995	靴	1031	著	1067	締	1103	密	1139	刻	1175	修
996	革	1032	諸	1068	純	1104	骨	1140	劇	1176	偏
997	命	1033	緒	1069	粋	1105	胃	1141	仮	1177	遍
998	令	1034	鏡	1070	迷	1106	腸	1142	版	1178	遇
999	領	1035	環	1071	惑	1107	肝	1143	片	1179	遺
1000	統	1036	境	1072	域	1108	臓	1144	皮	1180	貢
1001	補	1037	破	1073	越	1109	脳	1145	被	1181	献
1002	佐	1038	壊	1074	超	1110	悩	1146	彼	1182	僚
1003	臣	1039	激	1075	赴	1111	蔵	1147	徹	1183	寮
1004	巨	1040	攻	1076	更	1112	倉	1148	徴	1184	帳
1005	拒	1041	撃	1077	恵	1113	創	1149	微	1185	張
1006	否	1042	襲	1078	恋	1114	看	1150	妙	1186	緊
1007	距	1043	暴	1079	愛	1115	護	1151	秒	1187	繁
1008	離	1044	爆	1080	互	1116	弁	1152	砂	1188	栄
1009	推	1045	煙	1081	涙	1117	念	1153	劣	1189	挙
1010	哲	1046	犯	1082	房	1118	息	1154	勇	1190	厳
1011	掲	1047	罪	1083	雇	1119	応	1155	募	1191	派
1012	抱	1048	逮	1084	肩	1120	突	1156	墓	1192	閥
1013	包	1049	捕	1085	背	1121	穴	1157	幕	1193	閣
1014	均	1050	担	1086	胸	1122	容	1158	暮	1194	衆
1015	射	1051	批	1087	腰	1123	欲	1159	漠	1195	略
1016	占	1052	刑	1088	腹	1124	裕	1160	模	1196	異
1017	況	1053	健	1089	豚	1125	浴	1161	概	1197	圧
1018	祝	1054	康	1090	届	1126	河	1162	既	1198	至
1019	賀	1055	建	1091	属	1127	沿	1163	裁	1199	票
1020	競	1056	築	1092	展	1128	沈	1164	我	1200	標
1021	景	1057	策	1093	殿	1129	没	1165	武		
1022	影	1058	籍	1094	凍	1130		1166	輩		

第　4　水　準　　220字／計1420字

1201 戻	1235 隠	1269 兆	1303 畳	1337 鋼	1371 裂
1202 丘	1236 隔	1270 援	1304 翼	1338 鎖	1372 鈍
1203 匹	1237 融	1271 緩	1305 裸	1339 鉛	1373 鋭
1204 司	1238 邸	1272 丈	1306 軌	1340 銅	1374 克
1205 詞	1239 隅	1273 牧	1307 載	1341 胴	1375 児
1206 訂	1240 偶	1274 畜	1308 軟	1342 腕	1376 旧
1207 訴	1241 僕	1275 充	1309 硬	1343 肺	1377 慮
1208 訟	1242 偉	1276 玄	1310 柔	1344 胆	1378 寧
1209 譲	1243 俗	1277 豪	1311 炊	1345 肌	1379 寛
1210 購	1244 侵	1278 盲	1312 冊	1346 飢	1380 寂
1211 廷	1245 伺	1279 帽	1313 盤	1347 餓	1381 孤
1212 処	1246 伸	1280 昇	1314 盆	1348 飼	1382 触
1213 拠	1247 倣	1281 曇	1315 煮	1349 旨	1383 踊
1214 遣	1248 催	1282 糧	1316 署	1350 脂	1384 躍
1215 還	1249 債	1283 糖	1317 罰	1351 肪	1385 焦
1216 逐	1250 併	1284 粧	1318 型	1352 肥	1386 駐
1217 遂	1251 圏	1285 臭	1319 刺	1353 脈	1387 循
1218 墜	1252 宇	1286 鼻	1320 削	1354 肢	1388 衝
1219 悔	1253 宙	1287 憩	1321 剰	1355 膨	1389 征
1220 慎	1254 抽	1288 舌	1322 垂	1356 枯	1390 徐
1221 頻	1255 拍	1289 君	1323 華	1357 杉	1391 斜
1222 項	1256 摘	1290 含	1324 兼	1358 彫	1392 滑
1223 販	1257 握	1291 叫	1325 嫌	1359 髪	1393 潜
1224 贈	1258 探	1292 奇	1326 尋	1360 珍	1394 渇
1225 賄	1259 掘	1293 崎	1327 寿	1361 診	1395 沢
1226 賂	1260 堀	1294 峡	1328 闘	1362 療	1396 洪
1227 賢	1261 埋	1295 紅	1329 娯	1363 症	1397 津
1228 堅	1262 排	1296 繊	1330 妊	1364 癖	1398 浪
1229 臨	1263 拓	1297 維	1331 娠	1365 避	1399 汁
1230 幹	1264 抑	1298 紛	1332 妥	1366 恥	1400 渋
1231 稿	1265 拐	1299 紳	1333 威	1367 患	1401 淡
1232 稼	1266 扱	1300 縦	1334 戒	1368 菌	1402 滞
1233 稲	1267 撮	1301 索	1335 釣	1369 荘	1403 肯
1234 穏	1268 挑	1302 累	1336 鈴	1370 装	1404 齢

1405	履奮奪	1408	獲穫猫	1411	薦廃庶	1414	麻摩擦	1417	邪魔魅	1420	酸
1406		1409		1412		1415		1418			
1407		1410		1413		1416		1419			

第 5 水 準　　412字／計1832字

1421	伏	1451	怖	1481	揚	1511	濁	1541	班	1571	縫
1422	伐	1452	恨	1482	摂	1512	濫	1542	祥	1572	繕
1423	伴	1453	悦	1483	搭	1513	狂	1543	禍	1573	舶
1424	俊	1454	悟	1484	搾	1514	狩	1544	胎	1574	託
1425	倹	1455	惜	1485	操	1515	猟	1545	脚	1575	詐
1426	俵	1456	悼	1486	携	1516	猛	1546	膜	1576	詰
1427	俸	1457	惨	1487	搬	1517	猶	1547	騰	1577	該
1428	偽	1458	愉	1488	撤	1518	獄	1548	眺	1578	諾
1429	傍	1459	慌	1489	撲	1519	阻	1549	矯	1579	諭
1430	僧	1460	惰	1490	擁	1520	附	1550	砕	1580	諮
1431	傑	1461	慨	1491	汽	1521	陛	1551	硫	1581	謙
1432	吐	1462	憎	1492	泌	1522	陥	1552	硝	1582	謹
1433	唆	1463	懐	1493	泥	1523	陣	1553	礁	1583	譜
1434	喝	1464	憾	1494	沸	1524	陳	1554	称	1584	賊
1435	喚	1465	抄	1495	浄	1525	陰	1555	襟	1585	賦
1436	嘆	1466	扶	1496	浸	1526	陶	1556	褐	1586	跳
1437	嘱	1467	把	1497	涯	1527	旋	1557	粉	1587	跡
1438	塔	1468	披	1498	渦	1528	旗	1558	粒	1588	践
1439	塀	1469	拘	1499	溝	1529	朴	1559	粘	1589	軸
1440	壇	1470	拙	1500	滅	1530	枢	1560	粗	1590	轄
1441	如	1471	抹	1501	溶	1531	栓	1561	糾	1591	酌
1442	姻	1472	括	1502	漏	1532	桟	1562	紺	1592	酢
1443	岐	1473	挟	1503	漸	1533	棟	1563	紡	1593	酪
1444	帆	1474	拷	1504	滴	1534	棺	1564	紋	1594	酬
1445	壮	1475	捜	1505	漆	1535	棋	1565	絞	1595	酵
1446	弦	1476	措	1506	漬	1536	棚	1566	綱	1596	酷
1447	弧	1477	掛	1507	漂	1537	槽	1567	網	1597	鉢
1448	径	1478	挿	1508	潮	1538	欄	1568	縄	1598	銭
1449	衡	1479	控	1509	潤	1539	殉	1569	縛	1599	銃
1450	怪	1480	据	1510	澄	1540	殖	1570	緯	1600	銘

1601 鋳	1637 雄	1673 窃	1709 勲	1745 迭	1781 斎
1602 錬	1638 雅	1674 窒	1710 薫	1746 透	1782 耕
1603 錯	1639 雌	1675 窮	1711 紫	1747 逝	1783 耗
1604 錠	1640 培	1676 蛍	1712 誓	1748 逸	1784 垣
1605 鍛	1641 陪	1677 掌	1713 誉	1749 遮	1785 恒
1606 鎮	1642 賠	1678 奉	1714 貫	1750 遭	1786 巧
1607 鐘	1643 頂	1679 奏	1715 匠	1751 遵	1787 朽
1608 鑑	1644 頑	1680 泰	1716 匿	1752 鬼	1788 謡
1609 剖	1645 頌	1681 笛	1717 囚	1753 塊	1789 揺
1610 駄	1646 煩	1682 箇	1718 閑	1754 魂	1790 凝
1611 駆	1647 顕	1683 篤	1719 閲	1755 醜	1791 擬
1612 刈	1648 顧	1684 簿	1720 暦	1756 甚	1792 随
1613 剛	1649 嬢	1685 覇	1721 厄	1757 勘	1793 髄
1614 劾	1650 壌	1686 覆	1722 尼	1758 堪	1794 唇
1615 勧	1651 醸	1687 零	1723 尾	1759 某	1795 辱
1616 却	1652 亭	1688 霊	1724 尿	1760 媒	1796 幣
1617 叙	1653 棄	1689 霜	1725 層	1761 謀	1797 弊
1618 耐	1654 舎	1690 啓	1726 尽	1762 又	1798 墾
1619 彩	1655 傘	1691 召	1727 唐	1763 双	1799 懇
1620 彰	1656 冠	1692 堕	1728 庸	1764 貞	1800 敏
1621 邦	1657 呈	1693 塗	1729 廉	1765 偵	1801 侮
1622 敢	1658 宜	1694 墨	1730 腐	1766 叔	1802 炉
1623 欺	1659 宰	1695 妄	1731 磨	1767 淑	1803 炎
1624 款	1660 寡	1696 忌	1732 慶	1768 朱	1804 哀
1625 殴	1661 審	1697 怠	1733 扇	1769 珠	1805 衷
1626 殻	1662 賓	1698 悠	1734 扉	1770 卑	1806 喪
1627 穀	1663 崩	1699 愁	1735 疫	1771 碑	1807 晶
1628 朗	1664 崇	1700 愚	1736 疾	1772 享	1808 唱
1629 泡	1665 芳	1701 慰	1737 痢	1773 郭	1809 尚
1630 胞	1666 荒	1702 懲	1738 痴	1774 刃	1810 肖
1631 砲	1667 菓	1703 架	1739 癒	1775 忍	1811 凶
1632 飽	1668 慕	1704 香	1740 虐	1776 滋	1812 丹
1633 噴	1669 冒	1705 暫	1741 虚	1777 磁	1813 幻
1634 憤	1670 是	1706 脅	1742 膚	1778 慈	1814 弔
1635 准	1671 罷	1707 烈	1743 巡	1779 斉	1815 甲
1636 唯	1672 羅	1708	1744 迅	1780 剤	1816

1817	斥	1820	幽	1823	執	1826	疎	1829	憂	1832	麗
1818	亜	1821	栽	1824	粛	1827	鼓	1830	舗		
1819	奔	1822	瓶	1825	蛮	1828	碁	1831	覧		

第　6　水　準　　　　　115字／計1947字

	[自　然] （35字）	1852	堤	1871	奴	1892	艦	1911	壱	1932	痘
		1853	樹	1872	隷	1893	租	1912	弐	1933	曹
1833	菊	1854	柳	1873	后	1894	帥	1913	坪	1934	恭
1834	芋	1855	桑	1874	騎	1895	勅	1914	斤	1935	詔
1835	芽	1856	穂	1875	爵	1896	遷	1915	升	1936	褒
1836	茎	1857	畔	1876	侯	1897	赦	1916	勺	1937	騰
1837	苗	1858	暁	1877	伯	1898	賜	1917	屯	1938	朕
1838	薪	1859	昆	1878	侍	1899	謁	1918	隻	1939	畝
1839	藻	1860	蚊	1879	仁	1900	窯	1919	斗	1940	翁
1840	茂	1861	蛇	1880	仙	1901	戯	1920	凸	1941	逓
1841	滝	1862	巣	1881	孔	1902	婆	1921	凹	1942	錘
1842	沼	1863	鶏	1882	尉	1903	韻	1922	但	1943	銑
1843	渓	1864	獣	1883	吏	1904	吟	1923	且	1944	塑
1844	洞	1865	猿	1884	虜	1905	詠	1924	嚇	1945	虞
1845	瀬	1866	蚕	1885	嗣	1906	琴	1925	隆	1946	繭
1846	浦	1867	竜	1886	陵	1907	宵	1926	脹	1947	璽
1847	潟	[歴史・文学] （40字）		1887	楼	[特　殊] （40字）		1927	坑		
1848	峰			1888	墳			1928	呉		
1849	峠	1868	姫	1889	塚	1908	乙	1929	艇		
1850	岬	1869	妃	1890	藩	1909	丙	1930	佳		
1851	岳	1870	嫡	1891	儒	1910	厘	1931			

音訓索引
(*On-kun* Index)

All the readings for *kanji* entries are listed in *a-i-u-e-o* order with the corresponding *kanji* and *kanji* number. *On*-readings are indicated in bold type, and *kun*-readings are in regular type.

	あ	
あ	亜	1818
あい	哀	1804
	愛	1079
あい	相	391
あいだ	間	161
あう	合う	271
	会う	59
	遭う	1750
あお	青	47
あおい	青い	47
あおぐ	仰ぐ	1134
あか	赤	46
あかい	赤い	46
あかす	明かす	106
	飽かす	1632
あかつき	暁	1858
あからむ	赤らむ	46
	明らむ	106
あからめる	赤らめる	46
あかり	明かり	106
あがる	上がる	31
	挙がる	1189
	揚がる	1481
あかるい	明るい	106
あかるむ	明るむ	106
あき	秋	98
あきなう	商う	684
あきらか	明らか	106
あきる	飽きる	1632
あく	悪	114
	握	1257
あく	明く	106
	空く	461
	開く	215

あくる	明くる	106
あげて	挙げて	1189
あける	明ける	106
	空ける	461
	開ける	215
あげる	上げる	31
	挙げる	1189
	揚げる	1481
あさ	麻	1414
	朝	91
あざ	字	528
あさい	浅い	122
あざむく	欺く	1623
あざやか	鮮やか	916
あし	足	171
	脚	1545
あじ	味	311
あじわう	味わう	311
あずかる	預かる	571
あずける	預ける	571
あせ	汗	507
あせる	焦る	1385
あそぶ	遊ぶ	196
あたい	価	425
	値	426
あたえる	与える	713
あたたか	温か	839
	暖か	339
あたたかい	温かい	839
	暖かい	339
あたたまる	温まる	839
	暖まる	339
あたためる	温める	839
	暖める	339
あたま	頭	166
あたらしい	新しい	85

あたり	辺り	962
あたる	当たる	402
あつ	圧	1197
あつい	厚い	848
	暑い	119
	熱い	866
あつかう	扱う	1266
あつまる	集まる	224
あつめる	集める	224
あてる	充てる	1275
	当てる	402
あと	後	30
	跡	1587
あな	穴	1122
あなどる	侮る	1801
あに	兄	75
あね	姉	77
あばく	暴く	1043
あばれる	暴れる	1043
あびせる	浴びせる	1126
あびる	浴びる	1126
あぶない	危ない	789
あぶら	油	624
	脂	1350
あま	天	462
	尼	1722
	雨	232
あまい	甘い	345
あまえる	甘える	345
あます	余す	959
あまやかす	甘やかす	345
あまる	余る	959
あみ	網	1567
あむ	編む	883
あめ	天	462
	雨	232

いろ	色	316	うすまる	薄まる	799	うらめしい	恨めしい	1452
いろどる	彩る	1619	うすめる	薄める	799	うる	売る	187
いわ	岩	457	うすらぐ	薄らぐ	799		得る	643
いわう	祝う	1018	うすれる	薄れる	799	うるおう	潤う	1509
いん	引	257	うた	歌	200	うるおす	潤す	1509
	印	1136	うたい	謡	1788	うるし	漆	1505
	因	406	うたう	歌う	200	うるむ	潤む	1509
	姻	1442		謡う	1788	うるわしい	麗しい	1832
	音	620	うたがう	疑う	693	うれい	愁い	1700
	員	395	うち	内	152		憂い	1829
	院	230	うつ	打つ	771	うれえる	愁える	1700
	陰	1525		討つ	946		憂える	1829
	飲	132		撃つ	1041	うれる	売れる	187
	隠	1235	うつくしい	美しい	673		熟れる	864
	韻	1903	うつす	写す	194	うわ	上	31
				映す	234	うわつく	浮つく	820
う				移す	1101	うわる	植わる	678
う	右	35	うったえる	訴える	1207	うん	運	304
	宇	1252	うつる	写る	194		雲	844
	有	347		映る	234			
	羽	491		移る	1101	**え**		
	雨	232	うつわ	器	682	え	会	59
うい	初	440	うで	腕	1342		回	162
	憂い	1829	うとい	疎い	1826		依	890
うえ	上	31	うとむ	疎む	1826		恵	1077
うえる	飢える	1346	うながす	促す	1170		絵	617
	植える	678	うね	畝	1939	え	江	905
うお	魚	485	うばう	奪う	1407		柄	989
うかがう	伺う	1245	うぶ	産	574		重	115
うかぶ	浮かぶ	820	うま	馬	484	えい	永	1096
うかべる	浮かべる	820	うまる	埋まる	1261		泳	193
うかる	受かる	269	うまれる	生まれる	49		英	155
うかれる	浮かれる	820		産まれる	574		映	234
うく	浮く	820	うみ	海	454		栄	1188
うけたまわる	承る	819	うむ	生む	49		営	930
うける	受ける	269		産む	574		詠	1905
	請ける	878	うめ	梅	969		影	1022
うごかす	動かす	64	うめる	埋める	1261		鋭	1373
うごく	動く	64	うもれる	埋もれる	1261		衛	780
うし	牛	483	うやうやしい	恭しい	1934	えがく	描く	765
うじ	氏	744	うやまう	敬う	478	えき	役	609
うしなう	失う	594	うら	浦	1846		易	434
うしろ	後ろ	30		裏	436		疫	1735
うず	渦	1498	うらなう	占う	1016		益	921
うすい	薄い	799	うらむ	恨む	1452		液	906

	駅	56		桜	968	おさない	幼い	1099
えだ	枝	972		翁	1940	おさまる	収まる	828
えつ	悦	1453		黄	993		治まる	531
	越	1073		奥	71		修まる	1175
	謁	1899		横	34		納まる	733
	閲	1719	おう	生う	49	おさめる	収める	828
えむ	笑む	251		負う	717		治める	531
えらい	偉い	1242		追う	966		修める	1175
えらぶ	選ぶ	264	おうぎ	扇	1733		納める	733
えり	襟	1555	おえる	終える	130	おしい	惜しい	1455
える	得る	643	おお	大	87	おしえる	教える	214
	獲る	1408	おおい	多い	104	おしむ	惜しむ	1455
えん	円	14	おおいに	大いに	87	おす	雄	1637
	延	689	おおう	覆う	1686		押す	256
	沿	1128	おおきい	大きい	87		推す	1009
	炎	1803	おおせ	仰せ	1134	おそい	遅い	118
	宴	849	おおやけ	公	323	おそう	襲う	1042
	援	1270	おか	丘	1202	おそれ	虞	1945
	園	324	おかす	犯す	1046	おそれる	恐れる	759
	煙	1045		侵す	1244	おそろしい	恐ろしい	759
	猿	1865		冒す	1669	おそわる	教わる	214
	遠	110	おがむ	拝む	766	おだやか	穏やか	1234
	鉛	1339	おき	沖	912	おちいる	陥る	1522
	塩	924	おぎなう	補う	1001	おちる	落ちる	280
	演	616	おきる	起きる	128	おつ	乙	1908
	縁	732	おく	屋	54	おっと	夫	595
	お			億	650	おと	音	620
				憶	651	おとうと	弟	76
お	汚	907	おく	奥	71	おどかす	脅かす	1707
	和	352		置く	262	おとこ	男	67
	悪	114	おくらす	遅らす	118	おとしいれる	陥れる	1522
お	小	88	おくる	送る	206	おとす	落とす	280
	尾	1723		贈る	1224	おどす	脅す	1707
	雄	1637	おくれる	後れる	30	おとずれる	訪れる	783
	緒	1033		遅れる	118	おどり	踊り	1383
おいる	老いる	737	おこす	興す	631	おとる	劣る	1153
おう	王	577		起こす	128	おどる	踊る	1383
	凹	1922	おごそか	厳か	1190		躍る	1384
	央	706	おこたる	怠る	1698	おとろえる	衰える	1805
	応	1119	おこなう	行う	58	おどろかす	驚かす	477
	往	520	おこる	怒る	255	おどろく	驚く	477
	押	256		興る	631	おなじ	同じ	350
	欧	554		起こる	128	おに	鬼	1752
	殴	1625	おさえる	抑える	1264	おのおの	各	851
	皇	579		押さえる	256	おのれ	己	632

おび	帯	1065		花	314		皆	606
おびやかす	脅かす	1707		佳	1931		械	511
おびる	帯びる	1065		価	425		絵	617
おぼえる	覚える	208		果	502		街	371
おも	主	70		河	1127		開	215
	面	438		科	565		階	607
おもい	重い	115		架	1704		解	293
おもう	思う	202		夏	97		塊	1753
おもて	表	437		家	52		壊	1038
	面	438		荷	570		懐	1463
おもむき	趣	310		華	1323	かい	貝	719
おもむく	赴く	1075		菓	1667	がい	外	150
おや	親	249		貨	857		劾	1614
およぐ	泳ぐ	193		渦	1498		害	785
および	及び	1098		過	284		涯	1497
および	及ぶ	1098		嫁	599		街	371
およぼす	及ぼす	1098		暇	622		慨	1461
おり	折	772		禍	1543		該	1577
おりる	下りる	32		靴	995		概	1161
	降りる	136		寡	1660	かいこ	蚕	1866
おる	折る	772		歌	200	かう	買う	188
	織る	882		箇	1682		飼う	1348
おれる	折れる	772		稼	1232	かえす	返す	184
おろか	愚か	1701		課	669		帰す	134
おろし	卸	918	か	日	16	かえりみる	省みる	389
おろす	卸す	918		香	1705		顧みる	1648
	下ろす	32		蚊	1860	かえる	返る	184
	降ろす	136	が	我	1164		帰る	134
おわる	終わる	130		画	235		代える	413
おん	音	620		芽	1835		変える	222
	恩	757		賀	1019		換える	749
	温	839		雅	1638		替える	375
	遠	110		餓	1347	かお	顔	573
	穏	1234	かい	介	695	かおり	香り	1705
おん	御	919		回	162	かおる	香る	1705
おんな	女	68		灰	874		薫る	1710
	か			会	59	かかえる	抱える	1012
か	下	32		快	656	かかげる	掲げる	1011
	化	414		戒	1334	かがみ	鏡	1034
	火	18		改	726	かがやく	輝く	777
	加	295		怪	1450	かかり	係	447
	可	412		拐	1265		掛	1477
	仮	1141		悔	1219	かかる	係る	447
	何	80		海	454		架かる	1704
				界	157		掛かる	1477

	懸かる	450	かしら	頭	166	かな	金	21
かき	垣	1784	かす	貸す	183	かなしい	悲しい	341
かぎる	限る	975	かず	数	529	かなしむ	悲しむ	341
かく	各	851	かぜ	風	465	かなでる	奏でる	1679
	角	716	かせぐ	稼ぐ	1232	かならず	必ず	423
	画	235	かぞえる	数える	529	かね	金	21
	拡	768	かた	方	43		鐘	1607
	客	318		片	1143	かねる	兼ねる	1324
	革	996		形	509	かの	彼	1146
	格	852		肩	1084	かぶ	株	973
	核	986		型	1318	かべ	壁	1029
	殻	1626		潟	1847	かま	窯	1900
	郭	1773	かたい	固い	470	かまう	構う	991
	覚	208		堅い	1228	かまえる	構える	991
	較	500		硬い	1309	かみ	上	31
	隔	1236		難い	526		神	586
	閣	1193	かたき	敵	658		紙	243
	確	803	かたち	形	509		髪	1359
	獲	1408	かたな	刀	441	かみなり	雷	843
	嚇	1925	かたまり	塊	1753	かもす	醸す	1651
	穫	1409	かたまる	固まる	470	かよう	通う	204
かく	欠く	659	かたむく	傾く	1173	から	空	461
	書く	181	かたむける	傾ける	1173		唐	1727
がく	学	50	かためる	固める	470		殻	1626
	岳	1851	かたよる	偏る	1176	がら	柄	989
	楽	343	かたらう	語らう	154	からい	辛い	344
	額	861	かたる	語る	154	からす	枯らす	1356
かくす	隠す	1235	かたわら	傍ら	1429	からだ	体	165
かくれる	隠れる	1235	かっ	合	271	からまる	絡まる	300
かげ	陰	1525	かつ	括	1472	からむ	絡む	300
	影	1022		活	517	かり	仮	1141
かける	欠ける	659		喝	1434		狩	1514
	架ける	1704		渇	1394	かりる	借りる	182
	掛ける	1477		割	786	かる	刈る	1612
	駆ける	1611		滑	1392		狩る	1514
	懸ける	450		褐	1556		駆る	1611
かげる	陰る	1525		轄	1590	かるい	軽い	116
かこう	囲う	1062	かつ	且つ	1924	かれ	彼	1146
かこむ	囲む	1062		勝つ	263	かれる	枯れる	1356
かさ	傘	1655	がっ	合	271	かろやか	軽やか	116
かざ	風	465	がつ	月	17	かわ	川	101
かさなる	重なる	115	かつぐ	担ぐ	1050		皮	1144
かさねる	重ねる	115	かて	糧	1282		河	1127
かざる	飾る	603	かど	角	716		革	996
かしこい	賢い	1227		門	445		側	809

かわかす	乾かす	904		憾	1464		規	809
かわく	乾く	904		還	1215		喜	253
	渇く	1394		館	330		幾	408
かわす	交わす	504		環	1035		揮	776
かわる	代わる	413		簡	358		期	690
	変わる	222		観	805		棋	1535
	換わる	749		艦	1892		貴	855
	替わる	375		鑑	1608		棄	1653
かん	干	506	かん	神	586		旗	1528
	刊	1138	がん	丸	591		器	682
	甲	1816		元	245		輝	777
	甘	345		含	1290		機	334
	汗	507		岸	456		騎	1874
	缶	920		岩	457	き	木	20
	完	817		眼	976		生	49
	肝	1107		頑	1644		黄	993
	官	540		顔	573	ぎ	技	369
	冠	1656		願	862		宜	1658
	巻	715	かんがえる	考える	212		偽	1428
	看	1114	かんばしい	芳しい	1665		欺	1623
	陥	1522	かんむり	冠	1656		義	493
	乾	904		**き**			疑	693
	勘	1757	き	己	632		儀	936
	患	1367		企	701		戯	1901
	貫	1714		危	789		擬	1791
	寒	120		机	38		犠	937
	喚	1435		気	246		議	494
	堪	1758		岐	1443	きえる	消える	219
	換	749		希	888	きく	菊	1833
	敢	1622		忌	1697	きく	利く	248
	棺	1534		汽	1491		効く	501
	款	1624		奇	1292		聞く	179
	間	161		祈	823		聴く	645
	閑	1718		季	698	きこえる	聞こえる	179
	勧	1615		紀	634	きざし	兆し	1269
	寛	1379		軌	1306	きざす	兆す	1269
	幹	1230		既	1162	きざむ	刻む	1139
	感	431		記	633	きし	岸	456
	漢	527		起	128	きず	傷	835
	慣	655		飢	1346	きずく	築く	1056
	管	539		鬼	1752	きせる	着せる	190
	関	446		帰	134	きそう	競う	1020
	歓	1132		基	691	きた	北	42
	監	925		寄	1120	きたえる	鍛える	1605
	緩	1271				きたす	来す	133

きたない	汚い	907		虚	1741		極	679
きたる	来る	133		許	667	ぎょく	玉	575
きち	吉	893		距	1007	きよまる	清まる	754
きつ	吉	893	**ぎょ**	魚	485	きよめる	清める	754
	喫	752		御	919	きらう	嫌う	1325
	詰	1576		漁	914	きり	霧	845
きぬ	絹	880	きよい	清い	754	きる	切る	250
きびしい	厳しい	1190	**きょう**	凶	1812		着る	190
きまる	決まる	277		兄	75	きれる	切れる	250
きみ	君	1289		共	419	きわ	際	474
きめる	決める	277		叫	1291	きわまる	極まる	679
きも	肝	1107		狂	1513		窮まる	1675
きゃ	脚	1545		京	233	きわみ	極み	679
きゃく	却	1616		享	1772	きわめる	究める	298
	客	318		供	418		極める	679
	脚	1545		協	444		窮める	1675
ぎゃく	逆	386		況	1017	**きん**	今	27
	虐	1740		峡	1294		斤	1914
きゅう	九	9		挟	1473		均	1014
	久	1097		狭	560		近	109
	及	1098		香	1705		金	21
	弓	592		恐	759		菌	1368
	丘	1202		恭	1934		勤	525
	旧	1376		胸	1086		琴	1906
	休	138		脅	1707		筋	1059
	吸	272		強	111		禁	815
	朽	1787		教	214		緊	1186
	求	933		経	515		謹	1582
	究	298		郷	1024		襟	1555
	泣	252		境	1036	**ぎん**	吟	1904
	急	260		橋	313		銀	57
	級	410		興	631		**く**	
	糾	1561		矯	1549			
	宮	929		鏡	1034	**く**	九	9
	救	934		競	1020		久	1097
	球	935		響	1023		口	167
	給	618		驚	477		工	379
	窮	1675	**ぎょう**	仰	1134		区	548
ぎゅう	牛	483		行	58		功	378
きょ	去	309		形	509		句	663
	巨	1004		暁	1858		供	418
	居	535		業	307		苦	342
	拒	1005		凝	1790		紅	1295
	拠	1213	**きょく**	曲	625		宮	929
	挙	1189		局	228		庫	544

	結	302		原	405		誤	949
	傑	1431		現	578		護	1115
	潔	753		眼	976	こい	恋	1078
げつ	月	17		減	430		濃い	627
けむい	煙い	1045		嫌	1325	こいしい	恋しい	1078
けむり	煙	1045		源	854	こう	口	167
けむる	煙る	1045		厳	1190		工	379
けもの	獣	1864		験	793		公	323
けわしい	険しい	790					孔	1881
けん	犬	319	**こ**				功	378
	件	482	こ	己	632		巧	1786
	見	139		戸	534		広	113
	券	714		去	309		甲	1816
	肩	1084		古	86		交	504
	建	1055		呼	197		仰	1134
	研	297		固	470		光	464
	県	336		拠	1213		向	557
	倹	1425		孤	1381		后	1873
	兼	1324		弧	1447		好	244
	剣	791		故	722		江	905
	軒	508		枯	1356		考	212
	健	1053		個	469		行	58
	険	790		庫	544		坑	1928
	圏	1251		虚	1741		孝	738
	堅	1228		湖	453		抗	747
	検	792		雇	1083		攻	1040
	間	161		誇	950		更	1076
	嫌	1325		鼓	1827		効	501
	献	1181		顧	1648		幸	894
	絹	880	こ	子	69		拘	1469
	遣	1214		小	88		肯	1403
	権	804		木	20		侯	1876
	憲	787		粉	1557		厚	848
	賢	1227		黄	993		後	30
	謙	1581	ご	五	5		恒	1785
	繭	1946		互	1080		洪	1396
	顕	1647		午	28		皇	579
	験	794		呉	1929		紅	1295
	懸	450		後	30		荒	1666
げん	元	245		娯	1329		郊	503
	幻	1814		悟	1454		香	1705
	玄	1276		御	919		候	1174
	言	203		期	690		校	51
	弦	1446		碁	1828		格	852
	限	975		語	154		耕	1782

	仕	236		地	146	したう	慕う	1668
	史	705		字	528	したがう	従う	642
	司	1204		寺	328	したがえる	従える	642
	四	4		次	660	したしい	親しい	249
	市	547		耳	169	したしむ	親しむ	249
	矢	593		自	63	したたる	滴る	1504
	示	814		似	1172	しち	七	7
	旨	1349		児	1375		質	238
	次	660		事	237	しつ	失	594
	死	258		侍	1878		室	331
	糸	409		治	531		疾	1736
	自	63		持	142		執	1823
	至	1198		時	25		湿	838
	伺	1245		除	958		漆	1505
	志	756		滋	1776		質	238
	私	72		慈	1778	じっ	十	10
	使	199		辞	931	じつ	日	16
	刺	1319		磁	1777		実	672
	始	129		璽	1947	しな	品	683
	姉	77	じ 路	533	しぬ	死ぬ	258
	枝	972	しあわせ 幸せ	894	しのばせる	忍ばせる	1775
	社	896	しいたげる 虐げる	1740	しのぶ	忍ぶ	1775
	肢	1355	しいる 強いる	111	しば	芝	568
	姿	661	しお 塩	924	しばる	縛る	1569
	思	202	潮	1508	しぶ	渋	1400
	指	775	しき 式	796	しぶい	渋い	1400
	施	612	色	316	しぶる	渋る	1400
	師	967	織	882	しぼる	絞る	1565
	紙	243	識	512		搾る	1484
	脂	1350	じき 直	220	しま	島	455
	視	806	食	131	しまる	閉まる	216
	紫	1711	しく 敷く	724		絞まる	1565
	詞	1205	じく 軸	1589		締まる	1067
	歯	702	しげる 茂る	1840	しみ	染み	908
	嗣	1885	しず 静	247	しみる	染みる	908
	試	795	しずか 静か	247	しめす	示す	814
	詩	945	しずく 滴	1504		湿す	838
	資	853	しずまる 静まる	247	しめる	湿る	838
	飼	1348	鎮まる	1606		占める	1016
	誌	524	しずむ 沈む	1129		閉める	216
	雌	1639	しずめる 沈める	1129		絞める	1565
	賜	1898	静める	247		締める	1067
	諮	1580	鎮める	1606	しも	下	32
じ	仕	236	した 下	32		霜	1689
	示	814	舌	1288	しゃ	写	194

床	543		照	868	しらべる	調べる	210	
抄	1465		詳	944	しりぞく	退く	348	
肖	1811		彰	1620	しりぞける	退ける	348	
尚	1810		精	877	しる	汁	1399	
姓	598		障	1028		知る	143	
性	421		衝	1388	しるし	印	1136	
招	696		賞	711	しるす	記す	633	
承	819		償	712	しろ	代	413	
昇	1280		礁	1553		白	44	
松	970		鐘	1607		城	942	
沼	1842	じょう	上	31	しろい	白い	44	
青	47		丈	1272	しん	心	172	
政	530		冗	468		申	585	
星	463		成	377		伸	1246	
昭	867		条	750		臣	1003	
相	391		状	829		身	394	
省	389		定	289		辛	344	
宵	1907		乗	135		侵	1244	
従	642		城	942		信	640	
将	830		浄	1495		津	1397	
消	219		剰	1321		神	586	
症	1363		常	708		唇	1794	
祥	1542		情	654		娠	1331	
称	1554		盛	922		振	770	
笑	251		場	335		浸	1496	
唱	1809		畳	1303		真	242	
商	684		蒸	802		針	729	
渉	505		静	247		深	121	
清	754		縄	1568		紳	1299	
章	1027		壌	1650		進	267	
紹	694		嬢	1649		森	460	
訟	1208		錠	1604		診	1361	
勝	263		譲	1209		寝	127	
掌	1677		醸	1651		慎	1220	
晶	1808	しょく	色	316		新	85	
焼	218		食	131		審	1661	
焦	1385		植	678		請	878	
硝	1552		殖	1540		震	847	
粧	1284		飾	603		薪	1838	
装	1370		触	1382		親	249	
詔	1935		嘱	1437	じん	人	15	
証	666		織	882		刃	1774	
象	939		職	513		仁	1879	
傷	835	じょく	辱	1795		尽	1726	
奨	831	しら	白	44		迅	1744	

	臣	1003	すぎる	過ぎる	284		**せ**		
	甚	1756	すく	好く	244				
	神	586		透く	1746	せ	世	156		
	陣	1523	すくう	救う	934		施	612		
	尋	1326	すくない	少ない	105	せ	背	1085		
	す		すぐれる	優れる	1168		畝	1939		
			すけ	助	826		瀬	1845		
す	子	69	すける	透ける	1746	ぜ	是	1670		
	主	70	すこし	少し	105	せい	井	1064		
	守	537	すごす	過ごす	284		世	156		
	素	636	すこやか	健やか	1053		正	407		
	数	529	すじ	筋	1059		生	49		
す	州	553	すず	鈴	1336		成	377		
	巣	1862	すずしい	涼しい	340		西	40		
	酢	1592	すすむ	進む	267		声	619		
ず	図	329	すずむ	涼む	340		制	687		
	豆	471	すすめる	進める	267		姓	598		
	事	237		勧める	1615		征	1389		
	頭	166		薦める	1411		性	421		
すい	水	19	すたる	廃る	1412		青	47		
	出	185	すたれる	廃れる	1412		斉	1779		
	吹	259	すっぱい	酸っぱい	1420		政	530		
	垂	1322	すでに	既に	1162		星	463		
	炊	1311	すてる	捨てる	285		牲	938		
	帥	1894	すな	砂	1152		省	389		
	粋	1069	すべる	滑る	1392		逝	1747		
	衰	1805		統べる	1000		情	654		
	推	1009	すまう	住まう	141		清	754		
	酔	728	すます	済ます	516		盛	922		
	遂	1217		澄ます	1510		婿	600		
	睡	977	すみ	炭	875		晴	281		
	穂	1856		隅	1239		勢	865		
	錘	1942		墨	1695		歳	703		
すい	酸い	1420	すみやか	速やか	383		聖	580		
ずい	随	1792	すむ	住む	141		誠	943		
	髄	1793		済む	516		精	877		
すう	枢	1530		澄む	1510		製	686		
	崇	1664	する	刷る	1137		誓	1712		
	数	529		擦る	1416		静	247		
すう	吸う	272	するどい	鋭い	1373		請	878		
すえ	末	584	すれる	擦れる	1416		整	387		
すえる	据える	1480	すわる	座る	175	せい	背	1085		
すかす	透かす	1746		据わる	1480	ぜい	税	670		
すがた	姿	661	**すん**	寸	367		説	292		
すぎ	杉	1357				せき	夕	95		

	則	808		田	103	たかめる	高める	83
	促	1170	だ	打	771	たがやす	耕す	1782
	息	1118		妥	1332	たから	宝	576
	速	383		蛇	1861	たき	滝	1841
	側	809		堕	1693	たきぎ	薪	1838
	測	810		惰	1460	たく	宅	538
ぞく	俗	1243		駄	1610		択	764
	族	322	たい	大	87		沢	1395
	属	1091		太	124		卓	1030
	賊	1584		代	413		拓	1263
	続	211		台	532		度	333
そこ	底	745		対	363		託	1574
そこなう	損なう	396		体	165		濯	301
そこねる	損ねる	396		耐	1618	たく	炊く	1311
そそぐ	注ぐ	290		待	195	だく	諾	1578
そそのかす	唆す	1433		怠	1698		濁	1511
そだつ	育つ	879		胎	1544	だく	抱く	1012
そだてる	育てる	879		退	348	たくみ	巧み	1786
そつ	卒	306		帯	1065	たくわえる	蓄える	743
	率	615		泰	1680	たけ	丈	1272
そと	外	150		袋	685		竹	374
そなえる	供える	418		逮	1048		岳	1851
	備える	613		替	375	たしか	確か	803
そなわる	備わる	613		貸	183	たしかめる	確かめる	803
その	園	324		隊	779	たす	足す	171
そまる	染まる	908		滞	1402	だす	出す	185
そむく	背く	1085		態	451	たすかる	助かる	826
そむける	背ける	1085	だい	大	87	たすける	助ける	826
そめる	初める	440		内	152	たずさえる	携える	1486
	染める	908		代	413	たずさわる	携わる	1486
そら	空	461		台	532	たずねる	訪ねる	783
そらす	反らす	362		弟	76		尋ねる	1326
そる	反る	362		第	354	たたかう	戦う	360
そん	存	587		題	327		闘う	1328
	村	364	たいら	平ら	351	ただし	但し	1923
	孫	448	たいらか	平らか	351	ただしい	正しい	407
	尊	479	たえる	耐える	1618	ただす	正す	407
	損	396		堪える	1758	ただちに	直ちに	220
ぞん	存	587		絶える	734	たたみ	畳	1303
	た		たおす	倒す	225	たたむ	畳む	1303
			たおれる	倒れる	225	ただよう	漂う	1507
た	太	124	たか	高	83	たつ	達	384
	他	415	たかい	高い	83	たつ	竜	1867
	多	104	たがい	互い	1080		立つ	174
た	手	170	たかまる	高まる	83		建つ	1055

	読	180		泊める	207		鳴く	487
	篤	1683		留める	432	なぐさむ	慰む	1702
とく	溶く	1501	とも	友	79	なぐさめる	慰める	1702
	解く	293		共	419	なぐる	殴る	1625
	説く	292		供	418	なげかわしい	嘆かわしい	1436
とぐ	研ぐ	297	ともなう	伴う	1423	なげく	嘆く	1436
どく	毒	788	とらえる	捕らえる	1049	なげる	投げる	282
	独	559	とらわれる	捕らわれる	1049	なごむ	和む	352
	読	180	とり	鳥	486	なごやか	和やか	352
とける	溶ける	1501	とる	取る	270	なさけ	情け	654
	解ける	293		捕る	1049	なす	成す	377
とげる	遂げる	1217		執る	1823	なっ	納	733
とこ	床	543		採る	773	なつ	夏	97
	常	708		撮る	1267	なつかしい	懐かしい	1463
ところ	所	149	とれる	取れる	270	なつかしむ	懐かしむ	1463
とざす	閉ざす	216	どろ	泥	1493	なつく	懐く	1463
とし	年	24	とん	屯	1918	なつける	懐ける	1463
とじる	閉じる	216		団	366	なな	七	7
とつ	凸	1921		豚	1089	ななつ	七つ	7
	突	1121	とん	問	239	ななめ	斜め	1391
とつぐ	嫁ぐ	599	どん	鈍	1372	なに	何	80
とどく	届く	1090		曇	1281	なぬ	七	7
とどける	届ける	1090				なの	七	7
とどこおる	滞る	1402	**な**			なま	生	49
ととのう	調う	210	な	南	41	なまける	怠ける	1698
	整う	387		納	733	なまり	鉛	1339
ととのえる	調える	210	な	名	82	なみ	並	221
	整える	387		菜	774		波	913
となえる	唱える	1809	ない	内	152	なみだ	涙	1081
となり	隣	980	ない	亡い	582	なめらか	滑らか	1392
となる	隣る	980		無い	400	なやます	悩ます	1110
との	殿	1093	なえ	苗	1837	なやむ	悩む	1110
どの	殿	1093	なおす	治す	531	ならう	倣う	1247
とばす	飛ばす	265		直す	220		習う	201
とびら	扉	1734	なおる	治る	531	ならす	鳴らす	487
とぶ	飛ぶ	265		直る	220		慣らす	655
	跳ぶ	1586	なか	中	33	ならびに	並びに	221
とぼしい	乏しい	860		仲	1169	ならぶ	並ぶ	2221
とまる	止まる	217	ながい	永い	1096	ならべる	並べる	221
	泊まる	207		長い	89	なる	成る	377
	留まる	432	ながす	流す	279		鳴る	487
とみ	富	629	なかば	半ば	159	なれる	慣れる	655
とむ	富む	629	ながめる	眺める	1548	なわ	苗	1837
とむらう	弔う	1815	ながれる	流れる	279		縄	1568
とめる	止める	217	なく	泣く	252	**なん**	男	67

	南	41	にわとり	鶏	1863		農	626
	納	733	にん	人	15		濃	627
	軟	1308		任	639	のがす	逃す	283
	難	526		妊	1330	のがれる	逃れる	283
なん	何	80		忍	1775	のき	軒	508
				認	668	のこす	残す	223
に						のこる	残る	223
に	二	2	**ぬ**			のせる	乗せる	135
	仁	1879	ぬう	縫う	1571		載せる	1307
	尼	1722	ぬく	抜く	769	のぞく	除く	958
	弐	1912	ぬぐ	脱ぐ	191	のぞむ	望む	581
	児	1375	ぬげる	脱げる	191		臨む	1229
に	荷	570	ぬし	主	70	のち	後	30
にい	新	85	ぬすむ	盗む	268	のばす	伸ばす	1246
にえる	煮える	1315	ぬの	布	887		延ばす	689
にがい	苦い	342	ぬま	沼	1842	のびる	伸びる	1246
にがす	逃がす	283	ぬる	塗る	1694		延びる	689
にがる	苦る	342				のべる	延べる	689
にぎる	握る	1257	**ね**				述べる	963
にく	肉	561	ね	音	620	のぼす	上す	31
にくい	憎い	1462		値	426	のぼせる	上せる	31
にくしみ	憎しみ	1462		根	974	のぼる	上る	31
にくむ	憎む	1462	ねい	寧	1378		昇る	1280
にくらしい	憎らしい	1462	ねがう	願う	862		登る	472
にげる	逃げる	283	ねかす	寝かす	127	のむ	飲む	132
にごす	濁す	1511	ねこ	猫	1410	のる	乗る	135
にごる	濁る	1511	**ねつ**	熱	866		載る	1307
にし	西	40	ねばる	粘る	1559			
にせ	偽	1428	ねむい	眠い	978	**は**		
にち	日	16	ねむる	眠る	978	は	把	1467
になう	担う	1050	ねる	寝る	127		波	913
にぶい	鈍い	1372		練る	296		派	1191
にぶる	鈍る	1372	**ねん**	年	24		破	1037
にゃく	若	125		念	1117		覇	1685
にやす	煮やす	1315		粘	1559	は	刃	1774
にゅう	入	186		然	401		羽	491
	乳	821		燃	870		歯	702
	柔	1310	ねんごろ	懇ろ	1799		葉	569
にょ	女	68					端	680
	如	1441	**の**			ば	馬	484
にょう	女	68	の	野	404		婆	1902
	尿	1724	**のう**	悩	1110	ば	場	335
にる	似る	1172		納	733	はい	拝	766
	煮る	1315		能	411		杯	983
にわ	庭	542		脳	1109		背	1085

	肺	1343		漢	1159	ばつ	末	584
	俳	1167		暴	1043		伐	1422
	配	727		縛	1569		抜	769
	排	1262		爆	1044		罰	1317
	敗	718	はげしい	激しい	1039		閥	1192
	廃	1412	はげます	励ます	832	はて	果	502
	輩	1166	はげむ	励む	832	はてる	果てる	502
はい	灰	874	ばける	化ける	414	はな	花	314
ばい	売	187	はこ	箱	1060		華	1323
	倍	158	はこぶ	運ぶ	304		鼻	1286
	梅	969	はさまる	挟まる	1473	はなし	話	178
	培	1640	はさむ	挟む	1473	はなす	放す	723
	陪	1641	はし	端	680		話す	178
	媒	1760		橋	313		離す	1008
	買	188	はじ	恥	1366	はなつ	放つ	723
	賠	1642	はじまる	始まる	129	はなはだ	甚だ	1756
はいる	入る	186	はじめ	初め	440	はなはだしい	甚だしい	1756
はえ	栄	1188	はじめて	初めて	440	はなれる	放れる	723
はえる	生える	49	はじめる	始める	129		離れる	1008
	映える	234	はしら	柱	990	はね	羽	491
	栄える	1188	はじらう	恥じらう	1366	はねる	跳ねる	1586
はか	墓	1156	はしる	走る	177	はは	母	74
ばかす	化かす	414	はじる	恥じる	1366	はば	幅	897
はがね	鋼	1337	はずかしい	恥ずかしい	1366	はばむ	阻む	1519
はからう	計らう	288	はずかしめる	辱める	1795	はぶく	省く	389
はかる	図る	329	はずす	外す	150	はま	浜	911
	計る	288	はずむ	弾む	590	はやい	早い	117
	測る	810	はずれる	外れる	150		速い	383
	量る	435	はた	畑	872	はやし	林	459
	諮る	1580		旗	1528	はやす	生やす	49
	謀る	1761		端	680	はやまる	早まる	117
はく	白	44		機	334	はやめる	早める	117
	伯	1877	はだ	肌	1345		速める	383
	拍	1255	はだか	裸	1305	はら	原	405
	泊	207	はたけ	畑	872		腹	1088
	迫	964	はたす	果たす	502	はらう	払う	189
	舶	1573	はたらく	働く	192	はらす	晴らす	281
	博	798	はち	八	8	はり	針	729
	薄	799		鉢	1597	はる	春	96
はく	吐く	1432	ばち	罰	1317		張る	1185
	掃く	957	はっ	法	518	はれる	晴れる	281
	履く	1405	はつ	発	286	はん	凡	467
ばく	麦	637		鉢	1597		反	362
	博	798		髪	1359		半	159
	幕	1157	はつ	初	440		犯	1046

	帆	1444		碑	1771	ひや	冷や	662
	伴	1423		罷	1671	ひやかす	冷やかす	662
	判	899		避	1365	ひゃく	百	11
	坂	605	ひ	日	16	びゃく	白	44
	板	987		火	18	ひやす	冷やす	662
	版	1142		氷	1095	ひょう	氷	1095
	班	1541		灯	871		兵	994
	畔	1857	び	尾	1723		拍	1255
	般	648		美	673		表	437
	販	1223		備	613		俵	1426
	飯	604		微	1149		票	1199
	搬	1487		鼻	1286		評	948
	煩	1646	ひいでる	秀でる	1171		漂	1507
	頒	1645	ひかえる	控える	1479		標	1200
	範	1061	ひがし	東	39	びょう	平	351
	繁	1187	ひかり	光	464		苗	1837
	藩	1890	ひかる	光る	464		秒	1151
ばん	万	13	ひき	匹	1203		病	229
	伴	1423	ひきいる	率いる	615		描	765
	判	899	ひく	引く	257		猫	1410
	板	987		弾く	590	ひら	平	351
	晩	94	ひくい	低い	108	ひらく	開く	215
	番	551	ひくまる	低まる	108	ひらける	開ける	215
	蛮	1825	ひくめる	低める	108	ひる	昼	92
	盤	1313	ひける	引ける	257		干る	506
ひ			ひさしい	久しい	1097	ひるがえす	翻す	760
ひ	比	276	ひそむ	潜む	1393	ひるがえる	翻る	760
	皮	1144	ひたい	額	861	ひろい	広い	113
	妃	1869	ひたす	浸す	1496	ひろう	拾う	273
	否	1006	ひだり	左	36	ひろがる	広がる	113
	批	1051	ひたる	浸る	1496	ひろげる	広げる	113
	彼	1146	ひつ	匹	1203	ひろまる	広まる	113
	披	1468		必	423	ひろめる	広める	113
	泌	1492		泌	1492	ひん	品	683
	肥	1352		筆	355		浜	911
	非	707	ひつじ	羊	488		貧	859
	卑	1770	ひと	一	1		賓	1662
	飛	265		人	15		頻	1221
	疲	275	ひとしい	等しい	353	びん	便	227
	秘	1102	ひとつ	一つ	1		敏	1800
	被	1145	ひとり	独り	559		瓶	1822
	悲	341	ひびく	響く	1023		貧	859
	扉	1734	ひま	暇	622			
	費	858	ひめ	姫	1868			
			ひめる	秘める	1102			

	ふ								
				服	317		増やす	429
ふ	不	422		副	898	ふゆ	冬	99
	夫	595		幅	897	ふる	振る	770
	父	73		復	521		降る	136
	付	365		福	895	ふるい	古い	86
	布	887		腹	1088	ふるう	震う	847
	扶	1466		複	522		奮う	1406
	府	337		覆	1686		振るう	770
	怖	1451	ふく	吹く	259	ふるえる	震える	847
	歩	176		噴く	1633	ふるす	古す	86
	附	1520	ふくむ	含む	1290	ふれる	触れる	1382
	負	717	ふくめる	含める	1290	ふん	分	26
	赴	1075	ふくらむ	膨らむ	1354		粉	1557
	風	465	ふくれる	膨れる	1354		紛	1298
	浮	820	ふくろ	袋	685		雰	1063
	婦	597	ふける	老ける	737		噴	1633
	符	357		更ける	1076		墳	1888
	富	629	ふさ	房	1082		憤	1634
	普	427	ふし	節	699		奮	1406
	腐	1730	ふす	伏す	1421	ぶん	分	26
	敷	724	ふせぐ	防ぐ	781		文	320
	膚	1742	ふせる	伏せる	1421		聞	179
	賦	1585	ふた	二	2			
	譜	1583		双	1763		へ	
ぶ	不	422	ふだ	札	984	べ	辺	962
	分	26	ぶた	豚	1089	へい	丙	1909
	侮	1801	ふたたび	再び	992		平	351
	奉	1678	ふたつ	二つ	2		兵	994
	歩	176	ふち	縁	732		併	1250
	武	1165	ふつ	払	189		並	221
	部	53		沸	1494		柄	989
	無	400	ぶつ	仏	416		病	229
	舞	981		物	321		陛	1521
ふう	夫	595	ふで	筆	355		閉	216
	封	372	ふとい	太い	124		塀	1439
	風	465	ふところ	懐	1463		幣	1796
	富	629	ふとる	太る	124		弊	1797
ふえ	笛	1681	ふな	舟	646	べい	米	562
ふえる	殖える	1540		船	647	へき	壁	1029
	増える	429	ふね	舟	646		癖	1364
ふかい	深い	121		船	647	へだたる	隔たる	1236
ふかまる	深まる	121	ふまえる	踏まえる	266	へだてる	隔てる	1236
ふかめる	深める	121	ふみ	文	320	べつ	別	397
ふく	伏	1421	ふむ	踏む	266	べに	紅	1295
			ふやす	殖やす	1540	へび	蛇	1861

	埋	1261	まつり	祭	473	みず	水	19
まい	舞	981	まつりごと	政	530	みずうみ	湖	453
まいる	参る	294	まつる	祭る	473	みずから	自ら	63
まう	舞う	981	まと	的	380	みせ	店	55
まえ	前	29	まど	窓	231	みせる	見せる	139
まかす	任す	639	まどう	惑う	1071	みぞ	溝	1499
	負かす	717	まなこ	眼	976	みたす	満たす	555
まかせる	任せる	639	まなぶ	学ぶ	50	みだす	乱す	932
まかなう	賄う	1225	まぬかれる	免れる	941	みだれる	乱れる	932
まがる	曲る	625	まねく	招く	696	みち	道	66
まき	牧	1273	まぼろし	幻	1814	みちびく	導く	480
	巻	715	まめ	豆	471	みちる	満ちる	555
まぎらす	紛らす	1298	まもる	守る	537	**みつ**	密	1103
まぎらわしい	紛らわしい	1298	まゆ	繭	1946	みつ	三つ	3
まぎらわす	紛らわす	1298	まよう	迷う	1070	みつぐ	貢ぐ	1180
まぎれる	紛れる	1298	まる	丸	591	みっつ	三つ	3
まく	幕	1157		円	14	みとめる	認める	668
	膜	1546	まるい	丸い	591	みどり	緑	731
まく	巻く	715		円い	14	みな	皆	606
まける	負ける	717	まるめる	丸める	591	みなと	港	909
まげる	曲げる	625	まわす	回す	162	みなみ	南	41
まご	孫	448	まわり	周り	558	みなもと	源	854
まこと	誠	943	まわる	回る	162	みにくい	醜い	1755
まさ	正	407	**まん**	万	13	みね	峰	1848
まさる	勝る	263		満	555	みのる	実る	672
まざる	交ざる	504		慢	653	みみ	耳	169
	混ざる	837		漫	652	みや	宮	929
まじえる	交える	504				**みゃく**	脈	1353
まじる	交じる	504	**み**			みやこ	都	338
	混じる	837	み	未	583	**みょう**	名	82
まじわる	交わる	504		味	311		妙	1150
ます	升	1915		魅	1419		命	997
	増す	429	み	三	3		明	106
まずしい	貧しい	859		身	394	みる	見る	139
まぜる	交ぜる	504		実	672		診る	1361
	混ぜる	837	みえる	見える	139	**みん**	民	536
また	又	1762	みがく	磨く	1731		眠	978
またたく	瞬く	979	みき	幹	1230			
まち	町	549	みぎ	右	35	**む**		
	街	371	みことのり	詔	1935	む	矛	955
まつ	末	584	みさお	操	1485		武	1165
	抹	1471	みさき	岬	1850		務	388
まつ	松	970	みささぎ	陵	1886		無	400
	待つ	195	みじかい	短い	90		夢	800
まったく	全く	160	みじめ	惨め	1457		謀	1761

やっつ	八つ	8		憂	1829		洋	917
やど	宿	326		融	1237		要	424
やとう	雇う	1083		優	1168		容	1123
やどす	宿す	326	ゆう	夕	95		庸	1728
やどる	宿る	326		結う	302		揚	1481
やなぎ	柳	1854	ゆえ	故	722		揺	1789
やぶる	破る	1037	ゆか	床	543		葉	569
やぶれる	破れる	1037	ゆき	雪	842		陽	834
	敗れる	718	ゆく	行く	58		溶	1501
やま	山	100		逝く	1747		腰	1087
やまい	病	229	ゆさぶる	揺さぶる	1789		様	677
やむ	病む	229	ゆすぶる	揺すぶる	1789		踊	1383
やめる	辞める	931	ゆする	揺する	1789		窯	1900
やわらか	柔らか	1310	ゆずる	譲る	1209		養	675
	軟らか	1308	ゆたか	豊か	628		擁	1490
やわらかい	柔らかい	1310	ゆび	指	775		謡	1788
	軟らかい	1308	ゆみ	弓	592		曜	23
やわらぐ	和らぐ	352	ゆめ	夢	800	よう	八	8
やわらげる	和らげる	352	ゆらぐ	揺らぐ	1789		酔う	728
	ゆ		ゆる	揺る	1789	よく	抑	1264
			ゆるい	緩い	1271		浴	1126
ゆ	由	623	ゆるぐ	揺るぐ	1789		欲	1124
	油	624	ゆるす	許す	667		翌	492
	愉	1458	ゆるむ	緩む	1271		翼	1304
	遊	196	ゆるめる	緩める	1271	よこ	横	34
	諭	1579	ゆるやか	緩やか	1271	よごれる	汚れる	907
	輸	499	ゆれる	揺れる	1789	よし	由	623
	癒	1739	ゆわえる	結わえる	302	よせる	寄せる	1120
ゆ	湯	836		**よ**		よそおう	装う	1370
ゆい	由	623				よつ	四つ	4
	唯	1636	よ	与	713	よっつ	四つ	4
	遺	1179		予	403	よぶ	呼ぶ	197
ゆう	友	79		余	959	よむ	詠む	1905
	右	35		誉	1713		読む	180
	由	623		預	571	よめ	嫁	599
	有	347	よ	世	156	よる	夜	93
	勇	1154		代	413		因る	406
	幽	1820		四	4		寄る	1120
	郵	226		夜	93	よろこぶ	喜ぶ	253
	悠	1699	よい	宵	1907	よわい	弱い	112
	猶	1517		良い	602	よわまる	弱まる	112
	裕	1125		善い	676	よわめる	弱める	112
	遊	196	よう	幼	1099	よわる	弱る	112
	雄	1637		用	308	よん	四	4
	誘	274		羊	488			

わく	惑	1071		煩う	1646	わり	割	786
わく	枠	510	わずらわす	煩わす	1646	わる	割る	786
	沸く	1494	わすれる	忘れる	209	わるい	悪い	114
わけ	訳	761	わた	綿	881	われ	我	1164
わける	分ける	26	わたくし	私	72	われる	割れる	786
わざ	技	369	わたす	渡す	205	**わん**	湾	910
	業	307	わたる	渡る	205		腕	1342
わざわい	災い	873	わらう	笑う	251			
わずらう	患う	1367	わらべ	童	1026			

字形索引
（Form Index）

Kanji are arranged under each component heading according to the number of strokes, and the *kanji* number is given. The circled number indicates the number of strokes in the *kanji* excluding the component part. The number for each component can be found in the component chart inside the back cover.

| | | | レ　フ　ト　　（Left） | | | | | 1-73 |

—2画—

1	亻	
②	化	414
	仏	416
	仁	1879
③	仕	236
	付	365
	代	413
	他	415
	仙	1880
④	休	138
	伝	278
	件	482
	任	639
	仰	1134
	仮	1141
	仲	1169
	伏	1421
	伐	1422
⑤	何	80
	低	108
	作	137
	住	141
	体	165
	位	417
	佐	1002
	似	1172
	伺	1245
	伸	1246

	伴	1423
	伯	1877
	但	1923
⑥	使	199
	供	418
	価	425
	例	811
	依	890
	侮	1801
	併	1250
	侍	1878
	佳	1931
⑦	便	227
	係	447
	信	640
	保	665
	促	1170
	俗	1243
	侵	1244
	俊	1424
	侯	1876
⑧	倍	158
	借	182
	倒	225
	値	426
	個	469
	停	481
	倫	497
	側	809
	俳	1167
	候	1174
	修	1175

	倣	1247
	倹	1425
	俵	1426
	俸	1427
⑨	健	1053
	偏	1176
	偶	1240
	偽	1428
	偵	1765
⑩	備	613
	偉	1242
	傍	1429
⑪	働	192
	傷	835
	傾	1173
	催	1248
	債	1249
	僧	1430
	傑	1431
⑫	像	940
	僚	1182
	僕	1241
⑬	億	650
	儀	936
⑭	儒	1891
⑮	償	712
	優	1168

2	冫	
④	次	660

⑤	冷	662
⑧	凍	1094
	准	1635
⑭	凝	1790

3	忄	
⑥	協	444
⑩	博	798

—3画—

4	口	
③	吸	272
	叫	1291
	吐	1432
④	吹	259
	吟	1904
⑤	呼	197
	味	311
⑥	咲	261
⑦	唆	1433
⑧	喝	1434
	唯	1636
	唱	1809
⑨	喫	752
	喚	1435
⑩	嘆	1436
⑪	鳴	487

⑫	嘱	1437
	噴	1633
⑭	嚇	1925

5	土	
③	地	146
④	坂	605
	坊	782
	均	1014
	坑	1928
⑤	坪	1913
⑥	城	942
	垣	1784
⑦	埋	1261
⑧	域	1072
	堀	1260
	培	1640
⑨	場	335
	塔	1483
	塀	1439
	堪	1758
	堤	1852
	塚	1889
⑩	塩	924
	塊	1753
⑪	増	429
	境	1036
⑫	墳	1888
⑬	壊	1038
	壇	1440

	壌	1650

6	女	
②	奴	1871
③	好	244
	如	1441
	妃	1869
④	妨	784
	妙	1150
	妊	1330
⑤	姉	77
	妹	78
	始	129
	姓	598
⑥	姻	1442
⑦	娘	601
	娯	1329
	娠	1331
	姫	1868
⑧	婚	303
	婦	597
⑨	婿	600
	媒	1760
⑩	嫁	599
	嫌	1325
⑪	嫡	1870
⑫	嬢	1649

7 子		張 1185	
		⑨ 弾 590	
① 孔 1881			
⑥ 孤 1381		**13 彳**	
⑦ 孫 448			
		③ 行 58	
8 山		④ 役 609	
		⑤ 往 520	
④ 岐 1443		彼 1146	
⑤ 岬 1850		径 1448	
⑥ 峡 1294		征 1389	
峠 1849		⑥ 後 30	
⑦ 峰 1848		待 195	
⑧ 崎 1293		律 519	
		⑦ 従 642	
9 川		徒 641	
		徐 1390	
⑨ 順 952		⑧ 術 370	
		得 643	
10 工		⑨ 街 371	
		復 521	
② 功 378		御 919	
巧 1786		循 1387	
④ 攻 1040		⑩ 微 1149	
⑨ 項 1222		⑪ 徳 644	
		徴 1148	
11 巾		⑫ 徹 1147	
		衝 1388	
③ 帆 1444		⑬ 衛 780	
⑧ 帳 1184		衡 1449	
⑨ 幅 897			
帽 1279		**14 忄**	
12 弓		③ 忙 126	
		④ 快 656	
① 引 257		⑤ 性 421	
⑤ 弦 1446		怪 1450	
⑥ 弧 1447		怖 1451	
⑧ 強 111		⑥ 悔 1219	
		恨 1452	
		恒 1785	
		⑦ 悩 1110	
		悦 1453	

悟 1454		拝 766	
⑧ 情 654		拓 1263	
惜 1455		拐 1265	
悼 1456		披 1468	
惨 1457		拘 1469	
⑨ 愉 1458		拙 1470	
慌 1459		抹 1471	
惰 1460		⑥ 持 142	
⑩ 慎 1220		拾 273	
⑪ 慢 653		指 775	
慣 655		挑 1268	
憎 1462		括 1472	
⑫ 憤 1634		挟 1473	
⑬ 憶 651		拷 1474	
懐 1463		⑦ 振 770	
憾 1464		捕 1049	
		捜 1475	
15 扌		挿 1478	
		⑧ 捨 285	
② 払 189		授 312	
打 771		接 748	
③ 扱 1266		描 765	
④ 投 282		採 773	
技 369		掃 957	
抗 747		推 1009	
択 764		揭 1011	
抜 769		探 1258	
折 772		掘 1259	
批 1051		排 1262	
抑 1264		措 1476	
抄 1465		掛 1477	
扶 1466		控 1479	
把 1467		据 1480	
⑤ 押 256		⑨ 換 749	
招 696		提 767	
抵 746		揮 776	
拡 768		握 1257	
拒 1005		援 1270	
抱 1012		搭 1483	
担 1050		揚 1481	
拠 1213		揺 1789	
抽 1254		⑩ 損 396	
拍 1255		摂 1482	
		搾 1484	
		携 1486	

搬 1487		派 1191	
⑪ 摘 1256		洪 1396	
⑫ 撮 1267		津 1397	
撤 1488		浄 1495	
撲 1489		洞 1844	
⑬ 操 1485		⑦ 酒 144	
擁 1490		消 219	
⑭ 擦 1416		流 279	
擬 1791		浮 820	
		浜 911	
16 氵		涙 1081	
		浴 1126	
② 汁 1399		浪 1398	
③ 池 452		浸 1496	
汗 507		浦 1846	
江 905		⑧ 深 121	
汚 907		涼 340	
④ 決 277		渉 505	
沖 912		済 516	
沈 1129		清 754	
没 1130		混 837	
沢 1395		液 906	
汽 1491		添 1131	
⑤ 泳 193		渇 1394	
泊 207		渋 1400	
泣 252		淡 1401	
注 290		涯 1497	
法 518		淑 1767	
治 531		渓 1843	
油 624		⑨ 渡 205	
波 913		減 430	
況 1017		湖 453	
河 1127		満 555	
沿 1128		測 810	
泌 1492		湯 836	
泥 1493		湿 838	
沸 1494		温 839	
泡 1629		港 909	
沼 1842		湾 910	
⑥ 浅 122		渦 1498	
洗 198		滋 1776	
海 454		⑩ 漢 527	
活 517		源 854	
洋 917		漠 1159	
		滑 1392	

滞 1402	⑨ 猶 1517	⑦ 族 322	格 852	⑥ 胸 1086		**26 牛**		
溝 1499	⑩ 猿 1865	旋 1527	桜 968	胴 1341				
減 1500	⑪ 獄 1518	⑩ 旗 1528	梅 969	脂 1350		④ 物 321		
溶 1501	⑬ 獲 1408		桃 971	脈 1353		牧 1273		

滞 1402
溝 1499
減 1500
溶 1501
滝 1841
⑪ 演 616
漫 652
漁 914
漸 1503
滴 1504
漆 1505
漬 1506
漂 1507
漏 1502
⑫ 潔 753
潜 1393
潮 1508
潤 1509
澄 1510
潟 1847
⑬ 濃 627
激 1039
濁 1511
⑭ 濯 301
⑮ 濫 1512
⑯ 瀬 1845

⑨ 猶 1517
⑩ 猿 1865
⑪ 獄 1518
⑬ 獲 1408

19 阝

④ 防 781
⑤ 阻 1519
　 附 1520
⑥ 限 975
⑦ 降 136
　 院 230
　 除 958
　 陛 1521
　 陥 1522
　 陣 1523
⑧ 険 790
　 陸 833
　 陳 1524
　 陰 1525
　 陶 1526
　 陪 1641
　 陵 1886
　 隆 1926
⑨ 階 607
　 隊 779
　 陽 834
　 隅 1239
　 随 1792
⑩ 隔 1236
⑪ 際 474
　 障 1028
　 隠 1235
⑬ 隣 980

―4画―

20 方

④ 放 723
⑤ 施 612
⑥ 旅 153

⑦ 族 322
　 旋 1527
⑩ 旗 1528

21 日

④ 明 106
⑤ 映 234
　 昨 621
　 昭 867
⑥ 時 25
⑧ 晩 94
　 晴 281
　 暁 1858
⑨ 暗 107
　 暖 339
　 暇 622
⑭ 曜 23

22 木

① 札 984
② 机 38
　 朴 1529
　 朽 1787
③ 村 364
　 材 740
　 杉 1357
④ 林 459
　 枠 510
　 松 970
　 枝 972
　 枚 982
　 杯 983
　 析 985
　 板 987
　 枢 1530
⑤ 相 391
　 柄 989
　 柱 990
　 枯 1356
　 柳 1854
⑥ 校 51

格 852
桜 968
梅 969
桃 971
株 973
根 974
核 986
栓 1531
桟 1532
⑦ 械 511
⑧ 植 678
　 検 792
　 棒 988
　 棟 1533
　 棺 1534
　 棋 1535
　 棚 1536
⑨ 極 679
　 楼 1887
⑩ 様 677
　 構 991
　 模 1160
　 概 1161
⑪ 横 34
　 権 804
　 標 1200
　 槽 1537
⑫ 橋 313
　 機 334
　 樹 1853
⑯ 欄 1538

23 月

② 肌 1345
③ 肝 1107
④ 服 317
　 肪 1351
　 肥 1352
　 肢 1355
⑤ 肺 1343
　 胆 1344
　 胎 1544
　 胞 1630

⑥ 胸 1086
　 胴 1341
　 脂 1350
　 脈 1353
　 朕 1938
⑦ 脱 191
　 豚 1089
　 脳 1109
　 脚 1545
⑧ 勝 263
　 腕 1342
　 脹 1927
⑨ 腰 1087
　 腹 1088
　 腸 1106
⑩ 膜 1546
⑫ 膨 1354
⑬ 膳 1937
⑮ 臓 1108
⑯ 騰 1547

24 歹

② 死 258
　 列 812
⑥ 残 223
　 殊 813
　 殉 1539
⑧ 殖 1540

25 火

② 灯 871
④ 炊 1311
　 炉 1802
⑤ 畑 872
⑧ 焼 218
⑨ 煙 1045
　 煩 1646
⑫ 燃 870
⑬ 燥 903
⑮ 爆 1044

26 牛

④ 物 321
　 牧 1273
⑤ 牲 938
⑥ 特 398
⑬ 犠 937

27 王

⑤ 珍 1360
⑥ 班 1541
　 珠 1769
⑦ 理 241
　 現 578
　 球 935
⑬ 環 1035

28 ネ

① 礼 822
③ 社 60
④ 祈 823
　 祉 896
⑤ 神 586
　 祖 824
　 祝 1018
⑥ 祥 1542
⑦ 視 806
　 禅 589
　 福 895
　 禍 1543

―5画―

29 牙

③ 邪 1417
⑧ 雅 1638

17 丬

③ 壮 1445
④ 状 829
⑦ 将 830

18 犭

② 犯 1046
④ 狂 1513
⑥ 独 559
　 狭 560
　 狩 1514
⑧ 猫 1410
　 猟 1515
　 猛 1516

30 田		
②	町	549
⑤	畔	1857
⑥	略	1195

31 目		
⑤	眠	978
⑥	眼	976
	眺	1548
⑧	睡	977
⑬	瞬	979

32 矛		
⑥	務	388

33 矢		
③	知	143
⑦	短	90
⑫	矯	1549

34 石		
④	研	297
	砂	1152
	砕	1550
⑤	破	1037
	砲	1631
⑦	硬	1309
	硫	1551
	硝	1552
⑨	碑	1771
	磁	1777
⑩	確	803
⑫	礁	1553
⑬	礎	692

35 禾		
②	私	72
	利	248
③	和	352
④	科	565
	秒	1151
⑤	秋	98
	秩	954
	秘	1102
	称	1554
	租	1893
⑥	移	1101
⑦	税	670
	程	671
⑧	稚	1100
⑨	種	564
	稿	1231
	稲	1233
	穂	1856
⑩	稼	1232
⑪	積	886
	穏	1234
⑬	穫	1409

36 立		
⑨	端	680

37 ネ		
②	初	440
⑤	被	1145
⑥	補	1001
	裕	1125
⑧	裸	1305
	褐	1556
⑨	複	522
⑬	襟	1555

38 艮		
②	即	700
⑤	既	1162

—6画—

39 米		
④	料	240
	粋	1069
	粉	1557
⑤	粒	1558
	粘	1559
	粗	1560
⑥	粧	1284
⑧	精	877
⑩	糖	1283
⑫	糧	1282

40 糸		
③	約	381
	級	410
	紀	634
	紅	1295
	糾	1561
④	紙	243
	納	733
	純	1068
	紛	1298
	紡	1563
	紋	1564
⑤	細	123
	終	130
	経	515
	組	635
	紹	694
	紳	1299
	紺	1562
⑥	絡	300
	結	302
	絵	617
	給	618
		734
	絞	1000
	絞	1565
⑦	続	211
	絹	880
	継	901
⑧	練	296
	緑	731
	総	735
	綿	881
	緒	1033
	維	1297
	綱	1566
	網	1567
⑨	縁	731
	線	841
	編	883
	締	1067
	緩	1271
	縄	1568
⑩	縦	1300
	縛	1569
	緯	1570
	縫	1571
⑪	縮	884
	績	885
	繊	1296
⑫	織	882
	繕	1572
⑬	繰	902

41 耒		
④	耕	1782
	耗	1783

42 耳		
②	取	270
④	恥	1366
⑪	聴	645

	職	513
⑫	職	513

43 至		
②	到	287
④	致	725

44 舌		
①	乱	932
⑦	辞	931

45 舟		
④	航	649
	般	648
⑤	船	647
	舶	1573
⑦	艇	1930
⑮	艦	1892

46 虫		
④	蚊	1860
⑤	蛇	1861

47 艮		
③	郎	546
④	朗	1628

48 并		
⑤	瓶	1822

49 自		
③	帥	1894

	師	967
④	師	967

—7画—

50 臣		
⑪	臨	1229

51 角		
⑥	解	293
	触	1382

52 言		
②	計	288
	訂	1206
③	記	633
	討	946
	訓	951
	託	1574
④	設	611
	許	667
	訳	761
	訪	783
	訟	1208
⑤	証	666
	評	948
	詞	1205
	訴	1207
	診	1361
	詐	1575
	詠	1905
	詔	1935
⑥	話	178
	試	795
	誠	943
	詳	944
	詩	945
	誇	950
	詰	1576
	該	1577

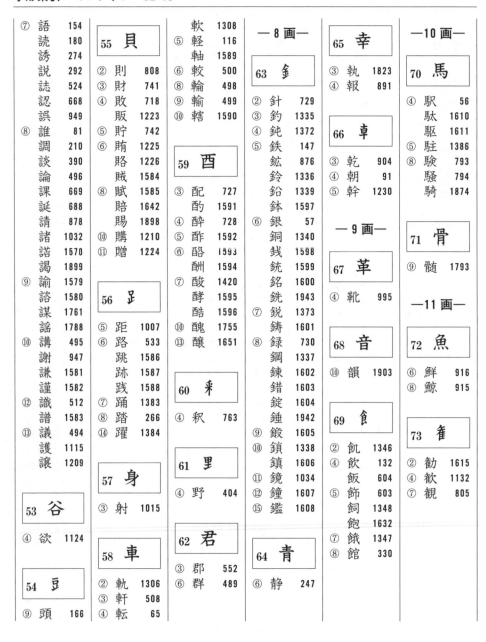

■ ライト (Right) 74-179

—1画—

74 し

③ 孔 1881
④ 礼 822
　 札 984
⑥ 乱 932
⑦ 乳 821

—2画—

75 几

④ 机 38
　 肌 1345
⑧ 飢 1346

76 刂

② 刈 1612
③ 刊 1138
④ 列 812
　 刑 1052
⑤ 利 248
　 別 397
　 判 899
⑥ 到 287
　 制 687
　 刷 1137
　 刻 1139
　 刺 1319
⑦ 則 808
　 削 1320
⑧ 剣 791
　 剖 1609
　 剛 1613
　 剤 1780

⑨ 副 898
　 剰 1321
⑩ 割 786
　 創 1113
⑬ 劇 1140

77 力

③ 功 378
　 幼 1099
⑤ 助 826
　 励 832
⑥ 効 501
　 劾 1614
⑦ 勅 1895
⑨ 動 64
　 勘 1757
⑩ 勤 525
⑪ 勧 1615

78 匕

② 比 276
　 化 414
③ 北 42
⑩ 靴 995

79 十

③ 汁 1399
⑦ 計 288
⑧ 針 729

80 卩

④ 印 1136
⑤ 即 700
　 却 1616

⑥ 卸 918

81 ム

② 仏 416
③ 払 189
⑤ 私 72

82 又

② 収 828
　 双 1763
⑥ 取 270
　 叔 1766
⑦ 叙 1617

83 丁

③ 打 771
④ 灯 871
⑤ 町 549
⑦ 訂 1206

—3画—

84 口

② 加 295
⑤ 知 143
　 和 352

85 寸

② 付 365
④ 対 363
　 村 364
⑥ 封 372

⑥ 卸 918

⑦ 討 946
　 射 1015
⑧ 尉 1882

86 己

③ 妃 1869
⑥ 紀 634
⑦ 記 633
　 配 727

87 干

③ 汗 507
④ 肝 1107
⑦ 軒 508

88 彡

④ 形 509
⑧ 彫 1358
　 彩 1619
⑪ 彰 1620
⑫ 影 1022
⑬ 膨 1354

89 阝

④ 邦 1621
⑤ 邸 1238
　 邪 1417
⑥ 郊 503
　 郎 546
⑦ 郡 552
　 郭 1773
⑧ 部 53
　 郵 226

耐 1618

都 338
郷 1024

90 テ

③ 行 58
⑧ 術 370
⑨ 街 371
⑫ 衝 1388
⑬ 衛 780
　 衡 1449

91 才

④ 材 740
⑦ 財 741

92 及

③ 吸 272
　 扱 1266
⑥ 級 410

93 也

② 他 415
③ 地 146
　 池 452

94 勹

⑤ 的 380
⑥ 約 381
⑦ 酌 1591
⑧ 釣 1335

—4画—

95 戈

② 成 377
　 伐 1422
③ 我 1164
　 戒 1334
⑤ 威 1333
⑦ 械 511
⑧ 滅 430
⑨ 戦 360
⑪ 戯 1901

96 支

③ 技 369
　 岐 1443
④ 枝 972
　 肢 1355
⑨ 鼓 1827

97 攵

③ 改 726
　 攻 1040
④ 放 723
　 枚 982
　 牧 1273
⑤ 政 530
　 故 722
⑥ 致 725
　 敏 1800
⑦ 教 214
　 敗 718
　 救 934
　 赦 1897
⑧ 敬 478
　 散 721

327

　敢 1622
⑨ 数 529
⑪ 敵 658
　敷 724

98 斗
⑤ 科 565
⑥ 料 240
⑦ 斜 1391

99 斤
③ 折 772
④ 祈 823
　析 985
⑦ 所 149
　断 900
⑨ 新 85
⑩ 漸 1503

100 方
③ 防 781
　坊 782
　妨 784
④ 放 723
　肪 1351
⑥ 紡 1563
⑦ 訪 783

101 欠
② 次 660
④ 欧 554
　炊 1311
⑦ 欲 1124
　軟 1308
⑧ 欺 1623
　款 1624
⑩ 歌 200

⑪ 歓 1132

102 殳
③ 投 282
　役 609
④ 殴 1625
⑤ 段 608
⑥ 殺 610
⑦ 設 611
　殻 1626
⑨ 殿 1093
⑩ 穀 1627

103 犬
③ 状 829
④ 献 1181
⑩ 獄 1518
⑫ 獣 1864

104 月
④ 明 106
⑥ 朗 1628
⑧ 朝 91
　期 690

105 卒
④ 枠 510
⑤ 砕 1550
⑥ 粋 1069
⑦ 酔 728

106 分
⑥ 紛 1298
　粉 1557

107 亢
③ 抗 747
　坑 1928
⑥ 航 649

108 反
② 仮 1141
③ 坂 605
④ 板 987
　版 1142
⑤ 飯 604
⑦ 販 1223

109 尺
④ 択 764
　沢 1395
⑦ 訳 761
　釈 763
⑩ 駅 56

110 少
③ 妙 1150
　抄 1465
⑤ 秒 1151
　砂 1152

111 艮
④ 服 317
⑧ 報 891

112 区
④ 枢 1530
⑩ 駆 1611

ー5画ー

113 生
③ 性 421
　姓 598
④ 牲 938

114 田
③ 畑 872
⑥ 細 123

115 白
③ 泊 207
　拍 1255
⑥ 舶 1573

116 皮
③ 波 913
　彼 1146
　披 1468
⑤ 破 1037
　被 1145

117 召
③ 招 696
　沼 1842
④ 昭 867
⑥ 紹 694
　詔 1935

118 㕣
③ 沿 1128
⑥ 船 647

⑧ 鉛 1339

119 台
③ 始 129
　治 531
④ 胎 1544

120 圣
③ 径 1448
⑥ 経 515
⑦ 軽 116

121 令
② 冷 662
⑧ 鈴 1336
⑫ 齢 1404

122 包
③ 抱 1012
　泡 1629
④ 胞 1630
⑤ 砲 1631
⑧ 飽 1632

123 主
② 住 141
③ 注 290
　往 520
④ 柱 990
⑩ 駐 1386

124 司
② 伺 1245

⑦ 詞 1205
⑧ 飼 1348
　嗣 1885

125 乍
② 作 137
④ 昨 621
⑦ 詐 1575
　酢 1592

126 且
③ 阻 1519
④ 祖 824
⑤ 租 1893
⑥ 組 635
　粗 1560

127 申
② 伸 1246
④ 神 586
⑥ 紳 1299

128 由
③ 油 624
　抽 1254
⑦ 軸 1589

ー6画ー

129 羊
③ 洋 917
④ 祥 1542
⑦ 群 489
　詳 944
⑪ 鮮 916

130 羽		
⑫	翻	760

131 聿		
③	律	519
	津	1397

132 舌		
③	活	517
	括	1472
⑦	話	178

133 艮		
③	限	975
	恨	1452
④	根	974
⑤	眼	976
⑧	銀	57

134 色		
⑦	絶	734

135 虫		
③	独	559
⑦	触	1382
⑩	融	1237

136 寺		
②	侍	1878
③	持	142
	待	195
④	時	25
	特	398
⑦	詩	945

137 各		
③	格	852
⑤	略	1195
⑥	絡	300
⑦	路	533
	酪	1593

138 交		
④	校	51
⑥	絞	1565
⑦	較	500

139 毎		
②	侮	1801
③	海	454
④	梅	969
	悔	1219

140 戋		
③	浅	122
④	残	223
	桟	1532
⑦	践	1588
⑧	銭	1598

141 朱		
④	殊	813
	株	973
	珠	1769

142 兆		
④	桃	971
⑦	跳	1586

―7画―

143 見		
④	現	578
	視	806
	規	807
⑨	親	249
⑪	観	805

144 谷		
②	俗	1243
③	浴	1126
⑤	裕	1125

145 豕		
④	豚	1089

146 辛		
⑥	辞	931

147 辰		
③	振	770
	娠	1331

148 里		
③	理	241

149 兑		
③	悦	1453
④	脱	191
⑤	税	670
⑦	説	292
⑧	鋭	1373

150 余		
③	除	958
	徐	1390

151 甫		
③	捕	1049
	浦	1846
⑤	補	1001
⑧	舗	1830

152 束		
⑤	疎	1826

―8画―

153 長		
③	帳	1184
	張	1185
④	脹	1927

154 隹		
②	准	1635
③	推	1009
	唯	1636
④	雄	1637
⑤	稚	1100

	雅	1638
⑥	雑	523
	維	1297
	雌	1639
⑦	誰	81
⑩	難	526
	離	1008

155 隶		
⑧	隷	1872

156 青		
③	情	654
	清	754
④	晴	281
⑥	精	877
⑦	請	878

157 僉		
②	倹	1425
③	険	790
④	検	792
⑩	験	794

158 侖		
②	倫	497
⑦	論	496
	輪	498

159 昔		
②	借	182
③	惜	1455
	措	1476
⑧	錯	1603

160 音		
②	倍	158
③	培	1640
	陪	1641
⑦	賠	1642

161 直		
②	値	426
④	植	678
	殖	1540

162 非		
②	俳	1167
③	排	1262

―9画―

163 頁		
②	頂	1643
③	順	952
	項	1222
④	預	571
	頑	1644
	頒	1645
	煩	1646
⑤	領	999
⑦	頼	572
	頭	166
⑧	頻	1221
⑨	類	563
	顔	573
	額	861
	顕	1647
⑩	願	862
⑫	顧	1648

164 扁
② 偏 1176
⑥ 編 883

165 俞
③ 愉 1458
⑦ 輸 499
　諭 1579

166 軍
③ 揮 776
⑥ 輝 777

167 単
③ 弾 590

④ 禅 589

168 易
③ 湯 836
　場 335
　揚 1481
　陽 834
④ 腸 1106

169 复
③ 復 521
④ 腹 1088
⑤ 複 522

—10画—

170 韋
① 偉 1242
⑥ 緯 1570

171 鬼
③ 塊 1753
④ 魂 1754
⑦ 醜 1755

172 冓
③ 溝 1499
④ 構 991
⑦ 講 495
　購 1210

—11画—

173 鳥
③ 鳴 487
⑧ 鶏 1863

174 曽
② 僧 1430
③ 増 429
　憎 1462
⑦ 贈 1224

175 責
② 債 1249
③ 漬 1506
⑤ 積 886

⑥ 績 885

176 商
③ 適 657
　摘 1256
　滴 1504
　嫡 1870

—13画—

177 義
② 儀 936
④ 犠 937
⑦ 議 494

178 蒦
③ 獲 1408
⑤ 穫 1409
⑦ 護 1115

179 喿
③ 操 1485
④ 燥 903
⑥ 繰 902

トップ　(Top)　180-233

—1画—

180 一
① 丁 550
② 三 3
　万 13
　下 32
③ 五 5
　不 422
　天 462
　互 1080
④ 平 351
　可 412
　丙 1909
⑤ 百 11
　両 556
　再 992
⑥ 否 1006
　更 1076
　亜 1818
⑦ 雨 232
　画 235
⑧ 面 438
⑨ 夏 97
⑭ 憂 1829
⑱ 璽 1947

—2画—

181 亠
① 亡 582
② 六 6
　方 43
　文 320
③ 市 547
　玄 1276
④ 交 504
　衣 889
　充 1275
⑤ 忘 209
⑥ 夜 93
　京 233
　卒 306
　育 879
　盲 1278
　享 1772
　斉 1779
⑦ 変 222
　帝 1066
　亭 1652
　哀 1804
⑧ 高 83

　恋 1078
　畜 1274
　衰 1805
　衷 1806
⑨ 産 574
　率 615
　商 684
　斎 1781
⑩ 蛮 1825
⑪ 裏 436
　棄 1653
⑫ 豪 1277
⑬ 褒 1936

182 人
② 今 27
　介 695
③ 令 998
④ 会 59
　全 160
　企 701
⑤ 余 959
　含 1290
⑥ 金 21
　食 131
　命 997
　念 1117
　舎 1654
⑧ 倉 1112
⑩ 傘 1655

183 八
② 分 26
　父 73
　公 323
⑤ 谷 458
⑦ 盆 1314
⑨ 貧 859

184 丷
④ 羊 488
⑤ 弟 76
⑥ 並 221
⑦ 前 29
　首 393
　美 673
⑧ 差 674
　益 921
　兼 1324
⑩ 着 190
　普 427

善尊 676
479
⑪ 義 493
慈 1778
⑬ 養 675

185 冖
② 冗 468
③ 写 194
⑦ 軍 778
冠 1656

186 十
② 支 368
③ 古 86
⑤ 克 1374
⑥ 直 220
⑦ 南 41
⑧ 真 242
索 1301

187 卜
① 上 31
③ 占 1016
⑥ 卓 1030
⑦ 点 399
貞 1764

188 厶
③ 台 532
弁 1116
⑥ 参 294
⑦ 息 1698

189 マ
② 予 403

③ 予 955
⑦ 勇 1154
柔 1310

190 勹
④ 色 316
危 789
争 361
⑤ 角 716
⑥ 免 941
負 717
⑨ 魚 485
⑩ 象 939

—3画—

191 口
② 兄 75
号 442
④ 足 171
呈 1657
呉 1929
⑥ 品 683
⑦ 員 395

192 土
② 去 309
③ 寺 328
④ 赤 46
走 177
⑤ 幸 894

193 士
③ 吉 893
④ 声 619
志 756
壱 1911

194 夂
② 冬 99
③ 各 851
④ 条 750

195 大
⑤ 奔 1819
奇 1292
⑪ 奪 1407
⑬ 奮 1406

196 宀
③ 安 84
字 528
守 537
宅 538
宇 1252
④ 完 817
⑤ 定 289
官 540
宝 576
実 672
宗 816
宙 1253
宜 1658
⑥ 客 318
室 331
宣 850
⑦ 家 52
案 305
害 785
宴 849
宮 929
容 1123
宰 1659
宵 1907
⑧ 宿 326
密 1103
寄 1120

寂 1380
⑨ 寒 120
富 629
⑩ 寝 127
寛 1379
⑪ 察 475
寧 1378
⑫ 寮 1660
寮 1183
審 1661
賓 1662
⑬ 憲 787

197 山
⑤ 岸 456
岩 457
⑥ 炭 875
⑧ 崩 1663
崇 1664

198 工
⑦ 貢 1180

199 ⺌
③ 当 402
④ 光 464
肖 1811
⑤ 尚 1810
⑦ 党 710
⑧ 常 708
堂 709
⑨ 掌 1677
⑫ 賞 711

200 ⺍
④ 労 443
⑤ 学 50

⑥ 単 359
栄 1188
⑦ 挙 1189
⑧ 蛍 1676
巣 1862
⑨ 覚 208
営 930
⑩ 誉 1713
⑭ 厳 1190

201 艹
③ 芝 568
芋 1834
④ 花 314
芸 566
芳 1665
⑤ 若 125
英 155
苦 342
芽 1835
茎 1836
苗 1837
茂 1840
⑥ 茶 145
草 567
荘 1369
荒 1666
⑦ 荷 570
華 1323
⑧ 菜 774
著 1031
菌 1368
菓 1667
菊 1833
⑨ 落 280
葉 569
葬 801
募 1155
⑩ 蓄 743
夢 800
蒸 802
墓 1156
幕 1157

⑪ 暮 1158
慕 1668
⑫ 蔵 1111
⑬ 薬 315
薄 799
薦 1411
薫 1710
薪 1838
⑮ 藩 1890
繭 1946
⑯ 藻 1839

202 亡
③ 妄 1696
④ 忘 209
⑤ 盲 1278

—4画—

203 日
② 早 117
④ 易 434
昇 1280
昆 1859
⑤ 星 463
冒 1669
是 1670
⑧ 暑 119
量 435
最 439
景 1021
晶 1808
⑪ 暴 1043
⑫ 曇 1281

204 木
⑤ 査 825
森 460

205 止	
④	歩 176
	肯 1403
⑧	歯 702
⑨	歳 703

206 罒	
⑦	貫 1714

207 宀	
③	妥 1332
④	受 269
⑨	愛 1079
⑬	爵 1875

208 耂	
②	考 212
	老 737
③	孝 738
④	者 148

209 龶	
③	麦 637
④	青 47
	表 437
	毒 788
⑥	素 636
⑦	責 638

210 六	
②	充 1275
④	育 879
⑨	棄 1653

—5画—

211 田	
②	男 67
④	界 157
	思 202
	胃 1105
⑥	異 1196
	累 1302
⑦	畳 1303
	塁 1692

212 癶	
④	発 286
⑦	登 472

213 禾	
②	秀 1171
③	委 697
	季 698
④	香 1705

214 穴	
②	究 298
③	空 461
	突 1121
④	窃 1673
	窓 231
	室 1674
⑩	窮 1675
	窯 1900

215 立	
②	辛 344
④	音 620
⑤	竜 1867
⑥	産 574
	章 1027
⑦	童 1026
⑧	意 291

216 罒	
⑦	買 188
⑧	置 262
	罪 1047
	署 1316
⑨	罰 1317
⑩	罷 1671
⑭	羅 1672

217 夫	
③	奉 1678
④	奏 1679
⑤	泰 1680

218 ⺌	
⑤	党 710
⑥	常 708
	堂 709
⑦	掌 1677
⑩	賞 711

219 ⺍	
②	労 443
③	学 50
④	栄 1188
⑥	蛍 1676
⑦	覚 208
	営 930

—6画—

220 竹	
④	笑 251
⑤	第 354
	符 357
	笛 1681
⑥	答 213
	等 353
	筆 355
	筒 373
	策 1057
	筋 1059
⑦	節 699
⑧	算 356
	管 539
	箇 1682
⑨	箱 1060
	範 1061
⑩	築 1056
	篤 1683
⑫	簡 358
⑬	簿 1684
⑭	籍 1058

221 羊	
③	美 673
④	差 674
⑥	着 190
	善 676
⑦	義 493
⑨	養 675

222 羽	
⑤	習 201
	翌 492
⑪	翼 1304

223 自	
③	臭 1285
④	息 1118
⑧	鼻 1286

224 血	
⑥	衆 1194

225 西	
③	要 424
⑤	票 1199
⑫	覆 1686
⑬	覇 1685

226 曲	
⑦	農 626
	豊 628

227 亦	
③	変 222
④	恋 1078
⑤	蛮 1825

—7画—

228 辰	
③	唇 1794
	辱 1795

229 釆	
⑤	番 551

—8画—

230 隹	
②	隻 1919
④	集 224
	焦 1385

231 雨	
④	雪 842
	雲 844
	雰 1063
⑤	電 61
	雷 843
	零 1687
⑥	需 681
⑦	震 847
	霊 1688
⑨	霜 1689
⑪	霧 845
⑬	露 846

232 灬	
④	無 400
⑦	舞 981

233 非	
④	悲 341
	輩 1166

ボトム (Bottom) 234-280

—2画—

234 儿
- ② 元 245
- ④ 先 48
- 兄 75
- 光 464
- 充 1275
- ⑤ 見 139
- 克 1374
- 児 1375
- ⑥ 免 941
- ⑧ 党 710
- ⑪ 寛 1379
- ⑮ 覧 1831

235 八
- ② 六 6
- ③ 穴 1122
- ④ 共 419
- ⑤ 貝 719
- 兵 994
- 呉 1929
- ⑥ 典 630
- 具 720
- ⑦ 貞 1764
- ⑧ 真 242
- ⑨ 黄 993
- 異 1196
- ⑭ 興 631
- ⑮ 翼 1304

236 力
- ④ 劣 1153
- ⑤ 男 67
- 労 443
- 努 827
- ⑦ 勇 1154
- ⑩ 募 1155
- ⑪ 勢 865

237 十
- ⑤ 辛 344
- ⑥ 卒 306
- 卓 1030
- ⑦ 草 567
- ⑧ 宰 1659
- ⑨ 率 615
- 章 1027
- ⑪ 準 614
- ⑦ 卑 1770

—3画—

238 口
- ② 右 35
- 古 86
- 石 102
- 台 532
- 占 1016
- ③ 名 82
- 召 1691
- 合 271
- 各 851
- 吉 893
- 舌 1288
- 后 1873
- ④ 谷 458
- 告 892
- 否 1006
- 君 1289
- 含 1290
- ⑤ 岩 457
- 舎 1654
- ⑦ 哲 1010
- 容 1123
- 唇 1794
- ⑧ 啓 1690
- ⑨ 喜 253
- 善 676
- 営 930

239 土
- ② 圧 1197
- ③ 至 1198
- ⑥ 型 1318
- ⑧ 基 691
- 堂 709
- ⑨ 堅 1228
- 塁 1692
- 堕 1693
- ⑩ 墓 1156
- 塗 1694
- 塑 1944
- ⑪ 塾 863
- 墨 1695
- ⑫ 墜 1218
- ⑬ 壁 1029
- 墾 1798

240 夂
- ④ 麦 637
- ⑥ 変 222
- ⑦ 夏 97
- ⑩ 愛 1079
- ⑫ 憂 1829

241 夕
- ⑩ 夢 800

242 大
- ⑤ 突 1121
- ⑥ 美 673
- 契 751
- 臭 1285
- ⑨ 奥 71
- ⑩ 奨 831

243 女
- ③ 妄 1696
- ④ 妥 1332
- ⑤ 妻 596
- 委 697
- ⑥ 要 424
- 姿 661
- ⑦ 宴 849
- ⑧ 婆 1902

244 子
- ③ 字 528
- ④ 孝 738
- ⑤ 学 50
- 季 698
- 享 1772

245 寸
- ③ 寺 328
- 守 537
- ④ 寿 1327
- ⑥ 専 797
- ⑨ 尊 479
- 尋 1326
- ⑪ 奪 1407
- ⑫ 導 480

246 山
- ③ 岳 920
- ⑤ 岳 1851
- ⑧ 密 1103

247 巾
- ② 市 547
- 布 887
- ④ 希 888
- ⑥ 帝 1066
- ⑦ 帯 1065
- ⑧ 常 708
- ⑩ 幕 1157
- ⑫ 幣 1796

248 廾
- ② 弁 1116
- ⑨ 葬 801
- ⑪ 算 356
- 鼻 1286
- ⑫ 弊 1797

—4画—

249 心
- ③ 忘 209
- 志 756
- 忌 1697
- 忍 1775
- ④ 忠 758
- 念 1117
- ⑤ 思 202
- 怒 255
- 急 260
- 息 1698
- ⑥ 恩 757
- 恐 759
- 恵 1077
- 恋 1078
- 息 1118
- ⑦ 悪 114
- 窓 231
- 患 1367
- 悠 1699
- ⑧ 悲 341
- 惑 1071
- ⑨ 意 291
- 想 392
- 感 431
- 愁 1700
- 愚 1701
- 慈 1778
- ⑩ 態 451
- ⑪ 慰 1702
- ⑫ 憲 787
- 憩 1287
- ⑬ 懇 1799
- ⑭ 懲 1703
- ⑯ 懸 450

250 小
- ⑥ 恭 1934
- ⑩ 慕 1668

251 手
- ⑥ 挙 1189
- ⑧ 掌 1677
- ⑪ 撃 1041

252 日
② 百 11
旨 1349
④ 者 148
昔 428
⑤ 春 96
⑥ 書 181
⑦ 曹 1933
⑧ 替 375
普 427
⑩ 暮 1158
暦 1720
⑪ 暫 1706

253 木
③ 来 133
条 750
④ 果 502
⑤ 染 908
栄 1188
柔 1310
架 1704
某 1759
⑥ 案 305
桑 1855
⑦ 菜 774
巣 1862
⑧ 葉 569
⑨ 業 307
楽 343
棄 1653
⑫ 薬 315
築 1056

254 灬
⑤ 点 399
⑥ 烈 1708
⑦ 黒 45
⑧ 無 400
然 401
煮 1315
焦 1385
⑨ 蒸 802
照 868
⑩ 熟 864
熱 866
黙 869
勲 1709
⑫ 薫 1710

255 月
③ 肖 1811
④ 青 47
育 879
④ 肩 1084
肯 1403
背 1085
胃 1105
骨 1104
脅 1707

256 王
③ 呈 1657
⑤ 皇 579
⑦ 望 581
⑨ 聖 580

257 友
⑩ 髪 1359

—5画—

258 田
② 苗 1837
⑤ 留 432
畜 1274
⑦ 番 551
富 629
⑧ 雷 843
⑪ 奮 1406

259 白
① 百 11
④ 皆 606
⑥ 習 201

260 皿
① 血 928
④ 盆 1314
⑤ 益 921
⑥ 盗 268
盛 922
盟 923
⑧ 監 925
盤 1313

261 目
③ 盲 1278
④ 省 389
首 393
看 1114
冒 1669
⑦ 着 190
⑧ 督 926

262 石
⑧ 碁 1828

263 示
③ 宗 816
票 1199
祭 473
⑧ 禁 815
⑨ 察 475

264 立
⑥ 翌 492

265 正
⑪ 整 387

—6画—

266 糸
① 系 449
素 636
索 1301
累 1302
紫 1711
⑨ 緊 1186
⑩ 繁 1187

267 羽
④ 翁 1940

268 虫
④ 蚕 1866
⑤ 蛍 1676
⑥ 蛮 1825

269 衣
④ 表 437
袋 685
装 1370
裂 1371
⑧ 製 686
⑯ 襲 1042

—7画—

270 見
⑤ 覚 208
⑩ 覧 1831

271 言
⑥ 誉 1713
⑦ 誓 1712
⑫ 警 476

272 豆
⑤ 登 472
⑥ 豊 628

273 豕
⑤ 象 939
⑦ 豪 1277

274 貝
② 負 717
貞 1764
③ 員 395
貢 1180
④ 責 638
貨 857
貧 859
貫 1714
⑤ 貸 183
買 188
貿 433
貴 855
費 858
賀 1019
⑥ 資 853
賃 856
賛 376
⑨ 質 238
賞 711
賢 1227

275 車
② 軍 778
⑧ 輩 1100

276 辰
⑥ 農 626
⑧ 震 847

277 里
⑤ 量 435
童 1026

—9画—

278 音
⑪ 響 1023

279 食
⑧ 養 675

—10画—

280 馬
⑫ 驚 477

トップ・レフト (Top & Left) 281-288

281 厂
② 反 362
厄 1721
③ 圧 1197
④ 灰 874
⑦ 厚 848
厘 1910
⑧ 原 405
⑫ 歴 704
暦 1720

282 ナ
② 友 79
③ 右 35
左 36

友 79
布 887
④ 有 347
存 587
在 588

283 尸
① 尺 762
② 尼 1722
③ 尽 1726
④ 局 228
尾 1723
尿 1724
⑤ 屈 349
居 535
届 1090
⑥ 屋 54
⑦ 展 1092
⑨ 属 1091
⑪ 層 1725
⑫ 履 1405

284 广
② 広 113
庁 541
④ 床 543
序 953
応 1119
⑤ 店 55
府 337
底 745
⑥ 度 333
⑦ 座 175
席 332
庭 542
庫 544
唐 1727
⑧ 康 1054
庶 1413
麻 1414
庸 1728
⑨ 廊 545
廃 1412
⑩ 廉 1729
⑪ 腐 1730
⑫ 慶 1732

285 戸
③ 戻 1201
④ 房 1082
肩 1084
⑥ 扇 1733
⑧ 雇 1083
扉 1734

286 疒
④ 疫 1735
⑤ 疲 275
病 229
症 1363
疾 1736
⑦ 痛 346
痢 1737
痘 1932
⑧ 痴 1738
⑫ 療 1362
⑬ 癖 1364
癒 1739

287 虍
③ 虐 1740
⑤ 虚 1741
⑦ 虜 1884
虞 1945
⑨ 慮 1377
膚 1742

288 麻
④ 摩 1415
⑤ 磨 1731
⑩ 魔 1418

レフト・ボトム (Left & Bottom) 289-294

289 又
④ 廷 1211
⑤ 延 689
⑥ 建 1055

290 辶
② 込 961
辺 962
③ 迅 1744
巡 1743
④ 近 109
返 184
迎 1133
⑤ 述 963
迫 964
迭 1745
⑥ 送 206
逃 283
退 348
逆 386
追 966
迷 1070
⑦ 通 204
連 299
速 383
途 960
造 965
逐 1216
透 1746
逝 1747
逼 1941
⑧ 週 163
進 267
逮 1048
逸 1748
⑨ 道 66
遅 118
遊 196
過 284
運 304
達 384
遍 1177
遇 1178
遂 1217
⑩ 遠 110
違 385
遣 1214
⑪ 適 657
遮 1749
遭 1750
⑫ 選 264
遺 1179
導 1751
遷 1896
⑬ 還 1215
避 1365

291 走
② 赴 1075
③ 起 128
⑤ 越 1073
超 1074
⑧ 趣 310

292 兔
② 勉 140

293 是
⑨ 題 327

294 鬼
⑤ 魅 1419

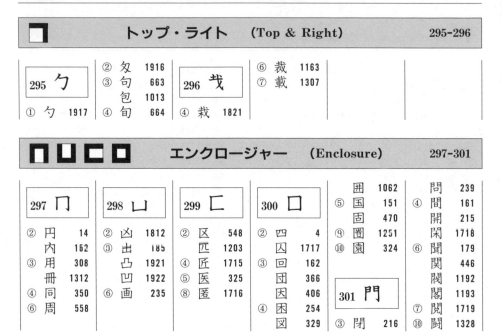

トップ・ライト (Top & Right) 295-296

295 勺	② 夂 1916	296 弋	⑥ 裁 1163
	③ 句 663		⑦ 載 1307
	包 1013		
① 勺 1917	④ 旬 664	④ 栽 1821	

エンクロージャー (Enclosure) 297-301

297 冂	298 凵	299 匸	300 囗					
					囲 1062		問 239
				⑤ 国 151	④ 間 161
					固 470		開 215
② 円 14	② 凶 1812	② 区 548	② 四 4	⑨ 圏 1251	閑 1718
内 152	⑨ 出 185	匹 1203	囚 1717	⑩ 園 324	⑥ 聞 179
③ 用 308	凸 1921	④ 匠 1715	③ 回 162		関 446
冊 1312	凹 1922	⑤ 医 325	団 366		閥 1192
④ 同 350	⑥ 画 235	⑧ 匿 1716	因 406	301 門	閣 1193
⑥ 周 558			④ 困 254		⑦ 閲 1719
			図 329	③ 閉 216	⑩ 闘 1328

総画索引
(Stroke Index)

This index includes 1) all the *kanji* not found in the form index, and 2) *kanji* which are included in the form index but considered difficult to find through it. These *kanji* are arranged by the number of strokes, and the corresponding *kanji* number is given.

語彙索引
（Vocabulary Index）

All the vocabulary contained in this book is listed in *a-i-u-e-o* order with the corresponding *kanji* number under which they appear.

347

さ

す

せ

そ

ち

ふ

む

め

字形構成素チャート (Component Chart)

■ レフト (Left)

2	亻 1	冫 2	十 3	**3**	口 4	土 5	女 6	子 7	山 8	川 9	工 10
巾 11	弓 12	彳 13	忄 14	扌 15	氵 16	斗 17	犭 18	阝 19	**4**	方 20	日 21
木 22	月 23	歹 24	火 25	牛 26	王 27	礻 28	**5**	牙 29	田 30	目 31	矛 32
矢 33	石 34	禾 35	立 36	衤 37	艮 38	**6**	米 39	糸 40	耒 41	耳 42	至 43
舌 44	舟 45	虫 46	艮 47	并 48	臼 49	**7**	臣 50	角 51	言 52	谷 53	豆 54
貝 55	足 56	身 57	車 58	酉 59	耒 60	里 61	君 62	**8**	釒 63	青 64	幸 65
革 66	**9**	革 67	音 68	食 69	**10**	馬 70	骨 71	**11**	魚 72	隹 73

■ ライト (Right)

1	し 74	**2**	几 75	刂 76	力 77	ヒ 78	十 79	卩 80	ム 81	又 82	丁 83
3	口 84	寸 85	己 86	干 87	彡 88	阝 89	疔 90	才 91	及 92	也 93	勹 94
4	戈 95	支 96	夂 97	斗 98	斤 99	方 100	欠 101	殳 102	犬 103	月 104	卒 105
分 106	亢 107	反 108	尺 109	少 110	艮 111	区 112	**5**	生 113	田 114	白 115	皮 116
召 117	台 118	台 119	圣 120	令 121	包 122	主 123	司 124	乍 125	且 126	申 127	由 128
6	羊 129	羽 130	聿 131	舌 132	艮 133	色 134	虫 135	寺 136	各 137	交 138	毎 139
戔 140	朱 141	兆 142	**7**	見 143	谷 144	豕 145	辛 146	辰 147	里 148	兌 149	余 150
甫 151	束 152	**8**	長 153	隹 154	隶 155	青 156	僉 157	侖 158	昔 159	音 160	直 161
非 162	**9**	頁 163	扁 164	俞 165	軍 166	単 167	易 168	复 169	**10**	韋 170	鬼 171
冓 172	**11**	鳥 173	曽 174	責 175	商 176	**13**	義 177	蒦 178	桌 179